JURISDICTION AND ARBIT
AGREEMENTS IN CONTRACT
CARRIAGE OF GOODS B

MARITIME AND TRANSPORT LAW LIBRARY

MARITIME AND TRANSPORT LAW LIBRARY

Ship Building, Sale and Finance
Edited by Bariş Soyer and Andrew Tettenborn

The Modern Law of Marine Insurance
Volume 4
Edited by D. Rhidian Thomas

Air Cargo Insurance
Malcom A. Clarke and George Leloudas

Offshore Oil and Gas Installations Security
An International Perspective
Mikhail Kashubsky

International Trade and Carriage of Goods
Edited by Bariş Soyer and Andrew Tettenborn

Maritime Law and Practice in China
Liang Zhao and Lianjun Li

Maritime Cross-Border Insolvency
Lia Athanassiou

The Law of Yachts and Yachting
Second Edition
Edited by Filippo Lorenzon and Richard Coles

Maritime Liabilities in a Global and Regional Context
Edited by Bariş Soyer and Andrew Tettenborn

New Technologies, Artificial Intelligence and Shipping Law in the 21st Century
Edited by Bariş Soyer and Andrew Tettenborn

The Law of Wreck
Nicholas Gaskell and Craig Forrest

Codification of Maritime Law
Challenges, Possibilities and Experience
Edited by Zuzanna Pepłowska-Dąbrowska and Justyna Nawrot

Transport Documents in Carriage Of Goods by Sea
International Law and Practice
Caslav Pejovic

Maritime Law
Fifth Edition
Edited by Yvonne Baatz

Ship Operations: New Risks, Liabilities and Technologies in the Maritime Sector
Edited by Bariş Soyer and Andrew Tettenborn

Maritime Safety in Europe
Edited by Justyna Nawrot and Zuzanna Pepłowska-Dąbrowska

For more information about this series, please visit: www.routledge.com/Maritime-and-Transport-Law-Library/book-series/MTLL

JURISDICTION AND ARBITRATION AGREEMENTS IN CONTRACTS FOR THE CARRIAGE OF GOODS BY SEA

LIMITATIONS ON PARTY AUTONOMY

JONATAN ECHEBARRIA FERNÁNDEZ

informa law
from Routledge

First published 2021
by Informa Law from Routledge
2 Park Square, Milton Park, Abingdon, Oxon OX14 4RN

and by Informa Law from Routledge
605 Third Avenue, New York, NY 10017

Routledge is an imprint of the Taylor & Francis Group, an informa business

British Library Cataloguing-in-Publication Data
A catalogue record for this book is available from the British Library

Library of Congress Cataloging-in-Publication Data
A catalog record has been requested for this book

ISBN 13: 978-0-367-24346-3 (hbk)

Typeset in Times New Roman
by Deanta Global Publishing Services, Chennai, India

CONTENTS

FOREWORD BY ERIK RØSÆG

I had the pleasure of studying the manuscript of the book you are now holding in your hands during the PhD phase of the work. I became acquainted with the author while he was visiting me at the Scandinavian Institute of Maritime Law at the University of Oslo, and I very much enjoyed our exchanges.

Jurisdiction and arbitration clauses are fascinating, and the studies responding to the four research questions of the current work certainly bring the debate forward. The interaction between EC law, English law, and Spanish law is well suited to demonstrating the complexities of these issues. The arrest dimension adds another layer of complexity. Thanks to Jonatan for his successful efforts in bringing better order to parts of this confusing area of law.

Despite these academic achievements, clarification also has its downsides. It is right that system and order are virtues of legal scholars, and predictability an ideal for the law. However, we have yet to reach full predictability, system, and order in the law because legislative interventions are lacking. As long as the system is imperfect and thus the ideals are not reached, clarification tends to assist rather than combat forum shopping. It is much easier to take advantage of flaws in systems when the flaws are clarified, as it is much easier to take advantage of differences in legal systems when the differences are pointed out clearly. In this way, academic clarification attempts in research, as well as clarification attempts in conventions harmonising the law, may be a problem as long as the system has not become all-embracing and perfect through legislation. The next-to-perfect is sometimes far from the best. Academic clarification can only create the next-to-perfect, as legislation is necessary to create the perfect system.

Jonatan proposes a new international convention to address the problems of jurisdiction and arbitration clauses. This may very well be a worthwhile attempt. However, there are strong commercial interests in maintaining the current complex legal situation. The jungle guides are likely to resist attempts to establish and maintain highways through the jungle. Governments are likely to their ears to commercial interests rather than the academic ideals of system and order.

The current skepticism regarding globalisation does not assist. The climate for allowing matters to be decided in foreign jurisdictions, and recognising and enforcing the foreign judgments that follow, is becoming more hostile. Furthermore, some states are tending to look to national solutions rather than those that are international and comprehensive. I do hope the wind will change.

While waiting for the legislators, the best we can do is to pursue our academic ideals. I wish Jonatan further success in his future academic pursuits.

Erik Røsæg
Professor of Law at the University of Oslo, Norway
Nesodden, Norway, 2 July 2020

FOREWORD BY ALFONSO-LUIS CALVO CARAVACA AND JAVIER CARRASCOSA GONZÁLEZ

One may think that the book written by Jonatan Echebarria Fernández dealing with party autonomy and its limitations in relation to jurisdiction and arbitration in the fascinating world of the carriage of goods by sea is just another reflection on the existing legal framework in the field. Not at all. It must be underlined that his analysis of the jurisdiction and arbitration clauses contained in contracts for the carriage of goods by sea considers these clauses as 'legal products' made by the parties. As such, these clauses are aimed at being recognised in different countries in order to enforce the contract where these are included. The more recognition these agreements gain, the better in terms of legal certainty – this enhances legal efficiency of international contracts for the carriage of goods by sea.

Conflict of laws needs to be analysed from an efficient perspective and that is one of the pillars of Jonatan Echebarria Fernández's book. The author complains about the fragmentation of the legal regime applicable to dispute resolution agreements and he is absolutely right. We need simpler rules for a complex world since Private International Law deserves to be more efficient. The ghost of 'forum shopping' strikes again.

Limitations on party autonomy might be regarded as a defence of the States' sovereignty or as a protection of the weaker party in the contracts for the carriage of the goods by sea. The effort made by the author with regard to this point is clear. Bills of lading are studied with care not only as proof of the contract of carriage but as a 'good itself' that can be transferred to third parties.

Particular attention is given to the rules that govern international jurisdiction determined by the content of jurisdiction and arbitration clauses in Spain, England and Wales. Anti-suit injunctions are also studied with attentiveness and a full picture of international litigation in the shipping sector is provided, supplemented by the arrest of ships, mandatory rules and public policy exceptions.

All previous considerations make this book extremely recommendable for those who are interested in the jurisdiction and arbitration clauses contained in contracts for the carriage of goods by sea from a practical and academic angle. Not only does the author consider *de lege data* legal provisions but he also provides some perspectives for improvement and a new convention proposal. The reader interested in international maritime law will be pleasantly surprised with the Jonatan Echebarria Fernández's most recent contribution to Private International Law.

Alfonso-Luis Calvo Caravaca
Full Professor of Private International Law at the
University Carlos III of Madrid, Spain
Javier Carrascosa González
Full Professor of Private International Law at the University of Murcia, Spain

Murcia and Madrid, Spain, 18 July 2020

ACKNOWLEDGEMENTS

This book has been written and composed during my employment at the Law Department (currently CBS LAW) of the Copenhagen Business School between 2014 and 2018. My contract was generously co-funded by the Danish Maritime Fund through CBS Maritime, for which I am grateful.

First and foremost, I am grateful to Professor Peter Arnt Nielsen (2018) (Copenhagen Business School) and Associate Professor George Theocharidis (World Maritime University) for their supervision. Also, I give my sincere thanks to Associate Professor Patrik Lindskoug (Lund University) and Professor Kim Østergaard (Copenhagen Business School).

Second, I want to extend a special thanks to Professor Juan José Álvarez Rubio (University of the Basque Country) for his continuous academic support and advice since 2010. Your comments and guidance have enriched this book. Professor Marta Casado Abarquero (University of Deusto) and Professor Jason Chuah (City University, London) have also provided vital advice and suggestions.

Third, I appreciate Eleanor Ayres' involvement in taking on the task of editor and Eryn Green for her assistance.

Thank you for your continuous support, guidance and fruitful discussions.

I want to express my gratitude for the financial support provided by the Otto Mønsteds Fond, Professor dr. jur. Max Sørensens Mindefond, Reinholdt W. Jorck og Hustrus Fond and Oticon Fonden. I employed the funds for my research stays in the following research centres, for which I am also very grateful: the Max Planck Institute Luxembourg for International, European and Regulatory Procedural Law; the Institute of Maritime Law (University of Southampton); the University of the Basque Country; the Scandinavian Institute of Maritime Law (University of Oslo); the Maritime Knowledge Centre (International Maritime Organization); the UCD Sutherland School of Law (University College Dublin) and the World Maritime University. The research stays have been milestones in the development of this book, providing me with access to relevant materials and the opportunity to exchange views with world-leading specialist academics in the field of maritime law and private international law.

Thanks to Gard AS for granting me the Claes Isacson Scholarship 2016 Award, handed out in Årendal (Norway). The scholarship allowed me to attend relevant courses, which helped me during the book writing process, at the Lloyd's Maritime Academy; the Judge Business School (University of Cambridge); the Harvard Negotiation Institute (Harvard Law School); the University of Columbia Law School; the Postgraduate Institute of European Studies (College of Europe); and the CBS Executive. The courses had a remarkable impact on the development of this book.

I would also like to express my thanks to the Head of Secretariat Pernille Brandt, Professor Christina D Tvarnø, and to all my former colleagues at CBS LAW, Copenhagen Business School. I sincerely appreciate your encouragement and support during difficult times, and your faith in me.

I want to express my heartfelt appreciation for the unconditional support with which my family has provided me during my studies: to my parents, Emilio and Estrella, and to all those who unfortunately are no longer with us; my uncle Pantxo Etxebarria, who passed away in 2017, and my grandparents, Emilia 'Amama', Maria Ángeles 'Tata' and Severino 'Tato', who will remain forever alive in my memory. I love you and you are the pillars that hold me up.

This book would not have been possible without all of you. As my father used to tell me when we were reaching the top of the mountain pass by bicycle: 'never say you can't!'

Jonatan Echebarria Fernández
London, United Kingdom, 1 July 2020

LIST OF ABBREVIATIONS

1952 Arrest Convention	International Convention Relating to the Arrest of Sea-Going Ships (Brussels, 1952)
1999 Arrest Convention	International Convention on Arrest of Ships (Geneva, 1999)
ADR	Alternative Dispute Resolution
BIMCO	Baltic and International Maritime Council
B/L	Bill of Lading
Brussels Convention	Convention of 27 September 1968 on jurisdiction and the enforcement of judgments in civil and commercial matters [1972] OJ L299/32 Consolidated text of 26 January 1998 [1998] OJ C27/1
Brussels I Regulation 44/2001	Council Regulation (EC) 44/2001 of 22 December 2000 on jurisdiction and the recognition and enforcement of judgments in civil and commercial matters [2001] OJ L12/1
Brussels I Regulation (recast)	Council Regulation (EU) No 1215/2012 on jurisdiction and the recognition and enforcement of judgments in civil and commercial matters [2012] OJ L351/1
CJEU	Court of Justice of the European Union
CJJA	UK Civil Jurisdiction and Judgments Act 1982
CMI	Comité Maritime International
CMR Convention	Convention on the Contract for the International Carriage of Goods by Road
COGSA 71	UK Carriage of Goods by Sea Act 1971
COGSA 92	UK Carriage of Goods by Sea Act 1992
CPR	Civil Procedure Rules (England and Wales)
EAPO	European Account Preservation Order Procedure
EU	European Union
Hague Choice of Court Convention	Hague Convention of 30 June 2005 on Choice of Court Agreements

Hague Rules	International Convention for the Unification of Certain Rules of Law Relating to Bills of Lading (Brussels, 1924)
Hague–Visby Rules	The Hague Rules as amended by the Protocol to amend the International Convention for the Unification of Certain Rules Relating to Bills of Lading 1924 (Brussels, 1968) and subsequent instruments
Hamburg Rules	United Nations International Convention on the Carriage of Goods by Sea (Hamburg, 1978)
ICC	International Chamber of Commerce
IMO	International Maritime Organization
INCOTERM	International Commercial Term
LCIA	London Court of International Arbitration
LMAA	London Maritime Arbitrators Association
LOI	Letter of Indemnity
LOU	Letter of Undertaking
Lugano Convention	Council Decision 2007/712/EC of 15 October 2007 on jurisdiction and the recognition and enforcement of judgments in civil and commercial matters [2007] OJ 2007, L339/3
Member State	EU Member State
MLM Convention	International Convention on Maritime Liens and Mortgages (Geneva, 1993)
New York Convention	United Nations Convention on the Recognition and Enforcement of Arbitral Awards (New York, 1958)
PIL	Private International Law
P&I Club	Protection and Indemnity Club
Rome Convention	Convention 80/934/ECC on the law applicable to contractual obligations [1980] OJ L266/1 Consolidated version [1998] C27/34
Rome I Regulation	Regulation (EC) No 593/2008 of the European Parliament and of the Council on the law applicable to contractual obligations [2008] OJ L177/6
Rome II Regulation	Regulation (EC) No 864/2007 of the European Parliament and of the Council of 11 July 2007 on the law applicable to non-contractual obligations [2007] OJ L199/40
Rotterdam Rules	United Nations Convention on Contracts for the International Carriage of Goods Wholly or Partly by Sea (New York and Rotterdam, 2008)
SAA	Spanish Arbitration Act 60/2003 of 23 December 2003
SAMN	Spanish Act on Maritime Navigation 14/2014
SLCP	Spanish Law 1/2000 of 7 January on Civil Procedure
SLCCGL	Spanish Law 15/2009 on Contracts for the Carriage of Goods by Land

SAILCCM	Spanish Act 29/2015 of 30 July 2015 on International Legal Cooperation in Civil Matters
SOLJ	Spanish Organic Law 6/1985 of 1 July on the Judiciary (Ley Orgánica 6/1985, de 1 de julio, del Poder Judicial)
TFEU	Treaty on the Functioning of the European Union
UCP 600	Uniform Customs and Practice for Documentary Credits
UKAA	UK Arbitration Act 1996
UNCTAD	United Nations Conference on Trade and Development
UNCITRAL	United Nations Commission on International Trade Law
UNCITRAL Model Law	UNCITRAL Model Law on International Commercial Arbitration (1985)
UNIDROIT	International Institute for the Unification of Private Law

TABLE OF CASES

In the United Kingdom section, ship names will be filed under both the ship name and the full title of the case. E.g., *The Ivan Zagubanski* will appear under *Navigation Maritime Bulgare v. Rustal Trading Ltd (The Ivan Zagubanski)* [2000] EWHC 222 (Comm); [2002] 1 Lloyd's Rep 106 as well as under *The Ivan Zagubanski*.

National Courts

United Kingdom

The Netherlands

Court of Justice of the European Union (CJEU)

TABLE OF LEGISLATION

National legislation

United Kingdom

Spain

France

United States

European Union (EU)

Primary sources

Secondary sources

Other non-binding sources

Opinion of the Court of Justice of the European Union (CJEU)

Proposals and communications

International

Conventions

'Soft law'

CHAPTER 1

Introduction

The carriage of goods by sea is the globally preferred method of international cargo transportation.[1] When a buyer and a seller agree on a contract for the sale of goods, they must set all conditions of purchase, including the transport of such goods by land, air or sea. Maritime transport documents (primarily charterparties and bills of lading (B/L)) are relatively complex and the uncertainty concerning dispute resolution clauses deserves particular attention.[2]

This book focuses on cargo claims related to the damage, loss, misdelivery or delay of merchandise during a sea venture. It sheds light on especially problematic scenarios, in which parties to the carriage contract might not be able to resolve their disputes, and examines the interface between party autonomy and dispute resolution clauses in B/Ls and charterparties in the context of restrictions imposed by different legal regimes in relation to procedure, substantive law and choice of law.

Private international law (PIL), or conflict of laws, shows that the law of treaties is not sufficient to solve the complex problems posed by the plurality of international, European and national sources that affect this subject. The global regulatory unbundling process has diminished the role that international conventions play in normative unification.[3] Their coexistence with more flexible instruments ('soft laws', reflecting both private and public interests and using normative principles and models[4]) ensures that trade usages and practices are suited to the complex modern reality of the shipping sector.[5]

---

1 In 2013, the European Union (EU) shipping industry directly contributed €56 billion to EU GDP and 615,000 employees, while the indirect impact was €61 billion to EU GDP and 1.1 million jobs. The total economic impact is estimated to have been €147 billion during 2013; Oxford Economics, *The Economic Value of the EU Shipping Industry: A Report for the European Community Shipowners' Associations* (report, April 2014); Jonatan Echebarria Fernández, 'Action Research and Efficient Maritime Transport Contract Negotiation' in Peter Arnt Nielsen, Peter Koerver Schmidt, Katja Dyppel Weber (eds), *Erhvervsretlige Emner: Jurisdik Institut CBS* (DJØF 2015) 49–63.

2 Felix Sparka, *Jurisdiction and Arbitration Clauses in Maritime Transport Documents* (Springer 2010) 19–38.

3 There is a trend in the literature to move towards international normative uniformity in maritime law. Tullio Treves, *Il nuovo diritto del mare e le convenzioni internazionali sulla protezione dell'ambiente marino* (1999) 101(1) Dir Marit 219; Sergio Maria Carbone and Francesco Munari, *Regole e organizzazione dei trasporti marittimi internazionali* (Giuffrè 1990) 7–10.

4 For the inadequacies of multilateral treaties for international codification and the European evolution of PIL, see Juan Carlos Fernández Rozas, 'La ordenación de las relaciones privadas internacionales a través de tratados en las postrimerías de su ciclo histórico' in Santiago Torres Bernárdez (ed), *El derecho internacional en el mundo multipolar del siglo XXI: obra homenaje al profesor Luis Ignacion Sánchez Rodríguez* (Iprolex 2013) 54.

5 Juan José Álvarez Rubio, *La dimensión procesal internacional en la Ley de navegación marítima* (2014–2015) 14–15 Anuario Español de Derecho Internacional Privado 159; see also Juan José Álvarez Rubio, *Derecho Marítimo y Derecho Internacional Privado: Algunos Problemas Básicos* (Servicio de Publicaciones Gobierno Vasco 2000) 19–42.

The issues in this book are considered within the framework of European Union (EU), English and Spanish law. Of these, English law is by far the dominant force, internationally, but even a limited consideration of Spanish law, as a civil law system, provides a different perspective and perhaps a different approach for the future. Maritime law is subject to international regulation, and the EU also has a significant role to play, particularly with regard to jurisdiction clauses. Excessive regulation does not protect shipping operators, as partial and sectoral regulatory harmonisation lacks sufficient legal certainty and predictability.[6] Attempts to solve the problems of party autonomy result in failure or ambiguity, as demonstrated by the Hamburg and Rotterdam Rules.[7] Such rules cannot adapt to the reality of the shipping industry and are not adequate instruments of international codification.

Limits on party autonomy are not only an English, Spanish or European problem. Parties may not be able to resolve their disputes under the terms of the contracts for the carriage of goods by sea, leading to problems that vary from case to case, despite the harmonisation and delimitation efforts of PIL and public maritime law.[8] The complexity in securing recognition of the seat chosen by the contracting parties points to the use of preventive advocacy, i.e., the avoidance of future disputes through legal advice.

Due to the nature of the industry, there are difficulties in setting out the legal regime under which the parties may enforce agreed jurisdiction or arbitration agreements. International instruments such as the Hague,[9] Hague–Visby[10] and Hamburg Rules[11] – as well as the still-not-in-force Rotterdam Rules – provide a liability regime for cargo claims. Some of these rules affect the validity of dispute resolution clauses along with EU law and the domestic legal regimes of England and Spain. Issues arising out of the incorporation of the charterparty terms (including the dispute resolution clause) into the B/L are proof of the limitations on party autonomy, depending on the applicable legal regime, the court or arbitral tribunal and the particularities of the case.

The international nature of shipping law[12] reflects the coexistence of a differentiated hierarchy of regulatory frameworks at national, EU and international level.[13] When an EU Member State court confirms its jurisdiction and the applicability of harmonised EU law over a (cargo) claim, such Member State court 'imposes' on non-EU countries European procedural and substantive legal standards. It implies that the same rules apply to trans-border conflicts between EU Member States and trans-border conflicts between Member States and non-EU states, with an overall shift away from substance to procedure in the external dimension of European private law.[14]

---

6 Álvarez Rubio, *Derecho Marítimo y Derecho Internacional Privado* (n 5) 19–42.

7 United Nations Convention on Contracts for the International Carriage of Goods Wholly or Partly by Sea ('Rotterdam Rules') adopted in New York on 11 December 2008, A/RES/63/122.

8 Giulio Diena, *Principes du Droit International Privé Maritime: Recueil des Cours,* vol 51, (Martinus Nijhoff 1935) 405 *et seq*.

9 International Convention for the Unification of Certain Rules of Law Relating to Bills of Lading ('The Hague Rules') (adopted 25 August 1924) 51 Stat 223, 120 LNTS 155.

10 Protocol to Amend the International Convention for the Unification of Certain Rules of Law Relating to Bills of Lading ('The Visby Rules') (adopted 23 February 1968) 1412 UNTS 121.

11 United Nations Convention on the Carriage of Goods by Sea ('The Hamburg Rules') (approved 30 March 1978, entered into force 1 November 1992) 1695 UNTS 3.

12 See the EU law projection on the maritime transport in Francesco Munari, *Il diritto comunitario dei trasporti* (Giuffrè 1996) 50–117.

13 See José Carlos Fernández Rozas, 'Comunitarización del Derecho internacional privado y Derecho aplicable a las obligaciones contractuales' (2009) 140 *Revista Española de Seguros* 595.

14 Hans-Wolfgang Micklitz, 'The internal vs. the external dimension of European private law – a conceptual design and a research agenda' (2015) EUI Working Paper LAW 2015/35, ERC-ERPL Project, 4,13.

This work seeks to untangle the issues at hand: the limits on party autonomy regarding dispute resolution clauses inserted into a charterparty or incorporated into a B/L by the shipowner and/or the charterer.

1 Limitations on party autonomy: background

In order to explore the problems arising from the incorporation of dispute resolution clauses into charterparties or B/Ls, and the resultant limitations on party autonomy, the roles of the parties involved and the types of carriage contracts need to be identified.

1.1 The parties

Contracts for the carriage of goods by sea derive from customs and traditions developed by merchants to provide proof of an agreement to hire a ship for the transport of the goods. A shipowner lets a charterer use the ship for a trip (voyage charter) or a set period of time (time charter), and the charterer agrees with the carrier on the transport of goods.[15] The charterer pays 'hire' (under a time charter) or freight (under a voyage charter) for the use of the vessel. This constitutes the remuneration payable to the ship interest (the carrier, referred to here as the 'shipowner') by the cargo interest (the shipper of the goods, consignee or charterer).[16]

Figure 1 illustrates the basic contractual arrangement for the carriage of goods by sea.[17] The shipowner owns the ship that carries the cargo and is often the contractual carrier of the cargo and liable for any loss or damage.

Nowadays, a shipowner may be a bank, a fund manager or a company with no shipping knowledge. In such cases, a ship management company will be vital for daily operations.[18] Charterers are entities that lease or charter the vessels.

The cargo interests are represented by the owner of the cargo, as shown in Figure 2.[19] However, they could be represented by another party. The 'consignor', also referred to as

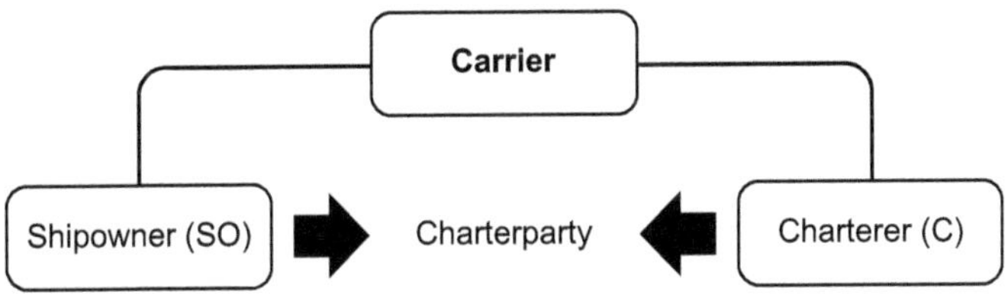

FIGURE 1 Charterparty.

15 James Whiteside Gray, *Shipping Futures* (2nd edn, LLP Professional 1990).

16 Lars Gorton, 'The Liability for Freight' in Ulf Bernitz and others (eds), *Festskrift till Jan Ramberg* (Juristförlaget 1996) 165.

17 Christopher J Giaschi, *Canadian Law of Carriage of Goods by Sea: An Overview* (November 2004) 3 <www.admiraltylaw.com/papers/carriage_of_goods_outline.pdf> accessed 6 December 2019.

18 Thomas Roslyng Olesen, *Value Creation in the Maritime Chain of Transportation* (CBS Maritime 2015).

19 For instance, the contract for the sale of goods may provide for ICC's CIF (Cost, Insurance and Freight) INCOTERM 2020, under which the seller arranges the transport by signing a charterparty for the carriage of goods by sea; alternatively, the buyer may protect itself to ensure good faith transmission of the charterparty terms in the B/L by inserting the ICC's FOB (Free On Board) INCOTERM 2020 and arranging the transport if possible.

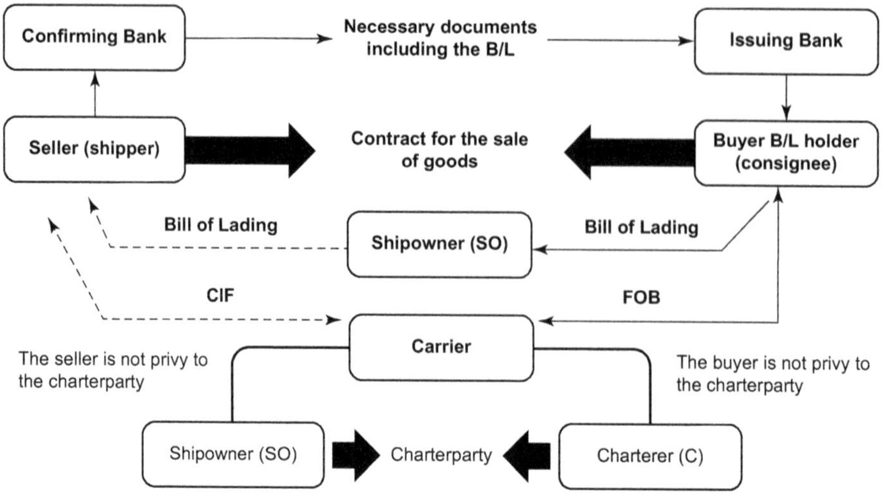

FIGURE 2 Sale of goods under CIF and FOB INCOTERMS, documentary credit and contract for the carriage of goods by sea. Source: Figure 2 is inspired by Corbett Haselgrove Spurin, 'The liability of carriers to cargo owners', *The Law of International Trade and Carriage of Goods* (Nationwide Mediation Academy for NADR UK Ltd 2004) 74, 75, 89.

the 'shipper', denotes the person actually handing over the cargo to the carrier and having the right of suit against the carrier. It may lose that right when the property of the goods passes from the shipper to the consignee. The 'consignee' is the 'receiver' or buyer of the goods and lacks a contractual link with the carrier.[20]

Banks often finance sale transactions using letters of credit. They have the right to sell the goods and may take possession of any negotiable B/L for security as a 'lawful holder', acquiring the right to the goods and title to sue the carrier, for example, if the B/L is delivered and endorsed to them, under s 5(2)(a) and (b) of the Carriage of Goods by Sea Act 1992 (COGSA 92).

The freight forwarder is an intermediary arranging the transport of goods by sea; it is not liable as a carrier unless it issues its own B/L.[21] It usually acts only as the 'contracting carrier' procuring transportation from one or several 'performing carriers' by concluding affreightment contracts with the carrier(s). When several means of transport are involved, it is more likely that a shipper will involve a freight forwarder.

1.2 The contracts

A contract of affreightment[22] or a contract of carriage is concluded when the shipowner, either directly or through an agent, undertakes to carry goods by sea or to provide a vessel

20 Christopher J Giaschi, *Canadian Law of Carriage of Goods by Sea: An Overview* (Giaschi & Margolis November 2004) 3 <www.admiraltylaw.com/papers/carriage_of_goods_outline.pdf> accessed 6 December 2019; Humphrey Humberto Pachecker, *Nafa's Blue Book: Legal Terminology, Commentaries, Tables and Useful Legal Information* (Xlibris Corporation 2010) 57.

21 ibid 3.

22 Contracts of affreightment used by the shipping industry worldwide generally use a standard form provided by major private international shipping organisations. These contracts govern the relationship between the carrier and the shipper; Anders Møllmann, *Delivery of Goods Under Bills of Lading* (Routledge 2016) 11.

for that purpose.[23] The classic division is between those embodied in charterparties and those contained in, or evidenced by, a B/L.[24] The distinction is not exhaustive. Other documents such as freight contracts, mate's receipts, non-negotiable receipts, sea waybills, ship's delivery orders and through transportation documents do not fall into either category.[25]

To determine contractual responsibility for cargo loss, damage or delay, legal regimes may vary, depending on the type of contract, and whether it is a vessel-oriented or a cargo-oriented contract.

1.2.1 Vessel-oriented contracts: the charterparty

Vessel-oriented contracts are those by which the shipowner, in return for a sum of money, agrees to perform a carriage of goods service or to furnish the services of a vessel for such purpose. The shipowner equips and mans the vessel, remaining responsible throughout the performance of the contract.[26]

A charterparty (known during the Roman Empire as a *carta partita*) is normally agreed when the shipowner agrees with a charterer to make available the vessel (or part of it), for a fixed voyage or period of time[27] for the conveyance of goods to one or more places or until the expiration of a specified time.[28] The B/L describes the goods, confirms that they have been received on board, states to whom they must be delivered at the destination and obtains a reference to the freight (pre-paid or payable on delivery). The charterparty represents the mere hiring of a ship, while a contract of affreightment supposes a carriage of goods by water and paid freight in exchange for the performance of the shipowner.[29]

The charterparty states the division of responsibilities between shipowners and charterers, as well as the intervention of charterer's agents and the servants of the shipowners, such as the captain, crew and stevedores. There are three main types of charterparty: voyage charterparties, time charterparties and demise (or bareboat) charterparties. In the first two, the shipowner will crew the ship and carry all expenses except for bunkers.[30] Through sub-chartering or subletting, two independent charterparties may run concurrently, placing

23 Other contracts included sales contracts between the buyer and the seller of the cargo, letters of credit that govern the payment for such cargo and contracts of insurance; see Møllmann (n 22) 11. Efficient communication and coordination among the different parties and the ports, operations management and all other managing functions reduce time and cost; Dimitrios v. Lyridis and others, 'Optimizing shipping company operations using business process modelling' (2005) 32(4) Maritime Policy & Management 403.

24 John F Wilson, *Carriage of Goods by Sea* (7th ed, Longman 2010) 3.

25 Bernard Eder and others, *Scrutton on Charterparties and Bills of Lading* (23rd edn, Sweet & Maxwell 2015) 1–3.

26 United Nations Conference on Trade and Development (UNCTAD) Secretariat, *Charter Parties* (UN 1974).

27 Wilson (n 24).

28 Charterparties have been standardised since the late 19th and early 20th century by organisations such as the Baltic and International Maritime Council (BIMCO), the Association of Shipbrokers and Agents (ASBA) and the International Chamber of Shipping. There is a large number of private charterparties (in-house charterparties). Large charterers such as major oil companies have their own forms of charterparties (e.g., Shell's SHELLVOY, BP's Beepeevoy) and they only use their own standard forms. A number of standard charter forms are available for use with all cargoes and some for special cargoes, such as grain. The most common charterparty standard forms include, for voyage charters, GENCON 1994 for general cargo and ASBATANKVOY, SHELLVOY, Exxonvoy or Beepeevoy for oil; for time charters, NYPE 1946 or 1993, BALTIME, ASBATIME, Shelltime 3 or 4; and for bareboat charters, BARECON; in Indira Carr, *International Trade Law* (5th edn, Routledge 2013) 160–172.

29 James Arthur Ballentine, *Law Dictionary with Pronunciations* (Lawyers Co-operative Publishing Company 1930) 280.

30 Allan Houtved, *Shipping* (Danmarks Skibsmæglerforening 2005); Bharath Krishna, *Chartering, Education PP* (2012) <http://www.slideshare.net/bharath_krishna/chartering?related=2> accessed 22 May 2018; Martin Stopford, *Maritime Economics* (3rd edn, Routledge 2009); as detailed in Olesen (n 18).

the original charterer in a dual position: a charterer against the owner of the vessel and an owner against the sub-charterer.[31]

A voyage charter is for the carriage of specified goods on a single voyage or a series of voyages between named ports.[32] The charterer is obliged to provide the cargo, pay freight (remuneration paid to the shipowner, usually a per-ton rate) and pay for any delay (demurrage) or time savings (despatch), subject to how the risk is allocated between shipowner and charterer.[33] Most contracts in dry bulk and liquid bulk are voyage charters.[34]

Time charterparties allow the charterer to hire the vessel for a concrete period of time 'without undertaking any financial commitments for ownership or responsibilities for the navigation and management of the vessel'.[35] The charterer is obliged to pay a hire cost but does not always issue the B/L. The shipowner under the charterparty has the obligation to insure, crew and maintain the vessel, under English law. Shipowners also have responsibility for navigation.

With a demise (or bareboat) charterparty, the possession and full control of the vessel, together with the legal and financial responsibility for it, are transferred from the shipowner to the demise charterer.[36] The demise charterer rents the ship – without crew – for a certain period and takes over all the shipowner's functions, as well as possession and control of the vessel and all responsibility for its navigation, management and operation.[37] The charterer will thus have commercial and technical responsibility for the vessel and will pay for maintenance, crew, insurance and so on.[38]

1.2.2 Cargo-oriented contracts: the bill of lading

The B/L is issued to the shipper when the goods have been loaded on board. If the vessel is chartered, the shipper may also be (but is not necessarily) the charterer.[39] The B/L can be a negotiable document of title that constitutes evidence and proof of the contract of affreightment.[40] It serves as an acknowledgement by the carrier of the receipt and possession of the loaded cargo on board the vessel. The signed B/L is handed by the master or the agent of the shipowner (or carrier) to the shipper, constituting a master's receipt for shipper's goods.[41] As a negotiable document of title, it is transferable and may be traded, and it carries an unconditional right to claim the goods referenced therein. In contrast, a non-negotiable instrument, such as a sea waybill, requires that the goods are not meant to be sold: a sea waybill is a non-negotiable document evidencing the terms and conditions of the contract of carriage, and, unlike the B/L, it is a document of title.

31 See Anthony Rogers, Jason Chuah and Martin Dockray, *Cases and Materials on the Carriage of Goods by Sea* (Routledge 2013) 3.

32 ibid 5.

33 See Olesen (n 18).

34 Ioannis N Lagoudis, Chandra S Lalwani and Mohamed Mohamed Naim, *A generic systems model for ocean shipping companies in the bulk sector* (2004) 43(1) Transportation Journal 56; in Olesen (n 18).

35 See Rogers, Chuah and Dockray (n 31).

36 Carole Murray, David Holloway and Daren Timson-Hunt, *Schmitthoff: The Law and Practice of International Trade* (12th edn, Sweet and Maxwell 2012) 282–352.

37 See Carr (n 28) 163.

38 Houtved, as detailed in Olesen (n 18).

39 UNCTAD Secretariat (n 26).

40 Roman T Keenan, 'Charter Parties and Bills of Lading' (1959) 42(3) Marq L Rev 346.

41 'A triangular relationship is established in all the scenarios once the shipper agrees on the transport of the cargo on a vessel hired by a charterer from a shipowner, which may also transport other cargo appertaining to different shippers', Rogers, Chuah, and Dockray (n 31) 6–7.

There are three types of B/L:[42] a 'straight' B/L, like a sea waybill, is non-negotiable or negotiable only once without further endorsement from the original shipper; an 'order' B/L is a negotiable B/L in which the goods are consigned to the order of a specific person (the seller or the seller's bank); and a 'bearer' B/L which is transferred by simple delivery: it might not specify a particular consignee, the party on whose order it is made, or it may be endorsed by its holder without specifying who ordered the cargo.

Article 1(b) of the Hague–Visby Rules, ratified by the most important maritime nations excluding the US, defines contracts of carriage only as those covered by a B/L or similar document of title

> in so far as such document relates to the carriage of goods by sea, including any bill of lading or any similar document … issued under or pursuant to a charterparty from the moment at which such bill of lading or similar document of title regulates the relations between a carrier and a holder of the same.[43]

González Pellicer comments on the negotiation of B/Ls:

> The carriage of goods by sea regime under the Bill of Lading is characterised, as is well known, by its regular ('line') and massive nature, with a multiplicity of shippers/partial shipments for a single ship/voyage. That demands a simplification and contractual standardisation (the result of which the Bill of Lading arises), but that also causes the negotiation imbalance between the parties, with the dominant situation of the shipowners over the shippers. The shipowner unilaterally prepares or drafts the general conditions of the bill of lading without taking into account the interests of the shipper.[44]

It should be noted that not all B/Ls create an imbalance between the carrier and the shipper. For instance, Ocean Liner Service Agreements (OLSA), known as service contracts, are the reason why the Rotterdam Rules have special provisions for volume contracts. These provide for the 'carriage of a specified quantity of goods in a series of shipments during an agreed period of time' according to Article 1(2) of the Rules.[45]

2 Party autonomy

Party autonomy[46] regarding choice of court and arbitration agreements generates intense debate in the PIL discipline and emerges in the study of the shipping law sector. Party autonomy provides speed, predictability and legal security to the contracting parties in the event

---

42 Peter G Pamel and Robert C Wilkins, 'Bills of Lading vs Sea Waybills, and The Himalaya Clause' (NJI/CMLA Federal Court and Federal Court of Appeal Canadian Maritime Law Association Seminar, Ottawa, 15 April 2011).

43 Under English Law, endorsement is required to obtain delivery of the goods according to COGSA 1992 s 1(1)–(3). The Law Commission and the Scottish Law Commission did not consider the straight B/Ls as documents of title: Law Commission and the Scottish Law Commission, *Rights of Suit in Respect of Carriage of Goods by Sea* (Law Com No. 196, 1991). S 5(5) COGSA 1992 points out that the Act shall have no prejudice to the application of the Hague–Visby Rules; Møllmann (n 22) 27. The House of Lords in *JI MacWilliam Co Inc v. Mediterranean Shipping Co SA (The Rafaela S)* [2005] UKHL 11, held that the Hague–Visby Rules apply to a straight B/L, i.e., it is a B/L or similar document of title; Richard Aikens, Richard Lord and Michael Bools, *Bills of Lading* (2nd edn, Informa 2015) [6.10].

44 José Manuel González Pellicer, 'Sobre el artículo 468 del Proyecto de Ley de Navegación Marítima y la nulidad de las cláusulas de elección de foro en los conocimientos de embarque' (2014) 8354 Diario La Ley 6.

45 Proshanto K Mukherjee and Abhinayan Basu Bal, 'A Legal and Economic Analysis of the Volume Contract Concept under the Rotterdam Rules: Selected Issues in Perspective' (2010) 77(1) Journal of Transportation Law, Logistics & Policy 27.

46 In the 19th century Friedrich Carl von Savigny contributed to the general acceptance of the party autonomy principle in Europe. Ole Lando, 'Private International Law: Contracts' in Kurt Lipstein (ed), *International Encyclopedia of Comparative Law* (vol 3, Mohr 1976) 11–12.

of a cargo claim and can be divided into procedural, material and 'conflictual'. The latter is also known as party autonomy in conflict of contract laws and allows parties to choose the law for the validity and effectiveness of the contract with no more limitation than the PIL of the forum. Procedural party autonomy provides for the recognition and enforcement of the choice of seat and dispute resolution mechanism. Substantive or material party autonomy sets the material content of the contract, contractual clauses normally incorporated by reference within a predetermined national system, subject to the mandatory rules of the forum.

It can be said that there is greater legal uncertainty regarding party autonomy from a procedural perspective (validity of choice of forum and applicable law), compared with conflictual (choice of law for the validity and effectiveness of a contract) or material (choice of contract clauses normally incorporated by reference within a predetermined national system) perspectives. This work will focus on procedural party autonomy, which influences material and conflictual party autonomies present in various instruments, to determine the most effective legal system for material and conflictual autonomy.

How does party autonomy impact contracts for the carriage of goods by sea? Contracts for the carriage of goods by sea carry legal risks that have to be balanced with the legitimate commercial interests of contracting parties. Charterparties and B/Ls will not have contradictory terms when the shipowner also acts as the carrier of the goods since it is a party to both the charterparty and the B/L. What are the components of party autonomy and in what circumstances does it come into play?

2.1 Procedural party autonomy

Procedural party autonomy is related to the recognition and enforcement of the choice of forum agreements, the cargo claims or the arrest procedures. It does not only apply to litigation. The different procedural rules either apply to contractual cargo claims between the shipowner and the charterer under the charterparty or to cargo claims between the B/L holder and the shipowner that will usually be in contract on the terms of the B/L, although not where it is a charterer's B/L.

In order to stress the importance of procedural party autonomy, different scenarios first need to be analysed. A problem may occur when a shipowner does not act as the carrier and does not sign the B/L. The terms in the charterparty and the B/L may differ, and the transferor of the B/L may not be aware of the negotiated terms of the charterparty. It may be necessary to clarify whether the transferor B/L holder can act against the carrier who is bound by both contracts. If the parties cannot settle the case on their own, the analysis of this issue by the court where the lawsuit is filed leads to a determination of the competent forum where the B/L holder is entitled to sue the carrier. Domestic procedural laws may or may not recognise the validity of dispute resolution clauses inserted in contracts of affreightment. Non-recognition may then lead to a conflict between different customary rules and practices established between the parties.

The principle of procedural party autonomy makes arbitration a flexible dispute resolution mechanism, providing parties with the freedom to contractually determine the circle of persons entitled to participate in the arbitration proceedings according to their commercial needs.[47] Parties may disagree on the designated dispute mechanism or the scope of its

47 Stavros Brekoulakis, 'The Relevance of the Interests of Third Parties in Arbitration: Taking a Closer Look at the Elephant in the Room' (2008) 113 Penn State L Rev 1165, 1166.

powers. Thus, a respondent may attempt to evade arbitration, perhaps making an allegation of violation of some limits or norms in order to attempt to invalidate the arbitration agreement.[48] Arbitration has a multiparty substantive background and third parties with an interest in the outcome of the arbitration should not be excluded from the arbitration process.[49]

The legal framework applicable to an arbitration agreement may involve different domestic or conventional laws applicable to the parties, the seat of arbitration, the contract and the arbitration agreement. Enforcement of the award may be subject to yet another law.[50] Parties are advised to make express choices of applicable law (ensuring that the arbitration clause meets the requirements of that law and that the dispute is regarded as arbitrable), the language of the arbitration and the method of appointing arbitrators. In the absence of express provisions agreed to by the parties, most arbitration rules afford arbitrators discretion to make these choices for the parties. The parties signing the arbitration agreement must have the capacity to do so and, where relevant, the authority to bind the party to the arbitration.[51] The substantive law applicable to the arbitration clause should also be specified, in case a dispute leading to arbitration occurs.[52]

Freedom of contract allows parties to choose a law applicable to disputes about the arbitration contract that is different from the one applicable to the main contract. To clarify whether the judge will uphold the clause or assume jurisdiction, it will be necessary to consider one of the more ratified conventions worldwide, the New York Convention[53] (see Chapter 2).

2.2 Substantive party autonomy

Substantive or 'material' party autonomy refers to the validity and scope of clauses incorporated into the contract for the carriage of goods by sea by the original parties. It includes the possibility available to the parties to establish pacts or clauses in the contract that regulate specific aspects of the contract dynamics, within the limits of a specific legal system. It does not refer to a choice of law but to the specific provisions of such laws that incorporate the contract under the party autonomy (incorporation by reference).[54] Legal norms incorporated by reference 'are private agreements between the parties', i.e., 'material clauses

48 See Klaus Peter Berger, *International Economic Arbitration* (Deventer 1993) 118; Mahmood Bagheri, *International Contracts and National Economic Regulation: Dispute Resolution Through International Commercial Arbitration* (Kluwer Law International 2000) 123.

49 Brekoulakis (n 47) 1187–1988.

50 Tony Cole and others, *Legal Instruments and Practice of Arbitration in the EU* (DG for Internal Policies, European Parliament 2014) 8.

51 J William Rowley, QC (ed), *Arbitration World: Jurisdictional Comparisons* (4th edn, Thomson Reuters 2012) 8–9.

52 Margaret L Moses, *The Principles and Practice of International Commercial Arbitration* (3rd edn, CUP 2017) 43–58.

53 International Convention on the Recognition and Enforcement of Foreign Arbitral Awards ('1958 New York Convention') (adopted 10 June 1958, entered into force 7 June 1959) 330 UNTS 38.

54 Jean-Michel Jacquet, *Le contrat international* (1st ed, Dalloz 1992) 112–120; Jean-Michel Jacquet, 'Retour sur la règle de conflit de lois en matière de contrats' (1991) 3 JDI 679; Jean-Michel Jacquet, 'Contrats' in *Encyclopédie Dalloz: Répertoire de droit international* (2nd edn, Dalloz 1998) 1–50; Alfonso-Luis Calvo Caravaca and Javier Carrascosa González (eds), *Derecho Internacional Privado: Vol II* (Comares 2016) 928–931; Javier Carrascosa González, *La Ley aplicable a los contratos internacionales: el reglamento Roma I* (Colex 2009) 164–168.

of the contract'.[55] They are not substantive law in the sense that they are applicable to the contract to the extent that the law of the contract allows it. The distinction between conflictual party autonomy (choice of law) and substantive (incorporation by reference) party autonomy according to the Rome I Regulation[56] requires a clear and unequivocal choice of law.[57] For example, a legislative change in the law incorporated by reference into a contract does not affect an *inter partes* agreement. The law chosen by the parties continues to apply to the same extent that the law allows.[58]

The contracting parties can incorporate by reference provisions that are not *per se* applicable to the contract, such as the Paramount Clause.[59] The parties cannot rule out certain parts of a convention, as some courts have pointed out; these rules are either fully applicable or non-applicable.[60] The validity of the incorporation of these rules depends on the law of the contract. Commercial usage, customs and clauses such as INCOTERMS 2020,[61] or general references to the *lex mercatoria* (merchant law) such as the UCP 600[62] are not part of any national law. However, a vague reference to *lex mercatoria* does not constitute an effective incorporation by reference, since it fails to identify the rule or rules incorporated into the contract.[63]

In order to analyse the limitations on party autonomy, it must be pointed out that a national judge decides the subject matter on the merits according to the substantive law. However, when the parties have made a conflictual choice of law, does the substantive law guarantee that the judge will apply English, Spanish or any other foreign law? It does not. The provisions of a predetermined set of national rules provide for the conflict rule of the domestic law that the judge hearing the case applies. The *lex fori* (law of the forum) is applied to determine the validity or not of such clause. However, the problem emerges by gathering the procedural party autonomy and the conflictual party autonomy applied to different and non-harmonised legal frameworks: domestic, conventional and EU procedural laws.

---

55 François Rigaux, 'Examen des quelques questions laissées ouvertes par la Convention de Rome sur la loi applicable aux obligations contractuelles' (1988) Cahiers de droit Européen 306.

56 Regulation (EC) No 593/2008 of the European Parliament and of the Council of 17 June 2008 on the law applicable to contractual obligations OJ 2008, L 177/6 (Rome I Regulation); in force on 17 December 2008, it applies to all EU Member States except Denmark; despite its doubts, the UK eventually opted in, replacing the Contracts (Applicable Law) Act 1990, which remained applicable to contracts signed before the Rome I Regulation came into force.

57 Recital 13 of the Rome I Regulation: 'This Regulation does not preclude parties from incorporating by reference into their contract a non-state body of law or an international convention'.

58 Calvo Caravaca and Carrascosa González, *Derecho Internacional Privado* (n 54); Carrascosa González (n 54) 164–168.

59 See case RJ 1980/4786 of the Spanish Supreme Court, *Banco Vitalicio de España v. Naviera Asón SA*, 21 June 1980; Dominique Bureau and Horatia Muir Watt, *Droit international privé: Tome II* (Presses Universitaires de France 2007) 324–325; Jonatan Echebarria Femández, 'Paramount Clause and Codification of International Shipping Law' (2019) 50(1) J Mar L & Com 45.

60 Paul Lagarde, 'Première Partie – Doctrine et Chroniques – Remarques sur la proposition de règlement de la Commision européenne sur la loi applicable aux obligations contractuelles (Rome I)' (2006) 95(2) *Revue Critique de Droit International Privé* 331, 336.

61 International Chamber of Commerce (ICC), 'Incoterms 2020: ICC Rules for the Use of Domestic and International Trade Terms' (2020).

62 International Chamber of Commerce (ICC), 'Uniform Customs and Practice for Documentary Credits (UCP), 2007 Revision, ICC Publication No. 600 (UCP 600)' (2007).

63 Andrea Giardina, 'La lex mercatoria e la certezza del diritto nei commerci e negli investimenti internazionali' 28 *Rivista di diritto internazionale privato e processuale* (1992) 461. Specific rules of a concrete state law can be also subject to incorporation, as well as rules prepared by experts and professors such as the UNIDROIT Principles of International Commercial Contracts or the Principles of European Contract Law; see Calvo Caravaca and Carrascosa González, *Derecho Internacional Privado* (n 54); Carrascosa González (n 54) 164–168.

The lack of harmonisation of commercial maritime laws in the EU leads to a chaotic situation since legislation varies from country to country. This probably is in accord with the interests of the shipping market, in this author's opinion.

2.3 Conflictual party autonomy

Conflictual party autonomy here refers to the choice of law applicable to contracts for the carriage of goods by sea. The law, *ius*, must be separated from the *forum*. The entire maritime transport sector is not governed by dispositive rules: agreements between parties face limitations.[64] 'Party autonomy in choice of law for contracts' is considered by this author to be a missing piece of the puzzle, that is, an international commercial regulation that does not exist globally in the shipping sector – although the Rome I Regulation applies in the EU.

3 The problem with party autonomy

This book reflects on limits on party autonomy regarding dispute resolution clauses incorporated into a charterparty by the shipowner and the charterer and any B/L issued pursuant to a charterparty, and the related challenges faced by the parties.

3.1 What are the limits on party autonomy regarding jurisdiction and arbitration clauses?

Party autonomy is an acknowledged principle that allows parties the freedom to choose methods of dispute resolution and the applicable law. It is present in domestic legislation worldwide and noticeably present in EU legislation, such as the Brussels I Regulation (recast).[65] The procedural, substantive and conflictual party autonomy to select a certain court or an arbitral tribunal, as well as the choice of applicable law, is limited by different normative frameworks due to a partial and sectorial harmonisation, preventing sufficient predictability[66] and legal certainty[67] in contractual relationships concerning parties' rights and obligations with regard to disputes.[68]

The potential limitations on the three types of party autonomy (procedural, material or substantial and conflictual) will be examined through a hypothetical cargo claim.

64 Pierre Mayer and Vincent Heuzé, *Droit international privé* (8th edn, Montchrestien 2004) 514–519.

65 Regulation (EU) No 1215/2012 of the European Parliament and of the Council of 12 December 2012 on jurisdiction and the recognition and enforcement of judgments in civil and commercial matters [2012] OJ 2012, L351/1 (Brussels I Recast Regulation).

66 On the analysis of the specific need for harmonisation of a specific normative sector, see Riccardo Luzzatto, *Metodi di unificazione del diritto marittimo e interpretazione uniforme* (1999) 1 Dir Marit 148–151.

67 In accordance with Recital 15 of the Brussels I Regulation (recast):

> The rules of jurisdiction should be highly predictable and founded on the principle that jurisdiction is generally based on the defendant's domicile. Jurisdiction should always be available on this ground save in a few well-defined situations in which the subject-matter of the dispute or the autonomy of the parties warrants a different connecting factor. The domicile of a legal person must be defined autonomously so as to make the common rules more transparent and avoid conflicts of jurisdiction; equally, Recital 16 of the Rome I Regulation specifies that to contribute to the general objective of this Regulation, legal certainty in the European judicial area, the conflict-of-law rules should be highly foreseeable. The courts should, however, retain a degree of discretion to determine the law that is most closely connected to the situation.

68 Among others, considerations on uniform law and PIL, as well as the Treaty regime, can be seen in A Malintoppi, *Diritto uniforme e diritto internazionale privato in tema di trasporto* (Giuffrè 1955) 38–84.

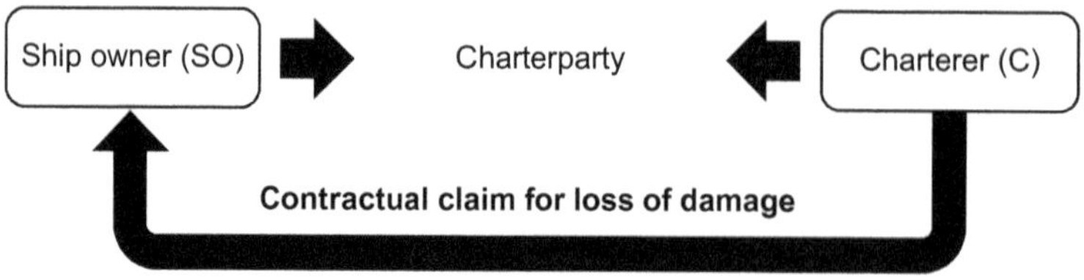

FIGURE 3 Contractual claim for loss or damage to the goods.

In the example shown in Figure 3, a charterer (C) and a shipowner (SO) sign a voyage charterparty under which SO agrees to perform the carriage of grain in return for freight. There are no intermediaries and a single contractual relationship between the parties is established. The carried grain is damaged, resulting in a cargo claim, and C will seek compensation for damages from SO under the contractual terms.

A contract for the carriage of goods between a shipowner employing its vessel in the liner trade and anyone interested in shipping goods is usually evidenced by a B/L. A charterparty and B/L are not mutually exclusive, since a party operating as a general carrier frequently charters the ship for a concrete period of time.[69]

Problems may arise if the quality and quantity of the goods described in the B/L do not coincide with what was agreed in the contract for the sale of goods and a dispute arises. Contracts of affreightment normally include a dispute resolution clause to provide legal certainty. The charterparty and B/L may contain the same or different express jurisdiction (*prorogatio fori*)[70] or alternative dispute resolution (ADR) clauses (usually arbitration).

In the example shown in Figure 4, a receiver (the buyer and B/L holder) may seek compensation from C after receiving the damaged grain cargo. This amounts to an extra-contractual claim. The seller has already received payment under the contract for the sale of goods from the buyer and only holds a B/L as the receipt and proof of the contract for the carriage of goods between S (shipper) and C. The extra-contractual responsibility of C for the damaged cargo shall not be dependent on the dispute resolution terms included in the B/L binding SO and S.

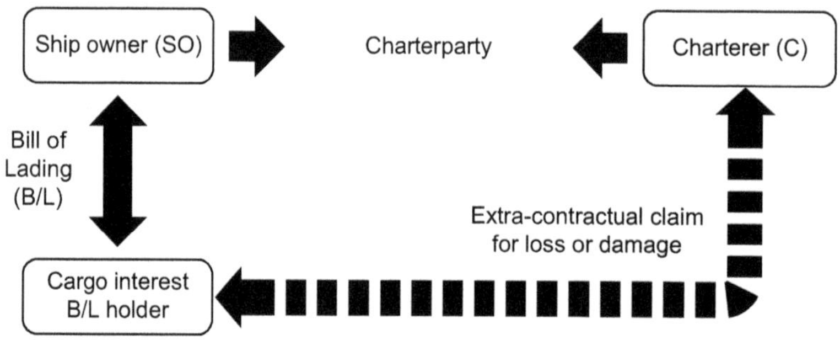

FIGURE 4 Extra-contractual claim for loss or damage to the goods.

69 cf Wilson (n 24).

70 Some B/Ls (e.g. CONGENBILL 2007 and CONLINEBILL 2000) provide solutions to incorporate jurisdiction clauses.

A contract between C and S for the carriage of goods may have contained a dispute resolution clause similar to or from the one included in the charterparty between SO and C. Such a contract may have had its terms superseded by those included in the B/L. If an agent signed a B/L on behalf of C, the contractual responsibility of C for any loss or damage to the cargo would depend on the dispute resolution clause included in the B/L.

When the cargo claim is filed, the judge will first analyse the court's competence to hear it, by analysing the relevant law and jurisdiction or ADR clauses. This will be more problematic if the cargo claimant starts proceedings in a country other than the one included in the contracts of affreightment and the judge in that country does not recognise the dispute resolution clause or its incorporation into the relevant contract based on procedural, substantive or conflict of laws grounds.[71] Third parties to a contract, such as S, may not be bound by incorporated dispute resolution clauses. The dispute resolution terms may be between the charterparty and B/L, leading to potential conflicts of interests due to erroneous incorporation of the charterparty dispute resolution clauses into the B/L. The question here is in what circumstances a *prorogatio fori* agreement is valid in case of a cargo claim by S against SO or C.

Party autonomy can be disregarded or limited in certain situations, leading to a different outcome in each case. A charterparty allows greater party autonomy to SO and C to decide the conditions for the use of the vessel. The situation may be different in relation to claims in tort or bailment, but these are outside the scope of this work.

3.2 When does the arrest of the ship frustrate the jurisdiction or arbitration agreement of the parties?

Dispute resolution clauses inserted into a charterparty or a B/L may not be recognised by a court when the claimant demands the arrest of the ship as an interim measure ancillary to the cargo claim. The clause has a separate nature from the rest of the contract and will be analysed as such. In the event of a cargo claim against the shipowner, the claimant may be able to obtain an arrest of the vessel for security for the claim in the vessel's present location, which may not be the same forum as that agreed in the relevant contract. In some countries, the issue of a writ for arrest may establish jurisdiction in that country, in contravention of the contractual jurisdiction clause.

In Figure 5, a shipper sues SO and applies for the arrest of the ship where the vessel is located. Will the arbitration or jurisdiction clause of the charterparty or B/L be recognised by the judge who issues the warrant of arrest? International arrest conventions applicable to the matter may constrain SO from resolving the dispute in the forum or ADR venue agreed to in the charterparty, or in the B/L, if applicable. If the judge issues an order for arrest, requiring the shipowner to provide security or provide a letter of indemnity (LOI) to release the ship, the court may hear the substance of the case on the merits, overriding the domestic legislation that would have applied had an arrest not been effected. The arrest of the ship, an interim measure having the nature of an action *in rem*, thus remains a contested issue for the recognition of clauses of jurisdiction or ADR contained in charterparties or B/Ls.

71 Procedural laws regulate the judicial process while the substantive law is composed of the applicable international, conventional or national rules; Sparka, *Jurisdiction and Arbitration Clauses in Maritime Transport Documents* (n 2) 19–38.

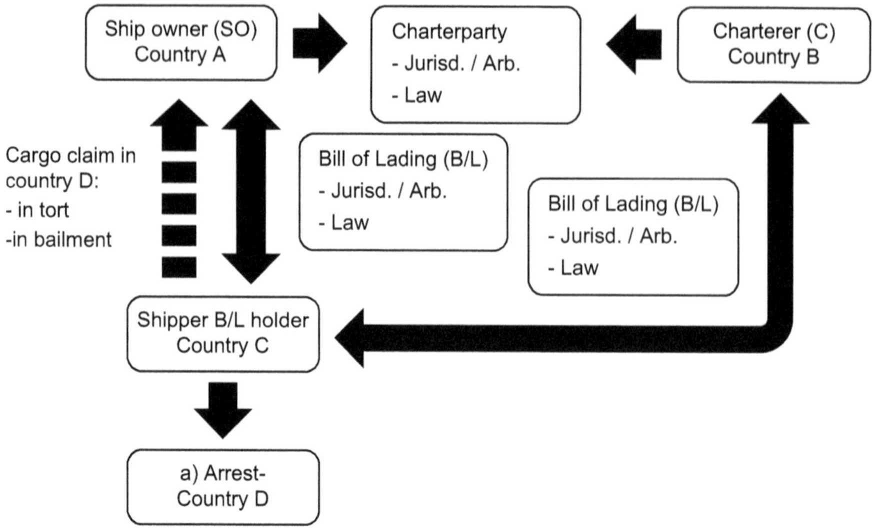

FIGURE 5 Arrest of ships.

3.3 When is the validity of a jurisdiction or arbitration agreement restricted by the substantive applicable law of the forum, including overriding mandatory rules?

Procedural law plays a fundamental role in the recognition of jurisdiction or arbitration agreements. International uniformity has not been achieved, although some regional frameworks, such as in the EU, are compulsory when parties have selected an EU Member State court, subject to formal requirements, regardless of where the parties are domiciled.

When jurisdiction has been determined, the mandatorily applicable legal regime may determine the minimum protective standards applied to the charterparty. When overriding mandatory rules apply, a court can take jurisdiction over a cargo claim dispute even if there is a relevant dispute resolution clause. If there is a conflict, domestic law or EU PIL rules will determine the applicable law and the jurisdiction or arbitration agreement may be overridden. Such practice may remarkably limit party autonomy. Courts in EU Member States will apply the Rome I Regulation or Rome II Regulation,[72] depending on the nature of the claim, if the contract for the carriage of goods by sea does not include an explicit choice of law.

Other problems are present in common law regimes, although not exclusively, where jurisdiction is declined due to public policy or other circumstances related to the nature of the claim. Moreover, the common law *forum non conveniens* doctrine may assist in avoiding irreconcilable judgments by two different courts. The EU regime is set up to

72 Regulation (EC) No 864/2007 of the European Parliament and of the Council of 11 July 2007 on the law applicable to non-contractual obligations (Rome II) OJ 2007 L 199/40 (Rome II Regulation).

avoid irreconcilable decisions while facilitating mutual trust between the EU courts and the execution of judgments generally.

The cargo claimant's risk of having a non-recognisable judgment and not recovering compensation may encourage it to apply for interim measures, such as arrest of the ship. Some international conventions, such as the 1952 Arrest Convention,[73] will take precedence over the EU jurisdictional framework in certain circumstances. The question of whether the chosen forum or arbitral seat will be recognised in security actions leads to legal uncertainty for the shipowner and the charterer.

The choice of applicable law may constitute an obstacle to the recognition of the chosen dispute resolution venue by the contracting parties. There are restrictions on the shipowner or the charterer in order to limit their responsibility when the substantive law is applied by the court or arbitral tribunal. These restrictions apply where a cargo claim is filed in a jurisdiction less favourable to their interests than that agreed in the contract of carriage. Depending on the identity of the contractual carrier, the shipowner and charterer may be able to limit their responsibility in a cargo claim from the shipper. The limitations on party autonomy concerning the dispute resolution clause incorporated into the B/L also exist in procedural laws and mandatory rules, such as ones related to limiting the responsibility (contractual defences) of the carrier, which may also be incorporated into the contract for the carriage of goods.

The international conventions in force, such as the Hague–Visby and Hamburg Rules, mandatorily applicable or not depending on the jurisdiction, regulate the liability regime in the B/L. However, since they are not directly applicable to charterparties, an express incorporation is required through a Paramount Clause.

4 Sources of law and the impact of Brexit

This book considers the national, international and EU aspects that apply to the incorporation of jurisdiction and arbitration clauses in bills of lading, with particular consideration of English law and comparisons with Spanish law. In the EU, the Brussels I Regulation (recast) is of particular significance, containing the jurisdictional regime that applies within the EU (with equivalent provisions found in the Lugano Convention,[74] which applies to the EU and EFTA states).

The exit of the UK from the EU (Brexit) is acknowledged. Companies need legal certainty in international economic relations. The EU legal framework will not apply in the UK after Brexit, including the Brussels I Regulation (recast), subject to whatever agreement or a new instrument is put in place to govern civil and commercial disputes. The European Union (Withdrawal Agreement) Bill of 21 October 2019 was passed by the House of Commons on 20 December 2019 and received royal assent on 23 January 2020. The European Parliament gave its consent to the agreement on 29 January 2020. At the time of writing, political tensions between the UK and the EU coupled with the coronavirus pandemic have not allowed Brexit negotiations to progress at a good pace.

73 International Convention for the Unification of Certain Rules Relating to the Arrest of Seagoing Ships (adopted 10 May 1952, entered into force 24 February 1956) (1952 Arrest Convention), 439 UNTS 193.

74 Council Decision 2007/712/EC of 15 October 2007 on jurisdiction and the recognition and enforcement of judgments in civil and commercial matters [2007] OJ 2007, L339/3 (Lugano Convention).

Current uncertainty looms as the Brexit negotiation process is stuck due to the current political impasse. The uncertainty over the eventual relationship between the UK and EU may give shipping companies pause when negotiating their contracts. Moreover, delays at European ports caused by customs checks may ensue if the UK quits the EU customs union on 31 January 2021. These factors potentially increase the risk of legal conflicts between shipping actors across Ireland, the UK and other jurisdictions. This research has been carried out without any legal changes to the status quo. This author has looked at the conflict of laws in this context because at the time of writing/publication the UK is still in the transition period.

4.1 International treaties

The law of merchant shipping was one of the early branches of private law to attract attention toward possible unification, primarily through international conventions. The unification of maritime law by international conventions is burdened by the same theoretical and practical problems as the unification of law in general. Not only are the necessity and limitations of unification themselves questionable but so also are the methods and procedures required to achieve and preserve formal and substantive uniformity. The adoption of these rules by a wide range of countries risks significant modifications and textual variations according to national legislative methods, which can lead to conflicting interpretations of legal texts embedding the same rules, in opposition to the original intention of creating uniformity.[75] The most successful international treaties are those with the most widespread ratification. The UK and Spain have not always ratified the same treaties, and therefore the approaches of English and Spanish law show further differences in their application of international law. There have been high hopes for further international unification and consolidation of maritime law through instruments such as the Rotterdam Rules, but these have not gained the traction that was originally anticipated, and are still not in force over 10 years after they were signed. The search goes on for a truly unifying international convention.

In order to ascertain the limits to the autonomy of parties to a charterparty in contracts of affreightment, the following international conventions are considered.

4.1.1 The Hague–Visby Rules

The Hague–Visby Rules[76] emerged as the result of the Hague Rules,[77] as amended by the Protocol to Amend the International Convention for the Unification of Certain Rules of

75 Athanassios N Yiannopoulos, 'The Unification of Private Maritime Law by International Conventions' (1965) 30 Law and Contemporary Problems 370.

76 International Convention for the Unification of Certain Rules of Law Relating to Bills of Lading (adopted 25 August 1924, entered into force 2 June 1931) ('The Hague Rules') 51 Stat 223, 120 LNTS 155, amended by the Protocol to Amend the International Convention for the Unification of Certain Rules of Law Relating to Bills of Lading (adopted 23 February 1968) ('The Visby Rules') 1412 UNTS 121, and the last Protocol amending the Hague–Visby Rules (adopted 21 December 1979) ('SDR Visby Protocol') UNTS 146.

77 In 1921, the Comité Maritime International (CMI) presented the so-called Hague Rules with the intention that they be voluntarily incorporated in all B/Ls. These rules were fundamental in the compromise between competing interests of carriers and shippers, and they were configured in the form of a B/L-type, aiming to have them adopted by the big shipping companies. However, since they were not compulsory, their effectiveness was reduced because the shipping companies were unwilling to give up the liability exemptions provided by numerous domestic laws.

Law Relating to Bills of Lading 1968 (the Visby rules) and the SDR Visby Protocol. The Rules are in force in both the UK and Spain.

The Hague–Visby Rules were intended to create a balanced model for jurisdiction respecting party autonomy that provides for freedom of choice. The Rules enhance party autonomy by allowing the parties to choose the applicable jurisdiction to apply to contracts for the carriage of goods by sea, as they do not contain any mandatory jurisdiction provisions. The Rules do impose minimum liability standards. Mandatory rules are commonly used in the industry to prevent a carrier from avoiding minimum liability standards by forcing on a shipper a forum where those standards have no effect.[78]

Charterparties are not subject to any statutory regime unless the parties choose to incorporate one, such as the Hague–Visby Rules.[79] A full set of defences for carriers is provided for in the Hague–Visby Rules, including:

a) Rule IV.2 (a)–(q), exempted perils;
b) Rule III.6, time limitation;
c) Rule IV.5, limitation of liability;
d) Rule III.3–4, B/L functions (such as receipt and the condition of the goods).

Usually the cargo claimant would sue on the B/L unless it is the charterer. Rule IV *bis* allows the carrier to invoke all the defences and limits provided by a liability limitation mechanism when sued in contract or in tort.[80]

The doctrine of *ius tertii* is the solution provided by continental law, while the privity of contract doctrine fetters contractors' freedom in the common law system. There are statutory exceptions to this doctrine in England such as the Carriage of Goods by Sea Act 1971 (COGSA 71), which gives force of law to the Hague–Visby Rules (see Article IV bis), and COGSA 92, which gives the consignee or endorsee of a transferable B/L title to sue the carrier: the obligations undertaken by the carrier are normally delegated and the B/L is transferred to the consignee who has to negotiate it to an assignee.[81] Therefore, parties have the possibility of establishing a statutory regime by contract, potentially based on conventions such as the Hague–Visby Rules.

4.1.2 The Hamburg Rules 1978

The Hamburg Rules were created with the aim of replacing the Hague Rules and the Hague–Visby Rules. They represent an attempt to harmonise the interests and curb the abuses committed by shipowner–carriers vis-à-vis shippers under the pretext of an alleged contractual

78 Rupert Coldwell, 'Jurisdiction and the UN Convention on Contracts for the International Carriage of Goods: Where the Freedom of Contract Prevails' (2014) 17(1) Intl Trade & Bus L Rev 108.

79 See Murray, Holloway and Timson-Hunt (n 36) 282–352.

80 George D Theocharidis, 'Mechanisms of Protection from Non-Contractual Modes of Recovery in Sea Carriage: A Comparison between Common Law and Civil Law Systems' (2013) 44(2) J Mar L & Com 219. An injured party can sue a third party that performed a delegated task and who is not party to the main contract – normally the servants or agents (including subcontractors who perform the real carriage). The problem arises under Rule IV.2(q) of the Hague–Visby Rules, which acknowledge that the carrier is liable contractually and in tort for all the servants and independent contractors it employs, giving rise to the most controversial question, not in the case of servants, but of independent contractors who are not precisely in breach of such a delegated duty.

81 Theocharidis (n 80).

negotiation. Under the new convention, a more balanced risk distribution policy between the cargo owner and the carrier is articulated, giving greater protection to the shipper.[82]

The debate during the drafting of what would become the Hamburg Rules revealed pressure from developing countries, with primarily shippers' interests, for a modification of the regime for the transport of goods by sea. The Hamburg Rules received significant support from these countries, but have not been widely accepted by major seafaring nations, and have not been ratified by the UK or Spain.

4.1.3 The Rotterdam Rules

The still-not-in-force Convention on Contracts for the International Carriage of Goods Wholly or Partly by Sea, known as The Rotterdam Rules, aims to establish a uniform and modern legal regime governing the rights and obligations of shippers, carriers and consignees under a contract for door-to-door carriage that includes an international sea leg. However, it has to be borne in mind that this set of rules is still not in force and requires ratification by 20 contracting states. As of 26 December 2019, only the Republic of the Congo, Spain, Togo, Benin and Cameroon have ratified the Convention.

The principal objective of the Rotterdam Rules is to achieve harmonisation and progressive unification of international maritime law and to enable a mandatory universal regime to standardise maritime transport contracts and contracts for the use of other modes of transport, to guarantee and promote legal security and sector efficiency. To this end, the Rules incorporate an autonomous definition of the contract of carriage and distinguish a list of contractual modalities, including volume contracts, regular line transport and non-regular transport. The Rules attempt to reconcile various interests, especially for the liability regime, including contractual and extra-contractual actions, providing a margin of manoeuvre to shipping operators while allowing party autonomy.

The Rotterdam Rules differentiate between various parties that might be involved in a transport relationship: these include the carrier, the performing party, the maritime performing party, the shipper, the documentary shipper, the holder and the consignee. The Rules include provisions concerning third-party claims against the carrier.

There is a tension between the different players in maritime transport, namely the developing economies versus the traditional seafaring powers that protect the shipping and insurance industries. The practical effect of choice of forum clauses is to reduce carriers' liability by choosing a forum that will award a very low level of damages.[83] If the carrier and the shipper agree on the competent court or courts designated under an exclusive jurisdiction agreement a third party may be bound by such agreement under Article 67(2) of the Rotterdam Rules if the relevant requirements are fulfilled.[84]

82 Pierre Bonassies, 'La responsabilité du transporteur maritime dans les règles de La Haye et dans les règles de Hambourg' (1989) 91(4) Dir Marit 949; Sergio Turci, 'Riflessioni in tema di responsabilità vettoriale secondo le convenzione di Bruxelles–Visby e di Amburgo' (1990) 91(1) Dir Marit 33; John O Honnold, 'Uniform Laws for International Trade: Early "Care and Feeding" for Uniform Growth' (1995) Intl Trade & Bus LJ 1.

83 Horatia Muir Watt, '"Party Autonomy" in International Contracts: from the makings of a myth to the requirements of global governance' (2010) 6(3) ERCL 250.

84 Yvonne Baatz, 'A Jurisdiction Race in the Dark' [2010] LMCLQ 364, 373–374.

4.1.4 The Hague Choice of Court Convention

The 2005 Hague Choice of Court Convention[85] aligns with the Brussels I Regulation (recast), stating in its Article 1(1) on the scope of application of the Convention that it 'shall apply in international cases to exclusive choice of court agreements concluded in civil or commercial matters'.[86] It was drafted under the auspices of the Hague Conference on Private International Law as an attempt to achieve the same effectiveness and legal certainty for jurisdiction agreements that arbitration agreements already enjoy under the New York Convention.

In Baatz's words, the Hague Choice of Court Convention shares three principles with the Brussels I Regulation (recast), 'subject to exceptions: if parties to a contract choose court jurisdiction or arbitration that choice should be given effect to; no other court should take jurisdiction; and any court judgment or arbitration award resulting from such choice should be recognised and enforced'. The scope of the Hague Choice of Court Convention is more restrictive than the Brussels I Regulation (recast) since it does not provide for the competent court where there is no jurisdictional agreement between the parties.[87]

The limitation of its scope of application excluding maritime disputes makes it inapplicable to the carriage of goods by sea and the limitation on liability for maritime claims.[88] However, it does apply to contracts of insurance (or reinsurance). It is arguable whether it applies to time charterparties. This author agrees with the assumption that it could be applicable to demise chartering, but not voyage charterparties.[89]

4.1.5 The 1952 Arrest Convention and the 1999 Arrest Convention

The 1952 Arrest Convention and the 1999 Arrest Convention[90] are of paramount importance since their rules, providing for jurisdiction, have a disproportionate influence over party-agreed dispute resolution clauses. These conventions may allow the claimant to benefit from 'forum shopping' tactics, where parties aim to benefit from the most advantageous jurisdiction offering the best procedural and substantive potential for arrest.

4.1.6 The New York Convention

The New York Convention of 1958 regulates the recognition and validity of arbitration agreements. This Convention is considered *erga omnes* as it is widely ratified by most countries worldwide, currently with 159 contracting states. It regulates a positive effect (that is, it confers jurisdiction for dispute resolution) and a negative one (that is, the obligation of courts to decline jurisdiction when a valid arbitration agreement exists).

---

85 The Hague Convention of 30 June 2005 on Choice of Court Agreements of the Hague Conference on Private International Law, 44 ILM 1294.

86 Juan José Álvarez Rubio and Unai Belintxon Martín, 'La Nueva Ley de Navegación Marítima desde la Perspectiva del Derecho Internacional' in Alberto Emparanza Sobejano and José Manuel Martín Osante (eds), *Comentarios Sobre la Ley de Navegación Marítima* (Marcial Pons 2015).

87 Yvonne Baatz, 'The Conflict of Laws' in Yvonne Baatz, *Maritime Law* (4th edn, Routledge 2018) 16–17.

88 Articles 2(2)(f)–(g) of the Hague Convention on Choice of Court Agreements, also exclude marine pollution, general average and emergency towage and salvage.

89 Yvonne Baatz, 'The Conflict of Laws' in Yvonne Baatz (ed), *Maritime Law* (4th edn, Routledge 2018) 17; Andrew Tettenborn, 'The Nuts and Bolts of Maritime Contracts: BREXIT and Choice of Law and Choice of Court Agreements' (Tribuna Profesional ANAVE, January 2018) <www.anave.es/images/tribuna_profesional/2018/tribuna_bia0118.pdf> accessed 15 January 2018.

90 International Convention on the Arrest of Ships 1999 (adopted 12 March 1999, entered into force 14 September 2011) (1999 Arrest Convention), 2797 UNTS 3.

The New York Convention has two aims: First, it prevents foreign arbitral awards from being discriminated against in its contracting states, favouring recognition and execution by them. Second, the text seeks to ensure that third-state courts recognise the full effect of arbitration agreements subscribed to by the original parties to the contract. There is no parallel international convention regarding the recognition and enforcement of judgments with such broad acceptance.

4.2 'Soft law': customs and usages

The *lex mercatoria* constitutes the commercial customs incorporated into contracts through the will of the parties. One example is the ICC's 'INCOTERMS', which are interpreted according to national laws (*lex fori*). On a worldwide scale, the UNIDROIT Principles of International Commercial Contracts (1994),[91] drafted at the International Institute for the Unification of Private Law, lack legislative force but are increasingly used in international commercial arbitration. The Principles of European Contract Law, drafted by a Commission on European Contract Law led by Ole Lando, are considered a blueprint for future legislation on European contract law.[92]

The 'soft law' developed by the United Nations Commission on International Trade Law (UNCITRAL) and its Model Law on International Commercial Arbitration[93] serves as the benchmark for the harmonisation of arbitration laws and statutes worldwide. Many domestic arbitration laws follow the model laws or general principles in international commercial law. The set of available rules vary between contracting states, depending on whether they apply the 1985 Model Law directly or domestic arbitration laws enacting it.

Lex mercatoria stems from a range of sources and institutions. These include the Baltic and International Maritime Council (BIMCO), the International Association of Independent Tanker Owners (INTERTANKO) and the International Association of Dry Cargo shipowners (INTERCARGO), as well as shipowners, shipping companies, freight forwarders, carriers and public organisations, such as national maritime administrations, in the decision-making process at the EU and international institutions.[94]

The customs and practices generated in the maritime environment have formed a specific *lex mercatoria* in this sector as a consequence of a 'flexibilisation' process of clauses that routinely appear in shipping documents. Such clauses determine which court will be competent (arbitral or jurisdictional) and clarify which legal regime will delimit the potential liabilities of international shipping contracts. These clauses pose the same problems of validity and effectiveness when invoked against third parties or contracting parties.[95] These rules have been gradually accepted by participants in the maritime transport sector, as well

91 Approved in 1994 and amended in 2004. The fourth edition was published in 2016 and contains a new section on illegality.

92 Mathias Reimann and Reinhard Zimmermann, *The Oxford Handbook of Comparative Law* (OUP 2006) 899.

93 UNCITRAL Model Law on International Commercial Arbitration adopted on 21 June 1985, and recognised in Resolution No. 40/72 by the 112th plenary meeting of the UN General Assembly on 11 December 1985 (UN document A/40/17), as amended by the bill approved in the UN General Assembly in Resolution No. 61/33 from 18 December 2006 (UN Document A/RES/61/33).

94 Echebarria Fernández, 'Action Research and Efficient Maritime Transport Contract Negotiation' (n 1) 49–63.

95 See Julio D González Campos, Diversification, spécialisation, flexibilisation et matérialisation des règles de droit Iiternational Privé: vol 287 (Martinus Nijhoff 2002) 156 *et seq.*; see Juan José Álvarez Rubio, 'Hacia un

as by courts. The real workhorse is the interpretation of arbitration and jurisdiction clauses typically included in shipping contracts or documents (both in liner and tramp traffic) as the *leitmotif* of lawsuits and claims subject to the customs and practices of international maritime traffic. These uses and practices determine not only the resolution of disputes, whether by arbitration, jurisdiction or national standards, but also the applicable law in this area.[96]

5 Limits of this work

Limitations on the choice of forum or arbitral seat by the shipowner and the charterer fall outside the scope of choice of law clauses contained in a charterparty or B/L. This is because the choice of law implies the application of international conventions implemented by courts through domestic law. In case of the absence of choice of law, the Rome I Regulation or Rome II Regulation do not apply to a negotiable B/L as it is excluded to the extent that the obligations arise out of its negotiable character.

This work does not address the recognition and enforcement of judgments and to a limited extent the applicable law. The applicable law is present to a certain extent in discussion on overriding mandatory rules or public policy, while the recognition and enforcement of arbitral awards (not judgments) are guaranteed through the New York Convention.

A contract of international transport constitutes a service contract[97] and is excluded from the concept of the sale of goods according to Article 7(1)(b) of the Brussels I Regulation (recast). As Lorente Martínez points out, a contract of international transport poses a highly conflictive area, unrelated to problems arising out of the contract for an international sale of goods.[98]

This analysis focuses on a specific sector, the carriage of goods by sea, for which conclusions will differ from those for other sectors, such as the carriage of passengers by sea.

6 Conclusions

The analysis from a comparative perspective brings different solutions and conclusions for practitioners and academics. Situations vary, depending on whether the parties have chosen an EU court. The Brussels I Regulation (recast) does not apply to a choice of jurisdiction of the court of a non-EU state or an arbitration clause. Differences may arise concerning the choice of an EU Member State court since the Brussels I Regulation (recast) requirements under Article 25 will prevail over different national legislation. The changes introduced by Article 25 of the Brussels I Regulation (recast) in comparison with Article

---

nuevo Derecho Marítimo Comunitario' in Julio D González Campos (ed), *Pacis Artes. Obra Homenaje al Profesor Julio D González Campos, vol 2* (Edifer 2005) 1165–1184.

96 Article 9(6) of the Spanish Arbitration Act, Law 60/2003 of 23 December on arbitration (Official State Gazette No 309 of 26 December 2003) (SAA), has introduced a number of innovations that may have some relevance to the interpretation of maritime arbitration clauses. It refers to the validity of the agreement and the arbitrability of the dispute; Rosario Espinosa Calabuig, 'Las cláusulas arbitrales marítimas a la luz de los usos del tráfico internacional' (2007) 13 Revista electrónica de estudios internacionales 2.

97 Pilar Jiménez Blanco, 'La aplicación del foro contractual del Reglamento Bruselas I a los contratos de transporte aéreo de pasajeros' (2009) 7294 Diario La Ley.

98 Isabel Lorente Martínez, 'Competencia Judicial Internacional y Compraventa Internacional de Mercaderías: Un Estudio de Meta Jurisprudencia Analítica' (Doctoral dissertation, Universidad de Murcia 2016) 299.

23 of the original Brussels I Regulation 44/2001[99] enabled the non-distinction between the claimant's and defendant's residence in order to allow an express choice of jurisdiction favouring an EU Member State. Outside the EU, domestic procedural rules of the seat of the court will apply. When the chosen seat of jurisdiction or arbitration is in a non-EU state, the Brussels I Regulation (recast) does not apply, requiring the validity of the agreement to settle any dispute unless the agreement is 'null and void as to its substantive validity under the law applied by the EU Member State court where the dispute resolution agreement is sought to be enforced by any party'.[100]

In addition to overriding mandatory rules, a court has jurisdiction based on merits unless a judge interprets that the claim is subject to *forum non conveniens* in common law countries, a public policy exception in civil law countries (i.e., *lis alibi pendens*) in a purely domestic context (but not an international one) or a valid choice of forum and arbitration clause under a court of arrest's *lex fori* as alleged by the defendant. However, there is no legal certainty for the contracting parties, which can lead to 'forum shopping' by claimants.

The primary problem is that shipowners are deprived of a vessel until a letter of undertaking (LOU)[101] or other security is provided in case of ship arrest, even if charterers are responsible for the cargo claim motivating the arrest. This issue is rooted in the limitations of party autonomy, which result in a high incidence rate for ship arrests that limit parties' chosen forum or arbitral tribunals. Two key factors play crucial roles in this issue. First is the subjective factor, formed by those who feel legally bound by the jurisdiction or arbitration agreement and those who are not parties to the agreements but are bound by the clause. Second is the objective factor formed by the contractual or non-contractual scope of a clause's effects.

Finally, the interactions between regulatory frameworks following EU, conventional or internal standards mean that even if relevant international conventions are ratified by a state as part of its PIL, a judge can apply the Brussels I Regulation (recast) in the EU when parties choose an EU court, arbitral tribunal or domestic laws to validate dispute resolution clauses, which can lead to diverse outcomes. Substantive international harmonisation has not yet been achieved.[102] It is highly desirable for it to be accompanied by international procedural unification, as there is a lack of substantive laws to recognise and enforce dispute resolution clauses in carriage of goods by sea contracts, as well as different procedural rules on issuing warrants of arrest in each jurisdiction.

---

99 Council Regulation (EC) 44/2001 of 22 December 2000 on jurisdiction and the recognition and enforcement of judgments in civil and commercial matters [2001] OJ 2001, L 012/1 (Brussels I Regulation).

100 Article 25 of the Brussels I Regulation (recast).

101 'The purpose of an LOU is to ensure that the vessel is not arrested in port by a creditor or to permit a ship already under arrest to sail. Whether the shipowner or managers are unwilling or unable to pay the underlying debt, their interest will be that the ship is enabled to continue trading and earning freight. A speedy release of the vessel is also in the interests of the creditor as it will help a shipowner or manager in financial straits to pay the debt. The Protection & Indemnity Club (P&I Club) provides security for the debt of the shipowner or manager by undertaking to settle the debt and to accept service of *in rem* proceedings in a competent court. This is provided by an LOU which the P&I Club is not obliged to give. An LOU is also a means to allow the parties the time to discuss the precise amount of the liability and acceptable ways of paying it while avoiding litigation for as long as possible'; Özlem Gürses and Johanna Hjalmarsson, 'Marine Insurance' in Yvonne Baatz (ed), *Maritime Law* (4th edn, Routledge 2018) 489.

102 Despite the high number of ratifications of international instruments such as the Hague–Visby Rules, the 1952 Arrest Convention, the International Convention on Maritime Liens and Mortgages (MLM Convention) and to a limited extent the Hamburg Rules and the 1999 Arrest Convention, the Rotterdam Rules are still not in force.

CHAPTER 2

International jurisdiction and arbitration

Chapter 2 focuses on international jurisdiction within the EU legal system and jurisdiction under international instruments. It illustrates how jurisdiction and arbitration clauses included in shipping contracts for the carriage of goods by sea may be found invalid and unrecognised by competent national judges. It also considers the limitations on party autonomy imposed by the EU legal framework regarding choice of jurisdiction and arbitration clauses.

1 International jurisdiction in the EU

International contracts for the carriage of goods by sea include jurisdiction and arbitration clauses, as well as clauses choosing the law applicable to the contract. The aim of this chapter is not to ascertain the limits on party autonomy related to applicable law clauses chosen by the parties but to analyse the framework that applies to jurisdiction and arbitration clauses. The incorporation of these clauses into B/Ls will not be treated here but in Chapter 3.

1.1 Separability of the jurisdiction clause from the main contract

> Separability, as a term of art, properly describes the disentangling of two contracts from what may appear in other respects to be a single agreement, in order that the invalidity of the one contract not affect the validity of the other.[1]

In other words, separability presumes the autonomy of the dispute resolution clauses (jurisdiction, arbitration or applicable law) or the rules on nullity or termination of the contract and its consequences as distinct from the contract, under the framework of the general principles of contract law. These clauses are independent of other clauses of the contract due to their purely procedural character and the overarching substantive or material party autonomy.[2] Examples are found in Article 22(1) of the Spanish Arbitration Act (SAA),[3] or Article 25(5) of the Brussels I Regulation (recast), which sets out the following: 'An agreement conferring jurisdiction which forms part of a contract shall be treated as an agreement independent of the other terms of the contract'.

---

1 Adrian Briggs, 'The subtle variety of jurisdiction agreements' (2012) 3 LMCLQ 364, 380.

2 José Carlos Fernández Rozas, 'Alternatives and uncertainties of the dispute settlement clauses in international maritime contracts' (2018) Cuadernos de Derecho Transnacional 10(2) 333, 336.

3 Law 60/2003 of 23 December on arbitration (Official State Gazette No 309 of 26 December 2003).

The determination of the validity of these dispute resolution clauses differs from the *kompetenz-kompetenz* principle that applies to arbitration. Article 3(d) of the Hague Choice of Court Convention states that: 'an exclusive choice of court agreement that forms part of a contract shall be treated as an agreement independent of the other terms of the contract. The validity of the exclusive choice of court agreement cannot be contested solely on the ground that the contract is not valid'.

These clauses require a constructive comparative legal analysis,[4] acknowledging that jurisdiction clauses aim to solve disputes by choosing a state court while arbitration ones are designed to evade state courts by entrusting the arbitrators with powers to undertake such duty.[5]

The Brussels/Lugano regime presupposes that the separability of the choice of forum clause from the main contract implies that if the main contract is null or void it does not affect the other independent agreement. That was the doctrine set out in the Court of Justice of the European Union's (CJEU) judgment in *Benincasa v. Dentalkit Srl.*[6] The court referred to legal certainty as the basis of its ruling, but there was no mention of the doctrine of separability.[7] The claimant agreed on a franchising agreement that included an Italian choice of jurisdiction clause. It raised a claim to a German court that referred to the CJEU the question of whether any court other than the one chosen under an exclusive jurisdiction agreement had jurisdiction to declare the main contract invalid.[8]

In *Benincasa*, the CJEU distinguished between choice of forum agreements, governed by the uniform jurisdiction rules of the Brussels Convention,[9] and the substantive contractual provisions, governed by the *lex causae* (paras 24–25 of the judgment). The CJEU distinguished between the choice of forum clause and other contractual provisions. As a result, the German court had to decide on its jurisdiction regardless of any consideration of the substance of the case (para 27). Legal certainty had to be ensured since the Brussels Convention could be invoked to frustrate the whole contract.[10]

The rule of separability can be found in other international conventions dealing with contractual issues: e.g., Article 81(1) of the UN Convention on Contracts for the International Sale of Goods (the Vienna Convention); Article 7.3.5(3) of the UNIDROIT Principles of International Commercial Contracts; Article 9:305(2) of the Principles of European Contract Law; Rule III–3:509(2) of the Draft Common Frame of Reference in Europe; Article 7.3.4(2) of the OHADAC Principles on International Commercial Contracts.[11]

---

4 Georges René Delaume, 'Clauses d'élection de for et clauses compromissoires: évolution et gestation d'un nouveau droit américain' (1975) JDI 486; Nathalie Coipel-Cordonnier, *Les conventions d'arbitrage et d'élection de for en droit international privé* (LGDJ 1999) 1–6.

5 Fernández Rozas, 'Alternatives and uncertainties of the dispute settlement clauses in international maritime contracts' (n 2) 336.

6 Case C-269/95 *Benincasa v. Dentalkit Srl* EU:C:1997:337, [1997] ECR I-3767 at [21]–[32].

7 Felix Sparka, *Jurisdiction and Arbitration Clauses in Maritime Transport Documents* (Springer 2010) 81–98.

8 Zheng Sophia Tang, *Jurisdiction and Arbitration Agreements in International Commercial Law* (Routledge 2014) 71.

9 Convention of 27 September 1968 on jurisdiction and the enforcement of judgments in civil and commercial matters OJ 1972, L 299/32, consolidated text of 26 January 1998 [1998] OJ 1998 C 27/1 (Brussels Convention).

10 ibid.

11 See José Carlos Fernández Rozas, Sixto A Sánchez Lorenzo y Gonzalo Stampa, *Principios Generales del Arbitraje* (Tirant lo Blanch 2018) 24; Fernández Rozas, 'Alternatives and uncertainties of the dispute settlement clauses in international maritime contracts' (n 2) 336.

The separability doctrine has been well accepted in England by courts[12] and scholars.[13] In *Mackender v. Feldia AG*,[14] a jurisdiction agreement was held to be valid despite the main contract being found to be voidable. A jurisdiction clause may be governed by a different law from the one that applies to the main contract.[15] Normally the procedure is governed by the *lex fori* (the law of the forum) and jurisdiction agreements are considered a matter of substantive law.[16] However, under English law, the *lex fori* generally governs their effect.[17] In *Deutsche Bank AG v. Asia Pacific Broadband Wireless Communication Inc*,[18] Longmore J held that the doctrine of separability applies, whereby: '... disputes about the validity of the contract must, on the face of it, be resolved pursuant to the terms of the clause and, indeed, the last sentence of the clause expressly so provides. It is only if the jurisdiction clause is itself under some specific attack that a question can arise whether it is right to invoke the jurisdiction clause. Examples of this might be fraud or duress alleged in relation specifically to the jurisdiction clause'.[19]

1.2 Brussels I Regulation (recast) in the EU

The Brussels I Regulation (recast) is the secondary EU legislation that provides for the recognition and enforcement of choice of forum clauses and judgments in 'civil and commercial' matters (Article 1).

In the absence of a *prorogatio fori* or the 'designation in an agreement of a specific tribunal to hear a dispute arising under or relating to that agreement',[20] subject to Article 25 of Brussels I (recast), the general forum is the domicile of the defendant (Article 4). If there is a 'sufficient link' between the subject matter of a dispute and a concrete EU Member State, under Section 2 (Articles 7–9 of Brussels I (recast)) special jurisdiction rules may apply. However, in several cases, the CJEU has restrictively interpreted derogations from the basic rule that the domicile of the defendant is the place to be sued.[21] This follows a uniform EU interpretation to ensure equal jurisdiction among EU Member States.[22] The situation may vary when there is a clause submitting to a foreign non-EU court since the domestic law of the forum will be applied to determine the validity of such a clause.

In the scope of its application, Brussels I (recast) displaces domestic laws and does not follow conflict of law rules, nor does it address the contractual validity of jurisdiction

12 *Crédit Suisse First Boston (Europe) Ltd v. Seagate Trading Co Ltd* [1999] 1 All ER (Comm) 261; *Sonatrach Petroleum Corp (BVI) v. Ferrell International Ltd* [2002] 1 All ER (Comm) 627 (QB).

13 Adrian Briggs, *Agreements on Jurisdiction and Choice of Law* (OUP 2008) 79–82.

14 *Mackender v. Feldia AG* [1967] 2 QB 590 (CA) 598.

15 David Joseph, *Jurisdiction and Arbitration Agreements and their Enforcement* (Sweet & Maxwell 2005) 108–109.

16 Michael Pryles, 'Comparative Aspects of Prorogation and Arbitration Agreements' (1976) 25(3) ICLQ 543, 544.

17 Otto Kahn-Freund, 'Jurisdiction Agreements: Some Reflections' (1977) 26(4) ICLQ 825, 835; Sparka (n 7).

18 [2008] EWCA Civ 1091, [2008] 2 Lloyd's Rep 619, para 24.

19 Simon Baughen, *Shipping Law* (7th edn, Routledge 2018) 363.

20 Aaron X Fellmeth and Maurice Horwitz (eds), *Guide to Latin in International Law* (OUP 2009), 233–234.

21 Case C-189/87 *Kalfelis v. Bankhaus Schröder, Münchmeyer, Hengst & Co and others* EU:C:1988:459, [1988] ECR 5565; Case C-45/13 *Kainz v. Pantherwerke AG* EU:C:2014:7; Case C-12/15 *Universal Music International Holding BV v. Michael Tétreault Schilling* EU:C:2016:449.

22 Yvonne Baatz, 'The Conflict of Laws' in Yvonne Baatz (ed), *Maritime Law* (4th edn, Routledge 2018) 31.

agreements. As a rule of thumb, national law as designated by a forum's PIL defines the validity of a dispute resolution clause when the judge analyses their own competence over a dispute and decides whether to proceed, to refer the parties to another court or even prohibit them from commencing proceedings in other forums or arbitral tribunals. The rules of judicial procedure only regulate what relief a claimant may seek when attempting to enforce a jurisdiction clause (i.e., the appropriateness of a transfer, dismissal or stay of the action).

Article 1(2)(d) and Recital 12 state that the Brussels I Regulation (recast) shall not apply to arbitration. The first two paragraphs of Recital 12 read as follows:

> This Regulation should not apply to arbitration. Nothing in this Regulation should prevent the courts of a Member State, when seised of an action in a matter in respect of which the parties have entered into an arbitration agreement, from referring the parties to arbitration, from staying or dismissing the proceedings, or from examining whether the arbitration agreement is null and void, inoperative or incapable of being performed, in accordance with their national law.
>
> A ruling given by a court of a Member State as to whether or not an arbitration agreement is null and void, inoperative or incapable of being performed should not be subject to the rules of recognition and enforcement laid down in this Regulation, regardless of whether the court decided on this as a principal issue or as an incidental question.

The third paragraph of Recital 12 states that where the EU Member State court has determined, through the exercise of its jurisdiction under the Regulation or national law, 'that an arbitration agreement is null and void, inoperative or incapable of being performed', its judgment on the substantive matter may be recognised and enforced (if necessary) according to the Regulation. Moreover, the Regulation recognises the competence of EU Member State courts 'to decide on the recognition and enforcement of arbitral awards' under the New York Convention regime, which takes precedence over Brussels I (recast).[23] Article 73 of the Regulation expressly states that the Regulation 'shall not affect the application of the 1958 New York Convention'.

1.3 Prorogatio fori *and* derogatio fori *under the Brussels I Regulation (Recast)*

A jurisdiction agreement in an international contract generally has two effects: it positively determines the jurisdiction of the chosen court (*prorogatio fori*) and it departs from the natural jurisdiction (*derogatio fori*).[24] This applies to the Brussels I (recast) system and how dispute resolution clauses included in contracts for the carriage of goods by sea are recognised by the EU Member States.

Article 25 of the Brussels I Regulation (recast) sets out the formal validity of jurisdiction agreements. The jurisdiction of an EU Member State court is exclusive if the parties have not agreed on the contrary. It also presupposes the contractual validity of a jurisdiction clause, which is determined by the applicable law:

> 1. If the parties, regardless of their domicile, have agreed that a court or the courts of a Member State are to have jurisdiction to settle any disputes which have arisen or which

---

23 Geert Van Calster, *European Private International Law* (Bloomsbury 2016) 82–89.

24 Beatriz Añoveros Terradas, 'Restrictions on Jurisdiction Clauses in Consumer Contracts within the European Union' (2003) Oxford U Comparative L Forum 1 <ouclf.law.ox.ac.uk> accessed 15 January 2018; Jerzy Jodłowski, 'Les conventions relatives à la prorogation et à la dérogation à la compétence internationale en matière civile' in *Collected Courses of the Hague Academy of International Law* (Vol. 143) (Sijthoff 1974-III) 483.

may arise in connection with a particular legal relationship, that court or those courts shall have jurisdiction, unless the agreement is null and void as to its substantive validity under the law of that Member State. Such jurisdiction shall be exclusive unless the parties have agreed otherwise. The agreement conferring jurisdiction shall be either:

a) in writing or evidenced in writing;
b) in a form which accords with practices which the parties have established between themselves; or
c) in international trade or commerce, in a form which accords with a usage of which the parties are or ought to have been aware and which in such trade or commerce is widely known to, and regularly observed by, parties to contracts of the type involved in the particular trade or commerce concerned.

2. Any communication by electronic means which provides a durable record of the agreement shall be equivalent to 'writing'.

...

5. An agreement conferring jurisdiction which forms part of a contract shall be treated as an agreement independent of the other terms of the contract.

The validity of the agreement conferring jurisdiction cannot be contested solely on the ground that the contract is not valid.

The jurisdiction agreement must be in writing, in accordance with practices established between the parties or in line with the prevailing usage in international commerce (i.e., according to the normal practices in international shipping, when analysing contracts for the carriage of goods by sea). However, the material validity is determined according to the substantive law applicable to the contract.[25]

The substantive validity of choice of forum agreements could be subject to different domestic laws. The consent of the parties is an autonomous criterion, independent of any *lex fori* in EU Member States.[26] The Rome I Regulation (in Article 1(2)(e)) excludes from its scope choice of law rules related to forum selection clauses and arbitration agreements. Article 25(1) of the Brussels I Regulation (recast) provides for a uniform conflict rule regarding the substantive validity of jurisdiction clauses, relying on the domestic law of the chosen EU Member State court by the parties: the nominated court will 'have jurisdiction, unless the agreement is null and void as to its substantive validity under the law of that Member State'.

Recital 20 of the Brussels I Regulation (recast) explains that the substantive validity is determined by *national* rules, including their conflict of laws rules:[27] 'Where a question arises as to whether a choice-of-court agreement in favour of a court or the courts of a

25 Michael Bogdan, *Concise Introduction to EU Private International Law* (Europa Law 2012) 64; Burkhard Hess, *Europäisches Zivilprozessrecht* (CF Müller 2010) para 6-137, 314; Miguel Virgós Soriano and Francisco Garcimartín Alférez, *Derecho procesal civil internacional: litigación internacional* (2nd edn, Thomson-Civitas 2007) 280. Different solutions are discussed by Hélène Gaudemet-Tallon, *Compétence et exécution des jugements en Europe: règlement no 44-2001, conventions de Bruxelles 1968, et de Lugano 1988 et 2007*, no 152 (4th edn, LGDJ 2010) 140–141; Jürgen Basedow, 'Exclusive Choice-of-Court Agreements as a Derogation from Imperative Norms', in Patrik Lindskoug and others (eds), *Essays in Honour of Michael Bogdan*, Juristförlaget i Lund (2013) 15–31.

26 Trevor C Hartley, *Choice-of-court Agreements under the European and International Instruments* (OUP 2013) 133.

27 *Renvoi* is valid concerning the choice of forum under Brussels I (recast), in contrast to Article 20 of the Rome I Regulation that excludes it: 'The application of the law of any country specified by this Regulation means

Member State is null and void as to its substantive validity, that question should be decided in accordance with the law of the Member State of the court or courts designated in the agreement, including the conflict-of-laws rules of that Member State'.

Thus the substantive validity is left to the *lex fori* or the national law of the EU Member State applying its conflict of laws rules (allowing *renvoi*). Article 25 of the Brussels I Regulation (recast) is applicable to the formal and substantive validity of the choice of forum agreement and not to the choice of law. However, rendering a jurisdiction agreement invalid due to the 'consequences on the substantive law to be applied' lies outside the scope of Article 25 of Brussels I (recast), according to Basedow.[28] Hence, the substantive national law does not determine consent, although it is applicable to the offer and acceptance, as well as to the legal capacity of the parties and, in cases of fraud, duress or mistake.

When the Brussels I Regulation (recast) is not applicable because the parties have agreed to another forum or an arbitral tribunal to discuss any dispute arising out of the contract, then domestic laws are applicable. Here are illustrative examples of such domestic laws:

(1) Under domestic Spanish law, there is a doctrinal discussion as to whether to consider jurisdiction agreements as a matter of procedural law or substantive law.[29]
(2) According to German scholars, choice of forum agreements are best classified as a matter of both substantive and procedural law. Garau Sobrino points out that German judges classify jurisdiction agreements as a 'substantive contract with procedural relations'.[30]
(3) Domestic English and Welsh Civil Procedure Rules (CPR)[31] deal only with the enforcement of arbitration clauses but not their validity; other instruments at the EU level such as the Brussels I Regulation (recast) may be applicable to the case; as Sparka points out, a choice of court agreement is valid according 'to its putative governing law' although a choice of English law is frequently suggested if the parties have agreed to refer any disputes to English courts.[32]

Basedow proposes the introduction of 'a more fine-tuned instrument' to 'address not the validity of the clause, but the exercise of the rights flowing from it. [These] may be abusive

the application of the rules of law in force in that country other than its rules of private international law, unless provided otherwise in this Regulation.'

28 Basedow (n 25).

29 Silvia Feliu Álvarez de Sotomayor, 'Nulidad de las cláusulas de jurisdicción y ley aplicable a la luz de la ley 3/2014 por la que se modifica el texto refundido de la ley general para la defensa de consumidores y usuarios' (2015) 29 Revista Electrónica de Estudios Internacionales (REEI), 5. In Germany, see Rainer Hausmann, 'Einheitliche Anknüpfung internationaler Gerichtsstands– und Schiedsvereinbarungen?' in Bernhard Pfister and Michael R Will (eds), *Festschrift für Werner Lorenz zum siebzigsten Geburtstag* (Mohr Siebeck 1991) 360–364; Dieter Martiny, 'vor Artikel 27', in Franz Jürgen Säcker and Kurt Rebmann (eds), *Münchener Kommentar zum Bürgerlichen Gesetzbuch* (CH Beck 1990) NM 50. In Spain, see Manuel Peláez del Rosal, *La competencia territorial en el proceso civil: el acuerdo de sumisión expresa* (Ariel 1974) 167; Alfonso-Luis Calvo Caravaca and Julio Diego González Campos, *La sentencia extranjera en España y la competencia del juez de origen* (Tecnos 1986) 74; Ana Quiñones Escámez, 'Evolución de la admisibilidad de la cláusula atributiva de competencia internacional en derecho español y comparado' (1987) 86(3) Revista jurídica de Catalunya 657, 660.

30 Federico F Garau Sobrino, 'Los acuerdos atributivos de jurisdicción en Derecho Procesal Civil Internacional español' (2010) 2(2) Cuadernos de Derecho Transnacional 52; Sparka (n 7) 81–98.

31 Civil Procedure Rules of England and Wales, approved by the Civil Procedure Act 1997 (amended 8 August 2016).

32 Sparka (n 7) 19–38.

in particular circumstances'. He remarks that 'the basis for the judicial review of the jurisdiction clause should not be sought in the national law of any Member State, but in the law of the Union'.[33] The Brussels I Regulation (recast) 'must be interpreted as meaning that an oral agreement on the place of performance which is designed ... to establish that the courts for a particular place have jurisdiction, is ... governed by' Article 25, 'and is valid only if the requirements set out therein are complied with'.[34]

In assessing agreements that choose a jurisdiction outside the EU, the EU Member State court will rely on its *lex fori* and not on Article 25 of the Brussels I Regulation (recast) to assess if the agreement is manifestly contrary to public policy.[35] Thus Article 25 of Brussels I (recast) permits *prorogatio fori* and *derogatio fori* and allows the parties, regardless of whether they are domiciled inside or outside the EU, to agree to submit their disputes to the courts of a Member State.

1.4 Declining jurisdiction, lis alibi pendens *and related claims in the EU*

Declining jurisdiction of one EU Member State court in favour of another when a claim is filed that relates to one already filed, and there is an exclusive jurisdiction agreement or exclusive competence in favour of another EU Member State, is regulated in Articles 25 and 24 of the Brussels I Regulation (recast). Article 26(1) provides jurisdiction in favour of a 'court of a Member State before which a defendant enters an appearance' (implied submission), unless that 'appearance was entered to contest the jurisdiction, or where another court has exclusive jurisdiction by virtue of Article 24'.

'Italian torpedo actions' intended as a tactic to delay proceedings in breach of an exclusive jurisdiction agreement in a charterparty or a B/L under the *prior in tempore, potior in jure* principle under the original Brussels I Regulation 44/2001 are no longer available under Brussels I (recast). Section 9 of Brussels I (recast) (*lis alibi pendens* and related actions) clearly states the mechanism to resolve pending decisions in related cases over the same cause of action and with the same parties. Article 29(1), under which 'any court other than the court first seised shall of its own motion stay its proceedings until such time as the jurisdiction of the court first seised is established' (such information to be provided on request, under Article 29(2)), should be read together with Article 31(2), which resolves the previous situation under Brussels I Regulation 44/2001, setting out that 'where a court of a Member State on which an agreement as referred to in Article 25 confers exclusive jurisdiction is seised, any court of another Member State shall stay the proceedings until such time as the court seised on the basis of the agreement declares that it has no jurisdiction under the agreement'.

Another important issue is that of jurisdiction agreements in favour of non-EU states, which introduces a *lis alibi pendens* rule with a limited and discretional scope of application. In *Owusu v. Jackson*,[36] the English Court of Appeal referred the interpretation of Article 2 of the Brussels Convention (now Article 4 of the Brussels I Regulation (recast)) to the CJEU. The CJEU ruled that jurisdiction could not be excluded in favour of a

33 Basedow (n 25).
34 Case C-106/95 *MSG v. Les Gravières Rhénanes SARL* EU:C:1997:70, [1997] ECR I-911 [35].
35 Basedow (n 25) 15–31.
36 Case C-281/02 *Andrew Owusu v. NB Jackson and others* EU:C:2005:120, [2005] ECR 1-1383.

more appropriate forum, due to the mandatory nature of the article.[37] As Lord Aikens remarked:

> To the consternation of many common lawyers, the CJEU ruled that courts of the Regulation countries could not invoke the doctrine of *forum non conveniens*, even where, to a common lawyer, it is plain that it should be exercised in favour of a non-Regulation State. The CJEU held that where the original jurisdiction in the courts of a Regulation State was correctly founded under Article 2 of Regulation 44/2001, based on the domicile of the defendant, there was no scope for the operation of the *forum non conveniens* doctrine.[38]

Articles 33 and 34 of the Brussels I Regulation (recast) introduce two new provisions in respect of *lis alibi pendens* and the connectedness of actions and proceedings between EU Members and non-EU states. These Articles reverse the *Owusu* v *Jackson* decision. As stated by Aikens:

> Under certain conditions they permit the court of a Member State to stay an action which is the same as or related to one in proceedings in a 'third State'. This introduces an approach akin to the common law doctrine of *forum non conveniens*, allowing a stay if certain conditions are fulfilled including a condition that the court of the Member State is satisfied that a stay 'is necessary for the proper administration of justice'. Article 33 applies where the causes of action in the two proceedings are the same and Article 34 applies when they are related, mirroring the distinction in (what are now) Articles 29 and 30 [of the Brussels I Regulation (recast)].[39]

Article 34 of the Brussels I Regulation (recast) sets out that where jurisdiction is based on Article 4 (domicile of the defendant) or Articles 7, 8 or 9 (special jurisdiction) and an action is pending in a non-EU court, when an EU court is seised relating to that pending action, the EU Member State court may stay proceedings if:

a) it is expedient to hear and determine the related actions together to avoid the risk of irreconcilable judgments resulting from separate proceedings;
b) it is expected that the court of the third State will give a judgment capable of recognition and, where applicable, of enforcement in that Member State; and
c) the court of the Member State is satisfied that a stay is necessary for the proper administration of justice.[40]

Article 34 goes on to set out the circumstances when the proceedings may be continued in the court of the Member State or dismissed.

Proceedings may therefore be stayed if a related action is pending in a non-EU court. The action must have been filed first in the non-EU State, and the EU Member State must be capable of recognising and enforcing the judgment of the non-EU State,[41] and the listed conditions must be satisfied.[42]

---

37 However, the English High Court stayed proceedings in favour of a non-EU state court in *Ferrexpo AG v. Gilson Investments Ltd* [2012] EWHC 721 (Comm).

38 Richard Aikens, Richard Lord and Michael Bools, *Bills of Lading* (2nd edn, Informa 2015) ch 14.

39 ibid.

40 Brussels I Regulation (recast), Art 34.

41 The EU Member State court 'does not have a discretion to stay where its jurisdiction is founded on Article 25' of the Brussels I Regulation (recast); see *UCP plc v. Nectrus Ltd* [2018] EWHC 380 (Comm); Baughen, *Shipping Law* (n 19) 389.

42 Adam Johnson, Anna Pertoldi, Nick Peacock and Hannah Ambrose, 'The recast Brussels Regulation: Implications for commercial parties' *PLC Magazine* (29 January 2015) 19–26.

In this author's opinion, Articles 33 and 34 of the Brussels I Regulation (recast) are an improvement on the previous position. They include the rules on *lis alibi pendens* and related claims in third states, allowing a stay of the proceedings in an EU Member State court when, among other conditions, the judgment issued in a third state is capable of recognition and enforcement.[43] As stated in Recital 24:

> When taking into account the proper administration of justice, the court of the Member State concerned should assess all the circumstances of the case before it. Such circumstances may include connections between the facts of the case and the parties and the third State concerned, the stage to which the proceedings in the third State have progressed by the time proceedings are initiated in the court of the Member State and whether or not the court of the third State can be expected to give a judgment within a reasonable time.
>
> That assessment may also include consideration of the question whether the court of the third State has exclusive jurisdiction in the particular case in circumstances where a court of a Member State would have exclusive jurisdiction.

Baatz considers it an unfortunate restriction on party autonomy that a mere residual discretion is available to the judge since Articles 33 and 34 of the recast Regulation are intended to be exclusive, save only for the exceptions in Articles 4, 7, 8 or 9.[44] Under Article 31(2), priority is given to the chosen court rather than the court first seised. She highlights that since there is no reciprocity between EU Member States and third states (unlike between EU Member States), third states that wish to protect their position when parties have chosen their tribunals can choose to ratify the Hague Choice of Court Convention. Under Recital 22 of the recast Regulation, the designated court 'has priority to decide on the validity of the agreement and on the extent to which the agreement applies to the dispute pending before it'[45] even if the court is the second seised or another court has already stayed the proceedings.

The *prior in tempore, potior in jure* principle applies when two courts have been designated as competent under the jurisdiction agreement. According to Recital 22, paragraph 2: 'This exception should not cover situations where the parties have entered into conflicting exclusive choice-of-court agreements or where a court designated in an exclusive choice-of-court agreement has been seised first. In such cases, the general *lis pendens* rule of this Regulation should apply'. No EU Member State court has the discretion to apply the *forum non conveniens* doctrine when there is a valid exclusive or non-exclusive jurisdiction clause in favour of another EU Member State,[46] although limited discretion is allowed

43 Marta Requejo Isidro, 'Recognition and Enforcement in the New Brussels I Regulation (Regulation 1215/2012, Brussels I recast): The Abolition of Exequatur' (European Judicial Training Network 2014) <http://www.ejtn.eu/PageFiles/6333/Requejo_Doc.pdf> accessed 29 May 2020.

44 Baatz, 'The Conflict of Laws' (n 22) 24–25.

45 Case C-352/13 *Cartel Damage Claims (CDC) Hydrogen Peroxide SA v. Akzo Nobel NV and others* EU:C:2015:335.

46 According to Article 25(1) of the Brussels I Regulation (recast), the choice of court will be exclusive 'unless the parties agree otherwise'. The parties agreed on: Belgian jurisdiction in Case C-322/14 *Jaouad El Majdoub v. CarsOnTheWeb.Deutschland GmbH* EU:C:2015:334, [24]; the exclusive jurisdiction of the courts of Paris in C-222/15 *Höszig Kft v. Alstom Power Thermal Services* EU:C:2016:525; English courts in *IMS SA v. Capital Oil and Gas Industries Ltd* [2016] EWHC 1956. Even where there is a non-exclusive jurisdiction clause, the court does not have the discretion to decline jurisdiction on grounds of *forum non conveniens* or *lis alibi pendens*: *UCP plc v. Nectrus Ltd* [2018] EWHC 380 (Comm); Yvonne Baatz, 'Choice of jurisdiction in bills of lading and cargo insurance' in Jason Chuah (ed), *Research Handbook on Maritime Law and Regulation* (Edward Elgar 2019) 342.

under Articles 33 and 34 when no EU Member State has jurisdiction under Article 25.[47] Baatz suggests that these provisions are a major improvement because they reverse previous CJEU case law[48] based on the Brussels Convention.[49] The *Gasser* decision has been reversed by Article 31(2) of the Brussels I Regulation (recast), which, in combination with Recital 22, aims 'to enhance the effectiveness of exclusive choice-of-court agreements and to avoid abusive litigation tactics'.[50]

A stay of proceedings by the court of an EU Member State exercising its discretion under Articles 33 and 34, in circumstances when a non-EU state court is first seised, is subject to its domestic law; but it is less clear what happens when it is the second seised. The court will determine whether there is an exclusive jurisdiction agreement in favour of another court or if the defendant enters into appearance. According to Article 28(2) of the recast Regulation, the defendant is worthy of protection: 'The court shall stay the proceedings so long as it is not shown that the defendant has been able to receive the document instituting the proceedings or an equivalent document in sufficient time to enable him to arrange for his defence, or that all necessary steps have been taken to this end'.

When dealing with clauses in favour of non-EU state courts, declining jurisdiction is subject to domestic law in relation to *lis alibi pendens*, or related actions, and exclusive dispute resolution clauses. Spanish courts can decline jurisdiction in non-EU forum agreements (see Chapter 3, section 3). The defendant must raise a specific motion called a *declinatoria*.[51] In England,[52] however, the courts are reluctant to permit service out of the jurisdiction in such cases, requiring strong arguments for submission to a foreign court to be overlooked.[53]

2 International arbitration

2.1 Introduction to alternative dispute resolution

There is no agreed technical definition for 'alternative dispute resolution' (ADR). It encompasses different resolution processes other than litigation in court. Arbitration, for example,

---

47 Article 29(1):

> 'Where proceedings involving the same cause of action and between the same parties are brought in the courts of different Member States, any court other than the court first seised shall of its own motion stay its proceedings until such time as the jurisdiction of the court first seised is established.'

Article 31(2):

> 'Without prejudice to Article 26, where a court of a Member State on which an agreement as referred to in Article 25 confers exclusive jurisdiction is seised, any court of another Member State shall stay the proceedings until such time as the court seised on the basis of the agreement declares that it has no jurisdiction under the agreement.'

48 Case C-116/02 *Erich Gasser GmbH v. MISAT Srl* EU:C:2003:657, [2003] ECR I-14693.

49 Baatz, 'The Conflict of Laws' (n 22) 24–25.

50 Fernández Rozas, 'Alternatives and uncertainties of the dispute settlement clauses in international maritime contracts' (n 2) 336

51 M Virgós and A Cambronero, 'Comparative Study of "Residual Jurisdiction" in Civil and Commercial Disputes in the EU: Spain' (2007) European Commission online publication.

52 Chris Woodruff and Karen Reed, 'Comparative Study of "Residual Jurisdiction" in Civil and Commercial Disputes in the EU: National Report for England' (2007) European Commission online publication.

53 *Mackender v. Feldia AG* [1967] 2 QB 590 (CA).

has existed at least since Ancient Greece.[54] Parties can avoid the inflexibility and the high costs of traditional dispute resolution institutions and procedures by using ADR methods to achieve the same or a better result, often for a lower cost. Some types of ADR may be used alongside litigation to improve the quality of negotiation in a dispute.[55] The ADR process usually has a more flexible structure, more confidentiality and can be shaped to the needs of the parties. Arbitration is usually a much more formal process compared with negotiation. The ADR process can be facilitated by one or more third-party individuals, and there are many commercial, maritime and not-for-profit organisations (among others) that can assist with identifying suitable people.[56] The substantive law governing the contract is not necessarily included in an ADR clause.[57]

Contracts of affreightment frequently include agreements on jurisdiction or ADR, as well as on choice of law. These ADR clauses may agree on arbitration, conciliation, negotiation or other dispute settlement techniques. It needs to be clear and effectively identified where (e.g., a concrete court or arbitral tribunal) and how (e.g., the applicable substantive law) disputes arising out of the contract are to be determined.

2.2 Maritime arbitration

Arbitration is an essential dispute resolution method in the maritime sector. The maritime sector has a particular set of concerns and conditions due to its international nature, and without dispute resolution agreements the sector would be inundated with the cross-border disputes that inevitably occur. This internationality distinguishes the field: on the one hand, it frees the sector from the strict control of a single legal system, but on the other, it requires some uniformity of regulation to deal with the problems and dangers that may arise due to the lack of barriers or geographical boundaries.[58]

An arbitration clause is a specialised type of forum selection clause, as suggested by Sparka.[59] It designates an arbitral tribunal that can be ad hoc or institutional. The parties can determine the form, structure, system and other details of the arbitration. Arbitrators are not vested with pre-existing jurisdictional powers, but their jurisdictional function is analogous to judges. However, arbitrators are not capable of using coercive powers over property and persons, which are conferred by a state on a national court in the exercise of

54 There are many different types of ADR besides arbitration, such as negotiation and mediation. Conciliation has gained increasing momentum in recent years; Susan Blake, Julie Browne and Stuart Sime, *A Practical Approach to Alternative Dispute Resolution* (2nd edn, OUP 2012) 3–6, 394.

55 Karl Mackie and others, *The ADR Practice Guide: Commercial Dispute Resolution* (3rd edn, Tottel Publishing 2007) 8–10.

56 Negotiation may involve lawyers, clients, specialists and experts, as well as independent third parties as in arbitration or mediation. Online dispute resolution is also an option and may include mediation in addition to arbitration or negotiation; Blake, Browne and Sime (n 54) 3–6.

57 Parties should specify the substantive law that they have agreed to govern their contract, in order to avoid disputes. Its incorporation within an ADR clause prevents one side from arguing that the substantive law governing the contract does not necessarily determine the substantive law that governs an ADR agreement, such as for arbitration. Parties should therefore consider including an agreement in an ADR clause on how costs will be allocated, such as legal fees and other disbursements; Margaret L Moses, *The Principles and Practice of International Commercial Arbitration* (3rd edn, CUP 2017) 46–62

58 Christina Zournatzi, *Arbitrato e Contratti di Trasporto Marittimo* (Cedam 2014) 3–9.

59 Sparka (n 7) 1–18.

its functions. By contrast, the source of the jurisdictional authority of arbitral tribunals is strictly private.[60]

The most significant legal principle in arbitration is party autonomy. The jurisdiction of an arbitral tribunal is derived from the will of the parties, whereas the competence of courts is derived from the procedural norms of the state or international convention. Freedom of contract encompasses two closely connected, yet distinct, concepts: 'contracts are based on mutual agreement, and the creation of a contract is the result of a free choice, without the influence of any external control'.[61]

The law of the seat of the arbitration, also known as *lex arbitri*, governs the operational framework of the arbitration (although not procedural details, which are dealt with between the parties). The seat of arbitration is not the geographical location of the proceedings but a purely legal concept that links the arbitration to a supervisory national legal system. It determines the circumstances under which an arbitration award can be set aside or annulled and any relevant procedure.[62] If the intervention of a court is requested during or after the arbitral process, the *lex arbitri* will apply.[63] The *lex arbitri* can be augmented by non-binding sets of rules, drafted by international organisations and business constituencies and based on existing practices, that parties can incorporate into their contracts.[64]

The *lex arbitri* may provide for the rights and duties of the arbitrators and parties and the intervention of the courts in the arbitral proceedings. However, it must be stressed that the *lex fori* may also override aspects of the agreement of the parties and set limits on the discretion of the arbitrators. According to Petrochilos: 'when the parties elect a forum they are conscious that they import the baggage of the *lex fori* of that court; they will at a minimum tolerate that law and at a maximum actively seek litigational advantages under it, but they are in either event making a deliberate choice'.[65]

The parties can choose between their own rules of arbitration (ad hoc) and ones provided by an arbitral institution ('institutional arbitration'),[66] a further form of 'soft law' designed to enhance party autonomy rather than curtail it. Although such rules are not statutes (by their nature they are private between the parties), they are considered binding on the parties (as 'soft law') when they agree to submit their dispute to institutional arbitration.[67] Well-known institutional arbitration rules include those provided by the London Court of International Arbitration (LCIA), the London Maritime Arbitrators Association (LMAA) or the International Chamber of Commerce (ICC). The UNCITRAL Arbitration Rules have been extensively applied (including to ad hoc arbitration) and are often viewed as the standard upon which other rules are predicated.[68]

60 Andrea Marco Steingruber, *Consent in International Arbitration* (OUP 2012) 12–13.

61 ibid.

62 J William Rowley, QC (ed), *Arbitration World: Jurisdictional Comparisons* (4th edn, Thomson Reuters 2012) 8–9.

63 Moses (n 57) 43–58.

64 Stefan Vogenauer, 'Introduction' in Stefan Vogenauer (ed), *Commentary on the UNIDROIT Principles of International Commercial Contracts (PICC)* (2nd edn, OUP 2015) 4.

65 Georgios Petrochilos, *Procedural Law in International Arbitration* (OUP 2004) 27.

66 Steingruber (n 60) 12–13.

67 Tony Cole and others, *Legal Instruments and Practice of Arbitration in the EU* (DG for Internal Policies, European Parliament 2014) 23.

68 ibid; see David D Caron and Lee M Caplan, *The UNCITRAL Arbitration Rules: A Commentary* (2nd edn, OUP 2013).

In the UK, the LMAA offers its terms of procedure to govern the proceedings while respecting the domestic arbitration Acts of the *lex arbitri.* This allows parties to choose the law applicable to the main contract of affreightment while maintaining the procedural elements that they consider necessary to achieve fairness, finality and functionality. The freedom of the parties to shape the arbitral tribunal and the arbitral process is very wide, but it is not unlimited. Limits are imposed by mandatory procedural norms of certain countries and various international conventions.[69]

2.3 The New York Convention

The New York Convention refers to both the *lex arbitri* and the laws of the country of enforcement. It applies to both ad hoc and institutional arbitrations (Article I(2)).

Article I(1) describes the territorial scope of the Convention. It is applicable 'to the recognition and enforcement of arbitral awards made in a territory of the State other than the State where the recognition and enforcement of such awards are sought, and arising out of differences between persons, whether physical or legal. It shall also apply to arbitral awards not considered as domestic awards in the State where their recognition and enforcement are sought'.

Simply put, the New York Convention applies to foreign or international arbitral awards, rather than domestic ones. It applies in three situations: (i) to arbitrations providing for a seat in a foreign state; (ii) to international arbitrations within the territory of a state containing foreign elements (e.g., nationality, domicile of the parties or other foreign elements), or any award rendered in the state considered non-domestic; and (iii) to arbitrations where no seat of arbitration has been provided, if they are likely to be considered non-domestic under Article I(1) or if the domestic court considers the agreement to be international.[70]

Contracting states may choose to apply the Convention only to commercial disputes and/or on a reciprocal basis only. These reservations are likely to also apply to the recognition of arbitration agreements.

Article II of the Convention is the international regulatory standard for arbitration agreements, and it aims to achieve harmonisation by establishing minimum requirements for their formal validity. Article II(2) provides clarity as to the format of an arbitration agreement, stating that 'the term "agreement in writing" shall include an arbitral clause in a contract or an arbitration agreement, signed by the parties or contained in an exchange of letters or telegrams'. Under Article V(1), the substantive validity of the arbitration agreement should be determined according to the *lex arbitri.*[71] There is almost uniform acceptance of the parties' autonomy to choose the law governing an international arbitration agreement.

Article II(3) provides that a court of a Contracting State, when seised of an action for which there is an arbitration agreement in force, should, on the request of the parties, refer the matter to arbitration, 'unless it finds that the said agreement is null and void, inoperative

69 Steingruber (n 60) 12–13.

70 International Council for Commercial Arbitration, *ICCA's Guide to the Interpretation of the 1958 New York Convention: A Handbook for Judges* (ICCA 2011).

71 Stacie I Strong, 'What Constitutes an Agreement in Writing in International Commercial Arbitration? Conflicts between the New York Convention and the Federal Arbitration Act' (2012) 48 Stanford J Intl L 47.

or incapable of being performed'. This is complemented by the positive *kompetenz-kompetenz* principle, by virtue of which an arbitral court may decide any case subject to a later judicial review. The negative effect is the prohibition of any objections on an interlocutory basis before the arbitrators have reached a decision for the same jurisdictional matter.[72]

Article V(1)(a) of the Convention allows the non-recognition of an arbitral award if the parties' agreement to arbitrate is invalid 'under the law to which the parties have subjected it or, failing any indication thereon, under the law of the country where the award was made'. In many cases, parties do not select the law governing their arbitration agreement but only the law governing the underlying contract. Authorities may adopt the default rule of the law of the putative arbitral seat, following Article V(1)(a), which provides that in the absence of a choice of law agreement, the 'law of the country where the award was made' shall apply.[73] The parties' choice of arbitral seat could imply a choice of the law of the seat to govern the arbitration agreement. Some countries apply the validation principle, stating that if the arbitration agreement is substantively valid under any of several laws that are potentially applicable to it, then the agreement will be upheld.[74]

According to Article V(1)(a), the parties can opt for the applicable law that will govern the formation and substantive validity of the arbitration agreement. However, they normally do not choose it beforehand.[75] The determination has to be made by the court first seised. From all the possibilities, the court normally adopts the *lex arbitri*, which can be different from the one where the tribunal is located (per Article V(1)(a), second rule), the law of the jurisdiction in which the tribunal is located or the law that governs the whole contract. Some countries uphold the validity of the arbitration clause by referring to the parties' common intention, instead of referring to their national rules.[76]

Party autonomy is at the heart of the New York Convention. This is enshrined in Article V(1)(d), which expressly affirms the supremacy of parties' agreements concerning the composition of the tribunal and arbitral procedure, and states that the law of the place of arbitration should apply only 'failing such agreement'. Courts have consistently recognised that the grounds in Article V(1)(d) must be measured, in the first instance, against the agreement of the parties.[77]

Recognition of an arbitral award is subject to Article III of the Convention, which allows for application of the most favourable domestic law or international treaty by the contracting state where the award is sought to be recognised or enforced according to Article VII. It is also applicable to the recognition and enforcement of arbitration agreements according to Article II.

Article VII(1) of the Convention also enshrines the principle of 'maximum efficiency' regarding the recognition and enforcement of arbitration awards. Contracting states must apply the more-favourable right provision between domestic law and treaties among the

72 Gabrielle Kaufmann-Kohler, 'How to Handle Parallel Proceedings: A Practical Approach to Issues such as Competence-Competence and Anti-Suit Injunctions' (2008) 2 DRI 110.

73 Articles 34(2)(a)(i) and 36(1)(a)(i) of the UNCITRAL Model Law reach the same conclusion.

74 Gary B Born, *International Arbitration: Law and Practice* (2nd edn, Kluwer Law International 2016) 59–60.

75 ICCA (n 70).

76 ibid.

77 UNCITRAL Secretariat, *Guide on the Convention on the Recognition and Enforcement of Foreign Arbitral Awards, New York, 1958* (UN 2016) 191.

available ones in the forum. The favoured right deviates from and prevails over the classic conflict of laws rules of international law on conflicting treaties, i.e., *lex specialis derogat legi generali* (where two or more norms deal with the same subject matter, priority should be given to the norm that is more specific) and *lex posterior derogat legi priori* (a later legal rule prevails over an earlier inconsistent rule),[78] which would otherwise apply.[79]

Article VII(1) also has the potential to overcome the writing requirement in Article II(2), by applying an expansive interpretation of Article VII(1), depending on the court where the recognition and enforcement is pursued. The requirement can be read expansively or by setting out examples of agreements in writing within the meaning of Article II(2). The article adapts to modern electronic commercial practices.[80]

The pro-enforcement bias of the Convention does not allow the parties to 'cherry-pick' a single more favourable rule of a legal regime for a particular issue during the recognition and enforcement process. Article VII(1) applies in a consistent and cohesive way and promotes the application of the most favourable provisions of the legal framework available where recognition and enforcement are sought.[81]

2.4 The doctrine of separability of the arbitration agreement from the contract

The presumption of separability of the arbitration clause has allowed national courts to uphold such clauses' validity by applying a different law from the underlying contract.[82] The arbitration clause may be subject to a law that is different from the law governing the substance of the contract in which it is contained or, in case of a separate agreement, the substantive law governing the dispute.[83]

Article 8 of the UNCITRAL Model Law, like Article II of the New York Convention, sets forth a substantive rule that international arbitration agreements are presumptively valid and enforceable and are therefore subject to a specialised legal regime not applicable to other contracts. Article 16(1) of the UNCITRAL Model Law expressly provides for the presumptive separability of international arbitration agreements, implicitly recognising the possibility of applying a different national law to the arbitration agreement than to the underlying contract.[84]

According to Born, the main consequences of the separability presumption are the following:

a) the invalidity or non-existence of an underlying contract does not necessarily entail the invalidity or non-existence of an arbitration agreement;

78 ibid 293.
79 ICCA (n 70).
80 ibid 50.
81 Karl Heinz Schwab and Gerhard Walter, *Schiedsgerichtsbarkeit: systematischer Kommentar zu den Vorschriften der Zivilprozeßordnung, des Arbeitsgerichtsgesetzes, der Staatsverträge und der Kostengesetze über das privatrechtliche Schiedsgerichtsverfahren* (Beck 2005) Ch 42 para 25; Claudia Alfons, *Recognition and Enforcement of Annulled Foreign Arbitral Awards: An Analysis of the Legal Framework and Its Interpretation in Case Law and Literature* (Peter Lang 2010) 51.
82 Gary B Born, 'The Law Governing International Arbitration Agreements: An International Perspective' (2014) 26 SAcLJ 814.
83 Cole et al. (n 67) 21.
84 Born, 'The Law Governing International Arbitration Agreements: An International Perspective' (n 82).

b) the invalidity of an arbitration agreement does not necessarily entail the invalidity of a main or underlying contract;

c) the law governing a main or underlying contract is not necessarily the same as the law governing an arbitration agreement (in particular Article II(2) of the New York Convention refers to the formal validity of arbitration agreements; Article II(3) and V(1)(a) *in fine* deals with the substantive validity of arbitration agreements; Article V(1)(a) states the capacity of the parties; Articles II(1) and V(2)(a) contain the arbitrability of the dispute);

d) different form requirements exist for the main or underlying contract and the arbitration agreement.[85]

These issues are all prerequisites for the validity of an arbitration agreement and may be dealt with in EU, international or national laws and regulations, which set out the requirements for the validity of arbitration agreements or include a conflict of laws rule, designating which law applies.

The idea of limiting the enforceability of an arbitration award through admiralty jurisdiction and the arrest of vessels by reference to separability raises more questions. National law is relevant for the enforcement of foreign awards. The result in *The Bumbesti*,[86] where the enforcement of a foreign arbitral award in order to secure an *in rem* claim was not executed, may be justified as a matter of shipping law or policy restricting the arrest of vessels; it should not be based on separability, since this is not the role of separability.[87] If there is enough security provided, as a general rule, a re-arrest might be an abuse of the authority of the court.[88] A choice of forum in the context of a contract for the carriage of goods by sea poses some challenges for the operators that succeed to rights under the contract. This means that the original parties are allowed to assign or transfer the forum agreement to a third party that may later exercise it in detriment to weaker or more vulnerable parties, in terms of business bargaining power.

Separability as a legal fiction prevents the paralysis of the dispute resolution clause, regardless of any potential invalidity of the underlying contract. Succession rights according to the applicable law between the parties in the original contract seem to have a formal or aesthetic purpose, obeying the internal logic of the law – that is, the non-transferability to third parties of the dispute resolution clause if the contract is invalid – rather than policy considerations.[89]

3 International jurisdiction and arbitration in maritime conventions

Aside from the Brussels I Regulation (recast) and the New York Convention, other international instruments may regulate procedural aspects concerning jurisdiction or arbitration

85 Born, *International Arbitration: Law and Practice* (n 74) 54–55.

86 *SC Rolinay Sea Star Srl v. Owners of the Bumbesti, SC Rolinay Sea Star Srl v. Compania de Navigatie Maritimie Petromin SA (The Bumbesti)* [2000] QB 559.

87 Adam Samuel, 'Separability of Arbitration Clauses – Some Awkward Questions about the Law on Contracts, Conflict of Laws and the Administration of Justice' (2000) 9 ADRLJ 36.

88 Aleka Mandaraka-Sheppard, *Modern Maritime Law Volume 1: Jurisdiction and Risks* (Informa 2013) 175.

89 Horatia Muir Watt, '"Party Autonomy" in International Contracts: from the makings of a myth to the requirements of global governance' (2010) 6(3) ERCL 250.

clauses when parties choose to refer their cargo claim disputes to an EU Member State court or arbitral tribunal.

Depending on whether the Hague, Hague–Visby, Hamburg or (once in force) Rotterdam Rules apply to a contract, the limits of liability will vary. Equally, parties may take into consideration the one-year time-bar of the Hague or Hague–Visby Rules compared with the two-year time-bar of the Hamburg Rules.[90]

3.1 The Hague–Visby Rules

Under the Hague–Visby regime, parties cannot avoid the minimum liability standards provided under its rules. For example, Article III.8 of the Hague–Visby Rules specifies that a contract for the carriage of goods, for example from Spain to Argentina, cannot oust the jurisdiction of a Spanish court if the Argentinian courts impose lower limits than those mandatorily imposed by the Hague–Visby Rules. Other than this, Hague–Visby provides no other mandatory jurisdiction provisions, leaving parties to negotiate an applicable jurisdiction or rely on national law where contracts are silent.[91]

As with choice of law clauses, jurisdiction clauses will be invalid if their effect is to derogate from a mandatory law. National provisions concerning jurisdiction clauses are still applicable when referring to non-EU state courts. However, some authors doubt that the Hague–Visby Rules would prevail over the Brussels I Regulation (recast) by virtue of Article 71 of the Regulation since they have no provisions regarding jurisdiction.[92]

The parties must expressly incorporate the Hague–Visby Rules into the B/L, or, in their absence, the contract of carriage must have a close connection to contracting states. This can be determined by the issuance of the B/L or by commencement of the carriage in a contracting state, as well as by the incorporation of a Paramount Clause.[93] The Hague–Visby Rules do not just cover the periods of loading or discharge of goods. The Rules also extend to 'the stage when the goods are in the custody of the carrier'[94] but will only have a contractual effect if provided.[95]

There is an interaction between conflictual (the Paramount Clause is the most complete example) and material party autonomy (the specific clauses that parties incorporate into their contracts). This is due to the existence of different tonnage limitation regimes and time-bars for legal actions available to parties engaged in the carriage of goods by sea.

90 Baatz, 'The Conflict of Laws' (n 22) 2–3.

91 Rupert Coldwell, 'Jurisdiction and the UN Convention on Contracts for the International Carriage of Goods: Where the Freedom of Contract Prevails' (2014) 17(1) Intl Trade & Bus L Rev 108.

92 See Julian Cooke and others, *Voyage Charters* (4th edn, Informa 2014) at [85.27] who favour the prevalence of Article 23 of the Brussels I Regulation over the Hague–Visby Rules; see also Trevor C Hartley, *International Commercial Litigation: Text, Cases and Materials on Private International Law* (CUP 2009) 187–189. On the other hand, Aikens, Lord and Bools (n 38) [10.55], fn 85, believe that 'the 1968 Visby Protocol is probably not within the terms of Article 57 of the Brussels and Lugano Conventions'; and Guenter Treitel and Francis MB Reynolds, *Carver on Bills of Lading* (4th edn, Sweet & Maxwell 2017), [9–077] fn 298, state that 'such a jurisdiction clause would however now normally require to be accepted by virtue of Art 25 of [Brussels I (recast)]'; see Baatz, 'Choice of jurisdiction in bills of lading and cargo insurance' (n 46) 357.

93 George D Theocharidis, 'Mechanisms of Protection from Non-Contractual Modes of Recovery in Sea Carriage: A Comparison between Common Law and Civil Law Systems' (2013) 44(2) J Mar L & Com 219.

94 *Trafigura Beheer BV v. Mediterranean Shipping Company SA (The MSC Amsterdam)* [2007] 2 Lloyd's Rep 594, 618 and 620–621.

95 Melis Özdel, *Bills of Lading Incorporating Charterparties* (Hart 2015) 166.

If the Hague–Visby Rules apply, a one-year time-bar for bringing a claim and a cap on recoverable damages, which favour the carrier, will apply. However, the bar on B/L clauses excluding or limiting the carrier's liability under Article III.8 will be relevant to cargo interests.

A Paramount Clause limits the responsibility of the shipowner for any loss or damage to the cargo.[96] The prevalence of the Hague Rules over the B/L terms depends on the wording of the Paramount Clause.[97] However, an old form of B/L used in a Paramount Clause caused the Hague Rules to be omitted from the B/L in *Vita Food Products Inc v. Unus Shipping Co Ltd.*[98] This gap allowed for the non-application of the Hague Rules 'by a choice of law clause for a jurisdiction which either had not adopted the Rules at all or did not apply them to that voyage'.[99]

3.2 The Hamburg Rules

3.2.1 Jurisdiction under the Hamburg Rules

Article 21(1) of the Hamburg Rules provides for jurisdiction:

> In judicial proceedings relating to carriage of goods under this Convention the plaintiff, at his option, may institute an action in a court which, according to the law of the State where the court is situated, is competent and within the jurisdiction of which is situated one of the following places:
>
> (a) The principal place of business or, in the absence thereof, the habitual residence of the defendant; or
> (b) The place where the contract was made provided that the defendant has there a place of business, branch or agency through which the contract was made; or
> (c) The port of loading or the port of discharge; or
> (d) Any additional place designated for that purpose in the contract of carriage by sea.

According to Article 21(2), a claim can be filed in a contracting state where a vessel is arrested, although the defendant has the right to remove the action to a jurisdiction provided in Article 21(1) after furnishing 'security sufficient to ensure payment of any judgment that may subsequently be awarded to the claimant in the action'. It is expressly provided by Article 21(3) that no action may be brought except in one of the places specified in Article 21(1) and (2) for provisional or protective measures, such as the arrest of the ship, unless a court of a Contracting State has jurisdiction. Article 21(5) states that a jurisdiction agreement made after the claim has arisen is valid.

Jackson suggests that the regime set out in the Hamburg Rules provides a jurisdictional framework with the purpose of displacing the one contained in the Hague–Visby Rules. Article 21(4) limits the *lis alibi pendens* by not allowing the cargo interests to start multiple claims based on the same grounds. However, any measures seeking enforcement of a judgment are not considered to start a new action; neither 'the removal of an action to a

96 For an in-depth analysis on the Paramount Clause, see Jonatan Echebarria Femández, 'Paramount Clause and Codification of International Shipping Law' (2019) 50(1) J Mar L & Com 45.

97 Özdel, *Bills of Lading Incorporating Charterparties* (n 95) 168.

98 [1939] AC 277.

99 Francis Reynolds, 'The Hague Rules, the Hague–Visby Rules, and the Hamburg Rules' (1990) 7 Australian and New Zealand Maritime Law Journal 16, 20; see also Yvonne Baatz, 'Clauses Paramount' in Barış Soyer and Andrew Tettenborn (eds), *Charterparties: Law, Practice and Emerging Legal Issues* (Informa 2017) 249, 252.

different court within the same country, [n]or to a court in another country' in accordance with Article 21(2).[100]

Baatz[101] points out that, in relation to court jurisdiction clauses, the CJEU in *Castelletti*[102] held that the original parties in a B/L contract (which applied the Brussels Convention) could choose a neutral forum. There is no requirement for any link between the relationship in dispute and the chosen court. But where any EU Member State has ratified and incorporated the Hamburg Rules into its domestic law, the provisions of those Rules that contain provisions in respect of jurisdiction or the recognition or enforcement of judgments and entered into force before the Brussels I Regulation (recast) could override the parties' choice of court as a result of applying Article 71 of the Regulation, giving them priority over the Regulation, 'if it conflicts', but probably not under the Hague–Visby Rules (see Section 3.1 of this chapter).[103] The Hague Rules and Hague–Visby Rules do not address jurisdiction and arbitration agreements and instead the provisions of the Brussels I Regulation (recast) or the New York Convention are likely to apply. Article 21 of the Hamburg Rules provides a cargo claimant with a choice of a number of different forums, thereby reducing the effect of a jurisdiction clause. Only a few EU Member States have ratified the Hamburg Rules (Austria, Czech Republic, Hungary and Romania), but some countries[104] that have not ratified it have chosen to incorporate the jurisdictional provisions of the Hamburg Rules into their national law.

The parties may elect to apply the Hamburg Rules by way of an agreement evidenced in writing that any dispute that may arise relating to the carriage of goods shall be referred to arbitration as per Article 22(1) of the Hamburg Rules. Problems arise when the cargo claimant can choose from a set of different forums linked to the carriage of goods and the venue chosen, reducing party choice to a mere option while restricting the effect of exclusive court or arbitration agreements.

Multimodal transport increases the number of potential locations related to the claim: cargo interests can obtain security by arresting the carrier's ship and enforce an arbitration award afterwards. However, in practice, the cargo interests' subrogated insurers usually sue the carrier, making further consumer protection unnecessary in such situations.

---

100 DC Jackson, *Enforcement of Maritime Claims* (4th edn, Informa 2013) ch 6.

101 Yvonne Baatz, 'Should Third Parties Be Bound by Arbitration Clauses in Bills of Lading?' (2015) 1 LMCLQ 85.

102 Case C-159/97 *Trasporti Castelletti Spedizioni Internazionali SpA v. Hugo Trumpy SpA* EU:C:1999:142, [1999] ECR I-1597.

103 International Conventions that entered into force before the Brussels I Regulation (recast) include the 1952 Arrest Convention, the 1999 Arrest Convention, the International Convention on Certain Rules Concerning Civil Jurisdiction in Matters of Collision 1952 and the Hamburg Rules; Yvonne Baatz, 'Jurisdiction and Arbitration in Multimodal Transport' (2011) 36 Tul Mar LJ 643.

104 Ukraine did not sign nor ratify the Hamburg Rules (<https://treaties.un.org/Pages/ViewDetails.aspx?src=TREATY&mtdsg_no=XI-D-3&chapter=11&clang=_en> accessed 15 June 2020). Ecuador signed but did not ratify the Rules. The Code of Commerce 1906 (Book III) incorporates Hague–Visby Rules (<https://www.standard-club.com/media/1813954/standard-bullet in-latin-america-special-edition-july-2015.pdf> accessed 16 June 2020; <https://treaties.un.org/Pages/ViewDetails.aspx?src=TREATY&mtdsg_no=XI-D-3&chapter=11&clang=_en> accessed 16 June 2020). Venezuela has a mixed regime (i.e. Hague–Visby/Hamburg Rules) (<https://www.standard-club.com/media/1813954/standard-bulletin-latin-america-special-edition-july-2015.pdf> accessed 16 June 2020; <https://treaties.un.org/Pages/ViewDetails.aspx?src=TREATY&mtdsg_no=XID-3&chapter=11&clang=_en). See <http://www.gard.no/web/updates/content/52959/hague-hague-visby-and-hamburg-rules-package-limitation-values-eastern-europe> accessed 16 June 2020.

3.2.2 Arbitration under the Hamburg Rules

The Hamburg Rules contain a specific response to the validity of arbitration clauses that are omitted from a B/L issued under a charterparty that lacks any express statement requiring the mandatory application of the clause to the B/L holder.[105] Assistance, salvage and ship construction contracts also fall under its scope, but the Rules exclude environmental protection and marine environment cases.[106] The binding effect of arbitration clauses on B/L holders has to be distinguished, depending on whether the arbitration clause is printed on or inserted into a B/L or is incorporated by reference into a B/L from a charterparty.[107]

According to Article 22(3), which mirrors the jurisdiction provisions in Article 21(1), the Hamburg Rules require arbitrations to be instituted in the state in which is located:

(i) The principal place of business of the defendant or, in the absence thereof, the habitual residence of the defendant;
(ii) The place where the contract was made, provided that the defendant has there a place of business, branch or agency through which the contract was made; or
(iii) The port of loading or the port of discharge.

Arbitration can also be held at any place designated for that purpose in the arbitration clause or agreement.

Article 22(2) of the Hamburg Rules states that where an arbitration clause in a charterparty is not incorporated expressly on the face of a B/L, the carrier may not invoke such provision against a B/L holder who has acquired the B/L in good faith. Bearing this rule in mind, the only way to maintain the validity of an arbitration clause in these cases is to distinguish between contracts where the clause is included and the document is related to the main contract. Some authors[108] suggest that if the B/L contains an express reference to a clause of the charterparty, such as its arbitration clause, that arbitration clause could be deemed valid while maintaining contractual distance between the B/L and the underlying charterparty.[109]

3.3 The Rotterdam Rules

The Rotterdam Rules aim to provide legal security, predictability and flexibility. These goals can be appreciated in the delimitation of objective forums that operate through alternative relationships and that can be superseded by a choice of a forum included in Article 66 that meets the formal, substantive and material requirements set out in the Rules. These agreements will be classified as concurrent or exclusive choice of forum agreements. The first yields in favour of the latter when an exclusive choice-of-court agreement is contained

105 Rosario Espinosa Calabuig, 'Las cláusulas arbitrales marítimas a la luz de los usos del tráfico internacional' (2007) 13 Revista electrónica de estudios internacionales 2, 15.

106 These are covered by exclusive forum clauses under the International Convention on Civil Liability for Oil Pollution Damage, 1969 (CLC Convention), replaced by the 1992 Protocol and International Convention on the Establishment of an International Fund for Compensation for Oil Pollution Damage, 1979 (FUND), superseded by the 1992 and 2003 Protocols.

107 Ling Li, 'Binding Effect of Arbitration Clauses on Holders of Bills of Lading as Non-Original Parties and a Potential Uniform Approach through Comparative Analysis' (2012) 37(1) Tul Mar LJ 107.

108 Eloy Gayán Rodríguez, 'El arbitraje internacional en las polizas de fletamento y en los conocimientos de embarque' [1996] Revista de la Corte Española de Arbitraje 22.

109 Espinosa Calabuig, 'Las cláusulas arbitrales marítimas a la luz de los usos del tráfico internacional' (n 105) 14–15.

in a volume contract that complies with the requirements set out in Articles 67 and 72.[110] A volume contract is defined as 'carriage of a specified quantity of goods in a series of shipments during an agreed period of time' (Article 1(2)).

The Rotterdam Rules amount to a *double* agreement because they regulate direct and indirect jurisdiction, based on Article 73, which defines the scope of application of the Brussels I Regulation (recast). The Rotterdam Rules also provide for consolidation and removal of actions, together with objective forums related to party autonomy.[111]

3.3.1 Jurisdiction under the Rotterdam Rules

The parties' freedom of choice has been slightly expanded in relation to volume contracts, subject to restrictions, but not otherwise compared with the Hamburg Rules. The parties have limited bargaining power over choice of jurisdiction or arbitration agreements under certain conditions, depending on whether the carrier and the shipper or the carrier and a third party rely on it.[112] Under the Rotterdam Rules, states can apply chapter 14 (jurisdiction). If a state has declared to be bound by chapter 14 (by application to the European Commission, which puts it to the Council of the EU), the claimant may institute proceedings in accordance with Articles 66 (actions against the carrier) and 68 (actions against the maritime performing party), or by reference to the *lex fori*. Under Article 74, the jurisdiction provisions 'shall bind only Contracting States that declare in accordance with article 91 that they will be bound by them'.[113]

The Rotterdam Rules distinguish between contracts in which the parties need to be mandatorily protected and volume contracts as defined in Article 1(2).

Article 66 (actions against the carrier) states:

> Unless the contract of carriage contains an exclusive choice of court agreement that complies with article 67 or 72, the plaintiff has the right to institute judicial proceedings under this Convention against the carrier:
>
> (a) In a competent court within the jurisdiction of which is situated one of the following places:
>
> (i) The domicile of the carrier;
>
> (ii) The place of receipt agreed in the contract of carriage;
>
> (iii) The place of delivery agreed in the contract of carriage; or
>
> (iv) The port where the goods are initially loaded on a ship or the port where the goods are finally discharged from a ship; or
>
> (b) In a competent court or courts designated by an agreement between the shipper and the carrier for the purpose of deciding claims against the carrier that may arise under this Convention.

110 Juan José Álvarez Rubio, 'Entre La Haya, Hamburgo y Rotterdam: La compleja opción legislativa interna ante las cuestiones de jurisdicción y arbitraje en el Derecho Marítimo' (2017) 17 Spanish Yearbook of Private International Law 596, 620.

111 Article 71 provides that unless there is a binding exclusive jurisdiction agreement, if an action is brought against 'both the carrier and the maritime performing party arising out of a single occurrence the action may be instituted only in a designated court'. If the carrier or maritime performing party seeks a declaration of non-liability or any other action depriving a party of a forum selection right under the Rules, they must withdraw that action on request once an appropriate court is selected.

112 Baatz, 'Should Third Parties Be Bound by Arbitration Clauses in Bills of Lading?' (n 101).

113 William Tetley, 'Transports de cargaison par mer, les Règles de Rotterdam, leur adoption par les États-Unis, le Canada, l'Union Européenne et les pays transporteurs du monde?' (Responsibility, Fraternity, and Sustainability in Law: A Symposium in Honour of Charles D Gonthier, Montreal, 20–21 May 2011).

Contractual parties are tackled in Article 67(1):

> The jurisdiction of a court chosen in accordance with article 66, subparagraph (b) is exclusive for disputes between the parties to the contract only if the parties so agree and the agreement conferring jurisdiction:
>
> (c) Is contained in a volume contract that clearly states the names and addresses of the parties and either (i) is individually negotiated or (ii) contains a prominent statement that there is an exclusive choice of court agreement and specifies the sections of the volume contract containing that agreement.

A person who is not a party to the volume contract can also be bound by an exclusive jurisdiction clause if it satisfies the requirements set out in Article 67(2)(a).[114] Parties to the B/L may include consignees, transferees, assignees and insurers exercising their subrogated rights against the carrier, excluding third parties (terminal operators, warehousemen and stevedores, governed by Article 68).[115] Third-party protection is incorporated into the Rotterdam Rules through various provisions. The general provisions in Article 79 state:

> 1. Unless otherwise provided in this Convention, any term in a contract is void to the extent that it:
>   (a) Directly or indirectly excludes or limits the obligations of the carrier or a maritime performing party under this Convention;
>   (b) Directly or indirectly excludes or limits the liability of the carrier or a maritime performing party for breach of an obligation under this Convention; or
>   (c) Assigns a benefit of insurance of the goods in favour of the carrier or a person referred to in Article 18.
> 2. …
>   (a) Directly or indirectly excludes, limits or increases the obligations under this Convention of the shipper, consignee, controlling party, holder or documentary shipper; or
>   (b) Directly or indirectly excludes, limits or increases the liability of the shipper, consignee, controlling party, holder or documentary shipper for breach of any of its obligations under this Convention.

Article 80 provides that certain volume contracts may provide for greater or lesser rights, obligations and liabilities than those imposed by the Rules. Article 80(2) provides that such a derogation is only binding if:

> (a) The volume contract contains a prominent statement that it derogates from this Convention;
> (b) The volume contract is (i) individually negotiated or (ii) prominently specifies the sections of the volume contract containing the derogations;
> (c) The shipper is given an opportunity and notice of the opportunity to conclude a contract of carriage on terms and conditions that comply with this Convention without any derogation under this article; and

114 That the court is designated under Article 66(a), the agreement is contained in the appropriate documents, appropriate notice of the exclusive jurisdiction is given and the choice is recognised by the court seised.

115 ibid.

(d) The derogation is neither (i) incorporated by reference from another document nor (ii) included in a contract of adhesion that is not subject to negotiation.

According to Berlingieri, it is clear that under Article 80(2)(d)(i), the derogation cannot be incorporated by reference from another document, but this statement does not affect choice of court agreements 'unless we have such exclusive agreement the plaintiff can sue the carrier in a competent court or courts designated by an agreement between the shipper and the carrier for the purpose of deciding claims against the carrier that may arise under this Convention' under Article 67(1)(a).[116] That exclusive jurisdiction agreement also must, according to Article 67(1)(b), 'clearly designate the courts of one Contracting State or one or more specific courts of one Contracting State'.

Briefly, the agreement must be contained in the volume contract and cannot be incorporated by reference to another document, as set out in Article 67(1)(a) and pursuant to Article 80(2)(d)(i). Baatz indirectly reaches the same conclusion as Berlingieri because Article 67(1)(a) requires a prominent statement that cements the jurisdiction and the court in the agreement.[117] The reasoning is less clear concerning Article 80(1)(d)(ii), if the contract is an adhesion contract that includes an arbitration clause.

Berlingieri explains the four conditions for exclusive jurisdiction agreements to bind third parties according to Article 67(2) of the Rules, including:[118]

(a) The chosen court must be in one of the places specified in Article 66(a): `(i) The domicile of the carrier; (ii) The place of receipt agreed in the contract of carriage; (iii) The place of delivery agreed in the contract of carriage; or (iv) The port where the goods are initially loaded on a ship or the port where the goods are finally discharged from a ship'.

(b) That agreement is contained in the transport document (in the volume contract) or electronic transport record' (being available to third parties).

A negotiable transport document or record, or a non-negotiable transport document that requires surrender, does not pose any problem. Berlingieri remarks that once an ordinary non-negotiable transport document or non-negotiable transport record is transferred to the consignee, that party may not be aware of any incorporated clauses, and there is doubt that they would bind the consignee.

(c) 'That person is given timely and adequate notice of the court where the action shall be brought and that the jurisdiction of that court is exclusive.

Berlingieri suggests timely and adequate notice before the third party brings proceedings against the carrier, with the intention of making it aware of where it is suing the latter in a different court by specifically quoting the text of such jurisdiction agreement.[119] In volume contracts, the interested parties are the ones that give such notice. However, a negotiable

116 Francesco Berlingieri, *International Maritime Conventions (Volume 1): The Carriage of Goods and Passengers by Sea* (Informa 2014) 237–239.

117 Yvonne Baatz, 'Jurisdiction and Arbitration' in D Rhidian Thomas (ed), *The Carriage of Goods by Sea under the Rotterdam Rules* (Informa 2010) 319, 326–327.

118 Berlingieri, *International Maritime Conventions (Vol. 1)* (n 116) 237–239.

119 ibid.

transport document or electronic record raises difficulties for identifying the relevant third party, probably the consignee, since it might be transferred several times.

(d) 'The law of the court seised recognises that that person may be bound by the exclusive choice of court agreement.' Any reference to the substantial law of a Contracting State shall be avoided, referring only to its procedural law, enabling the application of the 2005 Hague Convention on Choice of Court Agreements concerning third parties if it does not collide with internal procedural rules. However, as already stated its scope of application excludes the carriage of goods by sea and the limitation of liability for maritime claims. It could be applicable to contracts of insurance (or reinsurance) and arguably to time charter parties and bareboat or demise charter parties but not voyage charter parties.

The law of the court seised should recognise that the third party may be bound by the exclusive choice of court agreement. Any reference to the substantive law of a contracting state shall be avoided, referring only to its procedural law and enabling the application of the Hague Choice of Court Convention concerning third parties, if it does not collide with internal procedural rules. However, as previously stated, its scope of application excludes carriage of goods by sea and the limitation of liability for maritime claims. It could be applicable to contracts of insurance (or reinsurance), time charterparties and demise charterparties, but not voyage charterparties.

3.3.2 Arbitration under the Rotterdam Rules

Chapter 15 of the Rotterdam Rules deals with arbitration, requiring that, as with Chapter 14, states opt into the provisions (Article 78), creating uncertainty about the place of arbitration and the competency to determine the validity of the arbitration agreement. Furthermore, the Rules distinguish between volume contracts and other types of contract.[120]

According to Article 75(4)(d) of the Rules, a person that is not a party to the volume contract is bound by the designation of the place of arbitration in that agreement only if the applicable law permits that person to be bound by the arbitration agreement. It could lead to a contracting state refusing to recognise or enforce an arbitration award because its law as to whether there was an arbitration clause which bound the parties at all differed from that of the state in which the award was made.[121]

Article 76(1) states:

> Nothing in this Convention affects the enforceability of an arbitration agreement in a contract of carriage in non-liner transportation to which this Convention or the provisions of this Convention apply by reason of:
> (a) The application of article 7; or
> (b) The parties' voluntary incorporation of this Convention in a contract of carriage that would not otherwise be subject to this Convention.

120 Conversely, ss 5 and 6 of the UK Arbitration Act 1996 (UKAA) make no distinction between 'volume and other contracts; contracts between the original parties and consignees or transferees of the contract of carriage of goods; liner transportation and non-liner transportation; [therefore] commercial parties are effectively treated as guinea pigs while a system of arbitration is developed': Baatz, 'Jurisdiction and Arbitration' (n 117) 281–283.

121 ibid.

Arbitration (Chapter 15) prevails over the provisions on jurisdiction (Chapter 14), in the sense that the parties can agree to resolve any dispute by arbitration after it has arisen. Shipping interests seeking to be free from governmental limitations lobbied for the multiple opt-outs.[122]

As Baatz explains, the key question under Chapter 15 is where the arbitration will take place. To a large extent, mirroring the provisions on court jurisdiction, Chapter 15 draws a distinction between volume contracts, which satisfy certain requirements, and other contracts. Thus, choosing where the arbitration will take place is binding in the following situations according to Article 75(3):

> The designation of the place of arbitration in the agreement is binding for disputes between the parties to the agreement if the agreement is contained in a volume contract that clearly states the names and addresses of the parties and either:
>
> (a) Is individually negotiated; or
>
> (b) Contains a prominent statement that there is an arbitration agreement and specifies the sections of the volume contract containing the arbitration agreement.

Under Article 75(4), in order for a person who is not party to the volume contract to be bound by the arbitration agreement the following requirements must be met:

> (a) The place of arbitration designated in the agreement is situated in one of the places referred to in [Article 75(2)(b)];
>
> (b) The agreement is contained in the transport document or electronic transport record;
>
> (c) The person to be bound is given timely and adequate notice of the place of arbitration;[123] and
>
> (d) Applicable law permits that person to be bound by the arbitration agreement.[124]

According to Article 77, 'after a dispute has arisen the parties to the dispute may agree to resolve it by arbitration in any place'. The inconsistency of any term of the arbitration agreement with the previous requirements makes it void. Nevertheless, where the parties have not agreed on arbitration, after a dispute arises, if a non-volume contract does not fulfil Article 75(3) and (4) requirements, the cargo claimant can choose to arbitrate in any of the places detailed in Article 75(2):

> (i) The domicile of the carrier;
>
> (ii) The place of receipt agreed in the contract of carriage;
>
> (iii) The place of delivery agreed in the contract of carriage; or
>
> (iv) The port where the goods are initially loaded on a ship or the port where the goods are finally discharged from a ship.

In summary, cargo interests may bring litigation or arbitration actions against the shipowner in the locations included in Articles 66 or 75 of the Rotterdam Rules. Under Article

122 Tetley, 'Transports de cargaison par mer, les Règles de Rotterdam, leur adoption par les États-Unis, le Canada, l'Union Européenne et les pays transporteurs du monde?'(n 113).

123 In writing under Article 3 of the Rotterdam Rules.

124 *Raiffeisen Zentralbank Osterreich AG v. Five Star General Trading LLC (The Mount I)* [2001] EWCA Civ 68; in relation to an assignment; *Schiffahrtsgesellschaft Detlev von Appen GmbH v. Voest Alpine Intertrading GmbH (The Jay Bola)* [1997] 2 Lloyd's Rep 279, 286–285, per Hobhouse LJ (arbitration clause in time and voyage charterparties bound subrogated insurers); *Through Transport Mutual Insurance Association (Eurasia) Ltd v. New India Assurance Co Ltd (The Hari Bhum)* [2004] EWCA Civ 1598.

76(2), the Rotterdam Rules allow the incorporation of an arbitration clause when the transport document or electronic record 'identifies the parties to and the date of the charterparty or other contract excluded from the application of [the Rotterdam Rules and] incorporates by specific reference the clause in the charterparty or other contract that contains the terms of the arbitration agreement'.[125]

3.4 Remarks on the Hamburg and Rotterdam Rules

Berlingieri formulated two reflections of interest regarding the Hamburg Rules: first, the Hamburg Rules are not ratified by most of the important maritime powers in the world. Pro-carrier countries (many in Europe) are generally not in favour of the Hamburg Rules, which have mainly been ratified by pro-shipper countries, which creates an obstacle to the effective uniformity of laws and international harmonisation. Second, if there is already a certain degree of uniformity among a broad consensus of states, it is necessary to be prudent before promoting any new international regulation in order to guarantee a successful ratification and acceptance by most of the countries.[126]

Article 90 of the Rotterdam Rules does not allow any reservations, but Chapters 14 (jurisdiction) and 15 (arbitration) are optional, requiring an opt-in declaration in accordance with Article 91. This allows states to operate in accordance with domestic legal frameworks – whether autonomous, conventional or from bodies such as the EU – in the delimitation of the scope of jurisdictional forums and commercial arbitration.[127] Contracting states, including the EU, are the sole competent parties in matters set out in Chapter 14.

When a claimant sues a carrier – defined under Article 1(5) of the Rotterdam Rules as the person who concludes a transport contract with the shipper – the claimant is entitled to file a cargo claim before a competent court, as stated in Article 66 of the Rotterdam Rules. Both the Hamburg and Rotterdam Rules (Articles 21 and 66, respectively) provide lists of forums available to the claimant and include the jurisdiction of ports of loading or discharge or where agreed by contractual parties.

Additionally, the Hamburg Rules include the principal place of business of the carrier, while the Rotterdam Rules prefer the domicile of the carrier. The place 'designated' by the contract of carriage in the Hamburg Rules is a further option that is more restrictive under the Rotterdam Rules, which limit it to the place of receipt or the place of delivery under the contract of carriage. Under the Hamburg Rules, a claimant may choose to start proceedings against a carrier notwithstanding any jurisdiction clause between the carrier and the shipper.

Under the Rotterdam Rules, when a claim is filed against a maritime performing party (defined in Article 1(7) as a party that performs or undertakes to perform any of the obligations of the carrier between the ports of loading and unloading), the claimant can

125 Robert Force and Martin Davies, 'Forum Selection Clauses in International Maritime Contracts' in Martin Davies (ed), *Jurisdiction and Forum Selection in International Maritime Law* (Kluwer Law International 2005) 32.

126 Francesco Berlingieri, 'Uniformité du Droit Maritime. Quelques Problèmes' (1992) 3 Dir Marit 796; Jan Ramberg, 'Unification of Transport Law: Difficulties and Possibilities' (2010) Dir Marit 813; Francesco Berlingieri, 'The History of the Rotterdam Rules' in Meltem Deniz Güner-Özbek (ed), *The United Nations Convention on Contracts for the International Carriage of Goods Wholly or Partly by Sea: An Appraisal of the Rotterdam Rules* (Springer 2011) 1–63.

127 Álvarez Rubio, 'Entre La Haya, Hamburgo y Rotterdam' (n 110).

– according to Article 68 – file a claim that includes any cargo damage before a competent court located in: (a) the domicile of the maritime performing party; (b) the port where the goods were received or delivered by the maritime performing party; or (c) the port at which the maritime performing party performs activities with respect to goods.[128]

A subjective forum is optional (selected by the parties), so a claimant is able to choose between subjective or objective forums (available under the Rules). Article 67 of the Rotterdam Rules allows parties to agree on an exclusive jurisdiction clause for volume contracts that is only enforceable under certain conditions.[129] It states that jurisdiction derived from a choice of court agreement between the shipper and the carrier is exclusive and prevails over objective forums, unless an implied submission is agreed upon when conflict arises, according to Article 72.[130]

Another difference between the two sets of rules appears in jurisdiction at the place of arrest. According to the Hamburg Rules, a carrier can submit to another jurisdiction when providing security for a claim. Article 70 of the Rotterdam Rules does not provide jurisdiction when a vessel is arrested unless the usual requirements apply or if an international convention that applies in that state so provides.

Arbitration under Chapter 15 of the Rotterdam Rules allows the application of the limitation of liability and defences according to Article 4. When parties opt for specialised maritime arbitration, the arbitration provisions prevail over the jurisdiction provisions. Chapter 15 also distinguishes between volume contracts that satisfy certain conditions and other contracts.

The arbitration agreement must fulfil the requirements of the Rotterdam Rules and, as Berlingieri points out, the Rotterdam Rules differ from English law because under Article 66(a) or 75(2)(b) of the Rules, a subrogated insurer would not be bound by the jurisdiction or arbitration clause.[131] However, it is unclear what the result of a court testing the validity of the arbitration agreement and venue would be, both intra- and extra-EU. Such test would allow the court to focus on the merits of the dispute rather than determination of the venue, by not relying on different domestic laws that pose a risk of conflicting decisions on jurisdiction and merits of the dispute. The chosen court should assess the validity of a dispute resolution clause.[132]

Parties should have the opportunity to provide for a choice of a neutral (or not) location with arbitrators specialising in maritime matters. The parties would feel encouraged to choose arbitration despite the approach taken in the Hamburg or Rotterdam Rules. The international consensus has to focus on a test for whether an arbitration clause is binding. However, the Hamburg and Rotterdam Rules do not indicate which court should apply such tests and it remains unclear for any country or EU Member State court.[133] Focusing on jurisdiction issues rather than disputes on the merits is more costly and potentially creates

128 ibid.

129 Michael F Sturley, 'Jurisdiction and Arbitration under the Rotterdam Rules' (2009) 14(4) Unif L Rev 945

130 Álvarez Rubio, 'Entre La Haya, Hamburgo y Rotterdam' (n 110).

131 Berlingieri, 'Uniformité du Droit Maritime. Quelques problèmes' (n 126); Ramberg, 'Unification of Transport Law: Difficulties and Possibilities' (n 126); Berlingieri, 'The History of the Rotterdam Rules' (n 126).

132 Baatz, 'Should Third Parties Be Bound by Arbitration Clauses in Bills of Lading?' (n 101).

133 The arbitration agreement and venue is left to domestic law under Article 75(4)(d) of the Rotterdam Rules.

the problem of conflicting decisions and difficulties for the recognition and enforcement of arbitral awards.[134]

The problem regarding the ratification of the Hamburg and Rotterdam Rules by EU Member States and the multiple opt-outs is that the forum needs some connection to the dispute, allowing a consignee to reasonably foresee the court having jurisdiction. This solution limits the number of competent forums in claims related to the carriage of goods by sea.[135] Even if an express acceptance is not required, this limitation shows a will to protect the consignee. This argument is reinforced by the rejected European Parliament Resolution of 7 September 2010, which stated in its Recital O:

> Whereas third parties may be bound by a choice-of-court agreement (for instance in a bill of lading) to which they have not specifically assented and this may adversely affect their access to justice and be manifestly unfair and whereas, therefore, the effect of choice-of-court agreements in respect of third parties needs to be dealt with in a specific provision of the Regulation.[136]

The Brussels I Regulation (recast) is the relevant EU legislation that regulates jurisdiction and, under its Article 71, does not affect conventions that are already ratified by one or more EU Member States before the Regulation entered into force. Article 93(3) of the Rotterdam Rules allows economic integration organisations such as the EU the right to also opt into its arbitration provisions. The EU Commission could communicate such approval at the UNCITRAL Working Group Plenary Session. Alternatively, each EU Member State would have to opt in individually, as stated by Baatz.[137]

It is doubtful that the Rotterdam Rules will ever enter into force due to the low number of ratifications and the lack of international harmonisation concerning applicable rules.[138] The validity of the arbitration clause is subject to different rules even though most states are parties to the New York Convention. The incorporation of an arbitration clause could be stricter in jurisdictions outside English law, and there are no internationally uniform rules about the validity of an arbitration clause.

Baatz agrees. She emphasises the fragmented and confused international position, lacking international harmonisation on the applicable rules. A problematic issue for the parties' freedom of choice is that the choice of venue can be restricted – although they can submit a dispute to arbitration under the New York Convention. As stated before, the incorporation of the arbitration clause could be stricter in some jurisdictions compared with the UK. An example is *The Wadi Sudr* (see Chapter 4, Anti-suit injunctions).[139] The rules regarding

134 Yvonne Baatz, 'Incorporation of a Charterparty Arbitration Clause into a Bill of Lading and its Effect on Third Parties' in Miriam Goldby and Loukas Mistelis (eds), *The Role of Arbitration in Shipping Law* (OUP 2016) 107–131.

135 Binnaz Topaloğlu, 'The Validity of Jurisdiction and Arbitration Clauses as against Third Party Holders of Bills of Lading – a Comparative Study under French, English and EU Law' (2012) 44(61) Annales de la Faculté de Droit d'Istanbul 492.

136 Jurisdiction and the recognition and enforcement of judgments in civil and commercial matters, European Parliament resolution of 7 September 2010 on the implementation and review of Council Regulation (EC) No 44/2001 on jurisdiction and the recognition and enforcement of judgments in civil and commercial matters (2009/2140(INI)) [2011] OJ C308E/36; see Topaloğlu (n 135).

137 Yvonne Baatz, 'Jurisdiction' and 'Arbitration' in Yvonne Baatz and others, *The Rotterdam Rules: A Practical Annotation* (Informa 2013) 233–234, 242.

138 Twenty ratifications are needed for the Rules to come into force and only five have been received as at December 2019.

139 *National Navigation Co v. Endesa Generacion SA (The Wadi Sudr)* [2009] EWCA Civ 1397.

third parties may differ depending on whether the transferee of the transport document or a subrogated insurer is bound by an arbitration clause. There is no clear international agreement as to whether the chosen arbitral tribunal, the court of the seat of arbitration or even a different court may decide the validity of the arbitration clause.[140]

As Álvarez Rubio[141] remarks, the EU should pass new derivative or secondary legislation to rank and interpret norms as those contained in the Vienna Convention on the Law of the Treaties of 1969,[142] in accordance with the rule of speciality followed by the CJEU. A chosen forum should be connected to a dispute to allow a consignee to select an appropriate court. The main problems arising from the Hamburg and Rotterdam Rules are multiple opt-outs and difficulties in ratification by EU Member States. The limitation of competent forums to protect B/L consignees is an additional obstacle to ratification. Only Cameroon, Togo, Benin, the Republic of the Congo and Spain have yet ratified the Rotterdam Rules, while most maritime powers, such as the UK, the US and China have not expressed any interest in doing so.[143]

3.5 Future directions on multimodal transport

There may be new questions arising out of the plethora of international conventions that strive for uniformity and that have not achieved the expected results in terms of recognition and enforcement of jurisdiction and arbitration agreements included in charterparties and B/Ls. The Hamburg Rules do not provide for exclusive jurisdiction agreements while the Rotterdam Rules only refer to them in the case of volume contracts.

The Hague and Hague–Visby Rules only apply to tackle-to-tackle carriage of goods by sea (Article 1(e) of both Rules) and the Hamburg Rules to port-to-port carriage (its Article 1(6)).[144] The conventions are aimed at setting a liability regime for the carriage of goods by sea and only apply to B/Ls or charterparties if the contracting parties decide to incorporate them. Moreover, other legal instruments are applicable to the remaining parts of non-maritime carriage stressing the fragmented nature of multimodal transportation.[145]

The failure of the UN Convention on International Transport of Goods of 1980 resulted in the latest instrument, the Rotterdam Rules, which can be defined as a 'wet multimodal regime'.[146] The Rotterdam Rules are still not in force and thus do not provide for a comprehensive scope for multimodal transportation. Commentators consider the Rules 'an expanded maritime transport law convention ("maritime-plus")' that does not represent 'a step backwards' in this respect.[147]

140 Baatz, 'Incorporation of a Charterparty Arbitration Clause into a Bill of Lading and its Effect on Third Parties' (n 134).

141 Álvarez Rubio, 'Entre La Haya, Hamburgo y Rotterdam' (n 110).

142 Adopted 23 May 1969, entered into force 27 January 1980, 1155 UNTS 331.

143 ibid.

144 Michael F Sturley, 'Can Commercial Law Accommodate New Technologies in International Shipping?' in Barış Soyer and Andrew Tettenborn (eds), *New Technologies, Artificial Intelligence and Shipping Law in the 21st Century* (Informa 2019) 24–25.

145 ibid 27.

146 Carlo Corcione, *Third Party Protection in Shipping* (Informa 2019) [6.10] and [6.14].

147 ibid [9.26]; Manuel Alba and others, 'Montevideo Declaration: The Facts' (2010) <https://comitemaritime.org/wp-content/uploads/2018/05/Montevideo-Declaration-The-Facts.pdf> (accessed 25 May 2020).

In certain legal systems, for example, Spain, the unimodal internal regulations do refer to multimodal transport (claiming for itself the application of the regulations). The regulation of the land transport contract is set out in the Spanish Law on Contracts for the Carriage of Goods by Land (SLCCGL).[148] This includes 'the transport contract concluded by the shipper and the carrier to move goods by more than one mean of transport, one of them being land, regardless of the number of carriers involved in its execution'. Certainly, this regulation is intended for multimodal transport with at least one land leg; therefore, multimodal transport that is carried out exclusively by other means is excluded from its application. The regulation declares that this type of transport 'shall be governed by the regulations of each mode (of transport), as if the carrier and loader had concluded a contract of carriage different for each phase of the journey itself'.[149] The novelty that this law provides in land transport is that 'when the phase of the journey in which the damage occurred cannot be determined', the regime of responsibility for land transport will govern.[150]

In Spain, the Spanish Act on Maritime Navigation (SAMN)[151] (one of the newest national shipping acts in Europe) confirmed this approach by establishing that if the transport contract includes transport other than by sea, its rules will apply only to the maritime leg, with other legs being regulated by the specific regulations that correspond to them:

> in cases where the availability of a ship is contracted for purposes other than carriage of goods, the provisions established for charterparties that refer to availability and use of the ship, as well as to its charter and early termination, shall apply, to the extent that such are compatible with the purpose of the contract entered into.[152]

This is significant, because it expressly establishes that the type of transport will be governed, as it cannot be otherwise, by the regulations applicable to each separate mode of transport.

It is worth briefly considering the provisions of unimodal international standards for combined modes of transport, such as those stipulated in the Convention on the Contract for the International Carriage of Goods by Road (the CMR Convention).[153] Article 2 of the CMR Convention is clear (even more so after the introduction of the SLCCGL) that international road transport whose execution is carried out through other means of transport will be governed by the CMR regime. However, if the damage caused to the goods did not arise in the context of land transport, the current regime applicable to the relevant means of transport will apply. This regulatory model conceals the expression of the network liability system in which the responsible carrier must meet its obligations under the regulations applicable to the transport in which the damage has occurred. However, the implementation of this system can only be described as deficient. Firstly, because the scope of the prevailing regulation is not sufficiently specified when, by express mandate of the CMR Convention, its application is excluded. And, secondly, because it is not possible to foresee the exact moment when the damage occurs, so the means are not put in

148 Spanish Law 15/2009 of 11 November 2009 on Contracts for the Carriage of Goods by Land (Official State Gazette No 273 of 12 November 2009), Article 67.

149 Article 68(1) SLCCGL.

150 Article 68(3) SLCCGL.

151 Spanish Act 14/2014, dated 24 July, on maritime navigation (Official State Gazette No 125 of 26 May 2015).

152 Law 14/2014, Article 210 (contracts for use of the ship for purposes other than carriage of goods).

153 Adopted 19 May 1956, entered into force 2 July 1961, 399 UNTS 189.

place to remedy the situation. This highlights the impossibility of extrapolating this solution to multimodal transport in general, when it is noticeable that in this specific field of road transport plus other means of transport, neither the applicable regime nor its scope is effective. In short, it does not serve as a model for structuring a uniform liability system applicable to multimodal transport.

It is also worth noting that Article 1(6) of the Hamburg Rules declares 'a contract which involves carriage by sea and also carriage by some other means is deemed to be a contract of carriage by sea for the purposes of this Convention only in so far as it relates to the carriage by sea'. This reflects the predominance of unimodal regulation over multimodal regulation by clarifying that in multimodal transport, the maritime route of transport should always be governed by its own discipline. This view is in no way consistent with attempts to establish uniform regulation for all types of transport. Nor, therefore, do the Hamburg Rules lend themselves to being the foundation for a uniform model which may be extended to multimodal transport. In this situation, absent a harmonised international instrument in force and the reality of the failed attempt of the UN Convention on International Transport of Goods of 1980, it is logical that parties would want to provide themselves with a regulatory framework that provides a minimum of security to the legal and commercial relations that arise in multimodal transport.[154]

4 Conclusions

The interpretations offered by European legislators and the CJEU emphasise procedural party autonomy but are not based on subjective characterisation of claimants and defendants, due to a multitude of possible legal scenarios that complicate the harmonised application of procedural solutions. This problem could be overcome by using international conventions or EU legislation, avoiding isolationist attitudes towards international harmonisation. The comparative analysis provided here not only includes doctrine and jurisprudence but also explores the subjective characterisation of actors in the maritime sector, which varies between the Hague–Visby, Hamburg and Rotterdam Rules and comparative legislation. Formulating a universal definition for carriers is a characterisation problem of private international law.

Jurisdiction clauses often favour courts within the EU and protect parties once the requirements for formal validity are fulfilled according to the Brussels I Regulation (recast). The lack of procedural and substantive legal unification for resolving conflicting cargo claims is partially rectified through courts chosen by parties with appropriate legal instruments available and in force. However, there are obstacles to recognition of selected forums from a substantive legal perspective at a national level. For example, recognition

154 Juan José Álvarez Rubio and Unai Belintxon Martín, 'Una aproximación jurisprudencial a la Ley de Navegación Marítima desde la óptica del derecho internacional' in Alberto Emparanza Sobejano and José Manuel Martín Osante (eds), *Ley de Navegación Marítima: Balance de su aplicación práctica* (Marcial Pons 2019) 713–747; José Carlos Fernández Rozas, 'Alternatives and uncertainties of the dispute settlement clauses in international maritime contracts' (2018) 10(2) Cuadernos de Derecho Transnacional 333; see also in relation to multimodal transport, references in relation to the carriage of goods by rail: Alberto Emparanza Sobejano and Andrés Recalde Castells, *El contrato de transporte internacional de mercancías por ferrocarril* (Thomson Civitas 2008) 283–301; Unai Belintxon Martín, *Derecho europeo y transporte internacional por carretera* (Aranzadi 2015) 42–89; Francisco José Sánchez-Gamborino, *El contrato de transporte internacional. CMR* (Tecnos 1996) 56–68.

of dispute resolution clauses outside the EU depends on domestic procedural rules, while inside the EU, the Brussels I Regulation (recast) applies. The need for legal certainty stems from a lack of clarity regarding recognition of such clauses by different courts.

The chosen EU court and not the first seised has priority to hear the substance of a cargo claim dispute according to Article 31(2) of the Brussels I Regulation (recast), representing a limitation on party autonomy when a non-EU state court has been chosen by the parties. The possibility of introducing the *forum non conveniens* doctrine is prohibited under the recast Regulation when there is a valid jurisdiction agreement in favour of an EU Member State court. However, according to Article 25, there is a limited discretion under Articles 33 and 34 when related actions are pending in the courts of third states in the absence of a choice of forum clause in favour of an EU Member State court.

Conversely, arbitration clauses have a wider scope of application since the New York Convention ensures the uniform recognition and enforcement of arbitration agreements and arbitral awards almost worldwide. Arbitration clauses are excluded from the scope of application of the Brussels I Regulation (recast) and the CJEU has shaped the conditions. English courts have a pro-arbitration stance. The issuance of any declaratory judgment to ensure the enforcement of an arbitral award providing the best chances of enforcement (in order to take primacy over any subsequent conflicting foreign judgment) needs to comply with *lis alibi pendens* and mutual trust principles between EU Member State courts. Charterparties may not have been drawn up and signed by the parties, or may refer to previously concluded *pro forma* charterparties (see Chapter 3); moreover, multiple proceedings could be conducted out of a single incident. The Hamburg Rules allow arbitral proceedings in the country of the load or discharge port. The Rotterdam Rules address multimodal transport, and proceedings may take place in a landlocked country with no maritime expertise, where the multimodal transport began or ended.

CHAPTER 3

Incorporation of dispute resolution clauses contained in the charterparty into the bill of lading

This chapter sheds light on the incorporation of jurisdiction and arbitration clauses from the charterparty into the B/L in the EU, England and Spain, considering issues that arise when incorporating terms from a charterparty into a B/L. A B/L potentially contains rights and obligations that benefit or restrict parties who have no evidence of terms contained within the relevant charterparty. This analysis, from a comparative law perspective, of the submission to intra- and extra-EU forums and arbitral seats shows the limitations on party autonomy stemming from the legal frameworks and case law.

1 Incorporation of charterparty terms into the bill of lading

Party autonomy will generally have a major influence in dictating jurisdiction in maritime matters[1] because freedom of choice is usually preferred over the varied rules contained in international conventions, which may provide multiple different forums, depending on the circumstances. Parties might prefer a particular court for settling contractual disputes for reasons such as geographical proximity to elements in dispute, neutrality or the specialisation of a particular court.[2]

The B/L may contain provisions that incorporate some or all of the terms of the charterparty, distinguishing by general words three stages of the voyage: the shipment, carriage and discharge of the cargo[3] (as well as payment of freight).[4] The specific words used[5] may constitute a *prima facie* incorporation of a term, even if that term is not related to those stages of the voyage[6] or a certain degree of manipulation is required.[7] The wording used for incorporation and specific problems arising when referencing an arbitration clause rather than a jurisdiction clause in the charterparty will reflect the importance of the parties'

1 Adrian Briggs, 'The Validity of "Floating" Choice of Law and Jurisdiction Clauses' (1986) 4 LMCLQ 508; Jan Ramberg, 'Freedom of Contract in Maritime Law' (1993) LMCLQ 178.

2 Gabrielle Kaufmann-Kohler, 'La clause d'élection de for dans les contrats internationaux' (Helbing und Lichtenhahn 1980).

3 *Owners of the Annefield v. Owners of Cargo Lately Laden on Board the Annefield (The Annefield)* [1971] 1 Lloyd's Rep 1 (CA), explaining and following *Thomas v. Portsea* [1912] AC 1 (HL) and *TB&S Batchelor & Co Ltd v. Owners of the SS Merak (The Merak)* [1965] P 223 (CA). A clause in the charterparty concerning the approach voyage would not be incorporated: *Eridania SpA v. Rudolf A Oetker (The Fjord Wind)* [2000] 2 Lloyd's Rep 191.

4 *Thomas v. Portsea* (n 3) 6; *The Merak* (n 3).

5 *The Annefield* (n 3).

6 ibid; *The Merak* (n 3).

7 *Siboti K/S v. BP France SA (The Siboti)* [2003] EWHC 1278 (Comm).

intention,[8] and different judgments have had different results.[9] If there is any doubt, the judge will deem a provision not to be incorporated,[10] unlike in *The Channel Ranger*, which will be discussed in Section 4 of this chapter. An incorporation clause in a B/L that is not broad enough in its wording to incorporate the charterparty terms, cannot incorporate those terms (because that incorporation would not be feasible).[11]

If the clause is broad enough to effect a *prima facie* incorporation, the incorporated terms must make sense in the context of the B/L,[12] through an intelligent, not mechanical, reading[13] that respects common sense.[14] General words related to shipment, carriage or delivery may undergo a certain degree of manipulation to fit the B/L,[15] but not when referring to different matters.[16] Once the intention is clear, there can be a greater degree of manipulation to incorporate a specific clause.[17] Once incorporation is *prima facie* effective, the incorporated term must be consistent with the express terms of the B/L. If that is not possible,[18] terms related to those that are not incorporated will invalidate those terms that have been actively incorporated.[19] The compatibility of clauses raises numerous questions, and domestic laws differ depending on the jurisdiction, since the *lex fori* will determine the validity of such clauses.[20]

The court first seised may not declare itself competent, with no jurisdiction on the merits to hear a dispute, if the parties have incorporated a jurisdiction or ADR clause, such as an arbitration clause, into a charterparty or B/L. A conflict between case law of the nominated

---

8 *Caresse Navigation Ltd v. Zurich Assurances Maroc and others (The Channel Ranger)* [2014] EWCA Civ 1366; *Caresse Navigation Ltd v. Office National de l'Electricité (The Channel Ranger)* [2013] EWHC 3081 (Comm).

9 *The Merak* (n 3).

10 *The Annefield* (n 3) referring to *Thomas v. Portsea* (n 3) 9 and 11; *Ceval Alimentos v. Agrimpex Trading (The Northern Progress) (No 2)* [1996] 2 Lloyd's Rep 319.

11 *Skips A/S Nordheim v. Syrian Petroleum Co Ltd (The Varenna)* [1983] 2 Lloyd's Rep 592, 618 and 621–622; *Federal Bulk Carriers Inc v. C Itoh and Co Ltd (The Federal Bulker)* [1989] 1 Lloyd's Rep 103, 108, 110; cf. *The Merak* (n 3) and *The Annefield* (n 3). This issue was not determined in *The Channel Ranger* (n 8) [22]. Non-incorporated terms were consulted to understand the meaning of incorporated ones in *Tradigrain SA v. King Diamond Shipping SA (The Spiros C)* [2000] 2 Lloyd's Rep 319 [77].

12 *Hamilton & Co v. Mackie & Sons* (1889) 5 TLR 677; *Thomas v. Portsea* (n 3) 10 and 11; *The Merak* (n 3) 250; *The Annefield* (n 3); *Porteus v. Watney* [1878] 3 QBD 534, 542; *Gullischen v. Stewart Brothers* [1884] 13 QBD 317; *Serraino v. Campbell* [1891] 1 QB 283, 289; *The Phoenizien* [1966] 1 Lloyd's Rep 150.

13 *The Annefield* (n 3) 186, per Cairns LJ.

14 *Miramar Maritime Corp v. Holborn Oil Trading Ltd (The Miramar)* [1984] AC 676.

15 *The Annefield* (n 3) 184; *The Merak* (n 3) 260; *The Miramar* (n 14), in which a charterer remained liable for demurrage and the consignee under the B/L. A charterparty clause for payment was incorporated in the B/L by manipulation, providing for payment to a third party such as the shipowner in *The Spiros C* (n 11).

16 *The Merak* (n 3); *The Annefield* (n 3) 134. In *The Rena K* [1978] 1 Lloyd's Rep 545, it was not possible to incorporate an arbitration clause of the charterparty into the B/L.

17 *The Siboti* (n 7).

18 *Gardner v. Trechmann* [1884] 15 QBD 154, 157; *Akt Ocean v. Harding* [1928] 2 KB 371, 384; *Serraino v. Campbell* (n 12) 301; *Vergottis v. Robinson David & Co* [1928] 31 Lloyd's Rep 23, 28; *Hogarth Shipping v. Blyth* [1917] 2 KB 534, 549; *Red 'R' SS Co v. Allatini* (1909) 15 Com Cas 290; *Agrosin Pte Ltd v. Highway Shipping Co Ltd (The Mata K)* [1998] 2 Lloyd's Rep 614; Melis Özdel, *Bills of Lading Incorporating Charterparties* (Hart 2015) 61–69; Melis Özdel, 'Enforcement of Arbitration Clauses in Bills of Lading: Where Are We Now?' (2016) 33(2) J Int Arb 151; Yvonne Baatz, 'Should Third Parties Be Bound by Arbitration Clauses in Bills of Lading?' (2015) 1 LMCLQ 85.

19 See *The Spiros C* (n 11): even if the clause was not incorporated, it was unsuccessfully intended that the shipper would be responsible where an implied term in the B/L related to the charterparty's demurrage clause.

20 Bernard Eder and others, *Scrutton on Charterparties and Bills of Lading* (23rd edn, Sweet & Maxwell 2015) ch 6.

jurisdiction and the jurisdiction or arbitration terms contained in the charterparty and B/L may lead to different outcomes on a case-by-case basis. The shipping industry has promoted the standardisation of contracts of affreightment and the development of international maritime conventions. The standardisation process has led to a self-regulated and unified system as a representation of the customary laws and rules commonly used by different actors involved in the shipping industry.

One of the core issues when drafting a standard charterparty or B/L is the recognition and enforcement of the dispute resolution clause by a judge when a party files a claim in a jurisdiction other than that agreed under the terms of the charterparty or B/L. The autonomous and separable nature of a dispute resolution clause may allow such recognition and enforcement by the court; hence limitations on responsibility will vary depending on the applicable law in a dispute.

When the shipper endorses the B/L and ships the cargo to the receiver, there is no further opportunity to modify the terms of the B/L, including the dispute resolution clause. Subsequently, B/L holders have no possibility of modifying such terms through endorsements.

One of the main challenges for a B/L holder, as Özdel highlights, is when a B/L refers to a charterparty ('as per charterparty') and the B/L holder has no access to the charterparty, including the dispute resolution clause, as they are not a party to it. The terms of carriage of the B/L cannot be (re)negotiated between subsequent B/L holders and the carrier.[21] Shippers may choose to charter an entire vessel or load individual packages of cargo on board; they may use liner services that operate between major ports on a fixed schedule; they may choose tramp vessels that sail from port to port in search of cargo and carry them under B/Ls.[22]

The B/L holder will usually not have the chance to consult the charterparty. To overcome the legal uncertainty arising from this, the applicable rules of the relevant forum where the dispute resolution clause is to be recognised and enforced must be considered. Different material laws will lead to different results. In Spain, for instance, the forum selection clause must be specified in the B/L. The SAMN declares invalid any clause of submission to a foreign jurisdiction or arbitration contained in a charterparty or B/L if such clause has not been individually and separately negotiated. In addition, it specifies that the insertion of printed clauses on the front and back of any contract of affreightment does not serve as evidence of the parties' agreement.

The characteristics of the B/L are paramount when referring to dispute resolution clauses that may refer to or incorporate the dispute resolution clause stipulated in the charterparty. When goods are carried under a charterparty, the terms of that charterparty, including an arbitration clause, are often incorporated into B/Ls later issued under that charterparty.[23] Therefore, it is important to be clear whether, how and when charterparty clauses are incorporated into B/Ls.

21 Özdel, 'Enforcement of Arbitration Clauses in Bills of Lading' (n 18).

22 See Carole Murray, David Holloway and Daren Timson-Hunt, *Schmitthoff: The Law and Practice of International Trade* (12th edn, Sweet and Maxwell 2012) 282–352.

23 Felix Sparka, *Jurisdiction and Arbitration Clauses in Maritime Transport Documents* (Springer 2010) 63–80.

2 Incorporation of dispute resolution clauses in England

2.1 Incorporation of jurisdiction clauses in England

The incorporation of choice of forum clauses in England stems from shipping practice developed over centuries. One conceptual challenge for this chapter is whether and why a jurisdiction clause is considered to be a 'dispute resolution' clause especially in the context of English law – given that, as discussed in Chapter 2, English law has a divide between substance and procedure. In this regard, it is worth considering *The Mahkutai*, where the Privy Council did not consider a jurisdiction clause to relate to the substance of the legal relationship, stating:

> Their Lordships draw support for this view from the function of the Himalaya clause. That function is, as revealed by the authorities, to prevent cargo owners from avoiding the effect of contractual defences available to the carrier (typically the exceptions and limitations in the Hague–Visby Rules) by suing in tort persons who perform the contractual services on the carrier's behalf.[24]

This statement shows that the court was not prepared to entertain the argument that a jurisdiction clause relates to substantive rights (defences).

The rights and obligations under a B/L can be transferred to consignees and endorsees of any B/L. Under COGSA 92, the 'lawful holder of a B/L' to whom the B/L is transferred is supposed to have succeeded in 'all rights of suit' as well as liabilities under the B/L, in order to enforce the contract of carriage,[25] according to s 3 of COGSA 92.[26]

The endorsees or consignees must possess the B/L.[27] A straight B/L is excluded from COGSA 92,[28] being treated as a seaway bill[29] and not excluding shipper's rights that would be extinguished in other types of B/L under s 2(5). However, the situation differs when the B/L is issued 'to the order' and the shipper transfers it to the consignee. According to s 2(5)(a) of COGSA 92: 'where rights are transferred … the transfer … shall extinguish any entitlement to those rights which derives – (a) where that document is a bill of lading, from a person having been an original party to the contract of carriage'.[30]

Specific words of incorporation are required in the B/L, although there can be a certain degree of manipulation.[31] Consistency with express B/L terms must be kept. A clear clause

24 *The Mahkutai* [1996] 2 Lloyd's Rep 1 [166] (Lord Goff of Chieveley); the statement that is frequently 'found in one form or another in all the "Himalaya" clause cases' was reproduced by the House of Lords in *Makros Hout BV v. Agrosin Private Ltd (The Starsin)* [2003] UKHL 12 [151], acknowledging that ' the shipowners were attempting to enforce an exclusive jurisdiction clause against the bill of lading holders and failed as a matter of construction both under the "Himalaya" clause and the principle of bailment upon terms … The shipowners in the present case are, of course, not seeking to use the clause for any such purpose. They are not seeking to share the benefit of the contracting carriers' exceptions under the Hague Rules. That would not assist them. They are seeking to use the clause as the actual carriers to avoid all liability whatsoever. It is they not the cargo owners who are seeking to avoid the application of the contractual defences available to the carrier'; see Carlo Corcione, *Third Party Protection in Shipping* (Informa 2019) [7.59]–[7.84].

25 Section 1(2), 2(1) and 5(2) COGSA 92.

26 See *Borealis AB v. Stargas and others (The Berge Sisar)* [1998] 2 Lloyd's Rep 475 (CA).

27 Section 5(2) COGSA 192.

28 Section 1(2)(a) COGSA 92.

29 See *AP Moller-Maersk A/S (t/a Maersk Line) v. Sonaec Villas Cen Sad Fadoul* [2010] EWHC 355 (Comm).

30 Özdel, *Bills of Lading Incorporating Charterparties* (n 18) 61–69.

31 A B/L clause referring to 'disputes arising under this charterparty' exceeds the manipulation limits, but the incorporation was accepted in *The Annefield* (n 3) 186; *Navigazione Alta Italia SpA v. Svenska Petroleum*

in a B/L using general words of incorporation will not itself incorporate the jurisdiction or arbitration clause of the charterparty, according to English case law, even if the charterparty itself clearly states that any B/L issued under it should incorporate the jurisdiction clause: an English choice of law clause from the sub-charterparty was incorporated into a B/L but not an English arbitration clause since the reference was too general.[32]

The modern doctrine does not support a *prima facie* incorporation using insufficiently broad terms in the B/L.[33] A transferee of the B/L will have to check that the words of incorporation for jurisdiction or arbitration clauses are sufficiently clear and consistent with other express terms, as well as compatible with the language used in the charterparty.[34]

Consignees or endorsees can effectively succeed the shipper in all rights and obligations derived from a B/L, giving the carrier the possibility of suing the B/L holder under a jurisdiction clause in the B/L. However, as Özdel points out,[35] when the holder does not succeed the shipper in all rights or obligations under domestic law, Article 25(1)(c) of the Brussels I Regulation (recast) does not apply since the express or incorporated jurisdiction clause of the B/L is not considered to be a written one against such holders, unless the requirements of Article 25(1)(a) or (b) are fulfilled ('in writing or evidenced in writing or in a form which accords with practices which the parties have established between themselves').[36]

Nevertheless, as Baatz explains,[37] in *The Channel Ranger*[38] the English Court of Appeal went further than previous case law,[39] which led to the incorporation of an English jurisdiction clause from a voyage charterparty into a B/L, binding a third party. The panel found that the B/L contained no general words of incorporation but a specific reference to English law and an arbitration clause. The English jurisdiction clause was incorporated in the B/L, despite specific reference to the fact that the terms of the charterparty were recorded in an emailed fixture recap and the charterparty had not been drawn up. The flexibility of the English courts in adapting to business practice allows the incorporation of such clauses while keeping a liberal approach, as in another case where a charterparty was drawn up by the brokers but never signed.[40] In *The Merak*[41] the wording of the charterparty clause, which applied to claims under the B/L, led to an effective incorporation of the charterparty arbitration clause into the B/L. The Court of Appeal's judgment would not have been the

AB (The Nai Matteini) [1988] 1 Lloyd's Rep 452; *Astro Valiente Compania Naviera v. Government of Pakistan (The Emmanuel Colocotronis) (No 2)* [1982] 1 Lloyd's Rep 286. However, it was not possible in *The Rena K* (n 16); *Pride Shipping Corporation v. Chung Hwa Pulp Corporation and another (The Oinoussin Pride)* [1991] 1 Lloyd's Rep 126; *Daval Aciers D'Usinor et de Sacilor v. Armare SRL (The Nerano)* [1996] 1 Lloyd's Rep 1; *The Delos* [2001] 1 Lloyd's Rep 703 and *Skips A/S Nordheim and others v. Syrian Petroleum Co Ltd and Petrofina SA* [1983] 1 Lloyd's Rep 416, upheld in the Court of Appeal in *The Varenna* (n 11).

32 *The Siboti* (n 7) and *Navig8 Pte Ltd v. Al-Riyadh Co for Vegetable Oil Industry (The Lucky Lady)* [2013] EWHC 328 (Comm), respectively.

33 *The Varenna* (n 11) 618 and 621–622; *The Federal Bulker* (n 11) 108, 110; *The Siboti* (n 7).

34 *The Annefield* (n 3); *The Merak* (n 3); *Thomas v. Portsea* (n 3); *The Njegos* [1936] P 90; *The Phoenizien* (n 12); *The Federal Bulker* (n 11).

35 Özdel, *Bills of Lading Incorporating Charterparties* (n 18) 61–69.

36 See Case 71/83 *Partenreederei ms Tilly Russ and Ernest Russ v. NV Haven- & Vervoerbedrijf Nova and NV Goeminne Hout (The Tilly Russ)* EU:C:1984:217, [1984] ECR 2417).

37 Baatz, 'Should Third Parties Be Bound by Arbitration Clauses in Bills of Lading?' (n 18).

38 *The Channel Ranger* (n 8).

39 *Welex AG v. Rosa Maritime Ltd (The Epsilon Rosa)* [2003] EWCA Civ 938.

40 *Golden Ocean Group Ltd v. Salgaocar Mining Industries Pvt Ltd* [2012] EWCA Civ 265.

41 n 3.

same today, because the B/L referred to clause 30 of the charterparty (shipowner's right to substitute another vessel) and the arbitration clause was contained in clause 32.[42] The principles of construction of contracts may lead to a different decision.

This principle is an exception to the general approach of English law, which 'in principle ... accepts incorporation of standard terms by the use of general words'.[43] Third parties need certainty under negotiable B/Ls since they might not be aware of the charterparty terms, including the jurisdiction clause,[44] when a consignee is not a party to the charterparty or even when the carrier is the shipowner and is unaware of the terms of a voyage sub-charterparty incorporated into the B/L.[45]

According to *The Varenna*,[46] the operative words of incorporation must normally be found in the B/L itself, since incorporation can be achieved only by the agreement of the parties to that contract. If a general incorporation clause in a B/L 'catches' a term in a charterparty, that term must be read literally and disregarded if it is inappropriate in a B/L context or inconsistent with the B/L,[47] so a wish to incorporate a particular clause must be express. Specific words of incorporation, as found in *The Nerano*, will be sufficiently certain, even if it is necessary to manipulate[48] the wording of a charterparty clause.[49] In *The Nerano*, the B/L holder argued that the incorporated arbitration agreement between the shipowner and the charterer was not 'in writing' between the carrier and the B/L holder. The B/L holder's argument was dismissed by the court which treated such adapted wording as 'in writing' and thus binding the B/L.[50] The court held that the express reference of the clause in the B/L showed the clear intention of the parties to refer disputes arising under the B/L to arbitration. As a result, the clause was manipulated to cover also the disputes arising under the B/L. Thus to incorporate an arbitration clause requires an express reference to it in the B/L.[51]

Verbal manipulation in search of the parties' intentions is not permitted.[52] A demurrage clause that was not directly germane to the shipment, carriage and delivery of goods, could not substitute 'charterer' for 'consignee' or 'B/L holder' because it was not presumed to be incorporated into the B/L. 'Freight payable per charterparty' was held to incorporate the whole of the relevant charterparty's terms as to the payment of freight, not only the

42 See, for instance, Richard Aikens, Richard Lord and Michael Bools, *Bills of Lading* (2nd edn, Informa 2015), [7.92].

43 *Sea Trade Maritime Corp v. Hellenic Mutual Association (Bermuda) Ltd (The Athena)* [2006] EWHC 2530 (Comm) (Langley J).

44 *The Federal Bulker* (n 11); *The Channel Ranger* (n 8); *The Siboti* (n 7) [24].

45 *National Navigation Co v. Endesa Generacion SA (The Wadi Sudr)* [2009] EWHC 196 (Comm). See also The Channel Ranger (n 8), upheld on appeal, where Males J held that general words of incorporation were sufficient, applying *The Njegos* (n 34) and *Pacific Molasses Co and United Molasses Trading Co Ltd v. Entre Rios Compania Riviera SA (The San Nicholas)* [1976] 1 Lloyd's Rep 8, although in that case there were specific words referring to the law and arbitration clause, and *The Dolphina* [2011] SGHC 273, a decision of the Singapore High Court. General words of incorporation cannot incorporate an arbitration clause.

46 *The Varenna* (n 11).

47 *Hamilton v. Mackie* (n 12).

48 *The Nerano* (n 31), the clause referred to 'all disputes arising out of this charterparty to arbitration by adding and under any bill of lading issued hereunder'; see also *The Delos* (n 31) and *The Epsilon Rosa* (n 39).

49 Baatz, 'Should Third Parties Be Bound by Arbitration Clauses in Bills of Lading?' (n 18).

50 Özdel, *Bills of Lading Incorporating Charterparties* (n 18) 61–69.

51 *The Delos* (n 31).

52 *The Miramar* (n 14).

rate of freight payable but also 'the manner of payment, when and where and to whom freight shall be payable'.[53] The failure to insert the date of the relevant charter in a space provided in a B/L will not automatically mean it is not incorporated.[54] An incorporation clause in a B/L will not normally have the effect of incorporating oral terms that have not been reduced to writing;[55] however, such a clause may affect incorporation where the charter contract is contained in or evidenced by a recap telex or email and a standard form to which the telex or email refers.[56] In practice, most charterparties are concluded by email exchange, but the system is the same.

Under COGSA 92, a third-party consignee or endorsee of the B/L will also be bound by the arbitration clause in a B/L. In *The Epsilon Rosa*, the English Court of Appeal held that the consignee of the B/L was bound by an arbitration clause incorporated into the B/L from the charterparty, evidenced by the fixture recap. A subrogated cargo insurer would also be bound by the London arbitration clause in the B/L.[57] This decision was followed in *The Good Luck*.[58]

In *The Good Luck*, a dispute 'arising under the contract' was arbitrable despite the insurer's argument that it was not bound by the arbitration clause under the law of the People's Republic of China. It was held by the CJEU in *The Front Comor*[59] (English courts could no longer grant an anti-suit injunction restraining a party to an English arbitration agreement from litigating in the EU) and *The Ivan Zagubanski*[60] (anti-suit injunction was incompatible with the Brussels Convention) that the only rights transferrable to the insurers by subrogation were those that had to be enforced by arbitration, as an inseparable component of the claim transferred.

In recent years, English courts have taken a liberal approach to construction when there is a specific reference to arbitration in the B/L, but the charterparty clause was a hybrid court and arbitration clause or a court jurisdiction clause. In *The YM Saturn*,[61] in which the B/L incorporated a law and arbitration clause and the charterparty a law and litigation clause, the dispute had to be referred to arbitration under the LMAA's Small Claims Procedure.[62]

---

53 *India Steamship Co v. Louis Dreyfus Sugar Ltd (The Indian Reliance)* [1997] 1 Lloyd's Rep 52.

54 *The San Nicholas* (n 45); *Bangladesh Chemical Industries Corporation v. Henry Stephens Shipping Co and another (The SLS Everest)* [1981] 2 Lloyd's Rep 389.

55 *The Heidberg* [1994] 2 Lloyd's Rep 287.

56 *The Epsilon Rosa* (n 39).

57 In the *Schiffahrtsgesellschaft Detlev von Appen GmbH v. Voest Alpine Intertrading GmbH (The Jay Bola)* [1997] 2 Lloyd's Rep 279, 285–286, Hobhouse LJ stated, after examining earlier authorities:

> These authorities confirm that the rights which the insurance company has acquired are rights which are subject to the arbitration clause. The insurance company has the right to refer the claim to arbitration, obtain if it can an award in its favour from the arbitrators, and enforce the obligation of the [other party] to pay that award. Likewise, the insurance company is not entitled to assert its claim inconsistently with the terms of the contract. One of the terms of the contract is that, in the event of a dispute, the claim must be referred to arbitration. The insurance company is not entitled to enforce its right without also recognising the obligation to arbitrate.

58 *Niagara Maritime SA v. Tianjin Iron & Steel Group Co Ltd (The Good Luck)* [2011] EWHC 3035 (Comm).

59 Case C-185/07 *Allianz SpA (formerly Riunione Adriatica Di Sicurta SpA) v. West Tankers Inc (The Front Comor)* EU:C:2009:69, [2009] ECR I-663.

60 *Navigation Maritime Bulgare v. Rustal Trading Ltd (The Ivan Zagubanski)* [2000] EWHC 222 (Comm).

61 *YM Mars Tankers Ltd v. Shield Petroleum Co (Nigeria) Ltd (The YM Saturn)* [2012] EWHC 2652.

62 Baatz, 'Should Third Parties Be Bound by Arbitration Clauses in Bills of Lading?' (n 18).

Following the construction doctrine in *The YM Saturn*, the judgment in *The Channel Ranger*[63] regarding a vessel hired on time charter and sub-voyage charter, in turn, points to an incorrect incorporation of the charterparty clause. The term referred to 'English Law and the exclusive jurisdiction of the High Court of Justice of England and Wales', but the B/L terms included a generic law and arbitration clause. The *Channel Ranger* carried 39,000 mt of coal from the Netherlands to Morocco. The cargo was damaged due to self-heating, and being doused with seawater. The Protection & Indemnity Club (P&I Club) provided security accounting for a USS$1.1 million bank guarantee, which allowed the ship to be released. The receivers arrested the ship in Nador, Morocco. Clause 1 of the applicable Congenbill 2007 states: 'All terms and conditions, liberties and exceptions of the Charterparty, dated as overleaf, including the Law and Arbitration Clause/Dispute Resolution Clause, are herewith incorporated'.

In June 2011, the shipowners started proceedings in England in order to not be declared liable for any cargo damage, while the cargo insurers commenced proceedings against them in Morocco, alleging that there was no incorporation of English law and jurisdiction into the B/L. The English High Court considered that the intention of the parties in the charterparty prevailed over that of the B/L, as the Hague–Visby Rules were applicable and did not consider the *prorogatio fori*. Thus, it was found that the Hague–Visby Rules were applicable, and an anti-suit injunction was issued, effectively removing the possibility of the Moroccan courts' competence to resolve the merits of the dispute.[64]

Moroccan law would apply the Hamburg Rules rather than the Hague–Visby Rules, depriving the claimant from the benefit of the agreed jurisdiction (English High Court) and the applicable law (English law) and avoiding the time-bar of the Hague–Visby Rules at the hearing. The Court of Appeal upheld the decision, taking a slightly different approach to that followed in the High Court,[65] holding that the wording used for incorporation of the law and jurisdiction clause into the B/L must be considered in each case: the clause must have specific words of incorporation and then it is a matter of construction as to which clause is incorporated.[66]

A modern contextual approach to construction led to an effective incorporation of a 'law and arbitration' clause that referred to a 'law and jurisdiction' clause contained in the charterparty. Therefore, if a shipper, consignee, endorsee or their subrogated insurer intends to start or threaten to start proceedings at extra-EU or extra-Lugano Convention courts in order to breach an arbitration agreement, they can apply under English jurisdiction

63 *The Channel Ranger* (n 8) (HC), per Males J.

64 For Males J, the clause is that which the parties would incorporate according to the usual trade; Robert Veal, 'Case Update: How arbitration clauses refer to High Court jurisdiction' (2014) 14(10) Lloyd's Shipping & Trade Law 5.

65 *The Channel Ranger* (n 8) (CA), per Beatson LJ.

66 Beatson LJ followed the approach in *The Siboti* (n 7) [36]: the words of the B/L must be looked at as a whole in their context for the incorporation and 'in every case, the court is seeking to ascertain the intention of the parties and, when construing the language, it is necessary to have regard to the individual context and commercial background') and *The Delos* (n 31), but not *The Rena K* (n 16), *The Nerano* (n 31), nor *The Merak* (n 3), that Beatson LJ considered an 'old-fashioned and outdated approach to interpretation'. He treated the law and arbitration clause as 'a jurisdiction clause based on the modern approach on interpretation of contracts'; Serpil Yılmaz, 'Three Problems Caused by Arbitration Clauses Incorporated into Bills of Lading' (2016) 48(65) Annales de la Faculté de Droit d'Istanbul 193, 213.

for an anti-suit injunction to restrain the first party from commencing or pursuing the proceedings.[67]

Even if the evidence pointed to Morocco rather than to England, the express choice of England made it the most appropriate forum. In *The Lucky Lady*, the claimant could refer to 'a solid practical benefit' to having proceedings in England,[68] thus helping the owners to resist enforcement in a third country. The owners could show that the intention was to incorporate the dispute resolution clause of the charterparty in favour of English courts and that the parties were mistaken when referring to 'arbitration' instead of 'jurisdiction' in the B/L, so a reasonable person would have understood their real intention. Thus the cargo interests' challenge to English jurisdiction was dismissed and the owners' arguments were accepted.[69]

The difference with *The YM Saturn* lies in the fact that the law and litigation clause contained arbitration provisions only in certain cases and jurisdiction clauses in others. A problem arises when a B/L holder has not seen the terms of the head charterparty, in the case of a carrier under an incorporated voyage sub-charterparty and a consignee of a straight B/L or B/L holder to whom the B/L has been transferred, who is unaware of the dispute resolution clause. This stresses why, when transferring a B/L incorporating a charterparty, it is important that a copy of that charterparty is also presented.[70] As Baatz points out, however, the problem is that the presentation of documents under a letter of credit requires waiting until the goods are delivered at the discharge port, which may be too late.

Thus, when incorporating jurisdiction clauses in England, the reference must be clearly expressed, although the court will seek the 'real intention of the parties' if there is doubt. General words are not enough to incorporate a dispute resolution clause, although incorporation may be possible through an appropriate reference to a charterparty in the B/L. Disputes arising out of a jurisdiction or arbitration clause are normally resolved in accordance with the charterparty terms, since incorporation by reference is normally sufficient for a valid incorporation. English case law recognises dispute resolution clauses unless the claimant provides compelling reasons not to. However, English courts have no discretion if there is an arbitration clause or Article 25 of the Brussels I Regulation (recast) applies. English courts may not enforce a dispute resolution clause if or when it is not possible to

67 *Ust-Kamenogorsk Hydropower Plant JSC v. AES Ust-Kamenogorsk Hydropower Plant LLP* [2013] UKSC 35 (Kazakhstan); *Kallang Shipping SA v. Axa Assurances Senegal (The Kallang)* [2006] EWHC 2825 (Senegal); *Sotrade Denizcilik Sanayi ve Ticaret AS v. Amadou Lo (The Duden)* [2008] EWHC 2762 (Comm) (Senegal); *Noble Assurance Co v. Gerling-Konzern General Insurance Co* [2007] EWHC 253 (Comm); *C v. D* [2007] EWHC 1541 (Comm); *Markel International Co Ltd v. Craft (The Norseman)* [2006] EWHC 3150 (Comm); *Starlight Shipping Co v. Tai Ping Insurance Co Ltd* [2007] EWHC 1893 (Comm) (China); *Midgulf International Ltd v. Groupe Chimique Tunisien* [2010] EWCA Civ 66 (Tunisia); *Royal Bank of Scotland Plc v. Hicks* [2011] EWHC 287 (Ch) (Texas, US, where the defendant sought punitive damages); *The Good Luck* (n 58) (China). However, this was not true in *The Lucky Lady* (n 32) (Jordan), where the party sued in Jordan was not a party to the arbitration clause.For the position where the proceedings are in the court of an EU Member State or a Lugano contracting state, the position would be the same where there is a court jurisdiction clause in the B/L; see *The YM Saturn* (n 61), which involved a court jurisdiction clause in the charterparty incorporated into a B/L; *The Channel Ranger* (n 8); *Compania Sud Americana de Vapores SA v. Hin-Pro Logistics International Ltd* [2014] EWHC 3632 (Comm) (in which the anti-suit injunction was granted), [2015] EWCA Civ 401. See Baatz, 'Should Third Parties Be Bound by Arbitration Clauses in Bills of Lading?' (n 18).

68 *The Lucky Lady* (n 32).

69 Baatz, 'Should Third Parties Be Bound by Arbitration Clauses in Bills of Lading?' (n 18).

70 Article 22, UCP 600.

have a judicial process with guarantees, enforcement of the judgment, or the dispute resolution clause may be aimed at providing a procedural advantage, with no connection to the relevant facts of the case.[71]

As a general rule, a choice of forum clause is valid, except where one of the parties wants to resort to procedural or legal fraud or due to an international public policy (*ordre public*), for both EU and international law.[72] Thus, both public policy and overriding mandatory rules may constitute a limitation to the parties' intention. However, the court may issue anti-suit injunctions to restrain the parties from starting proceedings in other non-EU jurisdictions, in breach of an English arbitration agreement.[73]

2.2 Incorporation of arbitration clauses in England

The importance of maritime arbitration in the international commercial context is highlighted by Hill.[74] The popularity of arbitration is seen throughout different areas of maritime law: as well as the typical charterparty disputes, arbitration is frequently seen in relation to disputes over maritime assistance, salvage and ship-building contracts. Arbitration is excluded from environmental protection and marine environment cases because the CLC and FUND Conventions contain exclusive forums such as the place where the harmful event takes place or the place of adoption of preventive measures.[75]

London's prominence as a major centre of international maritime arbitration means that the regulations and business practices of English origin have widespread influence and a well-established framework. The 1996 UK Arbitration Act (UKAA)[76] represented a novel take on the traditional determination of the applicable law by the arbitrator in relation to the substance of the dispute at stake, as did the ICC Rules of Arbitration that have been in force since 1 January 2012.[77]

The UKAA's inception was influenced by the report from Lord Mustill in 1989.[78] It aims to 'restate and improve' the statutory and common law rules of commercial arbitra-

71 Ana María Sánchez-Horneros Adán, 'La ley 14/2014, de 24 de julio, de navegación marítima: Última llamada para la jurisdicción española en asuntos marítimos' (2016) 8802 Diario La Ley 2.

72 Aitor Zurimendi Isla, 'Responsabilidad del porteador frente al adquirente de un conocimiento de embarque con cláusulas de jurisdicción y arbitraje' in Pedro Jesús Baena Baena and Nieves López Santana (eds), *Estudios Sobre la Responsabilidad de los Operadores de Transporte en la Ley de Navegación Marítima* (Aranzadi 2017) 239–263.

73 Baatz, 'Should Third Parties Be Bound by Arbitration Clauses in Bills of Lading?' (n 18).

74 Jonathan Hill, *The Law Relating to International Commercial Disputes* (Informa 1994) 457 *et seq.*, in which the author reflects on the causes and origin of the growing importance of arbitration.

75 International Convention on Civil Liability for Oil Pollution Damage, 1969 (CLC Convention), replaced by the 1992 Protocol and International Convention on the Establishment of an International Fund for Compensation for Oil Pollution Damage, 1979 (FUND), superseded by the 1992 and 2003 Protocols.

76 Arbitration Act 1996 (Commencement No 1) Order 1996, SI 1996 No 3146 (c 96), Schedule 2; the UKAA is in force since 31 January 1997 in England, Wales and Northern Ireland according to section 2(1).

77 Article 21 (Applicable Rules of Law) states:

> The parties shall be free to agree upon the rules of law to be applied by the arbitral tribunal to the merits of the dispute. In the absence of any such agreement, the arbitral tribunal shall apply the rules of law which it determines to be appropriate. The arbitral tribunal shall take account of the provisions of the contract, if any, between the parties and of any relevant trade usages. The arbitral tribunal shall assume the powers of an amiable compositeur or decide *ex aequo et bono* only if the parties have agreed to give it such powers.

78 Michael J Mustill, *A New Arbitration Act? The response of the Departmental Advisory Committee to the UNCITRAL Model law on International Commercial Arbitration* (HMSO 1989).

tion[79] by following the structure and contents of the UNCITRAL Model Law. The seat of arbitration is 'the juridical seat' designated by the parties to the arbitration agreement or the institution, person or arbitral tribunal chosen by them. The juridical seat of arbitration can also be 'determined, in the absence of any such designation, having regard to the parties' agreement and all the relevant circumstances'.[80] 'The seat of arbitration is usually the physical location where the arbitration is located but in fact it may also be the legal place of arbitration'.[81] The parties may designate London as the seat of arbitration and English law as the applicable law. However, all or part of the proceedings can be conducted in another country.

According to the 'procedural party autonomy' principle, Article 19(1) of the UNCITRAL Model Law 1985 (last amended in 2006), regarding the determination of rules of procedure, states: 'subject to the provisions of this Law, the parties are free to agree on the procedure to be followed by the arbitral tribunal in conducting the proceedings'.

Similarly, the provisions of Part 1 of the UKAA are founded on principles among which 'the parties should be free to agree how their disputes are resolved, subject only to such safeguards as are necessary in the public interest' (s 1(b) UKAA).

Furthermore, the procedure in s 34(1) UKAA follows Article 19(1) of the UNCITRAL Model Law 1985: 'it shall be for the tribunal to decide all procedural and evidential matters, subject to the right of the parties to agree any matter'.

The limitations to procedural party autonomy in arbitration depend on the stage of arbitral proceedings. The arbitral procedural rules agreed before the constitution of the arbitral tribunal cannot normally be modified without the consent of the tribunal itself unless the parties to the contract never agreed on it.[82] If parties agree on institutional arbitration they will be bound by institutional rules.

Under s 31 UKAA (objection to substantive jurisdiction of tribunal), the respondent should object to the jurisdiction before contesting the merits of the matter:

1. An objection that the arbitral tribunal lacks substantive jurisdiction at the outset of the proceedings must be raised by a party not later than the time he takes the first step in the proceedings to contest the merits of any matter in relation to which he challenges the tribunal's jurisdiction. A party is not precluded from raising such an objection by the fact that he has appointed or participated in the appointment of an arbitrator.
2. Any objection during the course of the arbitral proceedings that the arbitral tribunal is exceeding its substantive jurisdiction must be made as soon as possible after the matter alleged to be beyond its jurisdiction is raised.

Section 6(1) UKAA defines an arbitration agreement as 'an agreement to submit to arbitration present or future disputes (whether they are contractual or not)'. The UKAA is applicable to arbitration agreements in writing: Andrews clarifies that 'an arbitration agreement not in writing might be valid at common law, that is, outside the scope' of the UKAA, and 'an unwritten arbitration agreement is not lacking in legal effect; but it

79 William W Park, *Arbitration of International Business Disputes. Studies in Law and Practice* (2nd edn, OUP 2012) 369–381.

80 UKAA, s 3.

81 *ABB Lummus Global Ltd v. Keppel Fels Ltd* [1999] 2 Lloyd's Rep 24; *Dubai Islamic Bank Pjsc v. Paymentech Merchant Services Inc* [2001] 1 Lloyd's Rep 65.

82 Michael Pryles, 'Limits to Party Autonomy in Arbitral Procedure' (2007) 24 J Int Arb 327, 339.

will not be governed by the Act'.[83] Section 5 UKAA sets out that there is an arbitration agreement in writing:

(a) if the agreement is made in writing (whether or not it is signed by the parties),
(b) if the agreement is made by exchange of communications in writing, or
(c) if the agreement is evidenced in writing.
... where parties agree otherwise than in writing by reference to terms which are in writing, they make an agreement in writing.

Furthermore, according to s 5(6), 'references ... to anything being written or in writing include its being recorded by any means' including electronic means (such as email, electronic B/L, fixture recap). If the agreement is not in writing it will be valid if it 'is recorded by one of the parties, or by a third party, with the authority of the parties to the agreement' (s 5(4)). The arbitration clause may be contained in a charterparty or a B/L. The ultimate B/L holder will be obliged to arbitrate in case of any claim arising from the breach of the B/L contract.[84]

Arbitration and jurisdiction agreements are subject to interpretation rules in English law. English and Welsh courts (or arbitral tribunals, under s 30 UKAA) will determine whether an arbitration clause complies with s 5. They will not determine the validity of the arbitration agreement following a foreign test when it is governed by a third country's law.[85] Judges have the 'power to recast botched text when the true intention is readily discernible' under s 5(5):[86]

> An exchange of written submissions in arbitral or legal proceedings in which the existence of an agreement otherwise than in writing is alleged by one party against another party and not denied by the other party in his response constitutes as between those parties an agreement in writing to the effect alleged.

Section 6(2) concerns arbitration clauses incorporated by reference: 'the reference in an agreement to a written form of arbitration clause or to a document containing an arbitration clause constitutes an arbitration agreement if the reference is such as to make that clause part of the agreement'.

Arbitration clauses can be incorporated by general words of incorporation. Although, as seen in *The Lucky Lady*, a B/L must specifically refer to the arbitration clause. The following provision could appear in a standard B/L issued under a charterparty:

> This shipment is carried under and pursuant to the terms of the Contract of Affreightment/Charterparty dated AS PER CHARTERPARTY at PER CHARTERPARTY between AS PER CHARTERPARTY and AS PER CHARTERPARTY as Charterer and all the terms whatsoever of the said Contract of Affreightment/Charterparty including the Arbitration clause, cargo line clause, and the conditions appearing on both sides of this Bill of Lading to apply and to govern

83 Lord Justice Saville, *Departmental Advisory Committee on Arbitration Law Report on the Arbitration Bill (1996)* (DTI 1997) [32]; UKAA s 81(2)(b); Lord Mustill and Stewart C Boyd QC, *Commercial Arbitration: 2001 Companion* (Butterworths 2000) 21, 371; Neil Andrews, *Arbitration and Contract Law: Common Law Perspectives* (Springer 2016) 24–26.

84 Sarah C Derrington and James M Turner, *The Law and Practice of Admiralty Matters* (OUP 2007) 298–313.

85 Andrews (n 83) 24–26.

86 ibid.

> the rights of the parties concerned in this shipment. A copy of the Contract of Affreightment/ Charterparty may be obtained from the Shipper or the Charterer upon request.

The arbitration clause provided in the charterparty becomes a provision in the B/L.[87] Under English law, the general rule is that an arbitration clause in a charterparty binds the B/L holder when it is expressly and specifically incorporated into the B/L.[88] The B/L holder is not an original signatory and has no power to negotiate the charterparty terms. This person has not acquired any responsibilities or rights under the B/L.[89] However, when the charterparty terms have been incorporated in the B/L and endorsed to the holder, this person is bound by the arbitration clause under the *lex fori*, raising reasonable doubts for B/L endorsees whether it might bind them.[90] The effect of arbitration clauses on B/L holders may be different, depending on whether the arbitration clause is printed on or inserted into a liner B/L or is incorporated by reference into a B/L from a charterparty.[91]

English courts take a strict approach to resolving the issue of effective incorporation. General words of incorporation in a B/L are not construed as effectively incorporating the arbitration clause from a charterparty.[92] While the B/L usually must include express reference to the charterparty's arbitration clause in order to bind a B/L holder to arbitration, English courts will allow some flexibility in situations where the intent of the parties is evident.[93] In addition, although English law does not necessarily require it, some courts have found that the provision being incorporated must be consistent with the B/L, and if it is inconsistent, the provision will be rejected.[94]

English courts may apply ordinary principles of construction to analyse the effect of an arbitration clause on non-contractual parties (i.e., the successors to the original contractual parties) if the circumstances warrant it,[95] but in most cases, they will require explicit words of incorporation to effectively incorporate an arbitration clause from one contract into another.[96] An arbitration clause must be incorporated expressly and precisely to bind a B/L holder because a B/L holder is not an original party to the contract of carriage and the arbitration clause is an ancillary dispute resolution provision that is not germane or *directly* relevant

87 Robert Force and Martin Davies, 'Forum Selection Clauses in International Maritime Contracts' in Martin Davies (ed), *Jurisdiction and Forum Selection in International Maritime Law* (Kluwer Law International 2005) 32. A liner B/L usually directs any dispute arising under the B/L to be heard by the courts of a certain country and sometimes stipulates an arbitration clause. When a liner B/L is issued, the carrier and the shipper are the original parties to such B/L, and a charterparty is not used. An arbitration clause will be included on the face of the B/L, so the B/L holder is fully aware of the terms. See Martin Davies, 'Forum Selection Clauses in Maritime Cases' (2002) 27(2) Tul Mar LJ 367; Martin Davies, 'Litigation Fights Back: Avoiding the Effect of Arbitration Clauses in Charterparty Bills of Lading' (2004) 35 J Mar L & Com 617; Ling Li, 'Binding Effect of Arbitration Clauses on Holders of Bills of Lading as Non-Original Parties and a Potential Uniform Approach through Comparative Analysis' (2012) 37(1) Tul Mar LJ 107.

88 See *Kallang Shipping SA v. Axa Senegal (The Kallang) (No 2)* [2008] EWHC 2761 (Comm) [64].

89 Joshua S Force and Robert J Zapf, *Benedict on Admiralty* (7th edn, LexisNexis 2011) [104], 1–13.

90 See, e.g., *The Duden* (n 67) [55]; *The Kallang (No 2)* (n 88), [15]; Li (n 87).

91 Li (n 87).

92 *The Federal Bulker* (n 11) 105.

93 E.g., *The Kallang (No 2)* (n 88) [64] (concluding that despite the existence of two charterparties with the same date, the parties' intent to incorporate the voyage charter was clear because the B/L specified that freight was 'payable', a term typically found in voyage charters).

94 See, e.g., *Hamilton v. Mackie* (n 12) [677]; *TW Thomas & Co v. Portsea SS Co* [1912] AC 3 [10].

95 As in *Habas Sinai ve Tibbi Gazlar Isthisal Endustri AS v. Sometal SAL* [2010] EWHC (Comm) 29 [46]–[47] and *The Athena* (n 43).

96 See *AIG Europe SA v. QBE International Insurance Ltd* [2001] 2 Lloyd's Rep 268, 271.

to the subject matter of the main contract of carriage. English courts intend to protect non-original parties, such as B/L holders, by requiring the original parties to expressly incorporate the arbitration clause into the B/L and thus provide notice of the arbitration clause to B/L holders.[97]

Li states:[98]

> The express incorporation requirement in English law means that, on its face, a B/L must specify that an arbitration clause from a charterparty is incorporated … in contrast to US law, English courts apply a rule that does not deal with the scope of the arbitration clause. Furthermore, English law does not require identification of the charterparty[99] … There are benefits and detriments to [this] approach.

When the charterparty intended to be incorporated in the B/L was not correctly identified and the claimant relying on the B/L terms was unaware that the Hague–Visby limitation period had already expired, a Singaporean court stayed court proceedings in favour of London arbitration, stating as a condition that the time-bar was waived.[100] As a general rule, words of incorporation in the B/L do not incorporate an arbitration or jurisdiction clause[101] in the charterparty by general reference to a standard form contract[102] or previous contracts between the same parties to incorporate an arbitration or jurisdiction clause.[103]

The differences between third countries and England can lead to a conflict of laws as well as 'forum shopping'.[104] Any proceedings other than as provided for in the arbitration agreement will be considered a breach of contract entitling the defendant to a stay under s 9(1) UKAA and even to apply for an anti-suit injunction and/or damages.[105] The choice of jurisdiction in the standard B/L terms and conditions has an important role as 'forum shopping' is not an option and a jurisdiction is chosen. Larger shippers often negotiate such clauses but seem eager to litigate in more favourable jurisdictions (i.e., forum shopping).

AP Moller Maersk A/S v. Sonaec Villas Cen SAD Fadoul and others[106] is another example of 'forum shopping'. A consignment of tiles was sold by Yekalon Inc to Sonaec SA, to be delivered from China to Benin. Sonaec (the consignee) did not pay the outstanding amount owed under the contract of sale to Yekalon (one of the shippers); Yekalon commenced action in the Chinese courts to obtain a B/L from the other shipper, obtained the original B/L, surrendered it to Maersk and, after obtaining a second set of B/Ls, sold the cargo to another buyer in Honduras with Maersk as the carrier. Sonaec commenced proceedings in Benin against Maersk when the third set of B/Ls was issued, and an interim order obliged Maersk to deliver it to Sonaec and to pay a daily US$4,800 fine until it arrived. Maersk commenced proceedings in the English High Court and, due to the exclusive jurisdiction

97 Li (n 87).
98 ibid.
99 Force and Davies (n 87) 32.
100 *The Duden* [2008] 4 SLR 984.
101 *The Siboti* (n 7).
102 See *Thomas v. Portsea* (n 3); *The Varenna* (n 11); *The Federal Bulker* (n 11); *The Lucky Lady* (n 32).
103 *Habas v. Sometal* (n 95); Yvonne Baatz, 'The Conflict of Laws' in Yvonne Baatz (ed), *Maritime Law* (4th edn, Routledge 2018) 6.
104 See Force and Davies (n 87) 37–40.
105 See Aikens, Lord and Bools (n 42) ch 14.
106 n 29.

and choice of law clause contained in clause 26 of Maersk's standard terms and conditions, the English court considered that the issuance of the first B/L was collateral to the main contract, equating it to an arbitration agreement.

After the first B/L was surrendered to Yekalon following the Chinese court order, the transfer of rights was without prejudice to any right deriving from an original party to the B/L, as s 2(5) of COGSA 92 stipulates. This decision followed *Pyrene Co Ltd v. Scindia Steam Navigation*,[107] in which another sale of goods under FOB terms made it possible for the buyer and the seller to be part of the carriage of transport of goods by sea.

Summing up, it is thus preferable to provide for express incorporation of the arbitration clause into the B/L by clearly stating the incorporation of that clause into the B/L.

2.3 The effect of Brexit on incorporation of dispute resolution clauses

Many scholars have written about the possible effect of Brexit in relation to jurisdiction agreements contained in charterparties and B/Ls. The status quo forms the *acquis communautaire* and, therefore, the Brussels I Regulation (recast) is still applicable by UK courts. It is unclear at the time of writing whether there will be an extension of the transition period after 31 December 2020 or a new Trade Agreement accompanied by new rules on international jurisdiction. The UK formally applied to become a party to the Lugano Convention on 8 April 2020. However, the European Commission does not seem inclined to accept the accession of the UK to that treaty, as it would allow the UK to apply an 'almost perfect copy of the old Brussels I Regulation',[108] and 'the UK is determined to leave the single market after the transition expires'.[109]

The choice of jurisdiction in favour of an EU Member State prescribed by Article 23(1) of the Brussels I Regulation 44/2001 has a narrower scope in comparison with Article 25 of the Brussels I Regulation (recast), requiring one of the parties to be domiciled in an EU Member State. The *lis alibi pendens* rules of Articles 33 and 34, as well as Recital 24 of the Brussels I Regulation (recast), apply when proceedings or an action are pending in non-EU courts and the foreign court is first seised or there is an exclusive jurisdiction agreement in favour of that third state. These rules have no equivalent in the Lugano Convention or the earlier Brussels regime. EU courts may find jurisdiction according to other provisions of the Brussels I Regulation (recast), and the jurisdictional and procedural standards of the non-EU courts may differ from those in the EU.[110] However, the 2005 Hague Choice of Court Convention excludes B/Ls and voyage charterparties from its scope, although it does apply to time charterparties, demise charterparties and marine insurance.[111]

107 [1954] 1 Lloyd's Rep 321.

108 Quim Forner-Delaygua, 'Changes to jurisdiction based on exclusive jurisdiction agreements under the Brussels I Regulation Recast' (2015) 11(3) *Journal of Private International Law* 379, 281–282.

109 Jim Brunsden and others, 'Britain risks losing access to valuable European legal pact' *Financial Times* (London 20 April 2020).

110 Pietro Franzina, 'Lis Pendens Involving a Third Country under the Brussels I-bis Regulation: an Overview' (2014) Rivista di diritto internazionale privato e processuale 23; Forner-Delaygua (n 108).

111 The UK would be able to uphold choice of court agreements in the case of direct actions against marine insurers without following the CJEU's judgment in C-368/16 *Assens Havn v. Navigators Management (UK) Ltd* EU:C:2017:546, that restricted the enforcement of an English law and jurisdiction clause in a direct action against the insurer in contravention of the P&I Club's insurance policy terms; Jonatan Echebarria Fernández, 'Limitations

It is noteworthy that the still-not-in-force Hague Convention of 2 July 2019 on the Recognition and Enforcement of Foreign Judgments in Civil or Commercial Matters,[112] in line with the Hague Choice of Court Convention, excludes from its scope of application the carriage of passengers and goods, as well as pollution, limitation of liability for maritime claims and general average.[113] This new Convention reflects the same restrictions on party autonomy as the Hague Choice of Court Convention, recognising any cargo claim judgment of another jurisdiction where this instrument has been ratified.

It is clear that in the absence of any temporary or permanent arrangement it would be plausible for the UK to ratify both instruments, covering not all but some maritime-related claims. The UK will continue to recognise and enforce any English or foreign choice of court agreement, binding any 'third party such as a consignee, B/L holder, assignee or subrogated insurer (in relation to third party matters, ie assignment or direct actions)', after the expiry of the transition period.[114] Furthermore, if there are no other arrangements in place between the UK and the EU, it is expected that there will be a revival of the bilateral agreements that existed prior to the accession of the UK to the European Communities in 1973 on jurisdiction and enforcement of judgments on civil and commercial matters.

Arbitral proceedings by way of exclusive arbitration clause should not be affected if a new trade agreement is not struck by the UK and the EU. Arbitration agreements are subject to the New York Convention, which was ratified by all the EU Member States and the UK. No substantial changes on arbitral proceedings – in the UK or an EU Member State – are foreseen. However, the UK may be able to issue anti-suit injunctions restraining the parties from commencing proceedings in EU Member States in breach of an English jurisdiction or arbitration clause. There remain many uncertainties regarding the future if the UK and EU reach a new agreement on the recognition and validity of jurisdiction agreements.

3 Incorporation of dispute resolution clauses in Spain

Under civil law, a right of action against a third party is restricted by the limitation of liability contained in the main contract.[115] However, such an obligation not to bring certain proceedings (in certain jurisdictions) has merely a promissory effect, sounding in damages for the breach. A jurisdiction clause creates mutual rights and obligations for the beneficiaries, meaning all original parties to a B/L and the endorsees bound by it. Third-party subcontractors do not necessarily receive any benefit from the clause, however, because their interests might be favoured in an alternative forum.

on Jurisdiction and Arbitration Agreements Based on Applicable Law and the Identity of the Carrier in Cargo Claim Disputes: Who and Where to Sue?' (2019) 11(1) Cuadernos de Derecho Transnacional 306.

112 The Convention was drafted by the Hague Conference on Private International Law and it is known as the Judgments Convention.

113 For more information on the Judgments Convention's scope of application see Peter Arnt Nielsen, 'The Hague 2019 Judgments Convention – From Failure to Success?' (2020) Journal of Private International Law 1; Francisco Garcimartín Alférez, 'The Judgments Convention: Some Open Questions' (2020) 67(1) Netherlands International Law Review 19.

114 Yvonne Baatz, 'Choice of jurisdiction in bills of lading and cargo insurance' in Jason Chuah (ed), *Research Handbook on Maritime Law and Regulation* (Edward Elgar Publishing 2019) 342.

115 As ascertained from the judgment of the Dutch Court of Appeal 10 April 1987, *Schip & Schade* (1988) n 5.

Although the clause may not be of benefit to subcontractors, they may benefit from suing endorsees, forcing them to submit to the jurisdiction agreed by the original parties, unless the subcontractor could communicate with the original promisor and reject such guarantees, including the defences and limits.[116] In Spain, the Spanish Organic Law on the Judiciary (SOLJ)[117] provides the general domestic rules on international jurisdiction. Article 22 *bis* (2) sets out the following concerning the choice of jurisdiction:[118]

> An express agreement to submit is understood to refer to the agreement by which the parties decide to assign the Spanish Courts responsibility for hearing certain or all disputes that have arisen or that may arise between them in relation to a given legal relationship, contractual or otherwise. Competence established via express submission will extend to the validity of the submission agreement itself.
>
> The express submission agreement must be recorded in writing, in a clause included within a contract or in an independent agreement, or must be made verbally with written confirmation, or in a manner that is in keeping with the habitual practices established between the parties, or within international trading is in accordance with the practices that the parties are acquainted with, or should be acquainted with and that, within such commerce, are fully known to them and regularly observed by the parties in contracts of this nature within this commercial sector. A written agreement will be understood to exist where it is the result of transmissions carried out via electronic channels obtained through a durable record.
>
> A written agreement will also be understood to exist where it is confirmed via the exchange of lawsuit documents and the response to them within proceedings initiated in Spain, wherein the existence of the agreement is affirmed by one party and not refuted by the other.

With regard to charterparties, Spanish law respects the autonomy of parties but keeps strikingly restrictive procedural provisions. It is necessary to note the translational efficiency of the B/L as a document of title under Article 251 SAMN (effectiveness of conveyance), which provides:[119]

> Conveyance of the bill of lading shall take the same effects as delivery of the goods represented, without prejudice to the relevant criminal and civil actions to which the party illegitimately dispossessed of such may be entitled. The acquirer of the bill of lading shall acquire all the rights and actions of the conveyor to the goods, with the exception of agreements regarding jurisdiction and arbitration, which shall require the consent of the acquirer pursuant to the terms stated in Chapter I of Title IX.

It is necessary to consider the requirement that sets the standard for the verification of consent by the purchaser in respect of jurisdiction and arbitration agreements. Regardless, transfer of the B/L has the same effect as the delivery of the goods, with the purchaser acquiring all rights and obligations of the transferor; however, the acquiring party will have to give its express consent to existing agreements on jurisdiction and arbitration under Articles 468 and 469 SAMN. This view diverges from the consolidated jurisprudential

116 Theocharidis (n 93).

117 The Spanish Organic Law 6/1985 of 1 July on the Judiciary (SOLJ) ['*Ley Orgánica 6/1985, de 1 de julio, del Poder Judicial*'] published in the Official State Gazette No 157 of 2 July 1985 and amended by the Organic Law 7/2015 of 21 July 2015.

118 Translation taken from *Legislation Online.org* <https://www.legislationline.org/download/id/6791/file/Spain_law_juidiciary_1985_am2016_en.pdf> accessed 2 July 2020.

119 Translation taken from Ministerio de Justicia, *Official Translation* (2014) <https://www.mjusticia.gob.es/cs/Satellite/Portal/1292427275074?blobheader=application%2Fpdf&blobheadername1=Content-Disposition&blobheadervalue1=attachment%3B+filename%3DAct_14_2014__dated_24th_july__on_Maritime_Navigation_%28Ley_de_Navegacion_Maritima%29.PDF> accessed 2 July 2020.

interpretation of the CJEU, which only requires verification of consent in those cases where the shipper's rights and obligations have not been transferred to the B/L holder under domestic law. The CJEU has repeatedly set out this doctrine in different judgments.[120]

Under Title IX, chapter 1 of the SAMN, certain specialties on international jurisdiction have to be addressed beforehand. Article 468 SAMN (jurisdiction and arbitration clauses) states the following:[121]

> Without prejudice to the terms foreseen in the international conventions in force in Spain and the provisions of the European Union, clauses of submission to a foreign jurisdiction or arbitration abroad shall be null and void and considered not to be included, as set forth in contracts for use of the ship, or in ancillary navigation contracts, when they have not been negotiated individually and separately.
>
> In particular, insertion of a jurisdiction or arbitration clause in the printed conditions of any of the contracts referred to in the preceding paragraph shall not provide evidence, in itself, of fulfilment of the requisites established therein.

Article 469 SAMN (criteria for attribution of competence), on the other hand, says the following:[122]

> 1. Except if the parties have validly introduced an exclusive jurisdiction clause or an arbitration clause as established in this Chapter, the criteria foreseen in this Article shall apply.
> 2. In contracts for use of the ship, the competent courts, to be chosen by the plaintiff, shall be those of:
>   (a) the domicile of the defendant;
>   (b) place where the contract is entered into;
>   (c) port of loading or unloading.
> 3. In ancillary navigation contracts, the competent courts, to be chosen by the plaintiff, shall be those of:
>   (a) the domicile of the defendant;
>   (b) place where the contract is entered into;
>   (c) place where the services are provided.
> 4. In order to hear the motion to challenge liquidation [adjustment or distribution] of the general average, both that made privately as well as that performed by a Notary Public pursuant to the relevant public certification proceedings, the competent court shall be that of the place of conclusion of the transport, or the place of arrival of the ship, if the latter is different.

Even before SAMN came into force, Spanish jurisprudence invalidated dispute resolution clauses where there is a fraudulent choice of forum or an intention to prevent an effective claim in accordance with Article 11(2) SOLJ and Article 7(2) of the Spanish Civil Code.[123] The limited practical applications of Articles 468 and 469 SAMN include situations where parties appoint non-EU courts or international agreements that take into account the possibility that parties may regulate international civil procedures. The individualisation and separate negotiation requirements of such articles are far from the regular international

120 See Case C-159/97 *Trasporti Castelletti Spedizioni Internazionali SpA v. Hugo Trumpy SpA* EU:C:1999:142, [1999] ECR I-1597 and Case C-387/98 *Coreck Maritime GmbH v. Handelsveem BV* EU:C:2000:606, [2000] ECR I-9337.

121 Official translation (n 119).

122 ibid.

123 Civil Code approved by Royal Decree of 24 July 1889 (Official State Gazette No 206 of 25 July 1889).

practice in the shipping sector and may conflict with Article 22 *bis* (2) SOLJ, which allows for an express submission agreement to be recorded in writing in a contract or an independent agreement, allowing the incorporation of the charterparty terms into a B/L and thus, respecting the habitual practice between the parties or within international trade.[124]

Article 22 *bis* regulates the *prorogatio fori* while Article 22 *ter* (4) contains *derogatio fori* rules. Their application is marginal and in most cases, the Brussels I Regulation (recast) will apply. The SOLJ supersedes the Brussels I Regulation (recast) in relation to remedies for non-compliance, akin to English anti-suit injunctions in certain scenarios. As to remedies for non-compliance, the SOLJ allows going beyond the Regulation. There is, therefore, nothing to prevent a Spanish judge from ordering a precautionary measure similar to an anti-suit injunction for breach of a jurisdiction clause in favour of Spanish courts by bringing a lawsuit in a third state, or for granting compensation for the loss caused by said action (the parties may also accompany the jurisdiction clause with a criminal clause).

For instance, in the judgment of the Spanish Supreme Court of 12 January 2009,[125] a contract between a US and a Spanish company included a jurisdiction clause in favour of the courts of Barcelona. The Spanish company filed a claim against the US defendant before the courts of Florida and the defendants alleged the existence of the jurisdiction agreement before the American courts. Once the courts of Florida declined jurisdiction in favour of the Spanish courts, the defendants started proceedings in Spain invoking the submission clause and requesting compensation for their losses caused by having to defend the case before the American courts in violation of the jurisdiction agreement. As Garcimartín Alférez points out, the Spanish Supreme Court rightly agreed to such request, 'understanding that the jurisdiction clauses impose behavioural duties on the parties, whose failure generates liability'.[126] This remedy can be found in contractual clauses such as the following:

> In the event that either party institutes any legal proceedings in any court other than the London District Court, that party shall assume all of the costs incurred in having such proceedings dismissed or stayed, including but not limited to the other party's attorney and paralegal fees.[127]

Article 22 *ter* (4) SOLJ contains the *derogatio fori* rules that Spanish courts must observe when a contract contains a submission clause in favour of third states. On one hand, the exceptions regarding matters outside the scope of exclusive rights and protection forums shall be considered since these are not negotiable by the contractual parties. On the other hand, the Brussels I Regulation (recast) (and the Lugano Convention) ensures uniformity across the EU for the acceptance of international jurisdiction by the court chosen by the parties when the requirements of Article 25 of the recast Regulation are met, through an implicit rule of recognition, since all Member States respect minimum procedural guarantees. However, a choice of a non-EU state with which Spain has no bilateral agreements in place does not offer those guarantees.[128]

---

124 M Virgós and A Cambronero, 'Comparative Study of "Residual Jurisdiction" in Civil and Commercial Disputes in the EU: Spain' (2007) European Commission online publication.

125 RJ 2009\544

126 Francisco Garcimartín Alférez, 'Competencia judicial internacional y autonomía de la voluntad' (*Almacén de Derecho*, 2 August 2017) <https://almacendederecho.org/competencia-judicial-internacional-autonomia-la-voluntad/> accessed 14 May 2020.

127 ibid.

128 ibid.

Spanish courts will assess if the defendant has invoked the jurisdiction or arbitration clause in favour of a third state, that the claimant opposes the *derogatio fori* of Spanish courts by proving that the foreign courts have not, or will not, assume international jurisdiction.[129] The defendant may also show that the chosen foreign courts will not offer adequate judicial protection, obliging the Spanish courts to continue the proceedings (see Article 33 Brussels I Regulation (recast)). As Garcimartín Alférez states, when the Brussels I Regulation (recast), the Lugano Convention or any international instrument ratified by Spain is not applicable, Articles 468 and 251 SAMN declare that jurisdiction or arbitration clauses should be negotiated individually and separately, excluding forms with general conditions, even among shipping parties.[130]

Summing up, the SAMN, in the view of the Spanish legislator, is meant to safeguard legal certainty[131] and to reduce the operability of the *favor negotii* principle (referring to maritime, commercial or business interests). Courts can decline jurisdiction in non-EU jurisdiction agreements according to Articles 22 *bis* and 22 *ter* (4) SOLJ.[132] The defendant must raise a specific motion called a *declinatoria*, regulated under Article 63 of the Spanish Law on Civil Procedure (SLCP)[133] or Article 8 SAA, regarding arbitral agreements before the oral proceedings.[134]

3.1 Incorporation of jurisdiction clauses in Spain

3.1.1 Jurisdiction agreements in favour of EU courts

The formalism of EU secondary legislation and CJEU case law in the past was overcome by recognising the convenience of commercial usages.[135] Likely due to inattention or a lack of foresight by the Spanish legislators, the SAMN[136] lacks any reference to the Brussels I Regulation (recast), with practical consequences for its application.

---

129 Article 22 *ter* 4 SOLJ applies when Spanish courts have no jurisdiction if there is a valid submission agreement to foreign tribunals or arbitration panels; moreover, Spanish courts will automatically decline jurisdiction (as stated in Article 38 SLCP) if the parties do not implicitly or tacitly agree to submit their dispute to them, according to Article 36(2)(3) SOLJ; Alfonso-Luis Calvo Caravaca and Javier Carrascosa González (eds), *Derecho Internacional Privado: Vol I* (Comares 2016) 390–392; see from the same authors, *Tratado de Derecho internacional privado* (1st ed, Tirant Lo Blanch, València 2020), 407–412.

130 ibid.

131 Spanish laws must observe legal security, according to Article 9(3) of the Spanish Constitution.

132 Article 22 *ter* (4) states: 'competence established in accordance with the stipulations of paragraph 1 of this Article can be overturned via an agreement to select a foreign court. In such cases, the courts will suspend proceedings and can only hear the claim deduced in the event that the assigned foreign courts decline their competence'.

133 Law 1/2000 of 7 January on Civil Procedure (Official State Gazette No 7 of 8 January 2000) amended by Spanish Law 42/2015 of 5 October.

134 Virgós and Cambronero (n 124).

135 Case C-106/95 *MSG v. Les Gravières Rhénanes SARL* EU:C:1997:70, [1997] ECR I-911.

136 Among SAMN's novelties are the new time charter and voyage charter expenses under Article 204(2), which states: 'The time charterer undertakes business management of the ship and, unless otherwise agreed, shall bear all the variable operating expenses. In voyage charters, such expenses shall be borne by the carrier, except if otherwise agreed'.Another positive aspect relates to the designation of the dock or loading place under Article 217 SAMN, under which, unless otherwise agreed, the charterer may assign the dock or loading place within the port where available, as long as it is safe and accessible for the ship before, during and after loading. If such assignment has not been established within a reasonable period, the carrier may keep the ship at anchor to await orders, or head for the usual dock or loading place, charging the charterer for the time elapsed.The loading and stowage as related operations for effective transportation of goods by sea and the possibility that the parties agree who is responsible for carrying out these activities and the assumption of risks that may occur are regulated under Article 218 SAMN (loading and stevedore operations), which states:

There is a problem of normative hierarchy between the SAMN and the SOLJ. An 'organic law' represents a category of hierarchically superior norm in the Spanish legal system. However, the specialised character of the SAMN creates doubt over the prevalence of the SOLJ by applying the principle of *lex specialis derogat legi generali*. Conversely, the *lex posterior derogat legi priori* principle validates the prevalence of the SAMN over the SOLJ. The issue is debatable considering the contradictory provisions of the SOLJ and the SAMN. Their compatibility has to be analysed since the general rule for jurisdiction and the procedural specialty of the SAMN have to be interpreted by Spanish judges in order to provide interpretative guidelines. However, it is accepted that the SOLJ and the SAMN are subordinate to the provisions of international treaties in force in Spain and in the EU that regulate the same matters as Articles 2(1) and 468 SAMN and Article 22 *bis* (2) SOLJ.

Article 4 *bis* (1) SOLJ clarifies that 'the judges and courts will enforce the law of the European Union in accordance with the jurisprudence of the Court of Justice of the European Union'. Moreover, according to Article 21(1) SOLJ, 'Spanish civil courts will hear claims that arise within Spanish territory in accordance with the stipulations of the international conventions and treaties to which Spain is a party, the regulations of the European Union and Spanish laws'. According to Article 2(1) SAMN: 'This Act shall be applied as long as it does not oppose the terms set forth in the international treaties in force in Spain and the legal provisions of the European Union that regulate the same matters'. Therefore, the current situation is not affected by internal legislative changes, acknowledging the validity of the clause of submission to a foreign jurisdiction or arbitration abroad in any of the forms required.[137]

Both Article 22 *bis* (2) SOLJ and Article 468 SAMN contain a rule concerning the express choice of jurisdiction agreements displaced by Article 25 of the Brussels I Regulation (recast) in the absence of applicable international agreements.[138] As already mentioned in relation to the incorporation of choice of forum clauses in the EU, Article 25 of the Brussels I Regulation (recast) leads to the *prorogatio fori* by allowing the parties, regardless of domicile, to agree to submit their disputes to the courts of an EU

1. Except if otherwise agreed, the charterer or stevedore shall place the goods alongside the ship and shall perform the loading and stacking thereof at its expense and risk, with the adequate diligence required by the nature of the merchandise and the voyage planned;
2. The above rules shall not be applicable to charter carriage of specific goods under the bill of lading regime, in which the carrier undertakes, except if otherwise agreed, to perform the loading and stacking;
3. Even when it is agreed that the loading and stacking be performed at the expense and risk of the charterer or consignor, the carrier shall be liable for the consequences arising from defective stacking that compromises the safety of the voyage.

137 Albert Badia, 'Jurisdicción y competencia' in Julio Carlos Fuentes Gómez and others, *Comentarios a la Ley de Navegación Marítima* (Dykinson 2015) 426. The author remarks on the minimum formal requirements set up by the EU regulatory framework and case law concerning attributive clauses of jurisdiction; Nerea Iráculis Arregui, 'La controvertida negociación individual y separada de las cláusulas de jurisdicción y arbitraje en la Ley de Navegación Marítima' (2017) 19 Revista de derecho del transporte: Terrestre, marítimo, aéreo y multimodal 173.

138 See Federico Garau Sobrino, 'Los acuerdos atributivos de jurisdicción en Derecho Procesal Civil Internacional Español' (2010) 2(2) Cuadernos de Derecho Transnacional 52; Juan José Álvarez Rubio, 'A correct jurisprudential orientation in relation to the validity and scope of the submission clause in favour of a foreign court contained in a bill of lading. Commentary on the Judgment of 13 February 2019 of the Provincial Court of Barcelona (Section 15)' (2019) 11(2) Cuadernos de Derecho Transnacional 388, 396.

Member State.[139] Moreover, a submission agreement drafted in a contract is considered to be independent of other clauses of the contract and can still be enforced even if the contract as a whole is declared null or invalid (Article 25(5) of the Brussels I Regulation (recast)).[140]

A *derogatio fori* effect takes place if the claimant starts proceedings in a tribunal other than the nominated one, staying the proceedings under the *lis alibi pendens* rules of Article 31(2) of the Brussels I Regulation (recast) unless the defendant enters an appearance according to Article 26 (implied choice of court agreement). Any clause in a contract for use of a vessel or an auxiliary navigation contract conferring jurisdiction over a particular dispute to an EU Member State court, regardless of whether the parties have their domiciles in the EU, will be governed by its provisions in terms of formal validity.[141]

The validity of a foreign jurisdiction clause included in a B/L is guaranteed by Spanish courts mainly by application of the CJEU doctrine. The interpretative doctrine of the Spanish Supreme Court is set out in the judgments of 29 September 2005 (case JR 2005/7156, respecting the trade usages of the sector), 2 August 2007 (case RJ 2007/558, where a dispute resolution clause was included on the reverse of a B/L), 7 June 2007 (case RJ 2007/5431, admitting the validity based on usages of the commercial sector) and 16 May 2008 (case RJ 2008/3080, admitting a choice of forum clause 'when it turns out that both the way to insert such conditions and the express clause itself are common in maritime trade').

In the Spanish Supreme Court case of 27 May 2008 (case RJ 2008/4155), the validity of the clause of attribution of competence was accepted by compliance with Article 17(a) of the Brussels Convention, requiring the written consent of the contracting parties: 'According to the Court of Appeal, the agreement of the parties had been proved, despite the absence of signature of the shipper, because the clause appeared on the front of the contract and in bold, perfectly highlighted'. However, there are some 'shocking' exceptions, in the words of Iráculis.[142]

The validity of jurisdiction clauses is recognised in Orders of the Provincial Courts of Madrid of 16 January 2012,[143] 19 September 2014[144] and 2 September 2015;[145] and

139 Pedro Alberto De Miguel Asensio, 'El nuevo reglamento sobre competencia judicial y reconocimiento y ejecución de resoluciones' (2013) 34(8013) La Ley 1; Ana Paloma Abarca Junco, 'La competencia judicial de los tribunales españoles: Foro de la autonomía de la voluntad' in Ana Paloma Abarca Junco and others (eds) *Derecho Internacional Privado* (UNED 2013) 134.

140 Álvarez Rubio, 'A correct jurisprudential orientation in relation to the validity and scope of the submission clause in favour of a foreign court contained in a bill of lading' (n 138) 397.

141 Zurimendi Isla (n 72) 239–263.

142 A judgment of 31 May 2012 (Case RJ 2012/4155) dismissed the validity of a choice of Saudi Arabian jurisdiction in the B/L under the pretext of it breaching the requirements set out in Article 23 Brussels I Regulation, since the signature of an employee of the shipper and its stamp on the back of the B/L did not constitute express consent, upholding the criteria adduced in the Court of Appeal's judgment; Iráculis Arregui (n 137).

143 Case AC 2012/437, where it was considered irrelevant that only the carrier signed the B/L, since it was regularly issued and received as in compliance by the shipper.

144 Case JUR 2015/247406, where it was held that the copies of the B/L did not include the signature and stamp of the parties because the parties consented on the content of an already-executed contract, and the B/L is just the instrument to externalise their will.

145 Case JUR 2015/248567, where an incomplete B/L was presented by the claimant.

in Orders of the Provincial Court of Pontevedra of 2 April 2010,[146] 19 May 2011[147] and 19 January 2016.[148] Other judgments that recognise jurisdiction clauses were issued by the Provincial Court of Valencia of 8 November 2016[149] and the Provincial Court of Barcelona of 21 December 2016.[150]

The same criteria are followed by Orders of the Commercial Courts No 1 of Barcelona of 4 March 2015[151] and No 6 of Madrid of 13 September 2016[152] and 5 July 2019,[153] confirming the validity of the choice of forum clauses in favour of intra-EU Member State courts.[154]

3.1.2 Jurisdiction agreements in favour of non-EU courts

The SAMN regime applies when the parties confer jurisdiction on a court or courts outside the EU or not part of an applicable international convention. If it applies, Article 468 sets a restrictive interpretation for the *derogatio fori* by Spanish courts from an agreement conferring jurisdiction on a foreign court, warning about the invalidity of any clause that has not been negotiated individually and separately from the main contract. If the conditions under SAMN are not met concerning contracts for use of a ship or ancillary navigation contracts, the clause containing this type of an express submission to a foreign tribunal would be void and disregarded.

If the choice of jurisdiction is deemed void, the Spanish courts would have jurisdiction under alternative forums set out in Article 469 SAMN (in contracts for the use of a ship: the defendant's domicile, the place where the contract was entered into and the port of loading

146 Case JUR 2010/135394 follows the doctrine established by the Supreme Court case of 8 February 2007.

147 Case JUR 2012/399815, dealing with a valid choice of English jurisdiction, deemed ineffective by subsequent implied submission.

148 Case JUR 2016/62443, in which an English jurisdiction clause in writing was incorporated into a B/L that documented an international contract for the carriage of goods by sea.

149 Case JUR 2017/14921, where the B/L included a submission to the English courts, and its nullity was invoked according to Article 468 SAMN by unilateral imposition, confirming its validity according to CJEU case law and the doctrine of the Spanish Supreme Court and Provincial Court, citing the Orders of 27 July 2016 issued in the Rolls of Appeal 450/2016 and 1271/2016, emphasising that the examination of validity of a jurisdiction clause in the field of maritime transport must be carried out individually in each specific case, not always depriving the Spanish courts from substantive jurisdiction.

150 Case JUR 2017/79290, dealing with the termination of a distribution contract containing a German jurisdiction clause, declaring a lack of territorial jurisdiction of the German courts, reversing the validity of the clause in the first instance.

151 Case AC 2015/1066 included a submission to the court of Marseilles, France.

152 In Case JUR 2016/209381, the B/L containing a submission clause to the High Court of England and Wales that was similar to previous formalised ones between the parties, under Article 23(1) of the Brussels I Regulation, now Article 25(1) of the Brussels I Regulation (recast).

153 In Case AC 2019/1354, the Spanish branch of Zurich Insurance PCL brought a subrogated claim against AP Møller-Maersk A/S for damage suffered to cargo carried by sea. The court dismissed the allegations by Maersk and recognised the validity of a choice of forum agreement in favour of the High Court of Justice in London included in the B/L, even if the shipper did not know about such clause until the cargo arrived to the port of destination. This commensurate with the trade usage in the maritime sector, and the Provincial Court of Madrid applied Article 25 of the Brussels I Regulation (recast) relying on CJEU case law; for an extensive analysis of the judgment and the lack of adequacy of the SMAN in relation to the Brussels I Regulation (recast), see Nerea Magallón Elósegui, 'Agreements Conferring Jurisdiction in Favour of a Foreign Court Included in a Bill of Lading: Customs and Contractual Freedom in the Maritime Sector: Commentary on the Order of 5 July 2019 of the AAP de Madrid (Section 28)' (2020) 12(1) Cuadernos Derecho Transnacional 619.

154 Iráculis Arregui (n 137).

or unloading; in ancillary navigation contracts: the defendant's domicile, the place where the contract was entered into and the place where the services are provided).

If the chosen jurisdiction lacks a minimum logical economic relationship to the carrier, the aim in choosing it may have been to hinder or prevent claims in practice. Such abuse falls within the scope of what Articles 251 and 468 SAMN aim to prevent. Regardless of who bears the burden of proof, in case of doubt, the carrier should at least provide a plausible explanation for choosing a particular forum since both parties agreed to it.[155]

Does Article 468 SAMN still have any bearing on the substantive validity of forum selection clauses as part of the *lex fori*? On the one hand, the validity of sectoral commercial usages in the EU prevails over individual and separate negotiations. This reinforces the presumed consent of the parties. On the other hand, in cases of a submission to a court of a non-EU state, it is not clear that the prevailing view is the one of requiring an individual and separate negotiation, although the Spanish courts have not clarified the requirement of express acceptance by the shipper, preferring to apply EU legislation and case law to declare validity. This is consistent with Article 22 *bis* (2) SOLJ and reinforces the idea of its prevalence over the SAMN. The Article allows for express submission agreements 'in a manner that is in keeping with the habitual practices established between the parties, or within international trading is in accordance with the practices that the parties are acquainted with, or should be acquainted with and that, within such commerce, are fully known to them and regularly observed by the parties in contracts of this nature within this commercial sector', including electronic means.

In certain cases, a jurisdiction clause was accepted by the court as a true commercial usage of the shipping sector.[156] However, there are some exceptions, as shown by the Spanish jurisprudence. Some judgments oppose the application of EU legislation by analogy.[157]

Articles 468 and 469 were applied in Order 615/17 of the Provincial Court of Valencia of 15 May 2017,[158] where the recipient sued the freight forwarder for breach of the duty '*in vigilando*'. The cargo was not received by the recipient. The B/L included a submission to

155 Zurimendi Isla (n 72) 239–263.

156 Judgment of the Provincial Court of Barcelona of 17 February 2011 (JUR 2011/203050), confirming the Order of the Commercial Court No 3 of Barcelona of 28 June 2010, granting full legal effectiveness to the agreement giving jurisdiction to the courts of Singapore; Court Order Provincial Court of Madrid of 2 April 2011 (JUR 2011/161665), which confirms the Order of the Commercial Court No 10 of Madrid of 5 April 2010, granting full validity to the agreement giving jurisdiction to the District Court of Tokyo, Japan; Judgment of the Provincial Court of Valencia of 27 January 2003 (JUR 2003/115264), granting full validity to the clause giving jurisdiction to the competent court of Rio de Janeiro; Order of the Commercial Court No 6 of Barcelona of 27 July 2009 (JUR 2013/153472), granting full validity to the clause giving jurisdiction to the courts of Seoul, South Korea.

157 Judgments opposing the application of EU legislation by analogy include: Order of the Commercial Court No 4 of Barcelona of 10 November 2006 (JUR 2007/388553), regarding submission to the courts of Turkey, rejecting the validity of the jurisdiction clause according to Law No 7/1998 of 13 April 1998 on General Contractual Conditions (*Ley 7/1998, de 13 de abril, sobre Condiciones Generales de la Contratación,* Official State Gazette No 89 of 14 April 1998, 12304) for not having been signed by the shipper (by itself or through its representatives). Likewise, the Spanish Supreme Court case of 31 May 2012 (RJ 2012/6551), regarding submission to the courts of Saudi Arabia, rejected the validity of the jurisdiction clause, considering that the Brussels I Regulation was not applicable since the defendant was not domiciled in an EU Member State. However, the Spanish Supreme Court dismissed the validity of such a clause as there was no acceptance present in the contract; Iráculis Arregui (n 137).

158 Case JUR 1811/2017.

the courts of Hong Kong that was not individually negotiated.[159] The grounds of the decision provide an interpretation that stresses the importance of fulfilling the general criteria set out by Article 22 *bis* (2) SOLJ with the individual negotiation of the choice of forum clause: 'Not always, nor in any case, the inclusion of a clause of extension of jurisdiction to courts of another State in the bill of lading … may have the effect of repealing the jurisdiction of the Spanish courts to hear the controversy that arises before them'.

Article 468 SAMN (granting jurisdiction to Spanish courts when a jurisdiction clause has not been validly introduced), on the basis of the rules of the SLCP, is located in Title IX of SAMN concerning 'procedural specialities'. The Valencia court's judgment of 15 May 2017 sets the following criteria regarding the normative hierarchy between the SOLJ and the SAMN:

> In this new context (after the enactment of the SAMN), when Regulation 1215/2012 does not apply, the legal regime resulting from Articles 468 and 469 of the Maritime Navigation Law [SAMN] must be applied and the clause of submission must be rigorously evaluated for the purposes of the determination of its validity.
>
> The examination of the clause inserted on the back of the bill of lading does not comply – in accordance with national regulations – with the requirements of incorporation referred to in Articles 5 and 7(b) of … the Law on General Contractual Conditions.[160] No signature or stamp appears on the face of the copies … nor on the back … since the amount of text per page and the 'font size makes it practically illegible'. Finally, the court could not observe any proof of 'an individual and separate negotiation that allows … to decline jurisdiction in favour of the courts of Hong Kong'.

A third state designated as competent by a clause conferring jurisdiction shall hear the dispute, regardless of the nullity of the forum submission clause under Spanish law and its application by the Spanish courts. Once such clause is declared void by the Spanish courts pursuant to Article 469 SAMN, some questions arise: could we consider the forum providing jurisdiction in favour of Spanish courts as a *forum exorbitantis* (that is, a forum attributing international competence to the courts of a state, in this case Spain, without a reasonable connection to that state), facing problems in its recognition by non-Spanish courts? Would a judgment issued by the court of a third state be designated as competent by a choice of jurisdiction agreement recognised in Spain?

The SAMN rule seems to be a constraint, limiting the autonomy of the parties to choose a competent jurisdiction and colliding with the current reality of the sector to the detriment of legal certainty. It also contains a conscious vagueness in the rules of *lis alibi pendens* and connectedness that reward the fastest to bring an action, allowing divergence in the final legal outcome depending on whether the action to decide whether a court has jurisdiction under its national law is brought before the court of a third state designated as competent by virtue of the agreement conferring jurisdiction. A cargo claimant may file a claim before the Spanish courts with the aim of achieving a declaration of invalidity concerning a jurisdiction clause not negotiated individually and separately (Article 468 SAMN). Equally, the claimant may ascertain the procedure before Spanish courts, as long as these have jurisdiction according to the stipulated forum in Article 469 SAMN.

159 Jacinto José Pérez Benítez, 'Algunas cuestiones sobre jurisprudencia marítima' (VIII Maritime Law Conference, University of the Basque Country, Bilbao, 30 October 2017).

160 Law 7/1998 (n 157), as amended by Law 3/2014 of 27 March 2014.

Domestic *lis alibi pendens* and connectedness rules do not offer any substantial difference from the Brussels I Regulation (recast) and do not contribute to a different solution. The aforementioned conscious vagueness stems from Article 39 of the Spanish Act on legal international cooperation in civil matters (SAILCCM)[161] (international *lis alibi pendens*),[162] which requires a stay of the proceedings of a Spanish court (at the request of the parties and after a report by the public prosecutor's office) where there is a pending foreign process with an identical object and cause and:

(a) The competence of the foreign court is due to a reasonable connection with the litigation (presumed when the foreign court has based its international jurisdiction competence on criteria equivalent to those provided for in Spanish legislation);
(b) It is foreseeable that if the foreign court issued a resolution it is likely to be recognised in Spain;
(c) The Spanish court considers the suspension of the proceedings necessary for the good administration of justice.

The Spanish court will continue with the proceedings in the following circumstances (Article 39(2) SAILCCM):

(a) The foreign court declares itself incompetent, had not ruled on its own competence following the request of the parties;
(b) The proceedings before the foreign court are suspended or have been dismissed;
(c) It is deemed unlikely that proceedings before the court of the other state will be concluded within a reasonable time;
(d) It is considered necessary for the good administration of justice; and
(e) On the basis that the final ruling of the other court may not be recognised and, where applicable, enforced in Spain.

Likewise, in Article 39(9), 'the Spanish court will put an end to the process and will close the proceedings if the proceedings before the court of the other state have concluded with a resolution capable of recognition and, where appropriate, execution in Spain'. However, Article 34 of the Brussels I Regulation (recast) displaces Article 39 SAILCCM when an action is pending in a non-EU court. In contrast, Article 33 of the Brussels I Regulation (recast) refers to proceedings pending in a non-EU court. Both Articles apply 'when a court in a Member State is seised involving the same cause of action and between the same parties as the proceedings in the court of the third state'.

The European Commission Green Paper on the matter already recognised that the extension of international jurisdiction rules may increase the risk of parallel proceedings between EU and non-EU state courts.[163] The Commission reviewed the *lis alibi pendens* rules in respect of Articles 22 and 23 of the Brussels I Regulation (now Articles 24 (exclusive jurisdiction) and 25 (submission agreements) of the Brussels I Regulation (recast)). The ensuing proposal only included *lis alibi pendens* rules in cases where there was the same cause of action between the same parties in non-EU courts. The proposal was criti-

161 Spanish Act 29/2015 of 30 July 2015 on International Legal Cooperation in Civil Matters (Official State Gazette No 182 of 31 July 2015).

162 Spanish Law 29/2015 of 30 July 2015 on International Legal Cooperation in Civil Matters.

163 European Commission, *Review of Council Regulation (EC) No 44/2001 on jurisdiction and the recognition and enforcement of judgments in civil and commercial matters* (Green Paper) COM (2009) 175 final.

cised and Article 34 finally included *lis alibi pendens* and related actions.[164] In other words, jurisdiction clauses contained in charterparties or B/Ls challenged before Spanish courts in favour of non-EU states would be subject to SAILCCM if the Regulation did not provide for *lis alibi pendens* with respect to claims filed outside the EU. When Recital 24 of the Brussels I Regulation (recast) refers to the assessment of all the circumstances of the case, jurisdiction agreements in favour of a non-EU state are included.[165]

The SAMN is a controversial act that the national legislature seeks to justify, stating in the preamble to the law itself certain inconclusive arguments of less relevance to the effect that it might have on the international maritime trade sector. The preferred application of international conventions and EU law is detailed specifically in this section of the law (paragraph XI of the preamble), setting out the aims of the chapter concerning jurisdiction and competence:

> On the basis of the rules of Act 1/2000, dated 7th January, on Civil Procedure, Title IX of the Act concerns the 'procedural specialities'.
>
> Chapter I contains what are known as specialities of jurisdiction and power that, based on the preferential application in this matter of the rules contained in the international conventions and in the provisions of the European Union, aims to avoid abuse detected, declaring the nullity of clauses of submission to a foreign jurisdiction or arbitration abroad, contained in ship use contracts or in ancillary navigation contracts, when these have not been negotiated individually and separately.

This type of scheming behaviour may occur when the parties make a choice of forum. It is possible to resort to the general prohibition on the abuse of law under Article 7(2) of the Spanish Civil Code, together with Article 11(2) SOLJ, which states that 'the courts and tribunals shall justifiably reject petitions, incidents and exceptions formulated in flagrant abuse of the law or which entail legal or procedural fraud'.

Even before the SAMN came into force, Spanish courts had declared such clauses invalid in these exceptional cases due to fraud in the choice of forum or an intention to prevent an effective claim.[166] In contrast, as reflected in the SAMN, it can be appreciated that the SAMN does not diminish the formal requirements for determining the validity of a choice of jurisdiction agreement.[167] Protecting contractual parties from surreptitiously introduced clauses must be balanced with avoiding any formalist anachronism that would immobilise international trade. No formal requirement should limit the adequacy and full validity of an agreement conferring jurisdiction according to the customs or usages established between parties within the specific sector of international trade.

The restrictive view projected by Article 468 SAMN constitutes a limitation on the freedom of will of the parties, reflecting the Spanish legislature's distrust of party autonomy

164 Pippa Rogerson, 'Lis pendens and Third States: The Commission's Proposed Changes to the Brussels I Regulation' in Eva Lein (ed), *The Brussels I Review Proposal Uncovered* (British Institute of International and Comparative Law 2012) 118; Julia Suderow, 'Nuevas normas de litispendencia y conexidad para Europa: ¿el ocaso del torpedo italiano? ¿flexibilidad versus previsibilidad?' (2013) 5(1) Cuadernos de Derecho Transnacional 184, 196.

165 Baatz, 'Choice of jurisdiction in bills of lading and cargo insurance' (n 114) 353–354.

166 Judgments of the Spanish Supreme Court of 31 May 2012 (Case RJ 2012/6551) and the Provincial Court of Biscay of 24 April 2009 (Case JUR 2009/309). See Alberto Emparanza Sobejano and José Manuel Martín Osante (eds), *Comentarios Sobre la Ley de Navegación Marítima* (Marcial Pons 2015) 769.

167 Zurimendi Isla (n 72) 239–263.

and contravening the customs and usages of the shipping sector. New criteria for determining party autonomy are hoped for to modify these requirements. However, the prevalence of Article 468 SAMN over Article 2 *bis* (2) SOLJ is doubtful. If the contracting parties comply with the usual practices between them or in the shipping sector, Article 468 will contribute to correct the abuses detected in case of an illegible or unsigned B/L. Gómez Jene considers the last paragraph of Article 468 SAMN as an 'escape clause' that opens up the possibility for recognition and enforcement of choice of court clauses in favour of non-EU state courts: 'the insertion of a jurisdiction or arbitration clause in the printed conditions of any of the contracts referred to in the preceding paragraph shall not provide evidence, in itself, of fulfilment of the requisites established therein'.[168]

In practice, there has been a limited application of the restrictions contained in Articles 468 and 469 SAMN in ancillary shipping contracts, in cases where the chosen foreign court is in a non-EU state or in an international convention contracting state where the convention (to which Spain is also a party) stipulates that parties can exercise their international civil procedural rights therein.

It is desirable that the SAMN respects the singularities of the international maritime law sector present in each type of contract, including parties' freedom of contract traditionally recognised in this area. The internationalisation of contractual relations for international trade favours self-regulation and generates denationalisation or delocalisation of regulatory frameworks. As Álvarez Rubio suggests,[169] it is necessary to enhance the collaboration and coordination among different institutions and specialised agencies due to the inevitable and feasible unification process in the maritime transport sector, in order to ensure that both private and geopolitical public interests are combined. This allows for the evaluation of different options, such as standard contracts or clauses, model laws, legal guidelines and principles of conduct.

Spanish legislators cannot neglect European and international regulations and must be aware of the priority ranking among normative sources in the shipping sector. Arbitral proceedings, whether institutional or ad hoc, reflect the autonomy of the parties in the sense of avoiding 'ordinary' court proceedings. This is reflected in all areas of maritime law, such as carriage of goods by sea, collisions, maritime assistance and salvage and shipbuilding contracts. In addition, business operators are aware that the arbitrators specialise in the relevant particular sector, ensuring knowledge of the rules and practices of the industry through their active role throughout the entire process.[170]

3.2 Incorporation of arbitration clauses in Spain

In private law, parties with full capacity based on autonomy – whether natural or legal persons – can resolve a dispute through civil and commercial arbitration. This is the case in

168 Miguel Gómez Jene, 'Las cláusulas de jurisdicción y arbitraje en la nueva Ley de Navegación Marítima' (2014) 6(2) Cuadernos de Derecho Transnacional 112.

169 Juan José Álvarez Rubio, 'Entre La Haya, Hamburgo y Rotterdam: La compleja opción legislativa interna ante las cuestiones de jurisdicción y arbitraje en el Derecho Marítimo' (2017) 17 Spanish Yearbook of Private International Law 596; Juan José Álvarez Rubio and Unai Belintxon Martín, 'La Nueva Ley de Navegación Marítima desde la Perspectiva del Derecho Internacional' in Alberto Emparanza Sobejano and José Manuel Martín Osante (eds), *Comentarios Sobre la Ley de Navegación Marítima* (Marcial Pons 2015).

170 ibid.

respect of international carriage of goods by sea, when there is sufficient evidence of internationality (foreign elements) to analyse *pro forma* contracts existing in business practice, the performance of international private organisations (that develop and promote arbitration work) and the regulations contained in the conventional norms of the industry regarding dispute resolution mechanisms, along with problems associated with current practices of so-called incorporation clauses.[171]

Application of the controversial rules contained in Article 468 SAMN concerning submission to arbitration would be virtually ineffective by virtue of the international conventions in force. Article 468 reflects the less convincing practice of the Spanish legislator in drafting articles on the order of preference of normative sources while being lax about the priority ranking of international rules over the Spanish *lex fori* derived from the SAMN. The rule contained in Article 468 does not favour arbitral recognition for contracts for use of a ship or ancillary navigation contracts, due to a lack of flexibility regarding the validity and effectiveness requirements for such individually and separately negotiated arbitration clauses.

The New York Convention regulates the recognition and validity of arbitration agreements. The form and content of arbitration agreements is regulated by Article 9 Spanish Arbitration Act (SAA).[172] The SAA introduced innovations that may have some relevance in the interpretation of maritime arbitration clauses. Article 9(6) provides more flexibility than the former Arbitration Act of 1988, applicable to the validity of an arbitration agreement on international arbitration.

Article 9 assesses the validity of the agreement and the arbitrability of the dispute by 'legal rules chosen by the parties to govern the arbitration agreement or to the legal rules applicable to the merits of the dispute' or Spanish law. However, there are some gaps in the SAMN, which prevents the SAA from providing a global response on the validity of arbitration agreements. For instance, the form of the arbitration agreement must be regulated by the New York Convention, but the capacity of the parties is regulated by Articles 9(1) and 9(11) of the Spanish Civil Code, a general solution provided by the Spanish PIL system. A positive step is the reference to 'legal norms', under which the *lex mercatoria* is admitted. In the shipping sector, this would refer to usages and specific practices in the sector, including the regular inclusion of clauses in the B/L, charterparties or other transport documents (choice of law and forum clauses, arbitration clauses, Paramount Clauses, etc). For instance, the Paramount Clause has become a territorial criterion for the application of international conventions that overlaps the parties' choice of law. Paramount Clauses have

171 Naón provides an excellent reflection on the nature and proper role of international commercial arbitration and the problem of applicable law by the arbitrator: Horacio A Grigera Naón, *Choice-of-Law Problems in International Commercial Arbitration* (Mohr Siebeck 1992); José Carlos Fernández Rozas, 'El Arbitraje Comercial Internacional entre la Autonomía, la Anacionalidad y la Deslocalización' (2005) 57(2) Revista Española de Derecho Internacional 605.

172 Spanish Act 60/2003 of 23 December on arbitration (SAA) [*Ley 60/2003, de 23 de diciembre, de Arbitraje*] published in the Official State Gazette no 309 of 26 December 2003 and amended by Act 13/2009 of 3 November 2009 and Act 11/2011 of 20 May 2011. It is inspired by the United Nations Commission on International Trade Law's UNCITRAL Model Law of 21 June 1985.

been useful in order to apply the most updated liability regime of the forum unless a court must apply the law of the forum (mandatory rule).[173]

This leads to a relaxation or 'flexibilisation' of the formal and substantial requirements under such terms and, for now, continues to pose the same problems of validity and effectiveness as invoked against third parties and original parties to the contract. Despite its shortcomings, Article 9(6) of the Spanish Civil Code may enable parties to voluntarily submit their disputes in accordance with the *lex mercatoria* to establish the validity of an arbitration agreement or to let arbitrators select *lex mercatoria* as the law governing the substance of the case if the parties do not choose it. This would assist in meeting the formal and substantive requirements for the acceptance and validity of dispute resolution clauses incorporated in maritime transport contracts, which affects the assessment and acceptance of jurisdiction and arbitration clauses, at least within the EU.[174]

By choosing a recognised arbitral institution, any abuse by the parties is almost impossible. In most cases, these entities were founded by commercial institutions at the request of shipping operators to achieve a faster and more specialised dispute resolution. These arbitral institutions are accessible and guarantee an impartial and equitable process.[175] Only in cases where the arbitrators or arbitration bodies lack recognition in the shipping sector might it even be possible to find abuse and invalidate an arbitration clause under Articles 251 and 468 SAMN. This is the same result as the application of Article 7 of the Spanish Civil Code and Article 11(2) SOLJ, which aim to prevent the abuse of rights and to allow judges to reject claims that involve procedural fraud. Zurimendi believes that, from a practical perspective, it would have been much better to drop Articles 251 and 468 SAMN, which do not bring anything new and generate confusion.[176]

The consent of the parties to a jurisdiction or arbitration clause incorporated in a B/L is presumed when their behaviour corresponds to a usage that governs the sector in which they operate and that they know or that they should be aware of. Nevertheless, there are the usual practical problems concerning the limits of freedom of contract, consent and validity of the choice of forum agreements, as well as the succession of the B/L holder of the goods to the shipper's rights and obligations.

In a general cargo carriage, a shipper makes a space reservation in the vessel by fax or email before receiving confirmation of the carrier or its agent. It, therefore, does not make practical sense that the B/L is a unilateral document which reflects clauses agreed in the original charterparty, to which the shipper is not a party. The carrier receives the cargo once the goods are loaded and issues the B/L. The acceptance by the shipper of a B/L should not imply acceptance of all the clauses in it, since the shipper has no choice in the matter. Even if it were aware of the agreed forum or arbitration clauses, if it wants to be paid for the cargo, it must accept the B/L and send it to the buyer.

---

173 Rosario Espinosa Calabuig, 'Cuestiones de jurisdicción y la ley aplicable al transporte maritimo tras las Reglas de Rotterdam y el reglamento Roma I' (2011) 113(1) Dir Mar 21, 24–25; see also Rosario Espinosa Calabuig, *El contrato internacional de transporte marítimo de mercancías: cuestiones de ley aplicables* (Comares 1999) 35.

174 Rosario Espinosa Calabuig, 'Las cláusulas arbitrales marítimas a la luz de los usos del tráfico internacional' (2007) 13 Revista electrónica de estudios internacionales 2.

175 Gómez Jene, 'Las cláusulas de jurisdicción y arbitraje en la nueva Ley de Navegación Marítima' (n 168).

176 Zurimendi Isla (n 72) 239–263.

In containerised cargo transport, the situation is similar. For instance, a BIMCO online booking form usually contains a reference to the principal place of business of the carrier (as in the Visconbooking BIMCO form used with the Visconbill B/L). Only with volume contracts does the situation vary, since the major shippers and carriers negotiate every technical and economic detail of the contractual conditions, including binding choice of forum, independent of it being included in any subsequent B/L issued to individual carriers.[177]

The effectiveness of clauses on compliance with formal requirements at the time of incorporation and the rules designed to protect the carrier have led to many discussions. The jurisprudence recognises the validity of submitting a clause to foreign arbitration under the SAA and Article II(2) of the New York Convention, which requires that 'the term "agreement in writing" shall include an arbitral clause in a contract or an arbitration agreement, signed by the parties or contained in an exchange of letters or telegrams'.

Article 9(3) SAA (form and content of the arbitration agreement) requires that:

> The arbitration agreement must be in writing, in a document signed by the parties or an exchange of letters, telegrams, telexes, faxes or other telecommunication methods that ensure a record of the agreement is kept. Where an arbitration agreement is accessible for subsequent reference on electronic, optical or other media, it will be regarded as compliant with this requisite.

What is decisive is the unequivocal will of the parties to submit their disputes to arbitration.[178]

The recognition of arbitral clauses is supported by judgments of the Spanish Supreme Court of 6 February 2003[179] and 9 May 2003.[180] The latter deals with a submission to London arbitration and considers the reasoning of the 6 February judgment that the claimant cannot disregard part of the content of the documents that serve as a basis for the claim, by arguing that it accepted all content except that which does not suit their interests. The unequivocal will of the parties to submit their disputes to arbitration in London was reinforced by having included the clause not only in the B/L but also in the booking note.

This interpretation was supported by the judgments of the provincial courts of Barcelona of 13 November 2007[181] and A Coruña of 19 March 2015.[182] The judgment of the Provincial Court of Valencia of 8 November 2016[183] is worth mentioning, even though it refers to a B/L including a choice of jurisdiction clause in reverse favouring the High Court of England and Wales. The Spanish Supreme Court's judgment of 6 February 2003[184] is referred to in this judgment, regarding the provision of consent, the signature on the document in which the clause is inserted and the inserted usages of the sector, stating:

> the judgment of 6 February 2003 admits the effectiveness of a clause of submission to arbitration in London, notwithstanding the signatures present in every B/L (provided by both parties),

177 Espinosa Calabuig, 'Las cláusulas arbitrales marítimas a la luz de los usos del tráfico internacional' (n 174); Federica Binocoli, 'Note e osservazioni a sentenza. La disciplina applicabile al lavoro portuale temporaneo. La sfera di applicazione del CCNL unico' (2006) 108(1) Diritto marittimo 221.

178 Gómez Jene, 'Las cláusulas de jurisdicción y arbitraje en la nueva Ley de Navegación Marítima' (n 168).

179 Case RJ 2003/850, in which a submission to London arbitration was respected due to the presence of a written form and the application to the commercial uses of the sector.

180 Case RJ 2003/3893.

181 Case JUR 2008/77240, which considers the validity of an arbitration clause inserted in a document managed by a third party, the so-called *minute* or *minuta* in Spanish, not signed by the parties, and finds that the way of contracting is adapted to the commercial usages of the cereal sector.

182 Case AC 2016/459 does not refer to the maritime transport sector.

183 Case JUR 2017/14921.

184 n 173.

> considering that such documents could not be questioned only in what would harm the party that wielded it as a transport document.[185]

Spanish and international legislation both require a written form as a guarantee of the real consent of the parties to an arbitration agreement, not just an express signature by the parties, since the unequivocal record of their will is paramount. Commercial usages are also crucial. Spanish jurisprudence admits the validity of a foreign arbitration agreement being included in a B/L by analogy with CJEU jurisprudence interpreting the formal requirements for the validity of choice-of-court agreements. Implied acceptance is admitted when these types of clauses are inserted into a form adapted to the usages of the shipping sector, which are known or ought to be known.[186]

The aim of achieving international harmonisation through the *lex mercatoria* developed by the shipping industry and the proliferation of new international contract standards, helped by the limited success of model laws, supports the interests of business operators that wish to avail themselves of a regulatory framework with the agility, legal certainty and efficiency demanded by the market.[187]

In summary, Article 468 SAMN is not applicable to international commercial arbitration, since the recognition and enforcement of arbitral awards is regulated by the New York Convention. Consent, as established by the jurisprudence of the Spanish Supreme Court, is regulated under the same article as a condition of the effectiveness or existence of an arbitration agreement. The recognition of an arbitral award is not subject to Article 468 but to Article VII of the New York Convention, allowing the application of Article 9 SAA. This distorted element leads to forum shopping, because a claimant may select a forum or an arbitral seat outside the EU that protects its interests.

3.3 *Transferability of a foreign jurisdiction clause contained in the B/L to third parties under Spanish law*

Obligations against third parties, other than the shipper of the choice of forum clause printed on the B/L, depend on domestic law provisions. In Spain, the subrogation requires express consent to the clause by the purchaser of the B/L in order to succeed the shipper or the transferor.

However, there is no succession in any jurisdiction or arbitration agreement under Article 251 SAMN. A third-party B/L holder may invoke it once the CJEU requirements are fulfilled, as set out in Chapter 2. Therefore, if by virtue of domestic law there is no succession to the rights and obligations under the B/L, the CJEU doctrine will apply. The individual

---

185 Iráculis Arregui (n 137).

186 Espinosa Calabuig, 'Las cláusulas arbitrales marítimas a la luz de los usos del tráfico internacional' (n 174).

187 ibid, Espinosa Calabuig points out that the question is whether to defend a broad or narrow interpretation of the notion of the usages of international maritime trade and its effect. Shippers and other parties, as participants in maritime transport services, would be exposed to and therefore must know the *usage* of such trade, including the regular presence of forum and arbitration clauses in a B/L or a charterparty. This would support the existence of consent and an acknowledgement, justifying the arbitration or jurisdiction clause, without requiring special formal and substantial requirements. A narrow interpretation involving the defence of third-party interests is desirable, being arguable only when the arbitration clause was somehow accepted (in line with most French jurisprudence). This requires a prudent assessment of such clauses being compatible with the development of maritime usages and practices while not disadvantaging third parties to the original contract.

and separate acceptance required by the third party when acquiring the B/L (under Article 251 SAMN and according to the conditions set out in Article 468 SAMN) surpasses the mandate of the CJEU. Iráculis[188] believes that, despite the matter of third-party succession, although the acquiring of a B/L is governed by national law, in the case of non-succession it is up to the CJEU to resolve the question of effective consent in order to have a direct relationship with the interpretation of international and European regulations. Presumed or implied consent by the third party should also be considered by the judge in respect of a foreign jurisdiction clause specified in the B/L.

Before the SAMN came into force, the Spanish courts were in favour of the effectiveness of the transfer of the B/L and the jurisdiction clause contained therein, with regard to a third party that acquires the document of title. Following the Spanish Supreme Court judgment of 29 September 2005,[189] the receiver of the goods normally succeeds the shipper in all the rights and obligations contained in the B/L, including the jurisdiction clause. This is confirmed by the following judgments of the provincial courts of Biscay of 10 February 2011,[190] Madrid of 19 September 2015[191] and 9 February 2015,[192] as well as Barcelona of 11 March 2010.[193]

After the entry into force of the SAMN in 2014 and the amendment of Article 22 SOLJ in 2015, the Commercial Court of Madrid No 6 in its judgment of 13 September 2016 (JUR 2016/209381) characterised the claimant insurance company as a third party when deciding on the effectiveness of a jurisdiction agreement under subrogation provisions derived from Article 43 of the Spanish Insurance Contract Act,[194] after indemnifying the insured shipper. However, this case does not deal with endorsement to the third party when acquiring the B/L. The Order of the Provincial Court of Barcelona of 23 July 2019 (appeal against the judgment of 13 February 2019) applies the restrictions placed on third parties to the contract based on who is the claimant.[195] If a shipper claims against a carrier, whether or not it has signed the B/L, the Brussels I Regulation (recast) applies. Nevertheless, when the recipient of the goods or successive B/L holders act against the carrier, the requirements of Article 468 and 251 SAMN apply. The previous judgments place an additional burden that is not in line with Article 25 of the Brussels I Regulation (recast) and CJEU case law such as *Coreck Maritime*, *The Tilly Russ* and *Castelletti*.[196]

---

188 Iráculis Arregui (n 137).

189 Case RJ 2005/7156.

190 Case AC 2011/1876.

191 Case JUR 2015/247406.

192 Case JUR 2015/248567.

193 In Case JUR 2011/35434, the judge considered the decision to decline the jurisdiction of the Spanish courts through an express foreign jurisdiction clause to also apply to the shipper, the consignee and their insurers (even if they did not sign the B/L providing for the dispute resolution clause).

194 Insurance Contracts Act 1980, approved by the Law 50/1980 of 8 October, on Insurance Contracts, (Official State Gazette No 250 of 17 October 1980).

195 Case AC 2019/1270 upholds the judgment of the Provincial Court of Barcelona of 13 February 2019, Case JUR 2019/59445, where a submission agreement in favour of the High Court of Justice of England and Wales contained in a sea waybill was considered valid according to Article 25 Brussels I Regulation (recast). However, the insurer that was subrogated in the position of the shipper could not be considered a third party to the B/L according to Article 251 SAMN. Moreover, the sea waybill, even though it is a document similar to a B/L, is not a negotiable document and therefore is not transferable. The claimant was not the shipper's insurer and was not bound by the clause. There was no connection with English jurisdiction since the transport was performed between two Spanish ports, the parties were Spanish and all the evidence was prepared in Spanish.

196 Francisco de Borja Langelaan Osset, 'Jurisprudencial examination on the legal and procedural regime of jurisdiction clauses inserted in bills of lading: current situation and foreseeable future' (2019) 11(1) Cuadernos de

Article 251 SAMN excludes automatic transmission and places strict requirements on the transfer of the dispute resolution clause.[197] However, as Álvarez Rubio points out, the Order of the Provincial Court of Barcelona of 13 February rightly stresses the primacy of Article 25 of the Brussels I Regulation (recast) over the provisions of the SAMN in determining the regulatory regime applicable to clauses conferring jurisdiction contained in B/Ls.[198] The Spanish courts acknowledge that the SAMN introduces modifications regarding submission agreements to foreign courts inserted in B/Ls or other contracts for the ships in Articles 468 and 251 that oblige them to review jurisprudential doctrine and the position of an arbitral tribunal. Article 25 of the Brussels I Regulation (recast) is 'not relegated by Spanish Law nor does it complement or introduce additional requirements'.[199] It establishes how submission agreements must be concluded and the applicable regime of the courts to which the parties have chosen to submit their dispute, by which the validity of the agreement must be examined.

It is worth considering the distinction between jurisdiction and arbitration agreements incorporated in a B/L and those in respect of a sea waybill. The Provincial Court of Barcelona, in its Order of 7 October 2019[200] addressed the validity or not in respect of third parties to a jurisdiction agreement in favour of the English courts inserted in the sea waybill signed by the contractual carrier (Rhenus Logistics) and the effective carrier (Maersk Spain), and in the absence of an express submission agreement contained in the B/L made between the shipper (Adagio) and the contractual carrier. The appellant insurer (in place of Adagio) succeeded in its appeal, dismissing the order which declined jurisdiction and favoured Rhenus Logistics and Maersk Spain's interests. The Provincial Court declared that the submission clause did not bind the appellant and, therefore, the Commercial Court of Barcelona had jurisdiction to hear the merits of the dispute.

A sea waybill signed by the contractual carrier and actual carrier, in addition to not being a document of title, like a B/L, has only and exclusively a probative value in the sense that it attests, unless proven otherwise, the conditions of the contract and of the receipt of the goods by the carrier. A sea waybill does not have to be tendered by the named consignee or its agent at the port of discharge and, normally, it will not be accepted by banks involved in documentary credit transactions, since it does not constitute a guarantee of the effective receipt and payment of the goods. It would be necessary to consider, although it is not the object of the present considerations, whether a third-party recipient, unaware of the controversy raised in this case, could be deemed submitted to a jurisdiction or otherwise linked by a jurisdiction clause inserted in the consignment note.[201]

Derecho Transnacional 408, 432–433.

197 Iráculis Arregui (n 137).

198 Álvarez Rubio, 'A correct jurisprudential orientation in relation to the validity and scope of the submission clause in favour of a foreign court contained in a bill of lading' (n 138) 400.

199 José Carlos Fernández Rozas, 'Cláusula de sumisión a tribunal extranjero en conocimiento de embarque (AAP Barcelona 13 febrero 2019)' (*El Blog de José Carlos Fernández Rozas*, 24 February 2019) <https://fernandezrozas.com/2019/02/24/clausula-de-sumision-a-tribunal-extranjero-en-conocimiento-de-embarque-aap-barcelona-13-febrero-2019/> accessed 14 May 2020. See also José Carlos Fernández Rozas, 'Alternatives and uncertainties of the dispute settlement clauses in international maritime contracts' (2019) 10(2) Cuadernos de Derecho Transnacional 333.

200 JUR 2019/293937.

201 Unai Belintxon Martín, 'Derecho internacional privado y Derecho marítimo internacional: competencia judicial internacional y acuerdos atributivos de jurisdicción en la LNM' (2020) 12(1) *Cuadernos de Derecho*

The CJEU in *Coreck Maritime* considered the effectiveness of the conveyance between the contractual parties according to Article 17 of the Brussels Convention (forerunner of Article 25 of the Brussels I Regulation (recast)) with respect to a third-party B/L holder. Spanish courts will analyse the effectiveness of the conveyance of a jurisdiction clause in each case – since arbitration is not subject to the same burden under the New York Convention. General and specific regimes for cargo claims are being currently developed by the judiciary. Espinosa Calabuig[202] points out that the validity of an arbitration clause subject to domestic law raises numerous questions in practice, depending on the jurisdiction. This is connected to the individualisation of the charterparty and the indication of the form used to contain the arbitration clause, whether it is generic, albeit by reference. The comparative examples favour a clear expression that the arbitration clause has been incorporated into the B/L and it can be enforced against B/L holders. The main hurdle is that in most cases, such as in regular container shipping, there is no individual negotiation of contracts for the use of a vessel that include jurisdiction or arbitration agreements. These are frequently signed by agents or are unilaterally issued by the carrier and received by the shipper once the cargo is loaded on board or is successively endorsed by buyers.

4 Incorporation of dispute resolution clauses under EU case law

Contracting parties have to balance legal risks under contracts for the carriage of goods by sea with their legitimate economic interests. Charterparties and B/Ls will not normally have contradictory terms when the shipowner is the carrier. However, if the terms in the charterparty and the B/L are different from each other and the transferor of the B/L is unaware of the negotiated terms of the charterparty, it is necessary to consider whether the B/L holder can act against the carrier, who is bound by both transport contracts.

In the EU, differences may arise since Article 25 of the Brussels I Regulation (recast) will prevail over national legislation in order to have such an agreement recognised (or not) under the chosen criteria. What happens if there is an arbitration agreement? The changes introduced in Article 25 enable an express choice of jurisdiction favouring an EU Member State. What happens when a jurisdiction agreement for the court of a non-EU state has been chosen? In such a case, national rules will decide whether the choice of court or arbitration agreement is valid.

Can a shipowner only invoke a jurisdiction or arbitration clause in a B/L when it has issued the B/L? Does it have to be invoked by the shipper? If the shipowner is the actual carrier, it may only rely on a jurisdiction or arbitration clause if it endorses the B/L to the shipper or if there is sub-bailment on terms (outside the scope of this work).

A jurisdiction agreement in a charterparty will normally fall within Article 25(1)(a) of the Brussels I Regulation (recast).[203] It is highly unlikely that the parties would not have a written record of the jurisdiction agreement. In the event they do not, however, Article 25 makes it is possible for the contractual parties to a charterparty to submit their disputes

Transnacional (forthcoming).

202 Espinosa Calabuig, 'Las cláusulas arbitrales marítimas a la luz de los usos del tráfico internacional' (n 174).

203 Simon Baughen, *Shipping Law* (7th edn, Routledge 2018) 262–263.

under certain conditions. Nonetheless, the court ought to regard the rules concerning the assumption of jurisdiction to be subject to Article 29 of the recast Regulation, which contains the rules on *lis alibi pendens*. When a clause refers to the exclusive or non-exclusive jurisdiction of a non-EU court, an EU court will decide according to its applicable national law whether the clause fulfils all the requirements to be valid. The results are uncertain and vary between EU Member States and their national conflict of laws rules. In the same manner, non-EU courts examining an exclusive or non-exclusive jurisdiction clause referring to an EU court or third country court will find the same issues at stake.

A jurisdiction agreement in a B/L can be troublesome if the contract of carriage has been orally agreed before the B/L has been issued. In *The Tilly Russ*,[204] the CJEU held that Article 17 of the Brussels Convention (now Article 25(1)(a) of the Brussels I Regulation (recast)) would be applicable where the parties had agreed a choice of court clause in writing or 'there had been prior oral agreement to the jurisdiction clause'.[205] Article 25(1)(b) (as it now is) would apply if these conditions are not met and the parties have a continuing business relationship, resorting to the jurisdiction clause included in carrier's general conditions. A contract referring to general conditions that includes a choice of court agreement fulfils the requirements of Article 25 of the recast Regulation. The general conditions and the jurisdiction agreement do not need to be specifically included in the contract. Moreover, the position of third-party B/L holders 'is determined by the application of this provision to the relationship of the shipper and the carrier'.[206]

According to *The Tilly Russ*, B/L holders, consignees and endorsees are accorded equal treatment to the original parties in relation to express or incorporated jurisdiction clauses in the B/L. Where they have fulfilled the same formalities in the jurisdiction agreement as the original parties, such agreement is also considered to be in writing between the carriers and the consignees or endorsees, as Özdel points out.[207]

However, it is a prerequisite that, according to the applicable national law, such consignees or endorsees have succeeded the shipper in all rights and obligations.[208] *The Tilly Russ* adds:

> If he did, there is no need to ascertain whether he accepted the jurisdiction clause in the original contract. In such circumstances, acquisition of the bill of lading could not confer upon the third party more rights than those attaching to the shipper under it. The third party holding the bill of lading thus becomes vested with all the rights, and at the same time becomes subject to all the obligations, mentioned in the bill of lading, including those relating to the agreement on jurisdiction.[209]

The CJEU reinforced the already-established criteria of *The Tilly Russ* in *Coreck Maritime* concerning Article 17 of the Brussels Convention:

> By its third question, the national court essentially asks whether a jurisdiction clause which has been agreed between a carrier and a shipper and appears in a bill of lading is valid as against any

204 *The Tilly Russ* (n 36); this case follows the line marked by the judgment of 14 December 1976, Case 25/76 *Galeries Segoura SPRl v. Société Rahim Bonakdarian* EU:C:1976:178, [1976] ECR 1851, 1860.

205 Baughen, *Shipping Law* (n 203) 262–263.

206 ibid.

207 Özdel, *Bills of Lading Incorporating Charterparties* (n 18) 61–69.

208 *The Siboti* (n 7) [41].

209 *The Tilly Russ* (n 36) [25].

> third party bearer of the bill of lading or whether it is only valid as against a third party bearer of the bill of lading who succeeded by virtue of the applicable national law to the shipper's rights and obligations when he acquired the bill of lading.
>
> It is sufficient to note that the Court has held that, in so far as the jurisdiction clause incorporated in a bill of lading is valid under Article 17 of the Convention as between the shipper and the carrier, it can be pleaded against the third party holding the bill of lading so long as, under the relevant national law, the holder of the bill of lading succeeds to the shipper's rights and obligations (*Tilly Russ*, paragraph 24, and *Castelletti*, paragraph 41).[210]

The doctrine of the CJEU regarding the effect that domestic law attributes to the legal relationship between the shipper or transferor of a B/L and a third party that acquires it also requires clarification. The judgment of 7 February 2013 in *Refcomp v. Axa Corporate* states that, concerning contracts for the carriage of goods by sea, foreign choice of forum clauses included in a B/L can be invoked against a third party to that contract, provided that the clause's validity has been recognised and, under the applicable national law, the B/L holder has subrogated the rights and obligations of the shipper upon acquiring the B/L.[211] According to paragraph 35 of the judgment, citing paragraph 54 of AG Jääskinen's opinion in *Refcomp v. Axa*, a B/L is defined as follows:

> An instrument of international commerce intended to govern a relationship involving at least three persons, namely the maritime carrier, the consigner of the goods or shipper, and the recipient of the goods. Under most legal systems of the Member States which agree on this matter the bill of lading is a negotiable instrument which allows the owner to transfer the goods, en route, to a purchaser who becomes as bearer of the bill of lading, the consignee of the goods and the holder of all the rights and obligations of the shipper in relation to the carrier.

The Advocate General, in his Opinion, stresses that:

> Although the bearer of the endorsed security is a third party in relation to the original transport contract, which it did not conclude, it is deemed to have agreed to the main content of that contract, in particular a jurisdiction clause, in so far as the applicable national law provides for the rights and obligations of the shipper to be transferred to it.[212]

The content of a B/L, as a document of title, is part of the factual matrix that a third party cannot ignore when acquiring it, so the B/L is always enforceable against third parties.[213] The causal relationship is opposable to the third-party B/L holder when reflected, either directly or by reference. Such an assumption does not invalidate the letter of the document – since the causal circumstances are reflected in the title, they constitute documentary exceptions and are therefore enforceable *erga omnes*.[214]

To what extent the rights and obligations under a B/L are transferable depends on the applicable national law. This generally does not cause divergent solutions among EU Member States: it is generally accepted that, by virtue of the acquisition of the B/L, the

210 *Coreck Maritime* (n 120) [22]–[23].

211 Case C-543/10 *Refcomp SpA v. Axa Corporate Solutions Assurance SA and others* EU:C:2013:62, EU:C:2012:637, Opinion of Advocate General (AG) Niilo Jääskinen, delivered on 18 October 2012.

212 ibid, Opinion of AG Jääskinen [43].

213 Alfred Hueck and Claus-Wilhelm Canaris, *Recht der Wertpapiere* (12th edn, Vahlen 1986) [9], II 2; Cándido Paz-Ares, 'Naturaleza Jurídica de la Letra de Cambio' in Aurelio Menéndez-Menéndez (ed), *Derecho Cambiario: Estudios sobre la Ley Cambiaria y del Cheque* (Cívitas 1986) 279 *et seq.*; Andrés Recalde Castells, *El Conocimiento de Embarque y Otros Documentos del Transporte* (Citivas 1992) 276 *et seq.*

214 Zurimendi Isla (n 72).

B/L holder succeeds the shipper in all rights and obligations with respect to the carrier and is bound by the jurisdiction clause. That such agreement does not exist with respect to the relationship between the initial purchaser and the sub-buyer in a chain of purchase contracts has the following consequences:

> It ... gives rise to different outcomes among the Member States liable to compromise the aim of unifying the rules of jurisdiction pursued by the Regulation. Any reference to national law would also be an element of uncertainty incompatible with the concern to ensure the predictability of jurisdiction which is ... one of its objectives (*Refcomp v Axa*, section 39). The concept of 'jurisdiction clause' ... must be interpreted as an independent concept ... to give full effect to the principle of freedom of choice on which Article 23(1) of the Regulation is based (*Refcomp v Axa*, section 40).[215]

However, the subrogation (or not) of all the rights and obligations of the shipper by the third-party B/L holder within the EU case law framework (as stated in *Coreck Maritime*) leaves room for national legislators to resolve the enforceability of the choice of forum clause inserted on the reverse of the B/L when it is expressly accepted by the purchaser. Obligations against third parties other than the shipper depend on domestic law provisions.

> If, under applicable domestic law, a third party to the initial contract does not succeed the shipper in all its rights and obligations, it must be verified that it has consented to the forum clause.[216]

As stated by the CJEU:

> Article 17 of the [Brussels] Convention imposes on the court ... the duty of examining first whether the clause conferring jurisdiction upon it was in fact the subject of consensus between the parties, which must be clearly and precisely demonstrated, and that the purpose of the requirements as to form imposed by Article 17 is to ensure that consensus between the parties is in fact established.[217]

The third-party B/L holder may invoke the jurisdiction clause once the requirements set out by the CJEU are fulfilled (*Coreck Maritime*, referring to the conclusions of AG Slynn in *The Tilly Russ*):[218]

> If the holder does not stand in the shoes of the original shipper under the applicable national law, then a new agreement has to be found between the holder and the carrier, either in writing or evidenced by writing, on a choice of jurisdiction clause. It does not seem to me that the mere presentation by the holder of the bill, who has already purchased the goods, to the carrier would in itself constitute such an agreement or evidence of an agreement for the purposes of Article 17.[219]

---

215 *Refcomp v. Axa* (n 211); Iráculis Arregui (n 137).

216 On transposing this response to other matters, for example a chain of contracts for the transfer of ownership of a property, AG Jääskinen pronounced in his conclusions in *Refcomp v. Axa* (n 211) [53] (considering that this jurisprudence cannot be applied beyond the specific scope of the B/L in which it arose): However, it is important not to lose sight of the fact that the dispute in the main proceedings relates to a direct action for a declaration of liability following a series of sales contracts, where the ownership of goods was transferred from one purchaser to another, and not to a tripartite relationship based on a bill of lading, the legal nature of which is very specific.

> In the CJEU's judgment in the same case, the CJEU admits that in a chain of contracts for transferring of ownership of goods, the competent court must verify the reality of the consent of the third party to the jurisdiction clause. (paras 37–41)

217 *Coreck Maritime* (n 120) [13]; see Iráculis Arregui (n 137).

218 *Coreck Maritime* (n 120) EU:C:2000:157, Opinion of AG Alber, delivered on 23 March 2000.

219 *The Tilly Russ* (n 36) EU:C:1984:119, Opinion of AG Slynn, delivered on 21 March 1984, p. 2444.

The conclusion drawn by the CJEU in *The Tilly Russ* and *Coreck Maritime* is that contractual parties are presumed to have consented to a jurisdiction clause incorporated in a B/L when their behaviour (i) corresponds to a usage common in the international trade in which they operate, and (ii) they are aware of it and acknowledge it. This allows consolidation of common practices in the shipping sector and guarantees that when the parties follow a concrete behaviour that, in a general way, governs their contractual relations. Furthermore, Briggs states that a practice is notorious if it is widely known and familiar to those engaged in a particular commercial operation in the port in question, although it is usually expressed in broad and imprecise terms, such as 'well-known at the place to which it applies and sufficiently widespread' within the particular commercial community.[220]

However, as Baatz and Özdel suggest, the CJEU decision in *The Tilly Russ* should be reviewed, since a shipper normally does not sign a B/L, which poses problems for carriers in proving the second requirement of the test. The grounds of the decision are based on Article 17 of the Brussels Convention, which did not contain any reference to practices of international trade and commerce when the case was decided. When the UK joined the EU, the phrase was added to Article 17 of the Brussels Convention (now Article 25(1) of the Brussels I Regulation (recast)), and was clarified with the Convention of San Sebastian of 26 May 1989, which amended the wording to read as follows:

> The agreement conferring jurisdiction shall be either:
>
> (c) in international trade or commerce, in a form which accords with a usage of which the parties are or ought to have been aware and which in such trade or commerce is widely known to, and regularly observed by, parties to contracts of the type involved in the particular trade or commerce concerned.[221]

Article 25(1)(c) of the Brussels I Regulation (recast) contains a lower threshold for the formality of jurisdiction agreements when parties are engaged in trade and commerce, than Article 17 of the Brussels Convention. A jurisdiction clause in a B/L in accordance with the usages of trade and commerce (e.g., on an international standard form) may bind the shipper independently whether or not it has signed the B/L. Asymmetric agreements fall within the scope of Article 25(1)(c) of the recast Regulation. These include choice of court agreements where a party can bring a claim in a competent jurisdiction while its counterpart will be only able to bring it in a specific jurisdiction.[222]

In *Castelletti*,[223] Article 25(1)(c) of the Brussels I Regulation (recast) was applicable to the jurisdiction agreement when its condition, 'a usage regularly followed in a particular

220 Briggs, 'The Validity of "Floating" Choice of Law and Jurisdiction Clauses' (n 1); Ramberg, 'Freedom of Contract in Maritime Law' (n 1).

221 The Convention on the accession of the Kingdom of Spain and the Portuguese Republic to the Convention on Jurisdiction and the Enforcement of Judgments in Civil and Commercial Matters, and to the Protocol on its interpretation by the Court of Justice, with the adjustments made to them by the Convention on the accession of the Kingdom of Denmark, of Ireland and of the United Kingdom of Great Britain and Northern Ireland and the adjustments made to them by the Convention on the accession of the Hellenic Republic (89/535/EEC), Article 7.

222 Baughen, *Shipping Law* (n 203) 262–263; e.g., in *Commerzbank Aktiengesellschaft v. Liquimar Tankers Management Inc* [2017] EWHC 161 (Comm); Baatz, 'Choice of jurisdiction in bills of lading and cargo insurance' (n 114) 342.

223 *Castelletti* (n 120).

branch of trade in which the parties operated', is met.[224] The CJEU held that the shipper and the carrier, both original parties to the B/L, were presumed to have consented in accordance with the accepted usages of trade and commerce, with the domestic courts having the burden of determining and recognising what amounts to an accepted usage.

In *Höszig Kft v. Alstom Power Thermal Services*,[225] following *Castelletti*, it was decided that, according to Article 25(1), the jurisdiction clause would follow Alstom's general terms and conditions since there was written proof of contracts between the parties that were forwarded once they were concluded. 'Paris court' and 'French law' were precise enough to allow the court to determine its own jurisdiction without requiring the explicit designation of an EU Member State, as the consent of the parties had been given. The Rome I Regulation did not apply to jurisdiction clauses according to its Article 1(2)(e), under which 'arbitration agreements and agreements on the choice of court' are excluded. Thus, the Hungarian court had no jurisdiction in the performance of the contract dispute started by *Höszig Kft*. The consignees and endorsees as B/L holders received treatment equal to that afforded to the original B/L parties concerning the express or incorporated jurisdiction clauses in the B/L, according to *The Tilly Russ*. Where they have fulfilled the same formalities in the jurisdiction agreement as the original parties, the agreement is considered to be in writing between the carrier and the consignees or endorsees. However, it is a prerequisite that, under the applicable national law, the consignees or endorsees have succeeded the shipper in all its rights and obligations.[226] As stated in *Coreck Maritime*:

> If he did, there is no need to ascertain whether he accepted the jurisdiction clause in the original contract. In such circumstances, acquisition of the bill of lading could not confer upon the third party more rights than those attaching to the shipper under it. The third party holding the bill of lading thus becomes vested with all the rights, and at the same time becomes subject to all the obligations, mentioned in the bill of lading, including those relating to the agreement on jurisdiction (*Tilly Russ*, paragraph 25).[227]

Article 25 of the Brussels I Regulation (recast) allows the parties, regardless of their domicile, to agree to submit their disputes to the courts of an EU Member State – unlike its predecessors Article 23 of Brussels I Regulation 44/2001 and Article 17 of the Brussels Convention. This means that any clause in a contract for the use of a vessel or auxiliary contracts of navigation conferring jurisdiction over a particular dispute to a court of a Member State of the EU, regardless of whether the parties have their domicile in the EU, will be governed by its provisions in terms of formal validity. The law used by a Member State to ascertain the validity of the jurisdiction agreement cannot itself contest the validity of such agreement, since Article 25(5) reaffirms the complete autonomy of the jurisdiction agreements, which form a separate contract from the rest of the contract.

Article 25(2) of the Brussels I Regulation (recast) states that any communication by electronic means which provides a durable record of the agreement shall be equivalent to 'writing'. For instance, if an electronic contract signed by both parties expressly refers to general conditions, one of which includes a clause conferring jurisdiction, the requirements of Article 25 will be satisfied. It is not necessary that the general conditions form part of the

224 Baughen, *Shipping Law* (n 203) 262–263.
225 C-222/15 EU:C:2016:525.
226 *The Siboti* (n 7) [41].
227 *Coreck Maritime* (n 120) [25].

contractual document itself, nor that there be express reference to the jurisdiction clause in the principal document.

Taser International[228] constitutes a creative and interesting resolution to reflect on the scope of party autonomy in determining the court having jurisdiction, the sound administration of justice, and the prevalence of tacit over express choice of jurisdiction. The judgment also raises awareness of the idea that the rules of international jurisdiction solve legal conflicts between individuals regulated by private law, abandoning the idea that the global character of international jurisdiction rules derives from the rules of conflict between states.[229]

The facts of the case are the following: a non-exclusive distribution agreement was signed between Taser International (whose seat is in the US) and Gate 4 Business, with the latter's administrator undertaking to assign to Taser International trademarks that were finally registered in Romania. Despite an exclusive jurisdiction agreement in those contracts in favour of the US courts, Taser International brought an action before the district court of Bucharest and the defendant appeared without contesting jurisdiction. Both parties undertook the necessary formalities to register the assignment following the court's order. After the preliminary ruling of the Romanian Court of Appeal, several questions were analysed by the CJEU involving the *prorogatio fori* of what is now Article 26 of the Brussels I Regulation (recast) when a choice of jurisdiction favours a non-EU State and the exclusive jurisdiction rules under Article 24(4) of the recast Regulation concerning the obligation to assign a trademark and its registration under domestic law. Article 26(1) states that:

> Apart from jurisdiction derived from other provisions of this Regulation, a court of a Member State before which a defendant enters an appearance shall have jurisdiction. This rule shall not apply where appearance was entered to contest the jurisdiction, or where another court has exclusive jurisdiction by virtue of Article 24.

Article 24(4) of the recast Regulation provides that the courts of an EU Member State shall have exclusive jurisdiction regardless of the domicile of the parties:

> In proceedings concerned with the registration or validity of patents, trade marks, designs, or other similar rights required to be deposited or registered, irrespective of whether the issue is raised by way of an action or as a defence, the courts of the Member State in which the deposit or registration has been applied for, has taken place or is under the terms of an instrument of the Union or an international convention deemed to have taken place.

Applying *CPP Vienna Insurance Group*,[230] Article 25 of the recast Regulation can be overruled by Article 26 (implied acceptance of jurisdiction); *Taser International* adds that this is possible even when the choice of court has been made in favour of a non-EU State. Although Article 33 and Recital 24 of the Brussels I Regulation (recast) regulate the choice of non-EU Courts, the CJEU did not enter into the discussion as in *Gothaer Allgemeine Versicherung and others*.[231] In *Taser International*, the CJEU points out:

> However, in the circumstances of the main proceedings, it is not necessary to determine whether a request for the enforcement of the contractual obligation to assign trade marks actually falls

228 Case C175/1 *Taser International Inc v. SC Gate 4 Business SRL and another* EU:C:2016:176, [2016] ETMR 28.

229 Isabel Lorente Martínez, 'Choice of court clause in favor of the courts of a third state and tacit submission in favor of the courts of a member state: the dilemma' (2017) 9(1) Cuadernos de Derecho Transnacional 444.

230 Case C-111/09 *CPP Vienna Insurance Group v. Bilas* [2010] EU:C:2010:290 ECR I-4545.

231 Case C-456/11 *Gothaer Allgemeine Versicherung AG and others v. Samskip GmbH* EU:C:2012:719.

> within Article 22(4) of Regulation No 44/2001, since the Romanian courts have, in any event, jurisdiction to decide this case. On the assumption that Article 22(4) is applicable to this dispute, the courts whose jurisdiction stems from that provision are the same as those whose jurisdiction is determined pursuant to the first sentence of Article 24 of that regulation, as the defendant in the main proceedings entered an appearance before the Romanian courts without challenging their jurisdiction.
>
> …
>
> Thus, the Court has held that, where the rules on exclusive jurisdiction within the meaning of Article 22 of Regulation No 44/2001 do not apply, the court seised must declare itself to have jurisdiction where the defendant enters an appearance and does not contest that court's jurisdiction, since entering an appearance in that way amounts to a tacit prorogation of jurisdiction for the purpose of Article 24 of the regulation …
>
> Indeed, that would still be the case where the jurisdiction of the court seised stems from Article 22 of Regulation No 44/2001.[232]

Whether or not the trademark assignment falls within Article 24(4) of the Brussels I Regulation (recast), the Romanian courts had jurisdiction under Article 31 of the recast Regulation, which states:[233]

> 1. Where actions come within the exclusive jurisdiction of several courts, any court other than the court first seised shall decline jurisdiction in favour of that court.
> 2. Without prejudice to Article 26, where a court of a Member State on which an agreement as referred to in Article 25 confers exclusive jurisdiction is seised, any court of another Member State shall stay the proceedings until such time as the court seised on the basis of the agreement declares that it has no jurisdiction under the agreement.
> 3. Where the court designated in the agreement has established jurisdiction in accordance with the agreement, any court of another Member State shall decline jurisdiction in favour of that court.

In summary, Article 26 ('implied submission') prevails over Article 25 ('exclusive jurisdiction agreement by the parties'). The jurisdiction is retained when the defendant does not contest jurisdiction, regardless of any valid agreement in favour of another EU Member State court.

The CJEU will apply certain invariable principles to its decisions, such as proximity, sound administration of justice, uniformity of approach and mutual trust. Apart from these, the CJEU takes the common law approach and creates 'sub-rules' for specific cases. It strikes a balance between principles and pragmatism in its approach, which is a hybrid of common law and civil law doctrines and procedures.

5 Conclusion

This chapter has sought to analyse the limitations on party autonomy regarding jurisdiction and arbitration clauses, including the transferability of the B/L from the carrier (shipowner or charterer) to the receiver through endorsement of the B/L as a document of title.

One of the main implications regarding the incorporation of dispute resolution clauses into EU, English and Spanish law is that the rights of the maritime industry are not necessarily equivalent to national rights. Article 25 of the Brussels I Regulation (recast) has been

232 *Taser International* (n 228) [28], [33]–34].

233 Geert Van Calster, *European Private International Law* (Bloomsbury Publishing 2016) 82–89.

uniformly interpreted by English and Spanish courts. EU Member State courts have followed a uniform interpretation of the Brussels I Regulation (recast) by applying the criteria set out by CJEU case law.

Some of the limitations on the recognition and enforcement of jurisdiction and arbitration clauses contained in charterparties and incorporated into B/Ls are that general words are not sufficient for their recognition by English courts. However, specific reference may be sufficient when the terms are consistent between the charterparty and the B/L.

The processes of economic and legal integration that have emerged worldwide in recent years have changed the traditional system of particular states incorporating so-called institutional law legal systems. However, in Spain, the effectiveness of the transfer of standardised terms by reference in the B/L poses questions with regard to the substantive validity of Article 468 SAMN when applied to jurisdiction clauses. The maritime speciality of Articles 468 and 469 should be read in conjunction with the general grounds for jurisdiction provided by Article 22 *bis* (2) SOLJ. Arbitration clauses are widely recognised and enforced under the arbitrability and formal validity criteria set out by the New York Convention.

CHAPTER 4

Anti-suit injunctions

Anti-suit injunctions provide interim relief in support of dispute resolution clauses contained in contracts for the carriage of goods by sea (charterparty or a B/L) or incorporated into a B/L. Anti-suit injunctions are powerful instruments that can be issued by a court to restrain a party from commencing proceedings, thus having a strong effect on jurisdictional or arbitral proceedings. The most common anti-suit injunction given by an English court is to restrain a party from commencing proceedings in breach of a London arbitration clause or an English jurisdiction clause.

Spain does not have such remedy, so under Spanish procedural rules, a defendant must enter an appearance in order to oppose the jurisdiction of the Spanish court in favour of a foreign court or an arbitral tribunal. Consequently, if the defendant is declared liable by a judgment or award rendered by a foreign court or by an arbitral tribunal, the only mechanism available to oppose the recognition and enforcement is that the Spanish courts declare it null or void, subject to the Brussels I Regulation (recast) for intra-EU judgments or the SOLJ for extra-EU judgments, and the New York Convention in case of arbitral awards. This chapter thus analyses anti-suit injunctions solely from an English law perspective.

Anti-suit or anti-arbitration proceedings are a common law mechanism that seeks to avoid duplicate proceedings and seeks to enforce party autonomy. An anti-suit injunction operates *in personam*, typically ordering a party not to commence – or to cease – proceedings in a foreign court. Despite being a discretionary or equitable remedy granted on an interim basis, it normally effectively determines where the parties will resolve their dispute.[1]

In the determination of jurisdiction and parallel proceedings in maritime disputes, in any EU Member State (including the UK) proceedings are limited when there is not yet a claim and the nature of such a limitation does not qualify the substantive rights of the claimant. As previously stated, under Article II(3) of the New York Convention

> the court of a Contracting State, when seized of an action in a matter in respect of which the parties have made an agreement within the meaning of this article, shall, at the request of one of the parties, refer the parties to arbitration, unless it finds that the said agreement is null and void, inoperative or incapable of being performed.

1 *Midgulf International Ltd v. Groupe Chimique Tunisien* [2009] EWHC 963 (Comm) [36] (Teare J); Geoffrey Fisher, 'Anti-suit injunctions to restrain foreign proceedings in breach of an arbitration agreement' (2010) 22(1) Bond LR i.

Furthermore, the positive and negative effects of the *kompetenz-kompetenz* principle have to be considered, i.e., an arbitral court may decide any case subject to a later judicial review and the prohibition of any objections on an interlocutory basis before the arbitrators have reached a decision for the same jurisdictional matter.[2]

One of the main limitations of Article II(3) of the New York Convention is that it refers parties to arbitration in cases that include existing valid agreements and does not include a *lis alibi pendens* rule, which is necessary not just within the EU but also internationally to achieve uniform conflict arbitral awards and judgments based on merits beyond those outlined in the Brussels I Regulation (recast) on maritime proceedings and cargo claims. There is a lack of international harmonised rules on arbitrability, as a fundamental expression of parties' freedom to arbitrate a cargo claim. The *lex arbitri* determines rules outside of arbitration agreements and sets out procedures for conducting arbitral proceedings. A choice of seat for arbitration sets the arbitrability of a dispute and the competence of the arbitral tribunal to rule within its own jurisdiction, while procedural rules give power to courts to intervene or assist in arbitral processes.

Anti-suit injunctions are heavily criticised from a public international legal perspective, as they are alleged to invade the sovereignty of foreign states to determine their own courts' jurisdiction,[3] while anti-arbitration ones undermine the arbitrators' *kompetenz-kompetenz* and the supervisory powers of the courts of the seat where the arbitration proceedings take place. This has been described as a 'unilateral judicialism' constraining international cooperation.[4]

1 Anti-suit injunctions and jurisdiction agreements in England

The material scope of application of the Brussels I Regulation (recast) according to its Article 1 is civil and commercial matters. Even if the aim is to avoid abusive litigation, it is clear that it will also restrain the English courts from issuing an anti-suit injunction when an EU or Lugano Member State court has to examine its own jurisdiction. However, this matter is unclear regarding arbitration clauses.[5]

Anti-suit injunctions should be followed since they can be used in parallel proceedings and halted at an EU level by the *lis alibi pendens* rule. The presumed mutual trust and equality principles between the EU courts operating under the *prior in tempore, potior in jure* role (first come, first served) of the Brussels I Regulation (recast) and CJEU case law since *Turner v. Grovit*[6] also have to be respected – even if the proceedings were started in bad faith.

2 Gabrielle Kaufmann-Kohler, 'How to Handle Parallel Proceedings: A Practical Approach to Issues such as Competence-Competence and Anti-Suit Injunctions' (2008) 2 DRI 110.

3 The regional court of appeal of Düsseldorf did not enforce an anti-suit injunction restraining the parties from continuing foreign proceedings in breach of a London arbitration clause in *Re the Enforcement of an English Anti-Suit Injunction* [1997] IL Pr 320 (Oberlandesgericht, Düsseldorf); Zheng Sophia Tang, *Jurisdiction and Arbitration Agreements in International Commercial Law* (Routledge 2014) 167.

4 Kaufmann-Kohler, 'How to Handle Parallel Proceedings' (n 2).

5 Alexander Sandiforth, 'Jurisdiction Agreements and Anti-Suit Injunctions' (University of Southampton Institute of Maritime Law Conference, London, 27 January 2017).

6 Case C-159/02 *Turner v. Grovit* [2004] ECR I-3565. Prior to this decision, the High Court had continued to grant anti-suit injunctions to restrain proceedings in Member States; see *Aggeliki Charis Compania Maritima SA v. Pagnan SpA (The Angelic Grace)* [1995] 1 Lloyd's Rep 87 (CA).

The English legal system provides two effective options when parties use procedural tactics to defend their interests: a declaration of non-liability and damages for breach of an exclusive jurisdiction clause.

A declaration of non-liability, according to s 31 of the Senior Courts Act 1981 and Civil Procedure Rules (CPR)[7] Rule 40.20, is an effective discretionary remedy[8] to avoid the risk of commencing proceedings in breach of an exclusive jurisdiction clause. If there is a London arbitration clause, a declaration of non-liability may be sought from the High Court according to the UKAA, s 32. Interim measures sought out of the UK to protect a London arbitration clause did not constitute a breach of such agreement in a dispute between two Zambian companies.[9] A declaration of non-liability may be also available when it has a useful purpose[10] for an innocent party seeking to seise an English court[11] and prevents the other party from starting proceedings in any other EU Member State or Lugano Contracting State.

The remedy for breach of an exclusive jurisdiction clause when a foreign court refuses its jurisdiction or such proceedings are dismissed on the merits[12] provides the innocent party with the recovery of any damages due to the costs incurred.[13]

1.1 Anti-suit injunctions and jurisdiction agreements under Brussels I Regulation 44/2001

Are claims by or against third parties (such as P&I Clubs) in breach of a contract's jurisdiction clause? Section 37 of the Senior Courts Act 1981 allows English courts to exercise their discretion when ordering injunctions. In *The Hornbay*,[14] an order was made against a German shipowner's agent by a Colombian consignee as an English jurisdiction clause was applicable under Article 23(1) of the Brussels I Regulation (Article 25(1) of the Brussels I Regulation (recast)).[15] The claimants had permission to join the claimants' agents in Colombia as a party.[16]

In *Gasser*,[17] it was declared that the second court seised, whether or not it had exclusive jurisdiction over the subject matter of the case, should stay its proceedings until the first court seised determined its own jurisdiction under the old Brussels I Regulation 44/2001.[18]

---

7 Civil Procedure Rules of England and Wales, approved by the Civil Procedure Act 1997, amended on 8 August 2016.

8 *Messier Dowty Ltd v. Sabena SA and others* [2000] 1 Lloyd's Rep 428 (CA), [41].

9 *U&M Mining Zambia Ltd v. Konkola Copper Mines Plc* [2013] EWHC 260 (Comm).

10 *Standard Bank Plc v. Agrinvest International Inc* [2007] EWHC 2595 (Comm). There was no exclusive dispute resolution clause in *Navig8 Pte Ltd v. Al-Riyadh Co for Vegetable Oil Industry (The Lucky Lady)* [2013] EWHC 328 (Comm).

11 Case C-406/92 *Owners of the cargo lately laden on board the ship 'Tatry' v. Owners of the ship 'Maciej Rataj' (The Tatry)* [1994] ECR I-5439, [45].

12 *Donohue v. Armco* [2001] UKHL 64, [181]–[182].

13 *Union Discount Co Ltd v. Zoller* [2001] EWCA Civ 1755, [2002] 1 WLR 1517 (CA), applied in *Swissmarine Services SA v. Gupta Coal India Private Ltd* [2015] EWHC 265 (Comm).

14 *Horn Linie GmbH & Co v. Panamericana Formas e Impresos SA* (*The Hornbay*) [2006] EWHC 373 (Comm).

15 Regarding the Colombian consignee's efforts in 'seeking to avoid the parties' contractual bargain by commencing proceedings in Colombia' Morison J stated: 'The only sensible course at this stage is to grant an anti-suit injunction in order to support the express terms of the bargain the parties made … this is an order directed only against the parties and not the Colombian Courts', ibid [33].

16 Richard Aikens, Richard Lord and Michael Bools, *Bills of Lading* (2nd edn, Informa 2015) ch 14.

17 Case C-116/02 *Erich Gasser GmbH v. MISAT Srl* EU:C:2003:657, [2003] ECR I-14693.

18 José Carlos Fernández Rozas, 'Alternatives and uncertainties of the dispute settlement clauses in international maritime contracts' (2018) Cuadernos de Derecho Transnacional 10(2) 333, 336; see also Chapter 2, Section 1 (International Jurisdiction in the EU).

Article 31(2) of the Brussels I Regulation (recast) changed the position on this, essentially rendering the *Gasser* decision no longer applicable.

If there is a breach of a dispute resolution clause, the English court has a discretionary power to issue an anti-suit injunction when a third party exercises rights of which it has been deprived under a contract.[19]

1.2 Anti-suit injunctions restraining the parties from commencing proceedings outside the EU

It is worth discussing the *Compania Sud Americana de Vapores SA v. Hin-Pro Logistics International Ltd* decision.[20] Goods had to be carried from Nanjing (China) to Puerto Caballo (Venezuela). The carrier, CSAV, alleged that the cargo was sent to the named consignee, Raselca, their agents in Venezuela, who delivered the goods to the buyers. Hin-Pro (the freight forwarder) claimed around US$24 million, which was the value of the cargo carried under standard form B/Ls plus freight and other costs. CSAV's sellers were Chinese companies who sold on C&F terms ('cost and freight' term of sale that charges all the transport costs until the port of destination to the buyer, excluding insurance) and were fully paid for the goods. CSAV successfully defended against Hin-Pro and alleged that the wrong delivery was made (without production of the original B/L in various ports in Venezuela), and it was dishonest.[21]

Chinese proceedings commenced by Hin-Pro against CSAV commenced in 2012 at the Wuhan Maritime Court (China) in breach of a London jurisdiction clause contained in five B/Ls. Clause 23 of the B/Ls provided, in relation to law and jurisdiction:

> This Bill of Lading and any claim or dispute arising hereunder shall be subject to English law and the jurisdiction of the English High Court of Justice in London. If, notwithstanding the foregoing, any proceedings are commenced in another jurisdiction, such proceedings shall be referred to ordinary courts of law. In the case of Chile, arbitrators shall not be competent to deal with any such disputes and proceedings shall be referred to the Chilean Ordinary Courts.

English proceedings started in November 2012. CSAV, domiciled in Chile, claimed against Hin-Pro. On 29 November 2013, Blair J granted CSAV an interim anti-suit injunction restraining further continuance of the Chinese proceedings in Wuhan, but Hin-Pro ignored the injunction, starting 23 judicial proceedings in the maritime courts of Guangzhou, Shanghai, Ningbo, Tianjin and Qingdao, based on 70 other B/Ls, where CSAV did not succeed in challenging Chinese jurisdiction.[22]

On 27 May 2014, the Ningbo court issued a judgment in one of the cases before it, awarding Hin-Pro damages of US$360,000 and legal costs for the value of the cargo claimed. However, the court prevented Hin-Pro's claim for freight on the basis that it was a seller on C&F terms. The sums awarded by the court were paid by CSAV to Hin-Pro. CSAV brought

19 *Royal Bank of Scotland Plc v. Highland Financial Partners LP* [2013] EWCA Civ 328.

20 *Compania Sud Americana de Vapores SA v. Hin-Pro International Logistics Ltd* [2015] EWCA Civ 401.

21 Yvonne Baatz, 'Choice of jurisdiction in bills of lading and cargo insurance' in Jason Chuah (ed), *Research Handbook on Maritime Law and Regulation* (Edward Elgar 2019) 342, 365.

22 ibid; *Compania Sud Americana de Vapores SA v. Hin-Pro International Logistics Ltd* [2014] EWHC 3632 (Comm).

proceedings against Hin-Pro in England, claiming a permanent anti-suit injunction, declarations and damages in respect of the latter's breach of clause 23 of the B/L. On 13 June 2014, the English Commercial Court issued an anti-suit injunction and a worldwide freezing order to the value of US$27.835 million over assets in Hong Kong.[23] The breach of an English court jurisdiction agreement was restrained.

On 10 September 2014, the Ningbo court handed down a further judgment, and a sum of US$652,936 was awarded to Hin-Pro in respect of cargo value, including legal costs. The claim in respect of freight was not allowed.[24] The judgment was under appeal and the sums awarded had not yet been paid by CSAV. The English Court of Appeal confirmed[25] the approach taken by the Commercial Court, that there was an exclusive choice of English law and jurisdiction – even if the word 'exclusive' was not included in clause 23 of the B/L and despite the fact that more than one year had passed according to Article III.6 of the Hague Rules and that Hin-Pro already had started proceedings in China.

This is justified by the Paramount Clause contained in clause 2 of the B/L leading to the application of the Hague Rules, unless the English courts sought to apply COGSA 1971, making the Hague–Visby Rules applicable. However, when the shipment was destined for or originated from the US the B/L would be subject to US Carriage of Goods by Sea Act (COGSA),[26] or to the Hamburg Rules in countries where they are mandatorily applicable. Furthermore, cargo interests may bring proceedings at the place of arrest under Article 21(2)(a) of the Hamburg Rules except when the defendants have sought a removal of the action and cargo interests must then choose between one of the places set out in Article 21(1) of the Rules.[27] If proceedings were to take place in Chile, the reference in clause 23 to English law and jurisdiction would be void, and Article 21 of the Hamburg Rules would lead to the application of Chilean law.[28] Judges are prone to giving an extensive interpretation of an English choice of court agreement, unless there is any clear statement pointing to a non-exclusive jurisdiction agreement. This expansive approach is in line with Article 3 of the Hague Choice of Court Convention and Article 25(1) of the Brussels I Regulation (recast).[29]

---

23 As in *Aggeliki Charis Compania Maritima SA v. Pagnan SpA (The Angelic Grace)* [1995] 1 Lloyd's Rep 87 (CA). Furthermore, on 14 November 2016 the Final Appeal Court of Hong Kong upheld in *Compania Sud Americana De Vapores SA v. Hin-Pro International Logistics Ltd* (FACV 1/2016) the worldwide freezing order (still called a Mareva injunction in Hong Kong); CSAV succeeded in most of the Chinese actions on appeal, when the Mareva injunction was issued; Baatz, 'Choice of jurisdiction in bills of lading and cargo insurance' (n 21) 366.

24 As a matter of construction, Cooke J considered clause 23 an exclusive jurisdiction agreement in contrast with the *Import Export Metro Ltd v. Compania Sud Americana de Vapores SA* [2003] EWHC 11, where the clause was treated as non-exclusive. Proceedings in relation to 14 B/Ls took place in Chile where the Hamburg Rules were applicable, with the two-year time-bar. The cargo interests were more interested in the Chilean time-bar and CSAV in the discharge of performance there. CSAV applied for a stay of the English proceedings. The case would have been decided under Chilean law and an arbitrator could have heard all the claims. Claims for loss and damage to the cargo in Chile are subject to mandatory arbitration, so the jurisdiction clause would be void; Baatz, 'Choice of jurisdiction in bills of lading and cargo insurance' (n 21) 365.

25 *Compania Sud Americana De Vapores SA v. Hin-Pro International Logistics Ltd* [2015] EWCA Civ 401.

26 United States Carriage of Goods by Sea Act (COGSA 1936) 46 USC § 30701; Felix Sparka, *Jurisdiction and Arbitration Clauses in Maritime Transport Documents* (Springer 2010) 19–38.

27 Baatz, 'Choice of jurisdiction in bills of lading and cargo insurance' (n 21) 370.

28 Felix WH Chan, 'Anti-suit Injunctions and the Doctrine of Comity' (2016) 79(2) MLR 341.

29 Baatz, 'Choice of jurisdiction in bills of lading and cargo insurance' (n 21) 370–371.

2 Anti-suit injunctions and arbitration agreements

The English High Court may grant an injunction when, in its view, it appears to be convenient and just. The High Court may thus grant an anti-suit injunction to protect a party's rights under an arbitration agreement in circumstances where there are no arbitral proceedings ongoing and none are intended. The parties can seek a declaration from the High Court that there is a binding arbitration clause,[30] or the High Court can refuse to determine the existence of an alleged arbitration clause prior to commencement of arbitration proceedings.[31]

2.1 Anti-suit injunctions and arbitration agreements under the old Brussels I Regulation 44/2001

Arbitration proceedings are excluded by Article 1(2)(d)[32] of the Brussels Convention. Under Article 5(3), the Italian court in *The Front Comor* had jurisdiction on the merits for damages in tort, since the Italian plaintiff's jetty was hit in Syracuse. However, the existence of an arbitration clause was a preliminary issue under the Brussels Convention. The case involved different issues, such as the claimant's estoppel in starting proceedings in its own courts, or procedural tactics that did not favour its interests such as the Italian torpedo injunctions. The case also involved a 'forum shopping' issue, since the negligent navigation exception under English law was preferable for the shipowners, while the interpretation under Italian law was preferable for the Italian insurers. It must be noted that the eventual favourable judgment by an Italian court would be enforceable in England under the Brussels I Regulation (recast), but the Italian court would first have to determine whether the English arbitration clause was valid.

The historical treatment of anti-suit injunctions within the scope of the old Brussels Convention helps explain how an arbitration agreement cannot restrain parties from commencing proceedings in an EU Member State court in breach of an arbitration agreement.

The CJEU's *Front Comor*[33] is a leading case. An English arbitral tribunal awarded equitable damages for breach of an exclusive London arbitration clause. Arbitration falls outside the scope of application of the old Brussels I Regulation 44/2001, according to its Article 1(2)(d). The charterers first initiated arbitral proceedings in London. The charterers' insurers brought a lawsuit in Italy. The shipowners sought and obtained an anti-suit injunction issued by Colman J on 21 March 2005, restraining the insurers from continuing the Italian process.[34] The case was referred to the CJEU by the House of Lords and the ruling

30 *Ust-Kamenogorsk Hydropower Plant JSC v. AES Ust-Kamenogorsk Hydropower Plant LLP* [2013] UKSC 35.

31 *HC Trading Malta Ltd v. Tradeland Commodities SL* [2016] EWHC 1279 (Comm).

32 Case C-190/89 *Marc Rich & Co AG v. Societa Italiana PA (The Atlantic Emperor)* [1992] ECR I-3855; *The Heidberg* [1994] 2 Lloyd's Rep 287, 298–303; *Toepfer International GmbH v. Société Cargill France* [1997] EWCA Civ 2811; Case C-391/95 *Van Uden Maritime BV trading as Van Uden Africa Line v. Kommanditgesellschaft in Firma Deco-Line* [1998] ECR I-7091; *Navigation Maritime Bulgare v. Rustal Trading Ltd (The Ivan Zagubanski)* [2000] EWHC 222 (Comm); *Through Transport Mutual Insurance Association (Eurasia) Ltd v. New India Assurance Co Ltd (The Hari Bhum)* [2004] EWCA Civ 1598; *A v. B* [2006] EWHC 2006 (Comm); [2007] 1 Lloyd's Rep 237.

33 Case C-185/07 *Allianz SpA (formerly Riunione Adriatica Di Sicurta SpA) v. West Tankers Inc (The Front Comor)* EU:C:2009:69, [2009] ECR I-663.

34 *West Tankers Inc v. RAS Riunione Adriatica di Sicurta SpA* [2005] EWHC 454 (Comm).

allowed the Italian court to decide whether the London arbitration agreement was valid, or whether the Italian courts had jurisdiction to hear the case. The CJEU forbade an anti-suit injunction from restraining an EU court starting proceedings to determine the validity of an English arbitration agreement, avoiding the applicability of the New York Convention, under which all EU Member State courts would be obliged to stay the proceedings.[35] The CJEU held that, being a preliminary issue in a claim for substantive relief, the existence of an arbitration agreement fell within the scope of the Brussels Convention. The London arbitral tribunal found that the shipowners did not incur liability and a London court upheld the award. In a separate hearing, the London court then awarded equitable damages following the breach of the exclusive London arbitration agreement.[36] After the CJEU's judgment was rendered on 10 February 2009, a third award was enforced following s 66 UKAA, and the English High Court and Court of Appeal upheld it, refusing to set it aside.[37]

In the more recent *Gazprom* case,[38] the CJEU held that an anti-suit injunction issued by a Lithuanian arbitral tribunal fell within the scope of the arbitration exception in Article 1(2)(d), as it was compatible with Brussels I Regulation 44/2001. The court allowed its recognition and enforcement by an EU Member State court.[39]

On 6 December 2008, a consignment of coal purchased by the Endesa Generación SA was shipped aboard the *Wadi Sudr*,[40] destined for the Spanish port of Ferrol. A clean on board CONGENBILL B/L was signed on behalf of the shipowners, National Navigation Co, with a standard clause incorporating an unidentified charterparty. During the voyage, the *Wadi Sudr* suffered a breakdown in the steering system. The ship was towed, and general average was declared. The cargo was discharged in Carboneras to be sent on to Ferrol. Endesa alleged that unloading the vessel in Carboneras caused problems which, in turn, caused significant delay, extraordinary costs and damage to the terminal. Endesa applied for an arrest of the vessel in Carboneras to ensure a maritime claim under the 1952 Arrest Convention, which would cover all damages suffered as a result of breach of contract of carriage (Article 1(1)(e)).

Shortly after Endesa applied for the arrest of the ship, National Navigation Co began proceedings before the English High Court, with the intention of solving the dispute in England. By order of 31 July 2008, the Spanish judge suspended proceedings and rejected the shipowner's plea until the High Court reviewed its jurisdiction to hear the case (and the validity of the arbitration clause). The Spanish judge considered that the arrest of the ship was an interim measure aligned with Article 28 of the Brussels I Regulation, rather than Article 27 (*lis alibi pendens*), because these were related actions.

The Spanish Court of Appeal rejected the shipowner's challenge to Spanish jurisdiction based on the High Court's ongoing proceedings, where the validity of the arbitration

---

35 Sandiforth (n 5).

36 *West Tankers Inc v. Allianz SpA* (*The Front Comor*) [2012] EWHC 854 (Comm); Yvonne Baatz, 'The Conflict of Laws' in Yvonne Baatz (ed), *Maritime Law* (4th edn, Routledge 2018) 10–14; Yvonne Baatz, 'Should Third Parties Be Bound by Arbitration Clauses in Bills of Lading?' (2015) 1 LMCLQ 85, 109–111; Sandiforth (n 5).

37 *West Tankers Inc v. Allianz SpA (The Front Comor)* [2012] EWCA Civ 27, [2011] EWHC 829 (Comm).

38 Case C-536/13 *Gazprom OAO v. Lietuvos Respublika* EU:C:2015:316.

39 Aikens, Lord and Bools (n 16) ch 14.

40 *National Navigation Co v. Endesa Generacion SA (The Wadi Sudr)* [2009] EWCA Civ 1397; Baatz, 'The Conflict of Laws' (n 36) 14–17.

clause included in the B/L was under scrutiny. In Spain, the formal validity of an arbitration clause inserted in a B/L by reference to a charterparty is regulated under the New York Convention. However, individual negotiation and the express and unequivocal consent of the parties were necessary requirements.

At first, the English High Court decided that any finding by an EU Member State court that had to be recognised in England creates an issue of estoppel with paragraphs 1 and 3 of s 32 of the UK Civil Jurisdiction and Judgments Act 1982 (CJJA) ('overseas judgments given in proceedings brought in breach of agreement for settlement of disputes'):[41]

> In determining whether a judgment given by a court of an overseas country should be recognised or enforced in the United Kingdom, a court in the United Kingdom shall not be bound by any decision of the overseas court relating to [proceedings] contrary to an agreement under which the dispute in question was to be settled otherwise than by proceedings in the courts of that country.

Gloster J acknowledged the relevance of *The Front Comor* – which was rendered while the High Court proceedings were taking place. She understood that these matters were outside of the scope of the Brussels I Regulation and that the statements made by the Spanish judge were not binding. She understood that the arbitration clause had been correctly incorporated into the B/L. The judge considered the issue as one of UK public policy.

The enforceability of an arbitral award is guaranteed by the New York Convention, despite the fact that an EU Member State's judgment may declare an arbitration agreement null and void. The fourth paragraph refers to ancillary proceedings, which requires interpretation as to whether it shall include a declaration about the existence of an arbitration agreement:

> This Regulation should not apply to any action or ancillary proceedings relating to, in particular, the establishment of an arbitral tribunal, the powers of arbitrators, the conduct of an arbitration procedure or any other aspects of such a procedure, nor to any action or judgment concerning the annulment, review, appeal, recognition or enforcement of an arbitral award.

The English Court of Appeal reviewed the matter again and concluded that Gloster J had erred in concluding that the Spanish judge's decision should not be recognised in the UK. This had to be considered under the scope of the Regulation and was, therefore, recognised in the UK. To the extent that the decision established that the arbitration clause had not been validly incorporated into the B/L, the English courts were not authorised to review the issue again. An EU Member State judgment must be always recognised in other EU Member States with the minimum formalities provided for in Article 34 of the Brussels Convention (now Article 45 of the Brussels I Regulation (recast)).

In relation to an alleged violation of public policy, the Court of Appeal held that a decision of an EU Member State court could not be considered contrary to public policy. The Court of Appeal decided to order an end to the arbitral procedure that the shipowners had begun in the UK, parallel to the court proceedings. Allowing the continuation of arbitral proceedings had been part of Gloster J's reasoning for ignoring the Spanish court's judgment (where incorporation of the arbitration clause into the B/L was invalid).

41 Aikens, Lord and Bools (n 16) ch 14.

In another case, in the Spanish Supreme Court,[42] the English law view was defended by the court regarding the recognition of an Italian judgment. The Spanish Supreme Court followed part of the doctrine that considered arbitration excluded from the material scope of the Brussels Convention according to Article 1(2)(4), avoiding review of the Italian court's international jurisdiction by the Spanish Supreme Court as prescribed in Article 28(3). The court held that, under certain circumstances, the decision of the Italian court concerning the validity and effectiveness of the arbitration agreement would not be binding on the receiving state. The Spanish Supreme Court considered that the Italian judgment respected the New York Convention and the 1961 Convention on International Commercial Arbitration. The Spanish entity did not prove the requirements of the applicable French law as the third state involved was France (where the award had to be rendered and respected by the Italian judgment) and it was not contrary to Spanish public policy.[43]

In *The Wadi Sudr*, there were several overlapping chartering contracts in place. The last voyage charterer was Carboex, SA, an entity from which Endesa had bought the coal on CIF terms (cost, insurance and freight). Carboex had chartered the ship for the trip to Morgan Stanley. Endesa was the receiver and B/L holder.[44]

The interpretation of the exception for navigational error by the Italian court was preferred by the Italian insurers. By way of comparison, in *The Wadi Sudr*[45] there was absolute liability under Spanish law rather than an English law due diligence requirement. In *The Front Comor*, the subrogated insurers started actions in Italy under Italian insurance law against the tortfeasor shipowner, while the charterer did the same for a contractual claim under an ASBATANKVOY[46] charterparty requiring English law and London arbitration proceedings to recover monies from the shipowner. That was held to be inconsistent by the CJEU according to Article 1(2)(d) of the Brussels Convention, which excludes arbitration from its scope.[47]

In contrast with *The Wadi Sudr*, in *The Front Comor* the arbitration clause was found to be binding; the Spanish Court decided that no incorporation into the B/L took place and that the shipowners waived their right to rely on such clause once they commenced jurisdiction proceedings in England before the arbitral tribunal could decide that the clause was valid.[48] The Court of Appeal of England and Wales confirmed that the judgment was binding, and the issue was about the substance of the matter.[49] These cases stress the importance of the recognition of dispute resolution clauses included in any charterparty or B/L in favour of EU Member State courts.

42 *Cerámicas Casao, SA v. IAG Impianti Automazione Gestione srl* (appeal) Case RJ 2007/3178, Civil Chamber, Section 1 Judgment No 558/2007, rendered on 17 May 2007.

43 Eduardo Albors Méndez and Javier Portales Rodríguez, 'Cuestiones jurisdiccionales en el derecho marítimo: Los casos "Front Comor" y "Wadi Sudr"' in José Luis García-Pita y Lastres, María Rocío Quintáns Eiras and Angélica Díaz de la Rosa (eds), *Estudios De derecho marítimo* (Thomson Reuters/Aranzadi 2012) 121–140.

44 ibid.

45 *The Wadi Sudr* (n 40).

46 This is a tanker voyage charterparty developed by the Association of Ship Brokers & Agents (U.S.A.), Inc. (ASBA); see <https://www.bimco.org/news/priority-news/20190527-asbagasvoy> accessed 15 September 2020.

47 *The Front Comor* (n 33).

48 *The Front Comor* (n 37) (High Court).

49 *The Front Comor* (n 37) (Court of Appeal).

2.2 Anti-suit injunctions and arbitration agreements under the Brussels I Regulation (Recast)

The wording of Article 1(2)(d) of the Brussels Convention has been kept in the Brussels I Regulation (recast), adding a still-controversial interpretation into Recital 12. The first two paragraphs of Recital 12 exclude any issue related to the existence of an arbitration agreement, in contrast with the English Court of Appeal's judgment in *The Wadi Sudr*.[50] According to Recital 12 of the recast regulation, any judgment by an EU Member State court on the validity of an arbitration clause would not be considered a judgment as such. If *The Wadi Sudr* had to be decided in light of the Brussels I Regulation (recast), Recital 12, paragraph 2, the result would be different. The Spanish judgment as to the validity of the arbitration clause would not be a judgment under the recast Regulation.

The third paragraph of Recital 12 of the Brussels I Regulation (recast) confirms that a judgment on the merits is within the scope of the Regulation, once an arbitration agreement has been declared null or void:

> On the other hand, where a court of a Member State, exercising jurisdiction under this Regulation or under national law, has determined that an arbitration agreement is null and void, inoperative or incapable of being performed, this should not preclude that court's judgment on the substance of the matter from being recognised or, as the case may be, enforced in accordance with this Regulation. This should be without prejudice to the competence of the courts of the Member States to decide on the recognition and enforcement of arbitral awards in accordance with the Convention on the Recognition and Enforcement of Foreign Arbitral Awards, which takes precedence over this Regulation.

It is unclear whether the Brussels I Regulation (recast) allows an anti-suit injunction to restrain proceedings brought in another EU Member State, even if the court that is second seised aims to restrain proceedings brought in breach of an arbitration clause. In *Gazprom*, the CJEU held that an anti-suit injunction issued by an arbitral tribunal was compatible with the Brussels I Regulation, falling within the scope of Article 1(2)(d). The CJEU considered that such anti-suit injunction was recognisable and enforceable in Lithuania. Advocate General Wathelet agreed on narrow terms[51] without any clear explanation of the type of anti-suit injunction restraining the Lithuanian court proceedings. Even though Recital 22 of the Brussels I Regulation (recast) aims to 'enhance the effectiveness of exclusive choice-of-court agreements and to avoid abusive litigation tactics', Recital 12 states in its third paragraph that the New York Convention 'takes precedence' over the Regulation.[52]

According to Sandiforth, before Brussels I Regulation 44/2001, it was possible for the parties to confer on an arbitrator the power to grant an interim anti-suit injunction under s 38(1) UKAA, complemented by s 48(5)(a), by which the arbitrator could render a final award in a form restraining the pursuit of foreign proceedings.[53] Nothing would prevent this happening now, according to Recital 12 of the recast Regulation, which establishes the primacy of the New York Convention over the Regulation; but timing is always important in a case requiring the involvement of an English court as arbitrators lack coercive powers.[54]

---

50 *The Wadi Sudr* (n 40); Baatz, 'The Conflict of Laws' (n 36) 14–17.

51 *Gazprom* (n 38), EU:C:2014:2414, Opinion of Advocate General (AG) Wathelet, delivered on 4 December 2014.

52 See Section 2.1 of this chapter.

53 This happened in *Welex AG v. Rosa Maritime Ltd (The Epsilon Rosa)* [2003] EWCA Civ 938, [35].

54 Sandiforth (n 5). According to Charles Debattista, 'Arbitrators' Powers to Order Interim Measures (Including Anti-Suit Injunctions)' (LMAA 50th Anniversary Conference, London 18 March 2010) 9–11, according to the

Since the main subject matter of the anti-suit injunction falls within the scope of the Brussels I Regulation (recast), the *Van Uden*[55] doctrine and *The Front Comor* criteria must be applied. In *Van Uden*, the Supreme Court of the Netherlands refused to allow the arrest of a ship for an interim payment, because the application of Article 24 of the Brussels Convention required a real 'connecting link' between the subject matter and the forum where the judgment was sought to be enforced.[56] An anti-suit injunction cannot be contrary to the principles of mutual trust and cooperation between EU Member State courts. In CJEU case law,[57] the status of EU public policy is considered equal to domestic public policy. An opinion of the Court of 18 December 2014 states that 'the principle of mutual trust between the Member States is of fundamental importance in EU law, given that it allows an area without internal borders to be created and maintained'.[58]

Mutual trust is guaranteed by Article 45(3) of the Brussels I Regulation (recast) under which 'the jurisdiction of the court of origin may not be reviewed [and] the test of public policy may not be applied to the rules relating to jurisdiction'. This imposes an obligation on the second court seised to accept such a presumption, as it aims to protect the mutual trust between courts of EU Member States. The principle of mutual trust has public policy status limiting the application of Article 45(1)(a), which establishes that 'on the application of any interested party, the recognition of a judgment shall be refused if such recognition is manifestly contrary to public policy (*ordre public*) in the Member State addressed'.

Corcione states that, according to Recital 12 of the recast Regulation,

> a court's decision that an arbitration clause is void does not preclude its award on the substance being enforced under the Regulation, without prejudice to the competence of courts to decide on the enforceability of an arbitral award under the New York Convention.[59]

UKAA 'the parties are free to agree on the powers exercisable by the arbitral tribunal for the purposes of and in relation to the proceedings' (s 38(1)) and 'the tribunal has the same powers as the court to order a party to do or refrain from doing anything' (s 48(5)(a)); ss 38–39 are aimed at interim measures, while s 48 is for substantive awards as per *Kastner v. Jason* [2005] 1 Lloyd's Rep 397, 401; there are no explicit powers granted for the arbitrators to grant interim anti-suit injunctions in both sections – however, it is possible that

> the parties have expressly agreed to give the [arbitral] tribunal the power to issue an anti-suit injunction through section 38(1) … directing the parties to desist from starting proceedings in another EU/EFTA jurisdiction or, if such proceedings had started, directing the party who started them to desist from pursing them.

That was the case in *CMA CGM SA v. Hyundai MIPO Dockyard Co Ltd* [2008] EWHC 2791 (Comm), which would provide a positive answer, according to Debattista, in a case where arbitrators awarded damages equal to the value of a French judgment obtained in breach of a London arbitration clause; moreover,

> if the party pursuing the foreign proceedings ignores the London tribunal's direction under section 38(1) … the respondent in the foreign court would apply to the arbitral tribunal for a peremptory order under section 41(5), setting a time for compliance with the anti-suit injunction.

English courts may be able to grant interim anti-suit injunctions after *Gazprom* while respecting *The Front Comor* in breach of a valid arbitration agreement: Robert Merkin QC and Louis Flannery QC, *Merkin and Flannery on the Arbitration Act 1996* (Taylor & Francis 2019) [38], fn 166.

55 *Van Uden* (n 32) 7122.

56 Gerry Maher and Barry J Rodger, 'Provisional and Protective Remedies: The British Experience of the Brussels Convention' (1999) 48(2) ICLQ 302–339.

57 Case C-126/97 *Eco Swiss China Time Ltd v. Benetton International NV* EU:C:1999:269, [1997] ECR I-3055.

58 Opinion C-2/13 of the CJEU (Full Court) pursuant to Article 218(11) TFEU, delivered on 18 December 2014.

59 Carlo Corcione, *Third Party Protection in Shipping* (Informa 2019) 424.

The decision of Males J in *Nori Holdings*[60] placed more emphasis on the recast Regulation's Recital 12 rather than Article 73(2), under which the Regulation shall not affect the application of the New York Convention, to stress that *The Front Comor* is still applicable and English courts cannot issue anti-suit injunctions in breach of English arbitration agreements, despite the silence kept by the Regulation on this matter.[61] As already stated, the enforcement of an arbitral award that restrains the parties from bringing proceedings in an EU Member State is possible under *Gazprom*, despite it being decided, along with *The Front Comor*, under the Brussels I Regulation 44/2001. If the anti-suit injunction is not rendered by a court but is in the form of an arbitral award, a party commencing or continuing litigation in breach of an arbitration clause may have an obligation to pay compensation, avoiding the presumption of incompatibility of an arbitral anti-suit injunction with the Brussels I Regulation (recast). Thus, under Article V(2)(b) of the New York Convention, an anti-suit injunction in the form of an arbitral award may not be recognised.[62] Baatz reinforces this message, as if an English court grants damages for breach of jurisdiction provisions, Articles 27 and 28 of the Brussels I Regulation (recast) provide a mechanism to resolve parallel proceedings or related actions, but this does not happen with the arbitration clauses.[63] Thus, it would be desirable to amend the recast Regulation to introduce such a mechanism. This was suggested in the Opinion of Advocate General Kokott in *The Front Comor* case,[64] after noting the prevalence of the New York Convention over the Regulation through application of Article 71 of the recast Regulation, infructuous attempts to introduce new EU legislation concerning arbitration[65] or, as the Heidelberg report suggests,[66] deleting Article 1(2)(d) of the recast Regulation.[67]

60 *Nori Holdings Ltd & Ors v. PJSC Bank Otkritie* [2018] EWHC 1343 (Comm). The arguments in this case at [28] were acknowledged in *Enka Insaat Ve Sanayi AS v. OOO 'Insurance Company Chubb' & Ors* [2020] EWCA Civ 574, [64], agreeing with Males J: 'when such an injunction is sought it is for the court to determine whether there is a binding arbitration agreement and whether the pursuit of the foreign proceedings constitutes a breach of the agreement'. An anti-suit injunction was issued on appeal to restrain parties from continuing proceedings in Russia but not in Cyprus. Arbitration was subject to ICC Rules in London. The Court of Appeal agreed with the High Court judgment of Andrew Baker J ([2019] EWHC 3568 (Comm), [41]) that Russian law was applicable to the arbitration agreement, following Chubb Russia's arguments supported by an opinion from Adrian Briggs, that by 'applying English law conflict of laws principles, in his view the arbitration agreement would be found to be governed by Russian law'. However, the Court of Appeal (at [95]) distinguished the law of the seat, English curial law, from the Russian law governing the main contract, stressing that the 'parties have necessarily chosen their relationship to be governed in some respects by two systems of law'. The Court also explained (at [61]) that CPR 62.5(1)(c) provides grounds on which to allow jurisdiction in respect of arbitration claims, but 'there is no requirement that England and Wales must be the proper place in which to bring the claim ... when the court is exercising the curial jurisdiction' as opposed to CPR 6.37(3) (which provides that 'the court will not give permission [for service] unless it is satisfied that England and Wales is the proper place in which to bring the claim'). Therefore, *forum non conveniens* considerations were rejected to stay English proceedings in favour of Russian courts, and the English court has the power to grant an anti-suit injunction, at [42].

61 Corcione (n 59) 424.

62 Pietro Ortolani, 'Anti-Suit Injunctions in Support of Arbitration Under the Recast Brussels I Regulation', (2015) MPI Luxembourg Working Paper 6.

63 Baatz, 'Should Third Parties Be Bound by Arbitration Clauses in Bills of Lading?' (n 36).

64 Case C-185/07 *Allianz Spa v. West Tankers* EU:C:2008:466, [2009] ECR I-663, Opinion of AG Kokott.

65 First proposed by Peter Schlosser: Professor Dr Peter Schlosser, 'Report on the Convention of 9 October 1978 on the Association of the Kingdom of Denmark, Ireland and the United Kingdom of Great Britain and Northern Ireland to the Convention on jurisdiction and the enforcement of judgments in civil and commercial matters and to the Protocol on its interpretation by the Court of Justice' [1979] OJ C59/71.

66 Burkhard Hess, Thomas Pfeiffer and Peter Schlosser, *The Heidelberg Report on the Application of Regulation Brussels I in the Member States* (Study JLS/C4/2005/03) (Beck 2008).

67 Baatz, 'Should Third Parties Be Bound by Arbitration Clauses in Bills of Lading?' (n 36).

2.3 Anti-suit injunctions restraining parties from commencing proceedings outside the EU

The High Court has jurisdiction regardless of whether the defendant is domiciled, resident or present within the English jurisdiction. In *The Anna Bo*,[68] an anti-suit injunction was granted under s 44 UKAA, restraining cargo receivers from litigating in China on matters subject to London arbitration. Section 37 was not applicable because the arbitration proceedings had already begun and the requirements to issue the anti-suit injunction restraining the parties from continuing foreign proceedings were not fulfilled by the cargo receivers in order to enforce a negative promise of not bringing parallel proceedings abroad.

Delays and engagements in foreign proceedings may be an obstacle for the party wishing to obtain an anti-suit injunction.[69] The justification adduced when England is the natural forum is to avoid 'vexatious or oppressive' foreign proceedings, exercising an anti-suit injunction within the 'ends of justice'.[70] In a more recent case,[71] an anti-suit injunction was granted to restrain an action already brought by a time charterer under their statutory rights recognised in Turkey in favour of a P&I Club, as the Turkish proceedings were 'vexatious and oppressive' and in conflict with their contractual right to arbitrate the dispute in England.[72]

When foreign proceedings are brought in breach of an English dispute arbitration clause (although proceedings to obtain security in a foreign jurisdiction will generally not be a breach of a dispute resolution clause, see *The Kallang (No 2)*[73]), the court may grant an interim anti-suit injunction to protect what the parties agreed to,[74] unless there are 'strong reasons' to the contrary.[75] There are some cases involving arbitration agreements where an English court has the discretionary power to issue an anti-suit injunction when a third party exercises rights deprived under a contract.[76]

A '*Scott v. Avery* clause' may be contained in a contract, restraining the parties from bringing court proceedings against each other until an arbitration award is issued.[77] Breach of such clause may allow the court to grant an anti-suit injunction.[78]

---

68 *Southport Success SA v. Tsingshan Holding Group Co Ltd (The Anna Bo)* [2015] EWHC 1974 (Comm).

69 *Magellan Spirit APS v. Vitol SA (The Magellan Spirit)* [2016] EWHC 454 (Comm); *ADM Asia-Pacific Trading PTE Ltd v. PT Budi Semesta Satria* [2016] EWHC 1427 (Comm); *HC Trading Malta Ltd v. Tradeland Commodities SL* (n 31).

70 *Société Nationale Industrielle Aerospatiale v. Lee Kui Jak* [1987] 1 AC 871 (PC). See also *Airbus Industrie GIE v. Patel* [1999] 1 AC 119; *Star Reefers Pool Inc v. JFC Group Co Ltd* [2012] EWCA Civ 14.

71 *Shipowners' Mutual Protection & Indemnity Association (Luxembourg) v. Containerships Denizcilik ve Tickaret AS (The Yusuf Cepnioglu)* [2016] EWHC Civ 386.

72 Aikens, Lord and Bools (n 16) ch 14.

73 *Kallang Shipping SA v. Axa Senegal (The Kallang) (No 2)* [2008] EWHC 2761 (Comm); see Baatz, 'Should Third Parties Be Bound by Arbitration Clauses in Bills of Lading?' (n 36).

74 See *Donohue v. Armco* (n 12); *Whitesea Shipping and Trading Corp v. El Paso Rio Clara Ltda (The Marielle Bolten)* [2009] EWHC 2552 (Comm); *Louis Dreyfus Commodities Kenya Ltd v. Bolster Shipping Co Ltd (The Giorgis Carras)* [2010] EWHC 1732 (Comm); *Joint Stock Asset Management Company 'Ingosstrakh-Investments' v. BNP Paribas SA* [2012] EWCA Civ 644.

75 See *Donohue v. Armco* (n 12) [179]; *The Eleftheria* [1969] 1 Lloyd's Rep 237; compare *Impala Warehousing and Logistics (Shanghai) Co Ltd v. Wanxiang Resources (Singapore) Pte Ltd* [2015] EWHC 811 (Comm).

76 For cases including anti-suit injunctions for breach of an arbitration clause, see *Schiffahrtsgesellschaft Detlev von Appen GmbH v. Voest Alpine Intertrading GmbH (The Jay Bola)* [1997] 2 Lloyd's Rep 279; *The Yusuf Cepnioglu* (n 71). For an analysis of the latter case see Jonatan Echebarría Fernández, 'Limitations on Jurisdiction and Arbitration Agreements Based on Applicable Law and the Identity of the Carrier in Cargo Claim Disputes: Who and Where to Sue?' (2019) 11(1) Cuadernos de Derecho Transnacional 306.

77 See *B v. S* [2011] EWHC 691 (Comm).

78 *Toepfer International GmbH v. Société Cargill France* (n 32).

As stated by Sandiforth,[79] when foreign proceedings are successful, damages can be awarded to reverse a decision on the merits rendered by a foreign tribunal, notwithstanding that estoppel[80] could preclude such claims, as well as an intended claim in tort regarding the breach of a contract.[81]

3 Conclusion

English courts are keen to protect party autonomy with regard to exclusive English jurisdiction clauses and are willing to issue anti-suit injunctions to do so. After the Brexit transition period is ended, if the Brussels I Regulation (recast) or the Lugano Convention are no longer in force in the UK (and no replacement instrument is agreed), and the country is no longer subject to the jurisdiction of the CJEU, it may then be possible to issue anti-suit injunctions restraining parties from commencing proceedings in EU Member State or Lugano-contracting country courts.

It can be said, although it is arguable, that intra-EU anti-suit injunctions issued by courts in breach of an arbitration agreement are prohibited unless the CJEU is willing to change its doctrine in a new judgment. Paradoxically, arbitral tribunals can issue an anti-suit injunction, as demonstrated in *Gazprom*, where the CJEU allowed the issue of an anti-suit injunction by an arbitral tribunal, judging it compatible with the Brussels I Regulation as the Regulation excludes arbitration from its scope. It should be borne in mind that this decision assessed the validity of an anti-suit injunction issued by an arbitral tribunal rather than by an EU Member State court, as in *The Front Comor*.

79 Sandiforth (n 5).
80 See *The Wadi Sudr* (n 40).
81 See *The Hornbay* (n 14) [26].

CHAPTER 5

Party autonomy and the arrest of ships

This chapter aims to demonstrate when the arrest of the ship frustrates the choice of forum or arbitration clauses of the parties in favour of a particular court or arbitral tribunal included in the charterparty or the B/L, by 'fixing' jurisdiction through the act of arrest. This is considered through a comparative study of the application of arrest conventions and the requirements for the arrest of vessels in the EU, as well as England and Spain, in particular. There is a lack of legal certainty due to the plethora of legal frameworks, and major efforts are required towards procedural unification to ensure the parties' will is carried out.

This chapter sheds light on when an abuse of sovereignty through the *lex fori* undermines the free will of the commercial parties in the case of arrest. The chapter considers why party autonomy is relevant, its limitations, the arguments in favour of and against protecting it and how national courts do not recognise party autonomy (jurisdiction and arbitration clauses specifically) in the case of arrest of ships. The application of specialised conventions may lead to a non-enforcement of the dispute resolution clauses and 'forum shopping' by cargo interests.

1 Ship arrest as an interim measure

1.1 Nature of actions in rem *under civil law and common law*

The clash between the party autonomy of the original parties and the dispute resolution terms of the B/L comes to a head in the arrest of ships, when the claimant charterer or third-party cargo interests sue the shipowner. The freedom of parties to start jurisdictional or arbitral proceedings demands at least that the seizure of the ship be fairly regulated from a procedural perspective in each EU or non-EU state. A legal analysis of judicial and the arbitral tribunal's powers to arrest ships requires a uniform global response to protect a claimant's adduced loss or damage in the claim. International judicial competence regarding arrest by different courts and arbitral tribunals varies, depending on the applicable rules. These include rules originating in the 1952 and 1999 Arrest Conventions, as well as national procedural rules. Special attention is drawn to the treatment of this issue under the SAMN.

The conditions for the arrest of a ship are contained in the *lex fori*. The 1952 Arrest Convention recognises two general principles: arrests should be permitted only for the purpose of obtaining security for a maritime claim,[1] and the proper subject of an arrest

1 Hans-Christian Albrecht and others (eds), *Maritime Law Handbook* (Kluwer Law International 1998).

should be either the vessel regarding which the claim arose or a sister ship registered under the same ownership.[2] As Theocharidis explains,[3] the jurisdictional basis provided for in the relevant rule reflects a preference in favour of the *forum arresti*, albeit in an indirect manner, since the choice is left to the *lex fori*, which almost invariably accords jurisdiction to the national court.

In common law jurisdictions, actions *in rem*, coupled with the arrest of a ship, may merge the potential functions of an arrest including: (a) obtaining security for the claim; (b) establishing jurisdiction on the merits (from the mere arrest of the vessel in the jurisdiction (unless another court claims exclusive jurisdiction), under the Brussels I Regulation (recast) or a lack of choice of jurisdiction or arbitration agreement between the parties); and (c) securing the position of statutory maritime claimants as preferred creditors over unsecured ones. These underlying claims may be preceded by a writ for arrest, under which an interim or protective measure is sought to prevent non-payment of any award made in relation to the underlying substantive claim.

A distinction between maritime claims and maritime liens must be drawn, to narrow the scope of the current analysis. Maritime liens pass with a ship irrespective of ownership, while maritime claims *in rem* may only be enforced against the vessel if the *in personam* defendant is still the owner of the vessel at the time of issue.[4] Maritime liens are true actions *in rem* and invisible: they are not subject to any scheme or registration and survive in the hands of a *bona fide* purchaser for value without notice, and are enforceable by an *in rem* claim. Besides being a charge on the ship, and thus enforceable against the owner or any subsequent purchaser, maritime liens differ from mortgages in not being required to be in a form prescribed by statute. Furthermore, maritime liens do not require registration to determine their priority over subsequent registered mortgages, as they have priority over all other maritime claims.

When advising the Privy Council in *The Bold Buccleugh*,[5] Sir John Jervis pointed out that maritime liens have their origin in civil law and noted that Lord Tenterden and Story J had defined a maritime lien as:

> A foundation of the proceeding *in rem* … Where such a lien exists … [it] gives a claim or privilege upon a thing to be carried into effect by legal process. This claim or privilege travels with the thing, into whosoever's possession it may come. It is inchoate from the moment the claim or privilege attaches, and when carried into effect by legal process, by a proceeding *in rem*, relates back to the period when it first attached.[6]

An international ship arrest is still conditioned according to the jurisdiction in which the arrest takes place, and the success of the arrest is determined by the applicable substantive laws of the place where the arrest takes place. Even if the procedural law allows arrest *in*

2 The term 'sister ship' is applied to vessels whose ownership is registered to the same legal entity. This is not always clear, because many ships have been separated into one-ship owning corporations to limit the liability of a single shipowner; see William Tetley, *Maritime Liens and Claims* (2nd edn, Les Éditions Yvon Blais Inc 1998) 1032; see also Sydney T Harley, *How to Secure a Maritime Lien: A Study* (Lampert & Selway 1981) 50–51.

3 George D Theocharidis, 'Jurisdiction for Provisional Relief under the Brussels Convention in the Maritime Context' (2002) 55 RHDI 453 *et seq*.

4 Aleka Mandaraka-Sheppard, *Modern Maritime Law Volume 1: Jurisdiction and Risks* (Informa 2013) 175.

5 *Harmer v. Bell (The Bold Buccleugh)* [1852] 7 Moo PC 267.

6 Discussed in Steven Rares, 'The Far from *Halcyon Isle*: Maritime Liens, Renvoi and Conflicts of Law' (2014) 28 MLAANZ Journal 1.

rem, the underlying claim may not be recognised as valid under the substantive law of the court. In addition, the order of priorities may rank the claim below others, even if it recognises the cause of action. After selling the vessel, the funds may not be enough to satisfy even a successful claim. But a state's substantive shipping law does not change a maritime claim to a lien. In short, a claimant may be successful on the merits but unsuccessful in recovering compensation. The claimant may then find that the claimed maritime lien is extinguished.[7]

Maritime liens receive a higher level of protection than other claims due to the right to attachment to the vessel itself, regardless of any change of ownership. The extent to which the holder of a ship mortgage or hypothecation faces the risk of being negatively affected by higher-ranking maritime liens depends on both the scope of the list of maritime liens under the relevant national law and the national law rules on the priority status of those maritime liens. Böger details the conflict of laws in the common law (private international law in civil law terms) concerning the governing law and the priority status of maritime liens. He provides three approaches leading to the application of the following: *lex fori*, since maritime liens are arguably primarily procedural; *lex causae* of the underlying maritime claim protected by the lien (the applicable law of its existence plus the *lex fori* determines its ranking among other security interests); and law of the flag.[8]

With regard to the civil law approach, three rules are provided for in civil procedure codes: (a) rules for a provisional pre-trial remedy (a conservatory measure to obtain security for a claim); (b) rules relating to establishing jurisdiction on the merits when there is a substantive link between the claim and the particular jurisdiction; and (c) rules relating to the status of some claims as preferred claims over unsecured creditors' claims.[9]

Therefore, a ship arrest differs between Spain and the UK. Under English law, only claims for crew wages, salvage and collision are to be brought against the vessel irrespective of its ownership (maritime lien). In contrast, in Spain under the SAMN, these claims are contained in Article 1 of the 1999 Arrest Convention. The pre-emptive embargo in civil law (a type of provisional measure) is defined as a maritime lien in common law. The arrest as such is a particular institution recognised in English law based on a maritime claim. Maritime liens against the offending ship are executed through 'attachment' after a judgment on such lien or credit, and constitute a security under English law.

According to Mandaraka-Sheppard,[10] an action *in rem* is deemed to enforce an existing maritime lien. The claimant becomes a secured creditor in relation to the vessel concerned. That interest will be enforceable against the purchasers of such property and is extinguished if the property is destroyed. The only security available is that property. The statutory extension to include liable property in most claims, enforced by an action *in rem* other than those attracting a maritime lien, reflects a proprietary interest

7 Robert W Lynn, 'A Comment on the New International Convention on Arrest of Ships, 1999' (2001) 55 U Miami L Rev 453, 460–461.

8 Ole Böger, 'The Case for a New Protocol to the Cape Town Convention Covering Security Over Ships' (2016) 5(1) Cape Town Convention Journal 73, 91.

9 Mandaraka-Sheppard (n 4) 24.

10 ibid 24–27.

in *all* appropriate assets of the defendant that could be seized as a security. Third parties should not be affected in their rights, so when the defendant appears the security shall be released.[11]

The enforceability of these claims in England and Wales is provided by s 20 of the Senior Courts Act 1981, which states the admiralty jurisdiction of the High Court is 'to hear and determine any of the questions and claims'. Under s 20(2), claims relating to the following subjects can be brought as *in rem* claims:

a) Possession or ownership (including claims between co-owners);
b) Claims between co-owners regarding the employment or earnings of the ship;
c) Mortgages or charges on a ship;
d) Damages received or done by a ship;
e) Loss of life or personal injury caused by any defect in a ship or through the fault or negligence of the owners, charterers or persons in possession or control of the ship. This category of claims includes the master or crew of a ship, as well as any third party falling within the category;
f) Loss of or damage to goods carried on a ship;
g) Arising out of any agreement relating to the carriage of goods on a ship or to the use or hire of a ship or towage and pilotage;
h) Salvage;
i) Goods or materials supplied for the ship's operation or maintenance;
j) Construction, repair or equipment of the ship, dock charges or dues;
k) Wages of the master or crew;
l) Disbursements made on account of a ship by a master, shipper, charterer or agent;
m) General average act;
n) Bottomry; and
o) Any claims for the forfeiture or condemnation of a ship or goods which are being, have been, or were attempted to be carried on a ship for the restoration of a ship or any such goods after seizure, or for droits of Admiralty.

The arrest has to be differentiated from recognised causes of action or a maritime lien as an enforceable interest being protected through an action *in rem* (typical from the common law jurisdictions), and the subsequent enforcement constituting a judicial sale to satisfy the claimed amount.[12] In civil law systems, the arrest of a ship is considered a kind of pre-trial attachment, so the ship may be arrested either to enforce a maritime lien or a personal claim against the shipowner. In both situations, there is a personal action directed against the shipowner and not against the vessel.[13]

In civil law jurisdictions, actions are addressed against a natural or legal person, combining *in personam* action with a *saisie conservatoire* or conservatory attachment to effect an arrest that allows the seizure of the debtor's property, such as the vessel, when there is

11 DC Jackson, *Enforcement of Maritime Claims* (4th edn, Informa 2013) 472.

12 William Tetley, 'Arrest, Attachment, and Related Maritime Law Procedures' (1998) 73 Tul L Rev 1895, 1898.

13 Caslav Pejovic, 'Civil Law and Common Law: Two Different Paths Leading to the Same Goal' (2001) 32(3) VUWLR 817.

a pending judgment.[14] In contrast with attachment in common law jurisdictions, a *saisie conservatoire* can be applied to other property and not just ships, extending arrest to most civil claims.[15]

In order to illustrate the relevance of the actions *in rem* in common law jurisdictions, let us consider an Australian case, *Brisbane Slipways Operations Pty Ltd v. Pantalon.*[16] The case dealt with a ship repair. The plaintiff had a cause of action against a defendant who was the charterer, not the shipowner as required by the case law. The plaintiff acted in good faith when commencing proceedings because the defendant had acted as if it had a proprietorial interest and had taken steps to perfect its apparent interest in order to claim ownership of the vessel. An Australian court granted a freezing order for funds paid by the defendant shipowner to secure the release of a vessel arrested beyond the court's jurisdiction as an action *in rem*. Improperly, this was brought together with an action *in personam*. The defendant joined proceedings and chose to plead to a contractual cause of action, as an original party to the agreement. The freezing order prevented the movement of funds and frustrated the jurisdictional process while the defendant's solicitors held the released money in a trust account. The action *in personam* succeeded even though the *in rem* claim was dismissed.[17]

Jurisdiction and security have become increasingly linked as issuing an action *in rem* carries with it an inbuilt remedy, that is, arrest.[18] The procedural approach of an action *in rem* has focused on the shipowners rather than the vessel since *The Indian Grace (No 2)*.[19] The significance of establishing a substantive claim *in personam*, that is, against the shipowner, has been stressed since this case, with the action *in rem* being a method of enforcement. In contrast to the view taken in *The Indian Grace (No 2)*, focusing on the action *in rem*, the Privy Council in *The Halcyon Isle*[20] held that a maritime lien is a procedural matter, ignoring its substantive characteristics. Moreover, the CJEU in *The Tatry* held that the substantive interests connected to an action *in rem* were disregarded, and concurrent actions *in rem* and *in personam* had no relevance at EU level, colliding with the subjective characterisation or personification concept.[21]

The enforcement of a lien is the primary justification for an arrest and action *in rem*. Liens have to be justified as a matter of policy, while an action *in rem* is the method of enforcing specified proprietary interests related to an asset against others that have different interests in that asset, and it is as a separate cause of action to enforce particular interests.[22]

An action *in rem* can even be persuasive or exhausted in order to induce a defendant to accept jurisdiction, continuing as an action *in personam*. Liability is attached to the property's existence and limited to its value. The rights created against third parties by a maritime

---

14 Tetley, 'Arrest, Attachment, and Related Maritime Law Procedures' (n 12).

15 Pejovic (n 13).

16 *Brisbane Slipways Operations Pty Ltd v. Pantaloni* [2010] FCA 654.

17 Kate Lewins and Ashwin Nair, 'International Recent Developments: Australia' (2012) 37 Tul Mar L J 559.

18 Jackson (n 11) 2.

19 *The Indian Grace (No 2)* [1997] 1 Lloyd's Rep 1; Jackson (n 11) 472.

20 *The Halcyon Isle* [1981] AC 221.

21 Case C-406/92 *Owners of the cargo lately laden on board the ship 'Tatry' v. Owners of the ship 'Maciej Rataj' (The Tatry)* [1994] ECR I-5439.

22 Jackson (n 11) ch 17.

lien or *in rem* claim are different from the substantive interests arising from a maritime lien or an action *in rem*. A lien (maritime or statutory) is a substantive interest enforced or created by the issue of an *in rem* claim and, if necessary, arrest and judicial sale.

In English law, the claim may include a lien and a method of enforcement (*in rem* or *in personam*): interlocutory and final remedies must be distinguished. The arrest of a ship is considered a security under English law, providing that the maritime lien holder maintains a sufficient interest in the ship in order to defend it as security, anticipating that the court orders a sale of the vessel to satisfy any award. The key elements are legal certainty and procedural law. However, we always assume that party autonomy is allowed to proceed, in regard to the consequences of a lawsuit. In Spain, on the other hand, SAMN provides for a negative example that shows, with regard to attributive clauses of jurisdiction, how over-regulation clashes with contractual freedom.[23]

1.2 Requirements for an arrest

The elements of precautionary measures are the risk in waiting (*periculum in mora*) and the reasonable prospect of success (*fumus boni iuris*), that is, a *prima facie* case for the claim. Whether this can benefit a judge or arbitrator is subject to the interpretations under continental and English legislation. The arrest of ships is a 'modern mixed legal institution' and 'several legal systems have departed from the universally recognised criteria such as in English law'. The reason is that the arrest of ships constitutes a component part of an action *in rem* under English law. It is viewed as a 'legal entitlement rather than a discretionary remedy'.[24]

In considering the requirements for the adoption of interim measures and whether their effectiveness is in accordance with conventional standards, this chapter will briefly compare the differences between the 1952 and the 1999 Arrest Conventions. It is common for P&I Clubs to provide security to avoid the arrest of a vessel, such as in LOUs. Jurisdiction is not determined by LOUs, but they often contain provisions on jurisdiction. There is a relationship between the 1952 Arrest Convention, the *in rem* jurisdiction of the court and Article 71 of the Brussels I Regulation (recast) which is in similar terms to Article 57 of the Brussels Convention and applies to claims under B/Ls.[25]

Bold tactics used by claimants, as shown in *The Kallang (No 2)*[26] or *The Duden*,[27] reflect the importance of the different tactics used, leading to the wrongful arrest of ships for the purpose of gaining time and avoiding the forum chosen by the parties. The old

23 Its worth consulting Juan José Álvarez Rubio and Unai Belintxon Martín, 'La Nueva Ley de Navegación Marítima desde la Perspectiva del Derecho Internacional' in Alberto Emparanza Sobejano and José Manuel Martín Osante (eds), *Comentarios Sobre la Ley de Navegación Marítima* (Marcial Pons 2015).

24 However, the criteria apply to freezing orders in relation to ships according to CJJA s 25; Verónica Ruiz Abou-Nigm, *The Arrest of Ships in Private International Law* (OUP 2011) 84.

25 Richard Aikens, Richard Lord and Michael Bools, *Bills of Lading* (2nd edn, Informa 2015) ch 14.

26 *Kallang Shipping SA v. Axa Senegal (The Kallang) (No 2)* [2008] EWHC 2761 (Comm), in which the defendant was not only seeking security but was using the arrest to frustrate the English arbitration and proceed in Senegal.

27 *Sotrade Denizcilik Sanayi ve Ticaret AS v. Amadou Lo (The Duden)* [2008] EWHC 2762 (Comm)

Evangelismos test developed by the Privy Council[28] requires proof by the shipowner of bad faith or *crassa negligentia*, implying malice on the part of the arresting party.[29]

An English court will not restrain a party to an English arbitration from arresting a vessel of the other party in another jurisdiction where the sole purpose of the arrest is to provide security for the English arbitration – as in *The Kallang*, where the cargo insurers tried to make the shipowner relinquish a London arbitration clause.[30] The cargo insurers were liable for damages on the basis of the tort of procuring breach of contract. The defendant also 'intended to procure a breach of contract'[31] in *OBG Ltd v. Allan.*[32] In the latter case, there was a wrongful arrest by inducement to breach the contract by unlawful means, distinguished from the loss in tort. In *The Duden*, the loss had been suffered by the bareboat charterer, a subsidiary, but not by the shipowner.[33]

2 Arrest of ships in the EU

Precautionary or interim measures and international shipping should be analysed through intra- and extra-EU judgments. A non-exhaustive comparative analysis of how to provide for the adoption of such measures within the scope of Brussels I Regulation (recast) offers much scientific value and originality to different states' legislation (in particular in comparison with the English vision, which is opposite to the continental perspective). This is done while considering the procedural, conflictual and material aspects of such measures.

Within the EU, provisional measures, including protective measures, were unlikely to be the subject of recognition and enforcement under Article 32 of the old Brussels I Regulation 44/2001, but they are now subject to this under the Brussels I Regulation (recast), contingent to a prior hearing of the defendant.[34] The choice of the judicial authority that will order the arrest is guided by domestic procedural rules.

The courts of the state where the arrest is applied for are also competent if proceedings to determine the merits of the dispute are commenced in a different jurisdiction. It could happen that different courts are competent for the arrest and the merits. The court of the country where the vessel is to be arrested has a separate subject matter for the claim and does not have the option of denying jurisdiction on the grounds of *lis alibi pendens*.[35] The need for an arrest may arise because the judgment or award is not yet enforceable or is not likely to be made enforceable before the departure of the ship from the territorial waters of the state where enforcement is sought. It is thought, in fact, that arrest is probably the most common protective measure.[36] The Brussels I Regulation (recast) provides that, in the

28 *The Evangelismos* (1858) 12 Moo PC 352; *Walter D Wallett* (1893) P 202.

29 Mandaraka-Sheppard (n 4) 158.

30 ibid 256–257.

31 Hugh Beale (ed), *Chitty on Contracts* (31st edn, Sweet & Maxwell 2012), ch 18-136, 1466.

32 [2007] UKHL 21, [8].

33 Mandaraka-Sheppard (n 4) 167–168.

34 Case 125/79 *Bernard Denilauler v. SNC Couchet Frères* EU:C:1980:130, [1980] ECR 1553.

35 The only precedent where the parties had such agreement was *Mike Trading and Transport Ltd v. R Pagnan Fratelli (The Lisboa)* [1980] 2 Lloyd's Rep 546.

36 See Francesco Berlingieri, *Berlingieri on Arrest of Ships Volume I: A Commentary on the 1952 Arrest Convention* (Informa 2017) 186.

event of an application for refusal of enforcement by the person against whom enforcement is sought, the court may, *inter alia*, limit enforcement proceedings to protective measures according to Article 44(1)(a).

In the case of an arrest of a ship initiated by a cargo interest B/L holder against the shipowner, if an EU court orders the arrest of a vessel (as in *The Tilly Russ*,[37] where there was a jurisdiction clause that, despite being printed on the reverse of the B/L, was deemed to be incorporated as an agreement in writing between the carrier and the shipper to which they intended to be bound) it ought to fulfil the following requirements:[38]

(i) Both parties signed the B/L;
(ii) The printed jurisdiction clause was specifically included in a prior oral or written agreement between the parties and the B/L acted as written confirmation; or
(iii) The clause was the product of an established course of dealing between the parties.[39]

Arbitration proceedings and court proceedings based mainly on arbitration were excluded from the Brussels I Regulation by Article 1(2)(d). The problems raised concern over the validity or existence of an arbitration agreement, the appointment of arbitrators and ancillary assistance to the arbitration proceedings, including the injunction to restrain a party from starting or continuing arbitral proceedings in breach of an arbitration agreement.

2.1 Compatibility of the Arrest Conventions with the Brussels I Regulation (recast)

The applicability and compatibility of the 1952 and 1999 Arrest Conventions have to be analysed under Article 71 of the Brussels I Regulation (recast). When a case needs to be governed by another convention,[40] the Brussels I Regulation (recast) regime is distorted and its Article 4 (domicile of the defendant in a Member State[41]) or Article 25 (exclusive jurisdiction agreements between the parties) cannot be invoked.[42] Clear compatibility rules provide a comfort zone for the legal operator. The 'rule of specialty' gives prevalence to certain specialised international conventions dealing with international jurisdiction over the rules of the Brussels I Regulation (recast).

The 'rule of specialty' follows the *lex specialis derogat lex generalis* principle. This means that the special rule prevails over the general one. The application of a specialised convention cannot be less favourable for an individual than the application of a general convention, since this would be against the proper functioning of the EU internal market.

37 Case 71/83 *Partenreederei ms Tilly Russ and Ernest Russ v. NV Haven- & Vervoerbedrijf Nova and NV Goeminne Hout (The Tilly Russ)* EU:C:1984:217, [1984] ECR 2417.

38 Under UKAA, s 5, the agreement shall be:

(i) Contained in writing whether signed or not by the parties;
(ii) Made by exchange of communications (including exchange of faxes, telexes, emails, etc);
(iii) Evidenced in writing.

39 Robert Force and Martin Davies, 'Forum Selection Clauses in International Maritime Contracts' in Martin Davies (ed), *Jurisdiction and Forum Selection in International Maritime Law* (Kluwer Law International 2005).

40 *The Tatry* (n 21) [28].

41 *The Anna H* [1995] 1 Lloyd's Rep 11.

42 *The Bergen* [1997] 1 Lloyd's Rep 380.

Therefore, the correct establishment of a transportation contract is according to Recital 4 of the Brussels I Regulation (recast):

> Certain differences between national rules governing jurisdiction and recognition of judgments hamper the sound operation of the internal market. Provisions to unify the rules of conflict of jurisdiction in civil and commercial matters, and to ensure rapid and simple recognition and enforcement of judgments given in a Member State, are essential.

In respect to other instruments, Article 71(1) of the Brussels I Regulation (recast) (formerly Article 57 of the Brussels and Lugano Conventions) clarifies that[43] – by virtue of a convention that governs jurisdiction or the recognition or enforcement of judgments – any forum will prevail over the forums provided by the Regulation itself, regardless of the non-ratification by the EU Member State in which the defendant is domiciled according to Article 72(2)(a). The same applies to the New York Convention, Article 73(2). Furthermore, while the specialised international conventions take precedence over the Brussels I Regulation (recast), the latter prevails over the domestic rules.[44]

However, it is unclear for the doctrine whether the 1999 Arrest Convention, unlike the 1952 Arrest Convention, does prevail over the Brussels I Regulation (recast) or not according to Article 71(1).[45] It shall be borne in mind that each treaty must be analysed individually in considering its applicability under the Brussels I Regulation (recast) in matters related to jurisdiction, recognition and enforcement of judgments. The judicial discretion of the CJEU has determined the application of the 'rule of specialty' to certain international conventions, but it still has not rendered any judgment concerning the prevalence or not of the 1999 Arrest Convention over the Brussels I Regulation (recast).[46]

In its case law, the CJEU has shaped the criteria in order to apply specialised conventions instead of the Brussels I Regulation (recast). A preliminary ruling concerning the interpretation of Article 71 of the Brussels I Regulation (recast) and Article 31 of the CMR Convention for road transport[47] was analysed by the CJEU in *TNT v. AXA*.[48] Paragraph 48 of the judgment states that Article 71 of the Brussels I Regulation (recast)

> is intended to ensure compliance with rules in whose enactment account was taken of the specific features of a particular matter … In the light of that objective, the Court has held that the rules laid down in specialised conventions have the effect of precluding the application of the provisions of the Brussels Convention relating to the same question.

According to *TNT v. AXA*, paragraph 51, citing *Nipponkoa*:[49]

> Article 71 of Regulation No 44/2001 cannot have a purport that conflicts with the principles underlying the legislation of which it is part. Accordingly, that article cannot be interpreted

43 Article 25 of the Rome I Regulation and Article 28 of the Rome II Regulation have the same wording as Article 71 of the Brussels I Regulation (recast).

44 Juan José Álvarez Rubio, 'La regla de especialidad como cauce para superar los conflictos normativos entre el Derecho comunitario y los Convenios internacionales en materias especiales' (2010) 7499 Diario La Ley 2.

45 José Luis Gabaldón García and José María Ruiz Soroa, *Manual de Derecho de la Navegación Marítima* (Marcial Pons 2006) 920 *et seq*.

46 cf Álvarez Rubio, 'La regla de especialidad como cauce para superar los conflictos normativos entre el Derecho comunitario y los Convenios internacionales en materias especiales' (n 44).

47 Convention on the Contract for the International Carriage of Goods by Road (CMR) 1956.

48 Case C-533/08 *TNT Express Nederland BV v. Axa Versicherung AG* EU:C:2010:243, [2010] ECR I-4107.

49 Case C-452/12 *Nipponkoa Insurance Co (Europe) Ltd v. Inter-Zuid Transport BV* EU:C:2013:858, [2014] 1 All ER (Comm) 288 [37].

> as meaning that, in a field covered by the Regulation, such as the carriage of goods by road, a specialised convention, such as the CMR, may lead to results which are less favourable for achieving sound operation of the internal market than those resulting from the provisions of the regulation at issue.

However, these principles have to be analysed in the light of the scope of application of the 1999 Arrest Convention and the Brussels I Regulation (recast). In fact, as Carballo Piñeiro highlights,

> the 1999 Arrest Convention lays down international jurisdiction rules along with uniform substantive rules. The latter are not included within the scope of the Brussels I Regulation (recast), meaning that Member States still hold exclusive competence for the ratification of the convention as regards these rules.[50]

The 1952 Arrest Convention also lacks uniform substantive rules.[51] Article 7(5) of the 1999 Arrest Convention lays down the rules determining the merits of the dispute following the warrant for arrest of a ship requiring that:

> a) The defendant has been given reasonable notice of such proceedings and a reasonable opportunity to present the case for the defence; and
> b) Such recognition is not against public policy.

However, the EU holds exclusive legislative competence concerning jurisdiction, as well as recognition and enforcement rules, according to CJEU Opinion 1/03.[52] The Brussels I Regulation (recast) has abolished the exequatur procedure in Article 39 but preserves the same grounds for refusal of the Brussels I Regulation in Article 46 (refusal of enforcement) in line with Brussels I Regulation 44/2001. If Spain, an EU Member State party to the 1999 Arrest Convention, renders a judgment the *favor executionis* principle could be compromised. The *favor executionis* principle clashes with the principle of the primacy (*primauté*) of EU law, since it cannot display any effect in case of conflict between EU and international law. The 1999 Arrest Convention does not belong exclusively to the EU legal system.

Tuo and Carpaneto[53] propose that Article 71 of the Brussels I Regulation (recast) should work as a coordination clause. The foundation is based on the application of the *règle de l'efficacité maximale* developed by French scholars, which 'consists in comparing the interests that each set of concurrent rules aims at protecting with a view to giving precedence to those of them which are deemed most capable of satisfying such interests to the maximum possible extent'.[54] Such rule would achieve the objectives of the Brussels I Regulation (recast) and the 1999 Arrest Convention. However, the doctrine[55] has set out, as

50 Laura Carballo Piñeiro, *International Maritime Labour Law* (Springer 2015) 34, 130–131.

51 Chiara Enrica Tuo and Laura Carpaneto, 'Connections and Disconnections between Brussels Ia Regulation and International Conventions on Transport Matters' (2016) 66 Zbornik PFZ 141, 162–164.

52 Opinion 1/03 of the CJEU of 7 February 2006, providing for the competence of the Community to conclude the new Lugano Convention on jurisdiction and the recognition and enforcement of judgments in civil and commercial matters EU:C:2006:81, [2006] ECR I-1145; cf. Carballo Piñeiro (n 50).

53 Tuo and Carpaneto (n 51).

54 Bernard Dutoit and Ferenc Majoros, 'Le lacis des conflits de conventions et leurs solutions possibles' (1984) 565 Rev crit. DIP (1984) 577.

55 Sergio Maria Carbone, 'Art. 2' in Fausto Pocar and others, *Commentario del nuovo diritto internazionale privato* (CEDAM 1996) 8, 12–14.

a prerequisite to such coordination mechanism, that the international commitments should be first respected.[56]

The Brussels I Regulation 44/2001 and its recast version shall not affect specialised conventions in order to allow EU Member States to respect their commitments to third states. As a rule of thumb, the CJEU follows the *favor executionis* principle when specialised conventions apply in order to provide a high degree of predictability and minimise the risk of *lis alibi pendens* or parallel proceedings in different states.[57] In this regard, paragraph 56 of *TNT v. AXA* set out that:

> Article 71 of Regulation No 44/2001 must be interpreted as meaning that, in a case such as the main proceedings, the rules governing jurisdiction, recognition and enforcement that are laid down by a specialised convention, such as the *lis pendens* rule set out in Article 31(2) of the CMR and the rule relating to enforceability set out in Article 31(3) of that convention, apply provided that they are highly predictable, facilitate the sound administration of justice and enable the risk of concurrent proceedings to be minimised and that they ensure, under conditions at least as favourable as those provided for by the regulation, the free movement of judgments in civil and commercial matters and mutual trust in the administration of justice in the European Union (*favor executionis*).

Carballo identifies the prevalence of the 1999 Arrest Convention according to Article 71 of the Brussels I Regulation (recast) as a 'complex dilemma that can only be resolved if the EU as a whole and individual EU Member States ratify the 1999 Arrest Convention'. Spain's ratification of the 1999 Arrest Convention took place prior to CJEU Opinion 1/03, *TNT v. AXA* and *Nipponkoa*, but after the Brussels I Regulation's entry into force.[58]

2.2 The arrest of ships of contracting and non-contracting states to the Arrest Conventions

If a vessel is flying the flag of another contracting state to the Arrest Conventions, the court of a contracting state will have the power to make a material arrest, since an arrest's provisional character in the Arrest Conventions is related to its temporary condition and its security function. It requires a reasonable prospect of success (*fumus boni iuris*) and a risk in waiting (*periculum in mora*), requiring an element of urgency.[59] *Periculum in mora* is presupposed when the arrest is sought and the *fumus boni iuris* when the party alleges its right.[60]

Concerning the arrest of a non-contracting state vessel by a contracting state court, national procedural rules may permit the arrest of such ship. But if the non-contracting state's company has its seat or is managed in that contracting state, interim relief may be

56 Tuo and Carpaneto (n 51).

57 Álvarez Rubio, 'La regla de especialidad como cauce para superar los conflictos normativos entre el Derecho comunitario y los Convenios internacionales en materias especiales' (n 44); Juan José Álvarez Rubio, 'Comentario a la sentencia del TJUE de 4 de mayo de 2010, Asunto C-533/08 *TNT Express Nederland BV c. AXA Versicherung AG*' (2011) 1 Revista Jurídica de Catalunya 266.

58 Carballo Piñeiro (n 50).

59 Ruiz Abou-Nigm (n 24) 78–91.

60 Belén Mora Capitán, 'El embargo preventivo de buques' in Alberto Emparanza Sobejano and José Manuel Martín Osante (eds), *Estudio sistemático de la propuesta de Anteproyecto de Ley General de la Navegación Marítima* (Servicio Central de Publicaciones del Gobierno Vasco 2006) 709, 715.

granted under Article 31 of the Brussels I Regulation (recast) in conjunction with national procedural rules.

The 'same' and 'related' actions must be distinguished: if actions are the same, the second court may be required to decline or stay its proceedings to avoid the risk of irreconcilable judgments. However, this would not happen in England since the claimant is not restrained from seeking the provisional remedies available in any jurisdiction. There is no room for irreconcilable judgments, since physical presence would be required in the first-seised court and security orders do not constitute a judgment on the merits of the dispute. Furthermore, in some civil law jurisdictions, it is possible to request arrest of a vessel irrespective of its physical presence within the territory of the court. All in all, if two proceedings take place in different EU Member State courts, reaching the vessel in the ports of the second, each Member State will decide under their national procedural rules whether to issue a warrant of arrest.

When a foreign company flags its vessel in a contracting state and the cargo claimant sues the shipowner in that contracting state, a *material* arrest may be granted according to the Arrest Convention. Furthermore, a *legal* arrest may be undertaken if the claimant sues the defendant according to the national procedural rules if that state's law provides for that. However, if the ship is berthing outside the territorial waters of the Arrest Convention and EU Member States, the court may provide interim relief outside the ambit of the Arrest Convention. The vessel must be within the territorial reach of the court that ordered the arrest.

If a company is not domiciled in an Arrest Convention contracting state, there is a possibility of invoking exorbitant jurisdiction (attributing international competence to the courts of a state without a reasonable connection) according to domestic jurisdictional rules. Once the conditions of Article 25 of the Brussels I Regulation (recast) are met, courts chosen by the parties shall have exclusive jurisdiction, as stated in *Gasser*.[61] The stay on the proceedings when a court is first seised on the main proceedings will have a limited impact on provisional and protective measures under Article 35 of the recast Regulation. This suggests that, even if the first court has to decide its own jurisdiction under Article 29 of the Brussels I Regulation (recast), interim relief may be provided according to Article 35.[62] However, Article 35 does not automatically grant jurisdiction.

2.3 Jurisdiction for arrest in non-EU states

Jurisdiction will be founded on domestic jurisdictional grounds if the defendant is domiciled in a non-EU state, and on the Brussels I Regulation (recast) grounds if it is domiciled in an EU Member State. The jurisdictional grounds of the Arrest Conventions prevail over those of the Brussels I Regulation (recast). The 1952 Arrest Convention only allows material arrest (see previous section) and not legal arrest when 'extreme urgency' is proved. When the vessel flagged in an Arrest Convention contracting state court is sailing out of reach of that court, a legal arrest will deter and impede the defendant from selling the

61 Case C-116/02 *Erich Gasser GmbH v. MISAT Srl* EU:C:2003:657, [2003] ECR I-14693.

62 Alexander Sandiforth, 'Jurisdiction Agreements and Anti-Suit Injunctions' (University of Southampton Institute of Maritime Law Conference, London, 27 January 2017).

vessel, limiting its proprietary rights, since the ship is registered in the state's shipping registry.

The Brussels I Regulation (recast) makes no distinction between actions *in rem* and *in personam*. An English 'Mareva injunction' or freezing order[63] *in personam* may deprive the shipowner of the possession of the ship, unless a sufficient link exists within England of it having sufficient means to cover the value of the claim by arresting sister ships and other assets, including bank accounts or any property abroad. Eventually, even if another EU Member State has started proceedings, the exorbitant forum provided by the freezing order will prevail. The Brussels I Regulation (recast) requires that a freezing order be provided *inter partes* but it operates *in personam*. The defendant can be deterred only from disposing of the property. This has minimal consequences if the defendant has no business in England.

The idea of requiring an *inter partes* procedure is reflected in Article 2(a) of the Brussels I Regulation (recast), where for the purposes of recognition and enforcement:

> "Judgment" includes provisional, including protective, measures ordered by a court or tribunal which by virtue of this Regulation has jurisdiction as to the substance of the matter. It does not include a provisional, including protective, measure which is ordered by such a court or tribunal without the defendant being summoned to appear, unless the judgment containing the measure is served on the defendant prior to enforcement.

The Brussels I Regulation (recast) does not define the nature of provisional measures, either in the Brussels Convention or in the Lugano Convention. The availability of such measures is left to national law. Accordingly, the Brussels I Regulation (recast)'s Recital 33 reinforces this idea:

> Where provisional, including protective, measures are ordered by a court having jurisdiction as to the substance of the matter, their free circulation to be ensured under this Regulation. However, provisional, including protective, measures which were ordered by such a court without the defendant being summoned to appear should not be recognised and enforced under this Regulation unless the judgment containing the measure is served on the defendant prior to enforcement. This should not preclude the recognition and enforcement of such measures under national law. Where provisional, including protective, measures are ordered by a court of a Member State not having jurisdiction as to the substance of the matter, the effect of such measures should be confined, under this Regulation, to the territory of that Member State.

The Brussels I Regulation (recast) does not prevail over the Arrest Conventions, but overlaps with them on many issues, contributing to limiting the applicability of the Arrest Conventions in the main proceedings. A claimant has many remedies at its disposal concerning ancillary proceedings, such as restraining the defendant from dealing with the assets or seizing the property (e.g., the ship). Both are possible in certain cases. But the judicially

63 The so-called Mareva injunction is named after a ship against which an injunction was issued, ordering that the debtor shall not remove the credit guarantee to the creditor: *Mareva Compania Naviera SA v. International Bulkcarriers SA* [1975] 2 Lloyd's Rep 509, CA. The freezing order is a judicial remedy that cannot be compared to the arrest in civil law systems; Christina Zournatzi, *Arbitrato e Contratti di Trasporto Marittimo* (Cedam 2014) 2–3. It is now regulated by s 37(1) and (3) Senior Courts Act 1981. The procedure has gradually evolved and was originally only allowed against a foreign debtor who had funds or properties in England; Frank Meisel, 'The Mareva Injunction – Recent Developments' [1980] LMCLQ 38. Only recently has it begun to be accepted, not without hesitation, that it may also be brought against an English debtor, following *Barclay-Johnson v. Yuill* [198] 3 All ER 190, as a remedy of a general nature. The absence of an interlocutory freezing order is known under English law – but not in North America, which has a writ of attachment.

produced remedies of the High Court of England and Wales can increase the effectiveness of other measures. The CJEU has strengthened the general rule of the Arrest Convention to arrest the vessel within the jurisdiction of the court that granted the measure.[64]

2.4 Jurisdiction for arrest in another EU Member State

Article 4 of the 1952 Arrest Convention provides for the physical arrest of the vessel within the geographical reach of a contracting state according to the national procedural rules of that state. The claimant may have multiple options, or be able to 'forum shop', but can the arrest order be enforced in another state where the ship is physically present? The recognition and enforcement conditions under the Brussels I Regulation (recast) must be examined.[65]

However, there is an alternative mechanism within EU Member States to allow the arrest of the ship ordered by an EU Member State court in another EU Member State territory. In *Allegro v. Fanty-GT*, the Rotterdam court[66] allowed *ex parte* leave to the owner of the Dutch-flagged pusher barge to arrest it in Germany or Austria due to an unpaid charter hire. The court granted the order for arrest because it was competent on the substance, according to the choice of forum clause included in the time charterparty. A conservatory measure for ownership rights was granted. The barge was not considered a ship within the meaning of the 1952 Arrest Convention, despite it flying a contracting state's flag. The conservatory attachment was enforceable abroad but the court did not issue a request for delivery of the barge.[67]

In *Allegro v. Fanty-GT*, it was provided that the judgment would be served on the debtor prior to enforcement. The court issued a certificate in accordance with Article 53 of the Brussels I Regulation (recast), under which 'the court of origin shall, at the request of any interested party, issue the certificate using the form set out in Annex I'. The judgment was enforceable, and the German and Austrian judicial authorities had to enforce it since the formalities of the Brussels I Regulation (recast) were observed. According to previous CJEU case law,[68] enforcement of such measures was not possible because they did not fall within the scope of chapter III of the Brussels I Regulation (recast). According to Article 2(a) of the Regulation, the requirements are that 'the court issuing the measure has jurisdiction as to the subject matter of the proceedings and provided the measure is served upon the defendant prior to enforcement'.[69] However, Recital 33 confines those measures ordered by an EU Member State court not having jurisdiction as to the substance of the matter to the territory of that Member State. As the Rotterdam court had jurisdiction as to the substance

64 Theocharidis, 'Jurisdiction for Provisional Relief under the Brussels Convention in the Maritime Context' (n 3).

65 ibid.

66 *Allegro BV v. Fanty-GT AD*, NL:RBROT:2015:3395.

67 Henning Jessen and George Theocharidis, 'National Translations of the Arrest Conventions: European Civil Law Jurisdictions' in Paul Myburgh (ed), *The Arrest Conventions: International Enforcement of Maritime Claims* (Hart 2019).

68 *Bernard Denilauler v. SNC Couchet Frères* (n 34).

69 Sebastiaan H Barten, 'Arresting vessels and attachment of other assets throughout Europe by "going Dutch" under the revised Brussels Regulation (*Lexology*, 2015) <www.lexology.com/library/detail.aspx?g=91b758d6-c590-47de-99c9-8328ba89db3f> accessed 20 August 2017.

of the matter, this case demonstrates that an EU-wide judgment for arrest was possible, even though the vessel was not located in the Netherlands. As Jessen and Theocharidis point out, this would contravene Article 4 of the 1952 Arrest Convention and the effectiveness of the national procedural laws of any EU or non-EU state.[70]

For example, in a hypothetical case an English shipper applies in England for a ship arrest in Italy. However, a warrant for arrest would require the vessel to be physically in England rather than in Italy, and the English courts would have no power under s 25 of the CJJA to grant interim relief. As in the previous Dutch case, in some continental systems it is possible to apply for the arrest of a vessel irrespective of its physical location. For example, if a shipper wants to arrest a ship in Spain, the vessel must arrive in a Spanish port; however, if the vessel moves to Denmark, the claimant may apply for arrest in Denmark as well. A Danish judge would then examine the conditions of the ship arrest under Danish procedural rules, even if the claimant tries to recognise the Spanish warrant in Spain. These are not irreconcilable judgments because they do not decide the merits of the case, and as protective measures are only applicable within the territory of each state. Therefore, the *lis alibi pendens* doctrine does not apply. If a claim form *in rem* is issued before a ship arrives at an English port, the claim form will expire one year after the date of issue, but there is the possibility of unlimited renewals.[71] Thus, if the *lis alibi pendens* doctrine did apply, a foreign court could be indefinitely prevented from hearing the case because the English court would always have jurisdiction based on such claim form *in rem*, leading to 'forum shopping'. The extraterritorial application of actions *in rem* within the EU falls within the scope of the Brussels I Regulation (recast).

2.5 The validity of the jurisdiction or arbitration clause for provisional measures

The effects and economic consequences of the arrest of ships and the recognition and validity of exclusive jurisdiction or arbitration clauses when the claimant issues a claim form *in rem* in an EU or non-EU state can vary, depending on the events involved.

Neither the Brussels I Regulation (recast) nor the Lugano Convention nor the Hague Choice of Court Convention tackles the issue of the validity of an arbitration clause. The Brussels I Regulation (recast) establishes requirements in Article 25, while the Lugano Convention requires a mere reference to the document containing the original jurisdiction agreement. Under the Hague Choice of Court Convention and the Brussels I Regulation (recast), the validity of such a clause is decided independently from that of the main contract, according to the *lex fori* and its conflict of laws rules. The effect of the applicability of such a clause on third parties is also decided by national law.

If there is a valid jurisdiction or arbitration agreement, other EU Member State courts have no jurisdiction over the substance of any dispute arising under the contract. Relief under Article 24 of the Brussels Convention cannot be provided for matters excluded from it, such as arbitration. The Contention will apply if the subject matter of court proceedings falls within its scope and the court proceedings are considered parallel to and not

70 For more information, see Jessen & Theocharidis (n 67).

71 Theocharidis, 'Jurisdiction for Provisional Relief under the Brussels Convention in the Maritime Context' (n 3).

ancillary to arbitral proceedings. The parties may try to exclude court jurisdiction completely, including proceedings brought before national courts. In such a case, if the court's jurisdiction is validly excluded, the parties cannot apply to the court for even provisional or protective measures, including proceedings ancillary to the arbitration. In such a case, parallel proceedings would still be subject to the Brussels I Regulation (recast) if their subject matter fell within the scope of the Brussels Convention.[72]

3 The arrest of ships: a comparative perspective

3.1 Arrest of ships in England

Regarding the procedural aspects in play concerning the arrest of ships in England, Aikens[73] considers that there are some linked procedural matters concerning the forum and applicable law for disputes involving a B/L. Actions *in rem* in England are heard by the Admiralty Court of the Queen's Bench division of the High Court and enable a vessel to be arrested to provide security for the underlying claim. The relevant parties and underlying contracts must be identified, as well as any valid choice of jurisdiction or arbitration clause (the applicable law). The claims that can be brought *in rem* and/or *in personam*, if the Brussels I Regulation (recast) or related conventions are applicable, must be equally identified, as well as the relevant procedure.[74] It must also be considered whether ancillary relief should be sought for a stay of court proceedings in favour of arbitration or an anti-suit injunction to avoid any party from initiating foreign proceedings, or a negative declaration.[75]

Aikens points out:

> Because the European regime is excluded by the invocation of the Arrest Convention, by the same token the English court's common law powers to stay an action must be preserved. Where there is an exclusive jurisdiction clause in favour of a Regulation country any English action *in rem* is likely to be stayed.[76]

In *The Nordglimt*,[77] it was held that under the Brussels Convention, *lis alibi pendens* (in relation to other EU Member State courts) does not preclude English courts from arresting a vessel – although, in the later case of *The Tatry*,[78] the contracting state participating in a convention of a specialised matter precluded the English courts from arresting a vessel. The *lis alibi pendens* provisions of the Brussels Convention were applicable as the 1952 Arrest Convention (applicable according to the rule of specialty of Article 57 of the

72 Christian A Heinze, 'Antisuit Injunctions in Support of Arbitration Proceedings and the Brussels Regulation – The Approach to Be Expected from the ECJ' (Seminar Series on Private International Law, British Institute for International and Comparative Law, 11 July 2007).

73 Aikens, Lord and Bools (n 25) ch 14.

74 Governed by the Civil Procedure Rules in England and Wales.

75 Aikens, Lord and Bools (n 25) ch 14.

76 ibid; *The Bergen* (No 2) [1997] 2 Lloyd's Rep 710.

77 *The Nordglimt* [1988] QB 183 (Hobhouse J):

> [I]t is permissible and proper that there should be an arrest of a vessel in one jurisdiction in support of a determination of the merits of a dispute by a court of competent jurisdiction in another contracting state and to provide security for the satisfaction of the judgment given by that court.

78 *The Tatry* (n 40).

Brussels Convention, currently Article 71 of the Brussels I Regulation (recast)) does not have any similar provisions.[79]

An order of arrest does not have to be issued in *ex parte* proceedings to be considered a judgment under the Brussels I Regulation (recast), but the Regulation's *lis alibi pendens* rules are seldom applied in these circumstances. The *Italian Leather* case recognised the possibility of recognising and enforcing a provisional (interim) measure.[80] The CJEU, interpreting Article 27(3) of the Brussels Convention, now Article 45(1)(c) of the Brussels I Regulation (recast), found that it was 'seised with two decisions of equal status and underlined that an interim judgment granting the measure conflicted with an interim measure refusing it'.[81]

Where a ship is arrested in England in support of an existing claim in another EU Member State, the English *in rem* proceedings will usually be stayed, in accordance with the Brussels I regime, although the court can order the retention of security under the court's discretion in s 26 of the CJJA. The discretionary power under s 26 of the CJJA also authorises an English court to dismiss proceedings *in rem* that have the single aim of obtaining security in support of substantive proceedings before a court of a foreign country or arbitration, whereas proceedings that are truly *in rem* are considered a matter of right. The property may be arrested and restrained as security for the satisfaction of a future judgment or award. A claimant who successfully starts *in rem* proceedings to secure a claim is not obliged to have the substantive claim heard by the Admiralty Court, and the claimant may apply to stay the substantive proceedings. The same possibility is available to the defendant.[82]

If a stay is ordered, the arrest or maintenance of any security may continue unless the court orders otherwise. This applies when the merits of the case are to be submitted to non-EU state courts, as *lis alibi pendens* only applies between EU Member State courts under Article 31 of the Brussels I Regulation (recast). An arrest can take place in England months or, exceptionally, years after the *in rem* claim form is issued.[83]

The *lis alibi pendens* rule applies between EU Member State courts under Article 31 of the Brussels I Regulation (recast). Articles 33 (*lis alibi pendens*) and 34 (related actions) of the Brussels I Regulation (recast) refer to actions or proceedings between EU and non-EU state courts. However, they are only applicable to actions and contested provisional proceedings (including default proceedings). Provisional measures are not judgments on the merits and do not require unification between countries. Even if two warrants for arrest

---

79 Berlingieri points out that in the judgment of the Tribunal of Ravenna, 15 June 2004, *Goldfish Shipping SA v. Odin Denizcilik Anonim Sirketi (The Pacific Trust ex Ahmet Bay)* (2005) Dir Marit 1423, 'an application for the arrest of a ship' was

> made by the same claimant in respect of the same claim in different jurisdictions and that the two actions may be pending at the same time before courts competent according to article 4 of the 1952 Arrest Convention because the ship has subsequently called at ports in two different countries. (*Berlingieri on Arrest of Ships* (n 36) 170–171)

80 Case C-80/00 *Italian Leather SpA v. WECO Polstermöbel GmbH & Co* EU:C:2002:342, [2002] ECR I-4995.

81 *Berlingieri on Arrest of Ships* (n 36) 171; Stéphanie Francq, 'Article 34' in Ulrich Magnus and Peter Mankowski (eds), *Brussels I Regulation* (2nd edn, Sellier 2012) 692.

82 Ruiz Abou-Nigm (n 24) 78–91.

83 ibid.

are granted (e.g., one in the UK, and another one in Greece, a country where the physical presence of a vessel in its territorial waters is not necessary to issue a warrant for arrest) the vessel may only be arrested in the country in which it is present.[84]

Even without the 1952 Arrest Convention, there would seem to be no reason why an arrest under CPR 61 in support of the proceedings of another EU Member State (in combination with Article 71 of the Regulation) should not be permitted under Article 35 of the Brussels I Regulation (recast):

> Application may be made to the courts of a Member State for such provisional, including protective, measures as may be available under the law of that Member State, even if the courts of another Member State have jurisdiction as to the substance of the matter.[85]

An arrest under English law (CPR 61.5) is not considered an interim remedy, and thus, should not be considered a 'protective or provisional' remedy within the meaning of Article 35 of the Brussels I Regulation (recast).[86] Nevertheless, Article 7 of the 1952 Arrest Convention prevails over Articles 4, 35 and 42(2) (enforcement of provisional, including protective, measures) of the Brussels I Regulation (recast).[87] The direct enforcement of the judgment (or the award) after the event by an *in rem* action raises some issues of *res judicata* and merger principles. The parties may prevent admission of evidence on the factual background by inserting a so-called merger clause[88] in their contract, stating that the document contains the entire contract.[89]

The claimant may re-litigate an *in rem* claim in full, even where the *in personam* claim is partially satisfied. There is a potential for double dipping.[90] In order to enforce judgments arising from B/L claims, freezing orders at a national or international level are discretionary and can provide protection to the defendant and third parties. The Third Parties (Rights against Insurers) Act 2010 (in force from 1 August 2016) is undermined by the carriers'

---

84 Theocharidis, 'Jurisdiction for Provisional Relief under the Brussels Convention in the Maritime Context' (n 3).

85 Nigel Meeson and John Kimbell, *Admiralty Jurisdiction and Practice* (4th edn, Informa 2013) 152–153.

86 ibid.

87 See Jessen & Theocharidis (n 67).

88 Under Article 2(17) of the UNIDROIT Principles of International Commercial Contracts (2016 edition):

> 'A contract in writing which contains a clause indicating that the writing completely embodies the terms on which the parties have agreed cannot be contradicted or supplemented by evidence of prior statements or agreements. However, such statements or agreements may be used to interpret the writing.

Moss states: Article 2.17

> recognises the validity of so-called merger clauses, provisions in which the parties affirm that their entire agreement is contained in the contract and that no other documents or evidence shall be admitted add to or modify the content of the contract. This clause is interpreted literally in the English system … and it reinstates the effects of the parol evidence in full. Unlike English law, the UNIDROIT Principles affirm that extrinsic evidence can still be produced in respect of the interpretation (i.e. establishing the meaning rather than the content) of the contract, even if the contract contains a merger clause. (Giuditta Cordero Moss, 'International Contracts between Common Law and Civil Law: Is Non-state Law to Be Preferred? The Difficulty of Interpreting Legal Standards such as Good Faith' (2007) 7(1) Global Jurist 3)

89 *McGrath v. Shaw* (1987) 57 P & CR 452.

90 Paul Myburgh, 'Private International Law (Conflicts) Issues in Maritime Litigation' (2nd Advanced Seminar on International Maritime Law, University of Athens, 28 May 2016).

standard P&I cover, which includes the 'pay to be paid' provision.[91] Third parties such as cargo interests (and cargo insurers) can rely on the insured's insurance policy, having the right to obtain information and act directly to recover damages.[92]

3.2 Arrest of ships in Spain

The 1999 Arrest Convention came into force in Spain on 14 September 2011, providing for jurisdiction based on arrest in combination with the new SAMN. There are some compatibility issues with Articles 33 to 35 of Brussels I Regulation (recast) regarding provisional and precautionary measures. Article 470 SAMN[93] sets the nature of such a measure, referring to the arrest of ships through the established application of the 1999 Arrest Convention, to the provisions of the law itself and additionally, to the provisions of the SLCP. The Article does not make any reference to the SOLJ or EU law. This is a surprising gap, since matters falling within the scope of the Brussels I Regulation (recast) displace national rules. This necessarily leads to the arrest in the port where the vessel is located. Article 35 of Brussels I Regulation (recast) states that the

> application may be made to the courts of a Member State for such provisional, including protective, measures as may be available under the law of that Member State, even if the courts of another Member State have jurisdiction as to the substance of the matter.

This interpretation has raised the question of whether the signing of the 1999 Arrest Convention by Spain might be a breach of EU law affecting the recognition and enforcement of judgments in civil and commercial matters, without any reservations regarding the application of the *lex fori* as grounds of jurisdiction to hear the merits of the case (Article 7). Three issues should be noted including the arrest for maritime claims in Article 472(1),[94] the arrest for other claims in Article 473 and the duty to initiate a process of constitution of the limitation fund within 10 days for every person who claims the right to limit liability according to Article 488 (invocation and term of constitution)[95] in civil proceedings.[96]

Article 472(1) SAMN defines ordinary maritime claims. Maritime liens set out in Article 4(1) of the MLM Convention 1993[97] are considered privileged claims:

---

91 The Spanish Law on Insurance Contracts 1980 and the Spanish Criminal Code, approved by the Organic Law 10/1995 of 23 November 1995 (Official State Gazette No 281 on 24th November 1995), constitute the analogous legislation in Spain; see *The London Steamship Owners Mutual Insurance Association Ltd v. Spain (The Prestige)* (No 2) [2015] EWCA Civ 333.

92 Aikens, Lord and Bools (n 25) ch 14.

93 Article 470(1) provides: 'The precautionary measure of arrest of ships, both domestic and foreign, will be regulated by the International Convention on Arrest of Ships, adopted in Geneva on March 12, 1999, by the provisions of this law and, additionally, so established in Law 1/2000 of 7 January, civil procedure'.

94 '1. In addition to decree arrest of a ship for maritime credit as defined in Article 1 of the International Convention on Arrest of Ships, it shall suffice to allege the right or claims claimed, the cause that gives rise to these and that the ship may be arrested'.

95 '1. All persons who invoke the right to limit the liability claimed in civil proceedings shall commence formalities to constitute a limitation fund within the maximum term of ten days from the invocation.

2. To that end, they shall file an application to constitute the fund, in the manner determined in this Act, before the same Court that hears the claim, which shall be processed in a separate Section to the main suit'.

96 Álvarez Rubio and Belintxon Martín (n 23).

97 International Convention on Maritime Liens and Mortgages (adopted 6 May 1993, entered into force 5 September 2004) 2276 UNTS 39 (MLM Convention).

Each of the following claims against the owner, demise charterer, manager or operator of the vessel shall be secured by a maritime lien on the vessel:

(a) Claims for wages and other sums due to the master, officers and other members of the vessel's complement in respect of their employment on the vessel, including costs of repatriation and social insurance contributions payable on their behalf;
(b) Claims in respect of loss of life or personal injury occurring, whether on land or on water, in direct connection with the operation of the vessel;
(c) Claims for reward for the salvage of the vessel;
(d) Claims for port, canal and other waterway dues and pilotage dues;
(e) Claims based on tort arising out of physical loss or damage caused by the operation of the vessel other than loss of or damage to cargo, containers and passengers' effects carried on the vessel.

These privileged maritime claims correspond with the ordinary claims defined under Article 472 SAMN by reference to Article 1 of the 1999 Arrest Convention (which contains a longer list than the 1952 Arrest Convention):

(a) Loss or damage caused by the operation of the ship;
(b) Loss of life or personal injury occurring, whether on land or on water, in direct connection with the operation of the ship;
(c) Salvage operations or any salvage agreement, including, if applicable, special compensation relating to salvage operations in respect of a ship which by itself or its cargo threatened damage to the environment;
(d) Damage or threat of damage caused by the ship to the environment, coastline or related interests; measures taken to prevent, minimise, or remove such damage; compensation for such damage; costs of reasonable measures of reinstatement of the environment actually undertaken or to be undertaken; loss incurred or likely to be incurred by third parties in connection with such damage; and damage, costs, or loss of a similar nature to those identified in this subparagraph (d);
(e) Costs or expenses relating to the raising, removal, recovery, destruction or the rendering harmless of a ship which is sunk, wrecked, stranded or abandoned, including anything that is or has been on board such ship, and costs or expenses relating to the preservation of an abandoned ship and maintenance of its crew;
(f) Any agreement relating to the use or hire of the ship, whether contained in a charterparty or otherwise;
(g) Any agreement relating to the carriage of goods or passengers on board the ship, whether contained in a charterparty or otherwise;
(h) Loss of or damage to or in connection with goods (including luggage) carried on board the ship;
(i) General average;
(j) Goods, materials, provisions, bunkers, equipment (including containers) supplied or services rendered to the ship for its operation, management, preservation or maintenance;
(k) Construction, reconstruction, repair, converting or equipping of the ship;
(l) Disbursements incurred on behalf of the ship or its owners;
(m) Insurance premiums (including mutual insurance calls) in respect of the ship, payable by or on behalf of the shipowner or demise charterer;
(n) Any commissions, brokerages or agency fees payable in respect of the ship by or on behalf of the shipowner or demise charterer;
(o) Mortgage or a 'hypothèque' or a charge of the same nature on the ship [not being privileged claims defined in Article 1 of the MLM Convention].

In comparison, Article 1(1) of the 1952 Arrest Convention has a narrower list of maritime claims arising out of the damage to the ship, loss of life and salvage.

Special maritime claims (not falling within the other two categories) are also contained in Article 1 of the 1999 Arrest Convention. These include disputes over ownership and employment/earnings, mortgages and disputes arising out of the sale of a ship.

Article 4(2) of the MLM Convention identifies some exclusions from Article 4(1), including pollution and radioactivity claims, which are dealt with under international law or mandatory provisions.

The backbone of the 1999 Arrest Convention (the arrest of the vessel) is contained in Article 3, which provides a more restrictive general rule than the one provided by the 1952 Arrest Convention: the shipowner must be the debtor when the arrest takes place,[98] or the 'demise charterer of the ship at the time when the maritime claim arose is liable for the claim and is demise charterer or owner of the ship when the arrest is effected'.[99] Mora Capitán criticises the confusing precept under which the ship could be sold while under arrest in accordance with the 1999 Arrest Convention.[100]

In Article 473 SAMN (in similar terms to Article 3(2) of the 1999 Arrest Convention), the arrest of sister ships is allowed when the maritime credit was obtained by the debtor who was 'the owner, demise charterer, manager or operator of the vessel':[101]

1. Arrest of Spanish ships that are physically within the Spanish jurisdiction, ordered on application by persons who have their usual residence or main establishment in Spain, or who have acquired the credit concerned by cession or subrogation of such, may be decreed both for the maritime claims as well as for any other rights or claims against the debtor pertaining to the ship or ships whose seizure is requested.
2. Spanish ships may also be arrested by the competent administrative body pursuant to the terms set forth in the specific provisions applicable.
3. In the arrests to which the preceding Section refers, the arrest may be replaced, at the discretion of the competent jurisdictional or administrative body, by an annotation of the measure on the Register of Moveable Assets and, where appropriate, of prohibition on disposal.
4. Arrest of ships flying the flag of a State that is not a party to the [1999 Arrest Convention], shall be governed by the provisions of that Convention, notwithstanding it being possible for them to be arrested both for maritime claims as well as for any other claims.

---

98 Article 3(1)(a) of the 1999 Arrest Convention:

> Arrest is permissible of any ship in respect of which a maritime claim is asserted if the person who owned the ship at the time when the maritime claim arose is liable for the claim and is owner of the ship when the arrest is effected.

99 Article 3(1) of the 1999 Arrest Convention also states:

> (c) the claim is based upon a mortgage or a 'hypothèque' or a charge of the same nature on the ship; or
> (d) the claim relates to the ownership or possession of the ship; or
> (e) the claim is against the owner, demise charterer, manager or operator of the ship and is secured by a maritime lien which is granted or arises under the law of the state where the arrest is applied for.

100 Mora Capitán, 'El embargo preventivo de buques' (n 60).

101 Eduardo Albors Méndez and Javier Portales Rodríguez, 'Embargo Preventivo De Buques' in Alberto Emparanza Sobejano and José Manuel Martín Osante (eds), *Comentarios Sobre la Ley de Navegación Marítima* (Marcial Pons 2015).

Article 472(2) SAMN determines the minimum amount of the required guarantee (of any class recognised by law, e.g., a bank guarantee) as '15 per cent of the alleged maritime claim', to order the arrest by the judge. The aim is to ensure responsibility for damages and costs that might be incurred. Article 473(3) concerns the seizure of vessels that fly the flag of a state that is not a party of the 1999 Arrest Convention, stating that such arrests are governed by the 1999 Arrest Convention. Furthermore, these vessels may be seized for any type of credit, including maritime ones. Spain made a reservation to the 1999 Arrest Convention in accordance with Article 10(1)(b), reserving the right to exclude the application of the 1999 Arrest Convention to ships that do not fly the flag of a state party.[102]

4 Arbitration and the arrest of ships

4.1 Party autonomy and shipping arbitration

Freedom of contract is imperative to business and must play a part in private international law. Synonymous with freedom of contract is the principle of party autonomy in contractual bargaining. Both principles enjoy global, universal support. With respect to jurisdiction, a party's autonomy to negotiate a convenient jurisdiction for its business is not only beneficial in that it achieves clarity but it may also contribute to the actual value of the contract.

Maritime arbitration, as the doctrine stands,[103] not only covers the transport sector under a charterparty but also matters related to ship collisions. The parties' choice of jurisdiction is further subject to restriction, because if there was another international convention in which the Member State was participating when the Brussels I Regulation (recast) came into force, which 'in relation to particular matters, govern[s] jurisdiction or the recognition or enforcement of judgments, the other conventions will prevail over the EU Jurisdiction Regulation if it conflicts'.[104] Such conventions of great significance (in relation to the carriage of goods by sea) include the International Convention on Certain Rules relating to Civil Jurisdiction in Matters of Collision 1952, the 1952 Arrest Convention and the 1999 Arrest Convention, which facilitates the arrest of the vessel based in the *forum arresti* in the absence of an arbitration agreement.

The approach taken to jurisdiction and arbitration clauses in the Arrest Conventions differs. The 1952 Arrest Convention refers to the domestic law of the state where a vessel has been arrested; the 1999 Arrest Convention gives priority to jurisdiction and arbitration clauses.

In certain jurisdictions, arbitral tribunals are granted the power to issue provisional and protective measures, including arrest. The exercise of such powers is in conflict with Article 4 of the 1952 Arrest Convention and, therefore, within the scope of application of such conventions, arrest may not be ordered by an arbitral tribunal. However, an arbitration agreement may state that the parties agree that arbitration proceedings must be conducted in accordance with the RMAC. In this case, the authority of the arbitral tribunal could be deemed to emanate from the arbitration agreement and, consequently, the parties could be

102 Álvarez Rubio and Belintxon Martín (n 23).
103 Jonathan Hill, *The Law Relating to International Commercial Disputes* (Informa 1994) 457 *et seq.*
104 Yvonne Baatz, 'Jurisdiction and Arbitration in Multimodal Transport' (2011) 36 Tul Mar LJ 643.

deemed to have authorised the tribunal to order the arrest, so the arrest might be considered as having a contractual origin.[105]

4.2 A procedural approach to maritime arbitration in England

The need for uniformity and legal certainty often leads to the choice of English law as the applicable law in voyage and time charterparty contract arbitration. Arbitration is also found in construction and sale of ships contracts, as well as in contracts related to the possession, holding or share ownership of the vessel. Equally, cooperation agreements among companies in the maritime transport sector provide for arbitration as the dispute resolution tool in their agreements. Arbitration is also provided in the Rules of P&I Clubs for any dispute between the Club and registered owners.

In England, the validity and the effect of an arbitration agreement are governed by provisions of the UKAA. In *The Deichland*, security was given to avoid arrest.[106] Since the defendant was domiciled in an EU Member State, the Court of Appeal held that the Brussels Convention applied, rather than the Arrest Convention. The claimant (to an *in rem* action) could not rely on Article 57 of the Brussels Convention,[107] which would have given primacy to the 1952 Arrest Convention, as Article 7 of the 1952 Arrest Convention does, since there was no actual arrest of a vessel and security was provided to avoid an arrest.

The Brussels Convention does not make any specific reference to an action *in rem*, and the defendant is liable *in personam*, in the same way as under English law. The defendant charterer will have to be sued in the court of its domicile and, if the domicile was in the UK, the Convention would have no relevance to an action *in rem*. The Convention is only concerned with the allocation of jurisdiction – not the methods of its exercise.[108]

After the 1952 Convention entered into force, we find legislative references to arbitral dispute settlements, particularly from the Comité Maritime International (CMI), the International Maritime Organization (IMO), and the Commissions of the United Nations (UNCTAD[109] and UNCITRAL), according to the type of reference made to arbitration. That reference can be as simple as recognising only the parties' opportunity to refer their disputes to arbitration articulated when the conventions provide such an opportunity to the parties, or the conditions for such a referral. In English law, in fact, the judgment rendered in *The Cap Bon*[110] case created sufficient legal precedent to prevent a grant of any kind of guarantee under arbitration to the exclusion – even for the possibility of ordering a precautionary measure – of alternative security when dealing with a foreign arbitration.

Following the entry into force, on 20 September 1984, of the CJJA, there was a new framework, giving courts the possibility of issuing deliberate precautionary measures to protect the rights of the parties in an arbitration hearing. Section 26 CJJA satisfactorily

105 Francesco Berlingieri, *International Maritime Conventions (Volume 2)* (Informa 2014) 246–258.
106 [1990] 1 QB 361.
107 See Article 71 of the Brussels I Regulation 44/2001 and Article 71 of the Brussels I Regulation (recast) in similar terms.
108 Jackson (n 11) 116.
109 United Nations Conference on Trade and Development.
110 *The Cap Bon* [1967] 1 Lloyd's Rep 543 *et seq.*

settled the question of granting an interim relief, in both domestic and foreign arbitrations, implementing the precautionary measures issued or ordering provisional measures:

> (1) Where in England and Wales or Northern Ireland a court stays or dismisses Admiralty proceedings on the ground that the dispute in question should be submitted to the determination of the courts of another part of the United Kingdom or of an overseas country, the court may, if in those proceedings property has been arrested or bail or other security has been given to prevent or obtain release from arrest –
> (a) order that the property arrested be retained as security for the satisfaction of any award or judgment which
> (i) is given in respect of the dispute in the legal proceedings in favour of which those proceedings are stayed or dismissed; and
> (ii) is enforceable in England and Wales or, as the case may be, in Northern Ireland; or
> (b) order that the stay or dismissal of those proceedings be conditional on the provision of equivalent security for the satisfaction of any such award or judgment.

Before the enactment of s 26 CJJA, when a ship was arrested for the purpose of obtaining security in satisfaction of an arbitration award, a court had a wide discretion either to release the ship from arrest by setting aside the warrant of arrest or to maintain the arrest until security was provided, if the claimant showed that an arbitration award in its favour would be unlikely to be satisfied by the defendant.[111] If the discretion were exercised in favour of ordering security to be provided, the claimant would thereafter pursue the action *in rem* to enforce the security. Such a wide discretion was abolished by s 26 CJJA, and, later, a similar provision was included (s 11) in the UKAA. If a ship has been arrested, the court can still order security under s 11 UKAA. However, s 26 CJJA is, naturally, wider in scope than s 11 UKAA, in that it empowers a court to make the same orders when the dispute should be submitted to another court, either in the UK or overseas.[112]

Both sections provide that, where Admiralty proceedings are stayed on the ground that the dispute in question should be submitted to arbitration and property has been arrested, the court may: (a) order that the property or security provided be retained for the satisfaction of the award or (b) order that the stay of the proceedings be conditional on the provision of equivalent security for the satisfaction of any such award. The maintenance of arrest is discretionary.[113]

A party subject to English arbitration may seek to arrest the vessel of the other party with the only intention of providing security and English courts will not impede it, as seen in *The Kallang (No 2)*[114] where the cargo receivers' insurance company arrested a ship in Senegal, not with the intention of obtaining security but to oblige the shipowners to relinquish a London arbitration clause. Section 26(2) CJJA allows the court to attach any other conditions when it makes orders under s 26(1), such as the prompt commencement

111 *The Rena K* [1978] 1 Lloyd's Rep 545; *The Vasso* [1984] 1 Lloyd's Rep 235 (CA); *The Tuyuti* [1984] 2 Lloyd's Rep 51 (CA).

112 Mandaraka-Sheppard (n 4) 256–257.

113 *The Bazias 3 and The Bazias 4* [1993] 1 Lloyd's Rep 101.

114 *The Kallang* (No 2) (n 26), in which the defendant was not simply seeking security but was using the arrest to frustrate the English arbitration and proceed in Senegal.

of the arbitration. However, the content of s 26(2) has been omitted from s 11 UKAA. The main reason is because, under the UKAA, it is for the arbitrators to enforce their directions and orders, and not the court (other than when the court's assistance is sought under s 44 UKAA). Since the stay of judicial proceedings is mandatory in all cases under the UKAA, it is difficult to see how any condition on the lifting of a stay could lawfully be imposed by the court. As the court has no right to refuse a stay, it cannot have any right to impose conditions on the grant of a stay, so that, on ordering the stay, the arrest must either be maintained or discharged. Its inclusion would have caused difficulties with regard to non-domestic arbitration under the New York Convention, which prevents the grant of a stay being made subject to any conditions.[115]

Regarding the power of the court under s 44 UKAA (which is relevant to this issue under s 11), there is an exceptional English case, *Phaethon International Co Sa v. Ispat Industries Ltd*, where Males J granted a mandatory injunction for the release of a ship from arrest in Mumbai, exercising jurisdiction under his discretion according to ss 44(1)(e) and 44(3) UKAA.[116] An Indian court instituted arrest proceedings in contempt of a previous order of the High Court of England and Wales, without disclosing the existence of the order to the court. The applicant shipowner sought an order for steps to be taken to ensure the release of its vessel from arrest in Mumbai.

The vessel was chartered to the respondent shipowner under a GENCON charterparty that contained a lien clause that extended to freight and damages for detention. The charterparty contained a London arbitration clause. According to the charterparty and B/L terms, the conduct of the respondent in arresting the vessel was unlawful. The court in Mumbai was misled and was not aware of the charterparty and B/L terms when ordering the arrest. An English court will not circumvent the power of the arbitrators to make orders under s 44, for example, orders for disclosure.[117]

In *NB Three Shipping Ltd v. Harebell Shipping Ltd*,[118] English courts had jurisdiction to hear any dispute between the parties according to the charterparty terms. However, any dispute that was not resolved under mutual agreement could be brought to arbitration by the shipowners, acting unilaterally. Such asymmetrical clause was enforced and the High Court stayed the judicial proceedings.[119] Morrison held (at para 14):

> As to the claim for section 44 relief, I am bound to say that I can see no grounds for making the orders sought. Disclosure of documents is a matter for the arbitrators; they have the necessary powers; if early disclosure is thought to be desirable then an application can be made to them for that relief. A mandatory order at this time was not appropriate.[120]

115 Mandaraka-Sheppard (n 4) 256–257.

116 *Phaethon International Co Sa v. Ispat Industries Ltd* [2010] EWHC 3466 (Comm).

117 Mandaraka-Sheppard (n 4) 77.

118 [2005] Lloyd's Rep 509.

119 A stay of the arbitral proceedings was granted in a similar case, *Law Debenture Trust Corp Plc v. Elektrim Finance BV and others* [2005] EWHC 1412 (Ch). All the parties were entitled to refer any dispute to arbitration, but the trustees had the option to litigate. Hakeem Seriki, *Injunctive Relief and International Arbitration* (Informa 2015) 9.

120 Mandaraka-Sheppard (n 4) 256–257.

The Duden represents another relevant example where the claimant pursued the arrest of a ship in order to obtain security and avoid arbitral proceedings in England.[121] The cargo insurer's conduct, knowledge and intent was to use arrest as a means of forcing the shipowner to accept Senegalese jurisdiction in order to make the insurer liable for the accessory tort of procuring the cargo receivers' breach of the relevant arbitration clause, which included an express agreement for London arbitration. Applying *The Kallang*[122] (arrest of a ship is intended to force the other party to avoid the chosen forum), the court held that, if a party seeks to use a foreign arrest for purposes beyond obtaining reasonable security for an arbitration claim, it will be in breach of the express agreement. An anti-suit injunction was granted.[123]

Aikens considers that there is confusion between a lien and the method of enforcement, phrased under the question of whether an action *in rem* will suffice to enforce an award or not. In *The Bumbesti*, it was held that an action to enforce an arbitration award on a charterparty claim could not be categorised as based on the claim itself so as to be enforceable by an action *in rem* under the Senior Courts Act 1981, s 20(2)(h).[124]

This isolates the award from its context and meaning. As a consequence, the statutory lien ends with an arbitration award but not under the civil rules of procedure by a judgment. Such a divergence is not only difficult to defend but also must make arbitration less attractive. If the claim submitted to arbitration attracts a maritime lien, admiralty jurisdiction depends on the continuation of the lien under s 20(3) of the Senior Courts Act. If, as argued above, that continues until satisfaction of the claim, an award will affect neither the lien nor any power of arrest.[125] The idea of limiting the enforceability of an arbitration award through admiralty jurisdiction and the arrest of vessels by reference to separability is nonsense. The result in *The Bumbesti* may be justified as a matter of admiralty law or policy restricting the arrest of vessels; it should not be based on separability, since this is not the role of separability.[126] If enough security is provided, as a general rule, a re-arrest might be an abuse of the authority of the court.[127]

4.3 Arbitral powers to request the arrest of ships in Spain

In Spain, the parties may (under Article 4 of the SAA) order the arbitrator to stick to arbitral rules during the procedure in a case of institutional arbitration. This also relates to Articles 730 to 743 SLCP or any other provisions of special procedural law. In the field of international arbitration, the parties can even determine that interim measures regarding the procedure may be sought according to the laws of a different country from the one where

121 *The Duden* (n 27).

122 See the discussion on *The Kallang* in Section 1.2 (Requirements for an Arrest) of the current chapter.

123 Mandaraka-Sheppard (n 4) 346–348.

124 *SC Rolinay Sea Star Srl v. Owners of the Bumbesti, SC Rolinay Sea Star Srl v. Compania de Navigatie Maritimie Petromin SA (The Bumbesti)* [2000] QB 559.

125 Jackson (n 11) ch 18.

126 Adam Samuel, 'Separability of Arbitration Clauses – Some Awkward Questions about the Law on Contracts, Conflict of Laws and the Administration of Justice' (2000) 9 ADRLJ 36.

127 Mandaraka-Sheppard (n 4) 175.

the arbitral procedure is held.[128] Article 23 SAA entrusts the arbitrators with the power to adopt interim measures:

> 1. Subject to any contrary agreement by the parties, the arbitrators may, at the request of a party, grant any interim measures deemed necessary in connection with the object of the dispute. The arbitrators may require the claimant to furnish sufficient security.
> 2. Irrespective of the form adopted by arbitral decisions on interim measures, the rules on setting aside and enforcement of awards will apply thereto.

The declaratory and executive dimensions of interim measures must be distinguished – except in cases where it has been agreed otherwise by the parties. The parties may apply to the court authority for the adoption of interim measures according to Articles 8 and 11 of the SAA, and Articles in the SLCP. In respect of interim measures, arbitral and court powers are alternative and concurrent, without having to call on the principle of procedural good faith. For instance, Article 15 (interim and provisional measures of an emergency arbitrator) of the procedural rules of the Spanish Court of Arbitration states:[129]

> 1. The arbitrators may, unless otherwise agreed by the parties, adopt the interim or provisional measures they deem necessary.
> 2. The arbitrators may subject the adoption of such measures to the prior creation of a sufficient security or guarantee that shall be required from the applicant in the manner, amount and time deemed advisable. This substitute security may be required after the adoption of the interim measure.
> 3. The applicable rules on compulsory annulment and enforcement of the Arbitration Law shall apply to arbitration decisions on interim or provisional measures regardless of how they are presented.
> 4. When a party requires an urgent measure prior to the constitution of the tribunal, the court may appoint an emergency arbitrator to decide on the application for urgent measures, after hearing from the parties and pursuant to the provisions of the rules. Their powers shall be identical to those of the Arbitral Tribunal laid down in Article 14 of the Rules, and their duties shall cease once the Tribunal is constituted. The Arbitral Tribunal may uphold, amend, or annul the provisional award or order issued by the emergency arbitrator. The emergency arbitrator cannot act as a member of the tribunal unless otherwise agreed by the parties.

In the framework of an international maritime procedure, can a cargo claimant apply to an arbitral tribunal for the arrest of a ship? Is it feasible that an arbitral tribunal (whose regulations do not provide for injunctions) can proceed? A comparative example is found in Article 1468 of the French Civil Procedure Code (amended by Decree No 2011-48 of 13 January 2011) that reforms the arbitration law and provides:

> The arbitral tribunal may order the parties, under the conditions it determines and if necessary financial penalty, any interim or conservatory measure it deems appropriate. However, the State jurisdiction is the only competent to order provisional seizures and judicial securities. The court may amend or supplement the interim measure it has ordered.[130]

128 Marcela Rodríguez Mejía, *Medidas Cautelares en el Proceso Arbitral* (Universidad Externado de Colombia 2014) 95–179, 183; see Alfonso-Luis Calvo Caravaca and Javier Carrascosa González, 'Medidas cautelares y comercio internacional' (2004) 18 Cuadernos de derecho judicial 409.

129 Author's translation.

130 Berlingieri, *International Maritime Conventions (Vol 2)* (n 105) 246–258.

The Chamber of Commerce, Industry and Navigation of Gipuzkoa (in Donostia–San Sebastián), among others, regulates the emergency arbitrator procedure *ex parte* (*inaudita parte* in Spanish terminology) to adopt interim measures as per Article 19 of the Arbitration Rules of the Chamber of Commerce, Industry and Navigation of Gipuzkoa (authority of the arbitrators to adopt interim measures).[131] An arbitrator has no jurisdiction, but if the parties have been subject to the chamber of commerce rules (*lex arbitri*) that provide for this possibility, then the arbitrator may apply these rules. The previous French and Spanish examples confirm the likelihood of arrest by arbitral tribunals in some countries. There is no question that the arbitrator will address the request for arrest directly to the judge, urging the adoption of the claim. On the contrary, in the absence of such coverage, the parties can propose an arbitrator if such protective injunction exceeds or is not within the arbitrator's competence. When analysing some of the chamber of commerce rules through case studies, it appears that an interested party may be able to stay the arbitrator's request for a protective injunction.

5 Can the court keep the case at the agreed court under the 1952 Arrest Convention?

The power of the court to hear the substance of the case when the arrest of ships is ordered by the court is contained in both Arrest Conventions. Article 7 of the 1952 Arrest Convention gives jurisdiction on the merits of the dispute if a ship is arrested in a contracting state even if the shipowner is domiciled in another EU Member State. If the arrest is threatened or an LOU or other security is provided by the shipowner, it is not sufficient to apply the 1952 Arrest Convention. If the cargo claimant agrees not to arrest it should ask the shipowner to agree to an EU Member State court's jurisdiction in the terms expressed by Articles 25 or 26 of the Brussels I Regulation (recast).[132]

The wording of Article 7 of the 1952 Arrest Convention does not directly recognise jurisdiction on the merits, unlike the 1999 Arrest Convention. However, the court will have jurisdiction in practice (unless the judge interprets the claim as subject to *forum non conveniens* in common law countries or a civil law public order exception, finds that there is *lis alibi pendens* or a valid choice of forum/arbitration clause under the court of arrest's *lex fori* is alleged by the defendant). Even if national civil procedure rules do not provide for such jurisdiction, the domestic PIL rules of a contracting state to the 1952 Arrest

131 Article 19 states:

1. The arbitrators may, by request of any party, take the precautionary measures they deem necessary regarding the subject of the dispute, unless it was prohibited in the arbitration agreement or by agreement of the parties. The arbitrator may require sufficient security from the applicant.
2. The arbitrators may adopt protective measures *inaudita parte*, in cases where this is required with the application for arbitration in accordance with the provisions of these regulations.
3. If either party believes that the circumstances that led to the adoption or rejection of the interim measures have changed, or had not urged the adoption of interim measures *inaudita parte* or on demand, at any time may request the adoption, modification or suppression of the interim measures, justifying the existence of supervening facts, request that will be resolved by the referees, after hearing the opposing party.

132 Yvonne Baatz, 'The Conflict of Laws' in Yvonne Baatz (ed), *Maritime Law* (4th edn, Routledge 2018) 41.

Convention may allow its incorporation into their legal system. The arrest conventions do not cover claims for wrongful arrest, which are governed by the *lex fori* as some principles are more difficult to prove in common law jurisdictions than civil law ones, such as bad faith or gross negligence.

Article 7(1) of the 1952 Arrest Convention should be read in conjunction with the provisions contained in the Brussels I Regulation (recast) in order to protect the domiciliaries of EU Member States from the exercise of exorbitant jurisdiction by the courts of other EU Member States. However, the Arrest Convention prevails over the recast Regulation in respect of a particular matter: Articles 4, 25, and 26 of the recast Regulation do not apply once an arrest has been effected. Any EU Member State court may, however, stay an action based on their national rules despite being entitled to hear the merits of the case.

Jurisdiction or arbitration clauses in common law and civil law countries, or intra- or extra-EU, lead to the application of international conventions (Hague Rules, Hague–Visby Rules, Hamburg Rules) that form part of their substantial law or *lex fori*, including national rules such as the Carriage of Goods by Sea Acts. A court deciding on its own jurisdiction to grant interim relief decides whether to issue a warrant of arrest by applying the arrest conventions or national law (*lex fori*), as well as national procedural laws that govern the process. If the courts have chosen not to tackle the substantive proceedings where there is a more suitable forum, the *forum non conveniens* doctrine in common law countries may be applied by the court.

The choice of law and jurisdiction clauses will be invalid if their effect is to derogate from the provision of an overriding mandatory law in England, such as COGSA 71. In *The Morviken* (discussed in Chapter 6, Section 2.2),[133] the House of Lords refused to enforce a Dutch jurisdiction clause in favour of the shipowner to avoid lessening the limitation figure, as the Netherlands was not part of the Hague–Visby Rules that were incorporated by COGSA 71. Equally, despite the 1952 Arrest Convention providing for jurisdiction, the English courts set aside the choice of law clause since overriding rules of the forum represents a limitation on party autonomy.

6 *Van Uden*: a real connecting link between subject matter and forum

The territorial scope of the 1952 Arrest Convention does not cover parties seeking an arrest in a country where the ship is not located. It entrusts the courts where the vessel is located to have jurisdiction to provide for the arrest. In *Van Uden*,[134] the Supreme Court of the Netherlands did not grant the arrest of a vessel for an interim payment since, according to Article 24 of the Brussels Convention, a real 'connecting link' between the subject matter and the territorial jurisdiction was needed to justify it. The definition of 'protective measures' as such does not call for enforcement outside the country in which it was granted. The court did not consider the recognition and enforcement provisions of the Brussels Convention in respect of other types of protective measures.[135]

133 *Owners of Cargo on Board the Morviken v. Owners of the Hollandia (The Morviken)* [1983] 1 AC 565.

134 Case C-391/95 *Van Uden Maritime BV trading as Van Uden Africa Line v. Kommanditgesellschaft in Firma Deco-Line* [1998] ECR I-7091, 7122.

135 Gerry Maher and Barry J Rodger, 'Provisional and Protective Remedies: The British Experience of the Brussels Convention' (1999) 48(2) ICLQ 302–339.

The main issue was the applicability of the Brussels Convention to the provisional measures applied for by a party to the arbitration. The Dutch company commenced arbitration proceedings against Deco-Line for unpaid invoices in the Netherlands and applied for an interim injunction to secure the debt. Deco-Line objected to the jurisdiction of the court, arguing that it could only be sued in Germany, where it was incorporated. No provisional measures were ordered based on Article 5(1) of the Brussels Convention when a contract refers the disputes to arbitration. When the subject matter falls within the scope *ratione materiae* of the Brussels Convention, it gives jurisdiction to the court to issue an arrest order although any other court or arbitration panel may hear the substance of the case.[136] It is relevant to the scope of the limitations on party autonomy that such real 'connecting link' between the subject matter – i.e., a cargo claim – and the country where the warrant is ought to be enforced. Arbitration proceedings are not within the scope of the Brussels Convention nor the Brussels I Regulation (recast), and provisional measures such as the arrest of a ship are excluded. Interim measures ancillary to arbitration proceedings are not allowed under the Brussels Convention, but only when they concern the performance of the contract.[137]

The arrest of a ship moving between countries can result in 'forum shopping' in favour of the shipowner because international interim justice cuts across international trade and has a force of attraction (*vis attractiva*) which can determine jurisdiction. For example, if a Danish shipper sues a Greek shipowner whose ship is registered in Spain but berthing in Italy, the arrest would require *urgency*, such as in *Van Uden*, and a *connecting link* to the forum where judgment is enforced.

7 Forum shopping and the arrest of ships

'Forum shopping' will continue unless a uniform procedure and a uniform substantive law are agreed to and ratified by maritime states. There are two types of forum shopping: the 'reactive model' allows a claimant to chase a debtor's vessel worldwide until the ship calls at a port in a jurisdiction in which the claimant is confident of recovery.[138] The vessel, however, may sail for long time without calling at a favourable jurisdiction, procedurally or substantially.[139] The 'proactive model' tries to avoid reactive forum shopping by the choice of a forum selection clause written into a contract. It serves its purpose only under contractual claims, but not collision- or pollution-related ones.

Spanish law discusses whether the ship may be arrested for different claims among those contained in Article 1 of the 1999 Arrest Convention (maritime liens), enabling arrest under the SAMN. This is possible due to temporary legislative measures adopted to extend

136 Burkhard Hess, Thomas Pfeiffer and Peter Schlosser, *The Heidelberg Report on the Application of Regulation Brussels I in the Member States* (Study JLS/C4/2005/03) (Beck 2008) [270].

137 Olga Troshchenovych, Jakob B Huebert and Samy Julien Hamama, 'Brussels I Regulation and Arbitration – Trading Torpedoes for Trust?' (European Judicial Training Network's Themis competition 2011) <http://www.ejtn.eu/Documents/Themis%202012/Written%20paper%20Lisbon/Written_paper_Germany_2_International_Cooperation_in_Civil_Matters%20%20%20.pdf> accessed 15 December 2017.

138 Lynn (n 7) 478.

139 Anna-Karin Niklasson, 'A Comparison between the Jurisdictional Rules in the EU and the US in the Light of the Arrest Convention and the Possibility to Shop for Forum' (School of Economics and Commercial Law, Göteborg University 2003) 47–48.

the application of the 1999 Arrest Convention to other vessels and not only these flagged in contracting states.[140] The answer is that all embargoes, notwithstanding the claims on which the action is based, are subject to the 1999 Arrest Convention.[141] This is incongruent since Spain made a reservation under Article 10(1)(b) of the 1999 Arrest Convention to reserve the right to exclude the application to non-state party-registered vessels. In Spain, under Article 472(2) SAMN, a minimum of 15 per cent of the alleged maritime claim must be provided as a security. The Spanish classification among the ordinary claims of Article 472(1) SAMN by reference to Article 1 of the 1999 Arrest Convention, privileged claims or maritime liens of Article 4(1) of the MLM Convention and special maritime ones also contained in Article 1, raises some questions regarding the nature of such actions. The court's order of arrest (*auto* in Spain) will distinguish between actions *in rem* directly affecting the vessel and other claims requiring the identity of the owner of the vessel and the debtor in order to proceed, adding an *in personam* element.

Since the choice of forum clauses in charterparties and B/Ls suggest different scenarios depending on where the ship arrest takes place, the validity will be determined by the *lex fori* in each case as a distorting element. Wherever the vessel is located, the parties are not prevented from choosing the most convenient place to apply for the arrest. The matter of providing an LOI[142] or enough security such as a bank guarantee due to the arrest of a ship depends on domestic substantive law. The claim may not be recognised as valid under the *lex fori*, even if the arrest is ordered by the judge. The interplay with other variables, such as the vessel's ownership, the operator, the flag, the law of the contracting state and the type of claim may allow a claimant to choose the preferable jurisdiction under a 'forum shopping' condition.[143]

In contrast with the 1952 Arrest Convention, the 1999 Arrest Convention makes the proactive model more efficient but enhances the uniformity of maritime law by constraining the reactive forum shopper, preventing the arrest of ship if the shipowners change the name of the proprietary company of the vessel. Cargo claims against a party other than the shipowner, for example, the charterer, will not succeed under such general rule. This will be possible only if the claim qualified under the limited lien status and the MLM Convention. Then, the judge will characterise the nature of the maritime lien as the basis of the claim when applying the *lex fori*, which normally provides for the ranking of those liens. Article 6 of the MLM Convention allows contracting states to grant maritime liens other than those

140 Royal Decree of Law 12/2011 of 26 August 2011 reforming the Civil Procedure Code, for the application of the [1999 Arrest Convention] of 12 March 1999 (Official State Gazette No 208 of 30 August 2011).

141 Albors Méndez and Portales Rodríguez (n 101).

142 A shipowner, having liability cover for, *inter alia*, loss of or damage to cargo carried has the option to request an LOI, provided by one of the International Group (IG) P&I Clubs, by a non-IG club or by a fixed premium insurer on terms similar to those maintained by IG clubs. A shipowner has the alternative to request a bank guarantee. However, they take longer time to arrange than LOIs and can be more expensive in comparison with LOIs that are provided free of charge to P&I Club members. Furthermore, certain P&I Clubs offer non-club bails. These letters are provided in a short-term period or an interim basis to non-club members until they can provide other types of security; Felipe Arizon and David Semark, *Maritime Letters of Indemnity* (Informa 2014) 262; Özlem Gürses and Johanna Hjalmarsson, 'Marine Insurance' in Yvonne Baatz (ed), *Maritime Law* (4th edn, Routledge 2018) 489.

143 Charles M Davis, *Maritime Law Deskbook* (Compass Publishing Company 1997) 65.

mentioned in Article 4, paragraph 1, under their national law that may include damage to the cargo.[144]

The finality of the claim plus the uncertainty of recovering any amount from such cargo claim magnifies the importance of the place where the arrest of the ship takes place. While claimants become aware of the most arrest-friendly jurisdictions, shipowners try to evade any liability by structuring the ship's ownership using sophisticated corporate structures and avoiding creditor-friendly jurisdictions. The 1999 Arrest Convention counterbalances proactive 'forum shopping' by allowing shipowners to change the company name in order to avoid an arrest. This is facilitated through 'one-ship owning corporations', that is, splitting ownership of different ships in order to limit the liability of a single shipowner.[145] Article 3(3) of the 1999 Arrest Convention allows the arrest of a bareboat-, time- or voyage-chartered vessel at port.[146]

> The main obstacle to proactive forum shopping is contained in Article 7(1) of the 1999 Arrest Convention, which allows an arrest in the jurisdiction where the vessel is located while the case proceeds on the merits in the forum stipulated by the parties. Once a judgment on the merits is issued, the judgment can be recognised where the ship is arrested,[147] according to Article 7(5) of the Convention.[148]

The avoidance of forum shopping, as already explained, involves difficulties. Recent developments involve the Danish ship fuel supplier OW Bunker's (OWB) bankruptcy,[149] and initiation of actions where shipowners faced double claims – one from the physical supplier (Rosneft Marine (UK) Ltd) under a maritime lien based on the retention of title clause (and thus ownership of the bunkers) that is only recognised in certain jurisdictions,[150] and another from ING (as assignee of OWB's rights by virtue of an English Omnibus Security Agreement) pursuant to the unpaid bunker supply contract with OWB. The latter gave permission only to use the bunkers under the chain of contracts.[151]

---

144 See William Tetley, 'Maritime Liens in the Conflict of Laws' in James AR Nafziger and Symeon C Symeonides (eds), *Law and Justice in a Multistate World: Essays in Honour of Arthur T von Mehren* (Transnational 2002) 439–457; see Francesco Berlingieri, *Berlingieri on Arrest of Ships Volume II: A Commentary on the 1999 Arrest Convention* (Informa 2017) 185.

145 Lynn (n 7) 460.

146 Belén Mora Capitán, 'Unificación internacional del embargo preventivo de buques del convenio de Bruselas de 1952 al convenio de Ginebra de 1999, 24 (2007) Español de Derecho Internacional Privado 91, 98.

147 Niklasson (n 139) 47–48.

148 Article 7(5) states:If proceedings are brought within the period of time ordered in accordance with paragraph 3 of this Article, or if proceedings before a competent court or arbitral tribunal in another state are brought in the absence of such order, any final decision resulting therefrom shall be recognised and given effect with respect to the arrested ship or to the security provided in order to obtain its release, on condition that:

(a) the defendant has been given reasonable notice of such proceedings and a reasonable opportunity to present the case for the defence; and

(b) such recognition is not against public policy (ordre public).

149 *PST Energy 7 Shipping LLC & Anor v. OW Bunker Malta Ltd & Anor (The Res Cogitans)* [2016] UKSC 23.

150 The ship was arrested in December 2015 by a commercial court of Beirut, which confirmed the debt in favour of Rosneft without appeal from the shipowner, while a London arbitration case was taking place.

151 A *sui generis* contract, not of sale, was agreed to allow consumption of bunkers prior to payment 60 days after delivery without any property transfer; such transfer only took place when the full price was paid.

Without further recourse, the shipowners (and this could be extended to charterers) had to face OWB's and ING's claims.[152] This constitutes a menace for the uniform international regime in addition to the comparative analysis of English and Spanish jurisdictional and arbitral procedures in connection with the different legal frameworks recognised under their domestic laws.[153]

The Brussels I Regulation (recast) does not distinguish between *in rem* and *in personam* proceedings. The jurisdiction *in rem* for the arrest of a vessel is conferred on the court provided that the ship is present within the territory. But, if the ship is out of England, a maritime creditor may apply for a freezing order that operates *in personam* if it can show a serious risk of dissipation of the defendant's assets, including the ship that may be abroad, when there is a 'sufficient link' that connects it with English jurisdiction. The shipowner can even be restrained from removing the vessel from that foreign jurisdiction if the amount is not enough to satisfy the claim in full. An ancillary search order can be issued if the claimant knows where the ship may be located, even if it is in a different and unconnected jurisdiction. When a ship is arrested in an English port, the court may continue the arrest even if a foreign court has jurisdiction on the merits. This tactical solution is particularly valuable when the merits of the case are pending in a non-EU court under Article 24 of the Brussels Convention (Article 35 of the Brussels I Regulation (recast)).[154]

For example, as shown in Figure 5, a Spanish receiver of damaged goods sues the shipowner in England. The B/L, signed by a Dutch charterer, includes a jurisdiction or arbitration clause in favour of the High Court of Justice of England and Wales or London arbitration, incorporated from the charterparty. The Spanish receiver requests an arrest from the English courts while the ship is located in the port of Southampton. However, the vessel leaves UK territorial waters and berths at the French port of Le Havre.

The territorial jurisdiction for the arrest appears in Articles 4 and 2 of the 1952 and 1999 Arrest Conventions, respectively, while in their absence Article 35 of the Brussels I Regulation (recast) would apply:

> Application may be made to the courts of a Member State for such provisional, including protective, measures as may be available under the law of that Member State, even if the courts of another Member State have jurisdiction as to the substance of the matter. The jurisdiction of the substance under Articles 7 and 8 of the 1952 and 1999 Arrest Conventions contain the procedural rules.

Articles 7 and 8 of the 1952 and 1999 Arrest Conventions show the mechanism and procedural rules to apply. If the conditions of Articles 2 and 53 of the Brussels I Regulation (recast) are fulfilled, the English court may issue an enforceable warrant for the arrest. The arrest order of the vessel may be helped by the European Account Preservation Order

152 The shipowners unsuccessfully started arbitral proceedings against OWB and ING, seeking to evade forum shopping by arguing that the property was transferred under ss 2(1) and 49 of the UK Sale of Goods Act 1979. This was disregarded on appeal by the Court of Appeal and dismissed by the Supreme Court.

153 This author believes that more uniformity is to be achieved by legislators, despite the fact that the shipping industry (and BIMCO, INTERTANKO, INTERCARGO, etc) is taking steps to protect parties' interests.

154 Theocharidis, 'Jurisdiction for Provisional Relief under the Brussels Convention in the Maritime Context' (n 3).

procedure (EAPO),[155] in force since 1 January 2017 other than in the UK and Denmark, creating a uniform procedure to preserve debtors' bank accounts and allowing creditors to preserve the amount owed in a debtor's bank account located in the EU.[156]

However, if the vessel left the port of Le Havre and berthed at the Moroccan port of Tangier, this would substantially change the situation, since such warrant for the arrest is not enforceable in Morocco. Such a situation leads to forum shopping with regard to the enforcement of any provisional measure between an EU and a non-EU state, as well as cases of *lis alibi pendens* or parallel proceedings. Such a situation would lead to irreconcilable judgments even if Article 4 of the 1952 Arrest Conventions provided jurisdiction for the arrest, allowing jurisdiction on the merits. The enforcement of a Moroccan judgment in the UK, or an English judgment in Morocco, could be refused for different reasons explained in this chapter.

8 Conclusions

As has been analysed in this chapter, the heterogeneous national regulations can generate distortions through various fragmented national responses in a globalised market context. Thus, the variety of dimensions of analysis exceeds the objectives of this work, but this autonomous or internal dimension should be stressed due to its important practical relevance.

In this author's opinion, the shipping sector lacks legal certainty from a comparative law perspective. The unification of procedural rules is embodied in conventional, European and national legal regulatory frameworks. Parties may be deprived of procedural freedom regarding the contractual rights of the original parties when an arrest takes place, leading to the jurisdiction on the merits of the dispute.

The *forum non conveniens* doctrine in common law countries, enabled under Article 7(2) of the 1952 Arrest Convention, may lead to a stay in the proceedings if there is a jurisdiction or arbitral agreement that could affect a third-party interest (e.g., other limits such as public policy in civil law countries). Articles 4 of the 1952 Convention and Article 2(1) of the 1999 Arrest Convention provide that a court is competent to arrest the vessel of a state party. However, the 1999 Arrest Convention allows other judicial authorities (e.g., an arbitral body in some countries) to order such measures.

In sum, 'forum shopping' is the outcome of the lack of procedural and substantive legal unification to ensure that the maritime claims are resolved in the jurisdiction or arbitral tribunal chosen by the charterparties. Currently, they face obstacles in terms of the recognition of their selected forum from a substantive legal perspective at a national level,

155 Regulation (EU) 655/2014 of the European Parliament and the Council establishing a European Account Preservation Order Procedure (EAPO).

156 'The Regulation provides common rules relating to jurisdiction, conditions and procedure for issuing an order, how it should be enforced by national courts and authorities, the remedies for the debtor and other elements of defendant protection. A single order can be made in the courts of one Member State that would be capable of freezing any bank account of a debtor in any Member State. The EAPO will be issued in an *ex parte* procedure. It is a protective measure in that it can be issued not only after judgment on the merits but also before. The Regulation contains a special procedure for obtaining information about the bank account of the debtor' Lawrence Collins, *Provisional Measures, Preparatory work of the 3rd Commission of The Institute of International Law* (23 December 2016) 337–338.

depending on whether a state has ratified either of the Arrest Conventions. This is also the case at the intra- and extra-EU level due to their different legal frameworks.

The recognition of dispute resolution clauses under the Brussels I Regulation (recast) or the domestic procedural rules of non-EU states constitutes a key issue. The need for legal certainty stems from a lack of clarity regarding the recognition of such clauses by different courts.[157]

157 Jonatan Echebarria Fernández, 'Party Autonomy and the Arrest of Ships from a Comparative Perspective' in José Manuel Martín Osante and Olga Fotinopoulou Basurko (eds), *New Trends in Maritime Law: Maritime Liens, Arrest of Ships, Mortgages and Forced Sale* (Thomson Reuters 2017) 498–521.

CHAPTER 6

Public policy and mandatory rules

Limitations on party autonomy

Chapter 6 considers when the validity of a jurisdiction or arbitration agreement is restricted by the substantive applicable law of the forum, including overriding mandatory rules. The chapter focuses on the limitations to the chosen jurisdiction or arbitration clauses by PIL national rules applied to a cargo dispute. These rules are part of the positive national law that a judge analyses in a case with foreign connections to determine the specific national law that applies to that case.

The main issue at stake is how the mandatory provisions applicable to the B/L, public policy, or the overriding mandatory rules of the forum may deprive parties of settling their dispute in the chosen forum or arbitral tribunal. The subjective characterisation of the parties may constitute a limitation on party autonomy.

The particular nature of the contract of affreightment is regarded under the scope of different legal frameworks. Each country's national laws or judicial interpretations include mandatory rules, overriding mandatory provisions and normative values that constitute their public policy or *ordre public international*. Indeed, the nature of the contract represents a symbiosis between the special nature of the maritime agreement and the application of the conflict rule.[1]

In some countries, arbitration and jurisdiction clauses are frequently linked to choice of law clauses in a way that contradicts the fundamental policies of the place where the contract is performed. The problems that may develop during litigation must be kept in mind when copying a dispute resolution clause that was good for one contract but may mean disaster for another contract – and a malpractice action for a lawyer.[2] As Guerra and others point out: a contract of affreightment

> normally includes liability clauses in the charterparties where the parties designate the applicable rules to the liability of the carrier. Placing the conflict of laws methods at the heart of the contract sets a link between its original nature and the applicable law to the dispute.[3]

A distinction between jurisdiction and applicable law has to be drawn. First, the mandatory rules, public policy and overriding mandatory rules are introduced. The applicable law analysis falls outside the scope of this work, but is necessary in order to introduce the

1 Miranda Guerra and Frank Nectali, 'Le conflit de lois en droit des transports de marchandises par mer' (University of Bourgogne 2013) 21–22.

2 See William W Park, *Arbitration of International Business Disputes: Studies in Law and Practice* (2nd edn, OUP 2012) 759–771.

3 Guerra and Nectali (n 1).

limitations on jurisdiction and arbitration agreements. Second, choice of forum clauses are analysed by revisiting the Brussels I Regulation (recast). An analysis of the intra- and extra-EU Member State courts submissions follows. Last, but not least, we consider the public policy limitations on arbitration agreements.

1 Mandatory rules, public policy and overriding mandatory rules

The unfettered freedom of choice of law of the parties engaged in commercial contracts is found in Article 3 of the Rome I Regulation.[4] However, such contractual freedom is subject to certain limitations. The litigants to a cargo claim cannot disregard the application of national mandatory rules, the fundamental principles of public policy (*ordre public international*) and overriding mandatory rules.[5]

Mandatory rules are different from the overriding mandatory rules. Neumayer[6] distinguishes between the non-derogable rules – mandatory rules – and overriding mandatory rules. Mandatory rules protect private interests, providing the backbone of the contract in case of national (without foreign elements) or foreign choice of law. Rome I Regulation's protective provisions regarding the contractually weaker party shall be observed considering the mandatory rules recognising that party autonomy has some limitations.[7] However, it can be said that party autonomy has been expanded in the Rotterdam Rules (that allow exclusive jurisdiction agreements for volume contracts) from that in the Hamburg Rules.

Depending on the circumstances, certain foreign mandatory national rules can be excluded by the parties. Such rules can be related to different sets of national legislation, such as consumer, labour, insurance or agency law. Mandatory rules can be domestic, regional (such as EU legislation), international (treaties) or transnational (e.g., the UNIDROIT[8] international principles of commercial contracts of 2016).

Mandatory rules contained in Articles 3(3) and 7 of the Rome I Regulation should be distinguished from those contained in Article 9, which are understood to be overriding

---

4 Article 3, paras 1 and 2 state:

1. A contract shall be governed by the law chosen by the parties. The choice shall be made expressly or clearly demonstrated by the terms of the contract or the circumstances of the case. By their choice the parties can select the law applicable to the whole or to part only of the contract.
2. The parties may at any time agree to subject the contract to a law other than that which previously governed it, whether as a result of an earlier choice made under this Article or of other provisions of this Regulation. Any change in the law to be applied that is made after the conclusion of the contract shall not prejudice its formal validity under Article 11 or adversely affect the rights of third parties.

5 Giuditta Cordero Moss, *International Commercial Arbitration: Party Autonomy and Mandatory Rules* (Tano Aschehoug 1999) 53.

6 Karl H Neumayer, 'Autonomie de la volonté et dispositions impératives en droit international privé des obligations' (1957) 4 Revue Critique de Droit International Privé 579.

7 Alfonso-Luis Calvo Caravaca and Javier Carrascosa González (eds), *Derecho Internacional Privado: Vol II* (Comares 2016) 901–905; Javier Carrascosa González, *La Ley aplicable a los contratos internacionales: el reglamento Roma I* (Colex 2009) 117–124.

8 'UNIDROIT is an independent intergovernmental organisation … Its purpose is to study needs and methods for modernising, harmonising and co-ordinating private and in particular commercial law as between states and groups of states and to formulate uniform law instruments, principles and rules to achieve those objectives'. UNIDROIT, 'History and Overview' (UNIDROIT, 28 January 2020) <https://www.unidroit.org/about-unidroit/overview> accessed 24 June 2020.

mandatory provisions. Article 3(3) of the Rome I Regulation (Article 14(2) of the Rome II Regulation is in similar terms for the event giving rise to the damage) states that domestic contracts having a foreign choice of law do not prejudice the application of the law of the country where all other elements relevant to the situation at the time of the choice are located, and that cannot be derogated from by agreement:[9]

> Where all other elements relevant to the situation at the time of the choice are located in a country other than the country whose law has been chosen, the choice of the parties shall not prejudice the application of provisions of the law of that other country which cannot be derogated from by agreement.

The Article applies to situations where all elements point to one EU Member State when parties have chosen the law of a third state (whether or not an EU Member State). The Article can also apply to non-Member States. The parties cannot derogate from the mandatory rules of the EU Member State or non-EU state where all the elements are closely connected to that state. The choice of law is a factor, unlike the choice of jurisdiction alone, according to Recital 15 of the Rome I Regulation.[10] The judge may enforce domestic laws in order not to apply a foreign choice of law selected *inter partes* that lessens their responsibility.[11]

Overriding mandatory provisions are more restrictive provisions that cannot be derogated by agreement, even in international cases. These must be construed more restrictively and codify some CJEU decisions from the 1990s and early 2000s.[12] Article 9(1) of the Rome I Regulation defines overriding mandatory provisions as

> provisions the respect for which is regarded as crucial by a country for safeguarding its public interests, such as its political, social or economic organisation, to such an extent that they are applicable to any situation falling within their scope, irrespective of the law otherwise applicable to the contract under the Rome I Regulation.

Overriding mandatory rules protect and defend public or collective interests and apply to any international contract regardless of the law chosen by the parties. Overriding mandatory rules cannot be derogated by agreement. The power to choose the applicable law to the contract derives from the law of the *lex fori*, which draws the limits of conflictual party autonomy.[13] Thus, the parties' free will faces limitations from the Hague Rules to the

9 Yvonne Baatz, 'The Conflict of Laws' in Yvonne Baatz (ed), *Maritime Law* (4th edn, Routledge 2018) 61–62.

10 Geert Van Calster, *European Private International Law* (Bloomsbury 2016) 225–226; Baatz, 'The Conflict of Laws' (n 9) 61–63.

11 Baatz, 'The Conflict of Laws' (n 9) 61–63.

12 For instance, in the joined Cases C-369/96 and C-376/96 *Arblade and Others (Criminal proceedings against Jean-Claude Arblade and Arblade & Fils SARL) v. Bernard Leloup, Serge Leloup and Sofrage SARL* [1999] ECR I-8453; Catherine Kessedjian, 'Mandatory Rules of Law in International Arbitration: What Are Mandatory Rules?' (2007) 18(1 2) Am Rev Intl Arb 147.

13 See Stefan Leible, 'La importancia de la autonomía conflictual para el futuro del Derecho de los contratos internacionales' (2011) 3(1) Cuadernos de Derecho Transnacional 214, 217; Leo Raape, *Internationales Privatrecht* (5th edn, Franz Vahlen 1961) 457; Kurt Siehr, 'Die Parteiautonomie im Internationalen Privatrecht' in Peter Forstmoser and others (eds), *Festschrift für Max Keller* (Schulthess 1989) 486; Frank Vischer, *Internationales Vertragsrecht: Die Kollisionsrechtlichen Regeln der Anknüpfung bei Internationalen Verträgen* (Stämpfli 1962) 24; Pierre Mayer and Vincent Heuzé, *Droit international privé* (8th edn, Montchrestien 2004) 514–519; Caravaca and González, *Derecho Internacional Privado* (n 7) 901–905; Carrascosa González (n 7) 117–124.

Hague–Visby, Hamburg and Rotterdam Rules. These conventions presume no full party autonomy.

Overriding mandatory rules may constrain party autonomy in related cargo claim proceedings and may limit the choice of non-EU law provisions against the law of the forum as will be discussed in relation to *The Morviken*. The enforcement of overriding mandatory provisions of the *ordre public international* where the choice of forum agreement is sought to be recognised can be considered as pertaining to form or to substance.[14] Article 21 of the Rome I Regulation (and Article 26 of the Rome II Regulation in similar terms) allows the application of a foreign law to be refused 'if such application is manifestly incompatible with the public policy (*ordre public international*) of the forum'. Article 23 lays down the relationship with other provisions of EU Law, while Article 25 deals with the conflict of laws rules in relation to existing international conventions.[15]

The mandatory overriding provisions of the law of the forum apply and stress that the choice of the forum or arbitral seat is paramount. The mandatory rules of the forum related to a B/L can affect jurisdiction or arbitration clauses when the parties have chosen a different jurisdiction or arbitral seat with the intention of applying a concrete set of rules that could be more favourable to the shipper. Article 9(1) of the Rome I Regulation (and Article 16 of the Rome II Regulation) restricts its scope of application to the 'law of the forum in a situation where they are mandatory irrespective of the law otherwise applicable' to contractual or non-contractual obligations. Mandatory overriding provisions constitute a general correction mechanism in conflict of laws that circumvents the parties' choice of foreign law under Articles 9(1) of the Rome I Regulation and Article 7 of the Rome Convention.[16] Such mandatory overriding provisions may lead to the application of the Hague, Hague–Visby or Hamburg Rules to a B/L when they constitute the law of the forum. However, a choice of English law does not automatically imply the application of the Hague–Visby Rules.[17] Even if such rules are voluntarily incorporated under a charterparty, they may not apply if they reduce the responsibility of any of the parties.[18]

Furthermore, Article 9(2) of the Rome I Regulation provides that 'nothing' in the Rome I Regulation 'restricts the application of the overriding mandatory provisions of the law of the forum', although some limits exist. Article 9(2) of the Rome I Regulation restricts the application of the Hague–Visby Rules to a contract, for instance, but not when they are applied mandatorily. The preliminary ruling of the CJEU in *Unamar* determined that the parties could choose Bulgarian law to be applicable to a commercial agency contract subject to arbitration.[19] However, Belgian laws provided a greater level of protection to

14 Jürgen Basedow, 'Exclusive Choice-of-Court Agreements as a Derogation from Imperative Norms', in Patrik Lindskoug and others (eds), *Essays in Honour of Michael Bogdan*, Juristförlaget i Lund (2013) 15–31.

15 Baatz, 'The Conflict of Laws' (n 9).

16 Convention on the law applicable to contractual obligations opened for signature in Rome on 19 June 1980 OJ 1980 L 266/1, consolidated version OJ 1998 C 27/34 (Rome Convention).

17 *Trafigura Beheer BV v. Mediterranean Shipping Co SA (The MSC Amsterdam)* [2007] EWCA Civ 794: the B/L expressly provided for English law but the Court of Appeal held that the Hague–Visby Rules did not apply because the B/L was not issued in a contracting state, was not from a contracting state, and did not provide for the Hague–Visby Rules or the ability to give them effect from Article X.

18 Case C-184/12 *United Antwerp Maritime Agencies (Unamar) NV v. Navigation Maritime Bulgare* EU:C:2013:663, [2014] 1 Lloyd's Rep 161. In this case, the national legislation's scope of protection for self-employed commercial agents surpassed the minimum requirements of the EU Directive.

19 ibid.

commercial agents, including laws related to shipping services during the transposition of the Commercial Agents Directive. Nevertheless, when applying the current Article 9(2) of the Rome I Regulation, Belgian courts may declare themselves competent by considering their national laws as mandatory provisions.

Considering the current analysis under English, Spanish and EU law, two different situations must be distinguished concerning the mandatory rules applicable to dispute resolution clauses contained in or incorporated into a contract for carriage of goods by sea: (i) the incompatibility of an imperative norm with the choice of forum; and (ii) the incompatibility of a choice of law agreement affecting the substantive validity of that clause under the Rome I Regulation.[20] The application of public policy and overriding mandatory provisions in non-EU jurisdictions can also make the law chosen by the parties inapplicable to contracts of affreightment, depriving the parties of the ability to resolve their cargo claim disputes in their selected forum or ADR venue.

2 The incompatibility of an imperative norm with a jurisdiction agreement

2.1 Incompatibility under the Brussels I Regulation (recast)

In Chapter 2, we drew a distinction between choice of forum and choice of law agreements. First, choice of court agreements in the EU must be assessed. The incompatibility of an imperative norm with the choice of forum is considered a matter outside the scope of the formal and substantive validity of the Brussels I Regulation (recast), under Article 25.

Such imperative norms of the forum are characterised as a matter of substance and cannot be applied out of the territory of the state. This is reinforced by Article 31(2) of the Brussels I Regulation (recast), in that when a choice of forum clause exists in favour of another EU Member State court then 'another Member State shall stay the proceedings until such time as the court seised on the basis of the agreement declares that it has no jurisdiction under the agreement'. Article 29(2) of the Brussels I Regulation (recast) sets out that 'upon request by a court seised of the dispute, any other court seised shall without delay inform the former court of the date when it was seised in accordance with Article 32'.

2.2 Intra-EU jurisdiction agreements

Next, we consider the effects of jurisdiction clauses on the practical implementation of parties' rights. According to Basedow, the assessment of the validity of a foreign and exclusive choice of forum clause when a court is seised may lead to the following choices:[21] first, the court may invalidate the agreement and engage in proceedings according to the *lex fori* or foreign law by giving 'effect to the imperative norms of the forum state'; second, the court may enforce the chosen foreign law and stay proceedings or dismiss the complaint.

The Morviken provides an example of an overriding mandatory rule voiding an express choice of law clause because it lessens the carrier's liability if the Hague–Visby Rules are mandatorily applicable.[22] The House of Lords stated that an express choice of law could be voided to prevent the lessening of the carrier's liability through the application of the

20 Basedow, 'Exclusive Choice-of-Court Agreements as a Derogation from Imperative Norms' (n 14).

21 ibid.

22 Baatz, 'The Conflict of Laws' (n 9) 47, 61–63.

Hague Rules under Dutch law, if the Hague–Visby Rules were mandatorily applicable. However, there is no compulsory rule under which the legal qualification must be made under EU law. A party cannot use a choice of law clause to evade the overriding mandatory rules of the forum. In *The Morviken*, a cargo claim for damaging the machinery was initiated in England, including *in rem* actions against the *Hollandia*, a sister ship to the *Morviken*. There was a Dutch choice of court, but the English judge did not stay the proceedings as the shipowners requested.[23] The jurisdiction clause was held invalid, applying Article III.8 of the Hague–Visby Rules under which clauses included in a B/L that may exclude or limit the carrier's liability are barred.[24]

It is noteworthy that normally 'no country applies the policy of another except where the law of that other country is selected by the conflict of laws rules of the first country as governing the issues in question'.[25] It was possible to except the application of the policy of another country under Article 7(1) of the Rome Convention. However, there are further restrictions under Article 9(3) of the Rome I Regulation.

The Hague–Visby Rules apply to B/Ls in the UK under s 1 of COGSA 71, regardless of the law governing the B/L, when the shipment is out of the UK or other contracting state, or issued in any circumstances under Article X of the Hague–Visby Rules. These are considered the overriding policy of the forum and thus, mandatory rules, according to Article 9 of the Rome I Regulation, independent of the chosen applicable law to the contract,[26] 'whatever may be the nationality of the ship, the carrier, the consignee, or any other interested person'.[27]

The Rules 'shall have the force of law' according to s 1(2) but the requirements of Article X have to be met. In *The Komninos S* case,[28] the Hague Rules did not apply even through there was 'a choice of British Courts' in the B/L and English law was applicable, since

23 *The Morviken* has the same effect as Article 9(2) of the Rome I Regulation, limiting the application of the Hague–Visby Rules to a contract but not when these Rules are mandatory.

24 The decision was followed in other jurisdictions. See *Akai Pty Ltd v. People's Insurance Co Ltd* (1996) 188 CLR 418, where the English High Court disagreed with the decision of the New South Wales Court of Appeal regarding the non-applicability of New South Wales law to a credit insurance policy containing the choice of English law and English jurisdiction; Guenter Treitel and Francis MB Reynolds, *Carver on Bills of Lading* (4th edn, Sweet & Maxwell 2017) [9-077].

25 *Carver on Bills of Lading* (n 24) [9-075].

26 See the dissenting opinion of Rix LJ on the application of Article 9(2) of the Rome I Regulation by the Court of Appeal in *Parsons Corporation v. CV Scheepvaartonderneming Happy Ranger (The Happy Ranger)* [2002] EWCA Civ 694, [19] and [42]; However, it was held in the judgment that the Rules applied compulsorily and that 'B/Ls issued in pursuance of the contract of carriage had contractual force by virtue of their incorporation, by express words, into the latter contract'. The case involved a shipment of three reactors from Italy, a contracting state, to Saudi Arabia. English law governed the contract but the B/L scheduled to it was governed by Dutch law. The latter was presumed to be equal to English law in that respect. 'The relevance of Article X(a) of the Hague–Visby Rules, which has the force of law, was not made obvious'. Furthermore, the Rules are not mandatorily applicable if they are excluded according to their own scope of application, e.g., in a case involving deck carriage, *Sideridraulic Systems SpA v. BBC Chartering & Logistic GmbH & Co KG (The BBC Greenland)* [2011] EWHC 3106 (Comm); *Carver on Bills of Lading* (n 24) [3-05] and [9-076]; the distinction between the 'contractual application to a contract' and the mandatory application of the Hague–Visby Rules is discussed by Filippo Lorenzon and others, *CIF and FOB Contracts* (Sweet & Maxwell 2012) 451, fn [64].

27 Article X(c) Hague–Visby Rules. There is no requirement to include a Paramount Clause. However, these clauses continue to be drafted in contracts for the carriage of goods by sea and Article X(c) of the Rules allows for such possibility; *Carver on Bills of Lading* (n 24) [9-076].

28 *Hellenic Steel Co v. Svolomar Shipping Co Ltd (The Komninos S)* [1991] 1 Lloyd's Rep 370.

the port of shipment was in Greece, which was not a Contracting State to the Rules.[29] The decision in *The Morviken* predated the CJJA and Article 17 of the Brussels and Lugano Conventions (current Article 25 of the Brussels I Regulation (recast)), as explained by Aikens.[30]

The Morviken was issued before the enactment of the Brussels Convention and the Brussels I Regulation. The Hague–Visby Rules would prevail over the Brussels I Regulation (recast) when a jurisdiction clause leads to the application of foreign rules that would lessen the carrier's liability. As Hartley points out, the Rules govern jurisdiction and invalidate forum selection clauses when such liability would be lessened. In this author's opinion, that is only possible in the case of a choice of non-EU courts. Hartley states that it 'solves the problem where there is an international convention' but not under the Brussels I Regulation (recast) of jurisdiction agreements 'concluded in order to allow the parties to evade mandatory rules of national law'.[31]

The feasible outcome of *The Morviken*, where overriding mandatory rules were applied, would be currently the same and the reason is twofold, according to Hartley.[32] The choice of court agreement would be invalid because it collides with English conflict of laws rules since it is contrary to the law of the forum. Similarly, the Hague–Visby Rules would not allow a lessening of the carrier's responsibility to be considered and would provide for English jurisdiction since the Rules in this situation prevail over the Regulation by virtue of its Article 71.[33] However, it is debatable whether the jurisdiction clause would be 'accepted by virtue of Article 25 of the Brussels I Regulation (recast)' or not since the doctrine is divided on this issue.[34]

Nowadays, any jurisdiction agreement in favour of an EU Member State court that complies with the requirements set out in Article 25 of the Brussels I Regulation (recast) will be referred to the EU Member State concerned, where the Hague–Visby Rules may not be in force. Therefore, the current legal framework would modify the outcome of *The Morviken.* However, if English courts have jurisdiction to hear the case, the Rules (by COGSA 71) would apply to a shipment from a contracting state independent of the applicable law to the B/L.[35] For instance, the court first seised would have jurisdiction following an order to arrest a vessel or a sister ship, since the 1952 Arrest Convention and the 1999 Arrest Convention are in force in the UK and Spain, respectively. The Rome I Regulation would apply only to a negotiable B/L according to its Article 1(2)(d). The overriding mandatory rules of the forum would be applicable under Article 9(2) of the Regulation that probably

29 Richard Aikens, Richard Lord and Michael Bools, *Bills of Lading* (2nd edn, Informa 2015) [10.50].

30 ibid [10.55].

31 Trevor C Hartley, *International Commercial Litigation: Text, Cases and Materials on Private International Law* (CUP 2020) 227–228, referring to Basedow, 'Exclusive Choice-of-Court Agreements as a Derogation from Imperative Norms' (n 14) 15.

32 ibid 187–189.

33 ibid.

34 Yvonne Baatz, 'Choice of jurisdiction in bills of lading and cargo insurance' in Jason Chuah (ed), *Research Handbook on Maritime Law and Regulation* (Edward Elgar 2019), 357 at fn 351.

35 Aikens, Lord and Bools (n 29) [10.55].

includes the Hague–Visby Rules. *The Morviken* solution would be achieved if an English court is seised and the Rome I Regulation does not apply.[36]

The example stressed in *The Morviken* is one of qualification. There is certainly not any compulsory rule in EU law that legal characterisation must be made under EU law. There is a procedural rule providing for an autonomous qualification in procedural matters in order to classify the subject as civil or commercial, not depending on the court with jurisdiction on the merits. Why is there no similar rule in substantive matters? Because there is no political will. Each state tries to preserve its traditions and status. Interests may also vary depending on the pro-carrier or pro-shipper interests of each country. There is no guarantee that a judge will apply the material law chosen by the parties.

The Morviken relates to substantive rights of the parties. The incompatibility of a choice of forum agreement with an imperative norm falls outside the scope of the formal and substantive validity provided by Article 25 of the Brussels I Regulation (recast). It is characterised as a matter affecting substance, and no EU Member State court can enforce its imperative rules of forum against a jurisdiction agreement that complies with the requirements set out in Article 25. The *lis alibi pendens* rules of Article 31(2) of the Brussels I Regulation (recast) prescribe that

> without prejudice to Article 26, where a court of a Member State on which an agreement as referred to in Article 25 confers exclusive jurisdiction is seised, any court of another Member State shall stay the proceedings until such time as the court seised on the basis of the agreement declares that it has no jurisdiction under the agreement.

The chosen court under the valid forum selection agreement will assess the validity of that clause.[37]

It shall be borne in mind that Article 45(3) of the Brussels I Regulation (recast) has a public policy status and does not allow the application of any rules relating to jurisdiction in respect of a jurisdiction agreement in favour of another EU Member State. The CJEU overruled the House of Lords' judgment in *The Morviken* in *Castelletti* when the Brussels Convention (currently the Brussels I Regulation (recast)) is applicable, as stated in paragraph 49 of *Castelletti*: 'it follows that the choice of court in a jurisdiction clause may be assessed only in the light of considerations connected with the requirements laid down by Article 17 (current Article 25 of the Brussels I Regulation)'.

Moreover, the judgment added that: 'any further review of the validity of the clause and of the intention of the party which inserted it must be excluded and substantive rules of liability applicable in the chosen court must not affect the validity of the jurisdiction clause (paragraph 51)'. In this author's opinion, unless there is a clear circumvention of EU law by a choice of foreign law (e.g., a non-EU country), as it will be explained in *Ingmar* (see Section 2.4 of this Chapter),[38] a choice of forum clause complying with the formal requirements set out in Article 25 of the Brussels I Regulation (recast) and the substantive ones related to the law of the chosen EU Member State court should not be set aside by the EU Member State tribunal seised to assess its validity.

---

36 Baatz, 'Choice of jurisdiction in bills of lading and cargo insurance' (n 34), 357.

37 Basedow, 'Exclusive Choice-of-Court Agreements as a Derogation from Imperative Norms' (n 14).

38 Case C-381/98 *Ingmar GB Ltd v. Eaton Leonard Technologies Inc* [2000] ECR I-9305.

2.3 Extra-EU jurisdiction agreements and imperative rules

In England, according to recent law, a third party would be bound by the applicable law of a B/L agreed between original parties. In *The Channel Ranger*,[39] there was an English choice of law in the B/L, enabling the English High Court to be competent for the purpose of issuing an anti-suit injunction, at a first glance.

The *Channel Ranger* carried coal from Rotterdam in the Netherlands to Nador in Morocco, and the cargo was damaged due to self-heating during transit. In June 2011, the shipowners started proceedings in England to declare their non-liability for any cargo damage, while the banks acting as cargo insurers commenced proceedings against them in Morocco alleging no incorporation of the English law and jurisdiction into the B/L. The Court of Appeal considered that the intention of the parties in the charterparty clause prevailed over the B/L, their intention being to apply the Hague–Visby Rules and not the Hamburg Rules in force in Morocco. The court considered beyond the construction of the clause and observed that the parties created an ancillary clause. The law and jurisdiction clause in the voyage charterparty was the only one that the parties could have intended to incorporate.[40]

General words of incorporation are sufficient to incorporate a charterparty governing law provision into a B/L, allowing a certain degree of manipulation. Having the B/L include two express references to the choice of English law in the voyage charterparty was judged sufficient to incorporate the choice of law into the B/L according to Article 3 (freedom of choice) of the Rome I Regulation, in force in England.

In *The Channel Ranger*, the English judge did not consider the *prorogatio fori* and eliminated the possibility that the Moroccan courts could become competent by issuing an anti-suit injunction (this applies only to extra-EU situations since it is not permitted between EU Member States). The choice of law clause was less favourable to the parties and would expose the carrier to a less favourable treatment under the Hamburg Rules in Morocco compared with England.

There are also examples of anti-suit injunctions targeting foreign proceedings by cargo interests against shipowners and of a P&I Club being considered vexatious and oppressive. In *Aline Tramp*,[41] the English Commercial Court rejected an anti-suit injunction targeting foreign Jordanian proceedings by cargo interests against the shipowners and the P&I Club. The Jordanian court declared itself competent to judge the case on the merits by applying Article 21(1)(d) of the Hamburg Rules, referring to the port of discharge of the cargo. The B/L contained a London arbitration clause determining that the Jordanian judge had competence under the Hamburg Rules. The English judge considered that, due to the principle of comity, any undesired parallel proceeding could not be considered vexatious and oppressive.

The cargo interests in *The Channel Ranger* argued that the obligation of the carrier to the named consignee under the B/L was to provide the chosen law on the face of the negotiable

---

39 *Caresse Navigation Ltd v. Zurich Assurances Maroc and others (The Channel Ranger)* [2014] EWCA Civ 1366; *Caresse Navigation Ltd v. Office National de l'Electricité (The Channel Ranger)* [2013] EWHC 3081.

40 Yvonne Baatz, 'Should Third Parties Be Bound by Arbitration Clauses in Bills of Lading?' (2015) 1 LMCLQ 85.

41 *Aline Tramp SA v. Jordan International Insurance Co* [2016] EWHC 1317 (Comm).

instrument and to not disclose the terms later after the dispute arose. In favour of their statement, Article 5(1) of the Rome I Regulation states:

> To the extent that the law applicable to a contract for the carriage of goods has not been chosen in accordance with Article 3, the law applicable shall be the law of the country of habitual residence of the carrier, provided that the place of receipt or the place of delivery or the habitual residence of the consignor is also situated in that country. If those requirements are not met, the law of the country where the place of delivery as agreed by the parties is situated shall apply.

The Moroccan port of Nador was the place of delivery. Males J emphasised that the real matter was the choice of law that had been made, according to Article 3 of the Rome I Regulation, by the original parties to the B/L contract.[42] The judge accepted previous case law showing that general words of incorporation are sufficient to incorporate such a choice of law clause.[43]

The AMWELSH charterparty for coal transportation did not include any limitation on transferring a B/L to a consignee who would bear the rights contained therein, including the choice of English law. It was assumed that English law applied to the question of validity of the choice of law clause, and the negotiable B/L seemed to fall outside the scope of the Rome I Regulation through the exclusion of Article 1(2)(d).[44] This led to the application of the Hague–Visby Rules under Article X, that is, carriage of goods between ports in two different states, if the B/L is issued in a contracting state or carried from a port in a contracting state, or if the law chosen by the parties in the B/L gives effect to the Hague–Visby Rules. Nevertheless, an express choice of law may be voided to prevent the carrier's liability from being reduced if the Hague–Visby Rules are mandatorily applicable.

A party could make use of the lack of legal uniformity to avoid substantive rules of liability. Baatz suggests that there should be a provision preventing any party from taking such action.[45] She states that at some point when substantive liability has been agreed between states, the freedom to contract as to jurisdiction or place of arbitration should not be limited to protecting the rights of cargo interests. The carrier has the choice of jurisdiction in standard form transport documents and can choose, for instance, the principal place of business of the carrier or a neutral venue.

2.4 Effects of forum selection agreements and effectiveness of imperative norms

The overriding mandatory or public policy rules should be effective in order to implement the judgments that give them effect. As stated by Basedow, 'the invalidity of the forum

42 Baatz, 'The Conflict of Laws' (n 9) 54–55.

43 *The Njegos* [1936] P 90; *Pacific Molasses Co and United Molasses Trading Co Ltd v. Entre Rios Compania Riviera SA (The San Nicholas)* [1976] 1 Lloyd's Rep 8.

44 Baatz, 'Should Third Parties Be Bound by Arbitration Clauses in Bills of Lading?' (n 40).

45 'If all States agreed to be bound by the same rules as to substantive liability it might be said that there was no need for any provisions on jurisdiction or arbitration as any court or arbitration tribunal chosen would apply the same rules. Unfortunately as there is no international uniformity on substantive law, it may be argued that that there needs to be some provisions which prevents a party from intentionally providing for a jurisdiction so that it may avoid the rules'; Yvonne Baatz, 'Thirty Years of Europeanisation of Conflict of Laws and Still all at Sea?' in Malcolm Clarke (ed), *Maritime Law Evolving: Thirty Years at Southampton* (Hart 2015) 268; see also Yvonne Baatz, 'Incorporation of a Charterparty Arbitration Clause in a Bill of Lading and Its Effect on Third Parties' in Miriam Goldby and Loukas Mistelis (eds), *The Role of Arbitration in Shipping Law* (OUP 2016) 107–148.

selection clauses relates to the substantive rights of the parties involved in the dispute'. In other words, it is a matter of substantive law. According to Basedow, there is no *tertium non datur* or third category along with the substantive validity of Article 10[46] and the formal validity of Article 11, both contained in the Rome I Regulation.[47]

Article 3(4) of the Rome I Regulation[48] is inspired by in the CJEU decision in *Ingmar*[49] and gives precedence to mandatory EU rules when, at the time of the choice of law of a contract, other elements are located in one or more EU Member States.[50] The German BGH as the last court of appeal could not rely on the *acte clair* doctrine and asked for a preliminary ruling of the CJEU according to Article 267(3) of the Treaty of Functioning of the European Union (TFEU).[51] There was no assessment by the CJEU of the English choice of court agreement but it did consider the choice of law.[52]

However, the parties must be located in one or more EU Member States, invalidating the doctrine set out by the CJEU in *Ingmar* where one of the parties, the principal, was based in California. The self-employed agent carried out its activity in England and the contract included a choice of Californian law. Article 6 of the Rome I Regulation regulates consumer contracts together with the special jurisdiction rules of the Brussels I Regulation (recast).[53] Article 17(1) of the Commercial Agents Directive[54] provided that 'Member States shall take measures to ensure that the commercial agent is, after termination of the agency contract, indemnified in accordance' with the Directive. The CJEU ruled the following in order to answer the preliminary question referred by the English Court of Appeal:[55]

> Articles 17 and 18 of [the Commercial Agents Directive], which guarantee certain rights to commercial agents after termination of agency contracts, must be applied where the commercial agent carried on his activity in a Member State although the principal is established in a non-member country and a clause of the contract stipulates that the contract is to be governed by the law of that country.

---

46 According to Article 10(1): 'the existence and validity of a contract, or of any term of a contract, shall be determined by the law which would govern it under this Regulation if the contract or term were valid'. Article 10(2) states:

> Nevertheless, a party, in order to establish that he did not consent, may rely upon the law of the country in which he has his habitual residence if it appears from the circumstances that it would not be reasonable to determine the effect of his conduct in accordance with the law specified in paragraph 1.

47 Basedow, 'Exclusive Choice-of-Court Agreements as a Derogation from Imperative Norms' (n 14).

48 Article 3(4) of the Rome I Regulation (Article 14(3) of the Rome II Regulation uses similar wording):

> Where all other elements relevant to the situation at the time of the choice are located in one or more Member States, the parties' choice of applicable law other than that of a Member State shall not prejudice the application of provisions of Community law, where appropriate as implemented in the Member State of the forum, which cannot be derogated from by agreement.

49 *Ingmar* (n 38).

50 Gian Paolo Romano, 'Le choix des principes UNIDROIT par les contractants à l'épreuve des dispositions impératives' (2007) 134(2) Journal du droit international 473.

51 Consolidated version of the Treaty on European Union and the Treaty on the Functioning of the European Union OJ 2012 C-326/13.

52 Basedow, 'Exclusive Choice-of-Court Agreements as a Derogation from Imperative Norms' (n 14).

53 Van Calster (n 10) 226–227.

54 Council Directive No 86/653/EEC on the coordination of the laws of the Member States relating to self-employed commercial agents [1986] OJ L382/17.

55 *Ingmar* (n 38) [26].

The Commercial Agents Directive was held to be part of EU mandatory law, constituting an overriding mandatory provision, but as one of the parties is based in a non-EU state (the US), the outcome would arguably be different applying Article 3(4) of the Rome I Regulation. National legislation implementing EU directives is also considered part of EU law. Article 3(4) extends the notion of Member State to Denmark for the application of Articles 3(4) and 7 (insurance contracts) of the Rome I Regulation.[56]

Similarly, in *Conseils et mise en relations (CMR) SARL v. Demeures terre et tradition SARL*[57] the CJEU ruled out the avoidance of paying a compensation or indemnity to commercial agents: 'The interpretation that no indemnity is payable in the event of termination of the commercial agency contract during the trial period is incompatible with the mandatory nature of the regime established by Article 17 of [the Commercial Agents Directive]'.

The derogation from imperative norms has to be treated differently: on the one hand, choice of law clauses concern the consistency of governmental action in a given state in a wider sense. On the other hand, jurisdiction clauses aimed to circumvent imperative norms of the forum offer limited examples. The choice of non-EU laws can be used to circumvent EU mandatory law. Intra-EU contracts with a non-EU jurisdiction clause can be exceptionally disregarded in terms of protection from abusive circumvention.[58]

3 Validity of arbitration agreements and incompatibility with public policy

The UK and Spain are both contracting states to the New York Convention. As already discussed in Chapters 2 and 3, the formal validity of the arbitration agreement is enshrined in Article V(1)(a) of the New York Convention, referring to Article II for its formal requirements. The parties' consent as a condition for the validity of an arbitration agreement is framed within the scope of Article II.

The UKAA states the conditions for the formal validity of an arbitration agreement in ss 5 and 6. The mandatory provisions as stated by s 4(1) of Schedule 1 UKAA detail the obligations of the arbitral tribunal, the parties and the right of supervision by a court. Section 2 (non-mandatory provisions) 'allows the parties to make their own arrangements by agreement but provide rules which apply in the absence of such agreement'.[59]

Article 468 SAMN (read with Article 251) requires the individual and separate negotiation by the contractual parties for the formal validity of an arbitration clause. However, the New York Convention is *erga omnes* and Article 468 SAMN would be inapplicable even in conjunction with Article VII of the Convention, which states:

> The provisions of the present Convention shall not … deprive any interested party of any right he may have to avail himself of an arbitral award in the manner and to the extent allowed by the law or the treaties of the country where such award is sought to be relied upon.

Article VII(1) of the New York Convention allows for the application of international conventions or domestic laws that would not only provide for the enforcement of an arbitral

56 Van Calster (n 10) 226–227.

57 Case C-645/16 *Conseils et mise en relations (CMR) SARL v. Demeures terre et tradition SARL* EU:C:2018:262.

58 Basedow, 'Exclusive Choice-of-Court Agreements as a Derogation from Imperative Norms' (n 14).

59 Baatz, 'The Conflict of Laws' (n 9) 5–9.

award but would also provide for the enforcement of an arbitration agreement when this is not possible under the New York Convention. The outcome would be similar since Article 468 SAMN imposes tougher conditions. The Spanish *lex fori* would not comply with Article VII (see Chapter 3, Section 4.2). The *lex posterior derogat anterior* principle or the *lex specialis* character of Article 468 SAMN do not serve as reasoning to make its application effective.

However, if Spanish courts decided to apply the strict conditions prescribed by Article 468 SAMN they would be in breach of Spain's international obligations. Article 9 SAA (form and content of the arbitration agreement) is the domestic rule that reduces the threshold for the formal validity of an arbitration agreement imposed by Article 468 SAMN. It sets out the separability of the arbitration clause from the main contract, the expression of parties' willingness to submit to arbitration all or certain disputes or the requirement of being in writing through different means (e.g., letters, telegrams, telexes, faxes and emails). The final requirement in paragraph 6 states:

> In international arbitration, the arbitration agreement will be valid and the dispute arbitrable if the requirements laid down in any of the following are met: the legal rules chosen by the parties to govern the agreement; the rules applicable to the substance of the dispute; or the rules laid down in Spanish law.

English courts have normally adopted a liberal approach concerning the incorporation of arbitration clauses into B/Ls as confirmed in *The Wadi Sudr*:[60]

> it is well-established that where a bill of lading purports to incorporate a charter, but fails to identify its date or other details of the charter concerned, that is not fatal to the incorporation of the charter if it can otherwise be properly identified.[61]

Article 73(2) and Recital 12 of the Brussels I Regulation (recast) give precedence to the New York Convention over the Regulation. Thus, in accordance with the New York Convention, English courts may question the agreement's validity and are obliged to give it effect. In *The Wadi Sudr*, *lis alibi pendens* between English arbitration and Spanish court proceedings regarding the validity of an arbitration agreement were resolved in favour of the Spanish court. The English Court of Appeal enforced the Spanish judgment that did not accept the incorporation of an arbitration clause, even though arbitration proceedings are excluded from the Brussels I Regulation (recast). The decision in *The Wadi Sudr* is now reversed by Recital 12 of the Brussels I Regulation (recast). The CJEU in *Gazprom* held that an anti-suit injunction issued by an arbitral tribunal was compatible with the Brussels I Regulation, since arbitration is excluded from its material scope of application.

Article V(2) of the New York Convention allows contracting states to refuse not only an arbitral award but also an arbitration agreement in the country where recognition is sought, if the subject matter is not arbitrable or if it is contrary to public policy. The latter is known as the 'public policy exception' under which the *ordre public international* is applied by contracting state courts.

The *ordre public international* has a wider scope than *ordre public interne* or domestic public policy. Definitions of public policy differ in each country and, as stated by

60 Miguel Gómez Jene, 'El convenio arbitral: statu quo' (2017) 9(2) Cuadernos de derecho transnacional 7.

61 *National Navigation Co v. Endesa Generacion SA (The Wadi Sudr)* [2009] EWHC 196 [109]; *The San Nicholas* (n 43); *Bangladesh Chemical Industries Corporation v. Henry Stephens Shipping Co and another (The SLS Everest)* [1981] 2 Lloyd's Rep 389.

UNCITRAL, 'case law tends to refer to a public policy basis for refusing recognition and enforcement of an award under Article V(2)(b)' of the New York Convention when 'the core values of a legal system have been deviated from'. Public policy is an exception that constitutes a 'safety valve to be used in those exceptional circumstances when it would be impossible for a legal system to recognize an award and enforce it without abandoning the very fundaments on which it is based'.[62]

English courts have not clearly defined public policy. This is because it addresses cases where

> there is some element of illegality or that the enforcement of the award would be clearly injurious to the public good or, possibly, that enforcement would be wholly offensive to the ordinary reasonable and fully informed member of the public on whose behalf the powers of the state are exercised.[63]

Spanish courts have construed a narrowed concept of public policy in terms of judicial control of arbitral awards. The judicial control of foreign arbitral awards recognises party autonomy in international arbitration when it does not collide with the fundamental principles of the legal systems of the parties involved or the international community in general.[64]

England and Spain may refuse to enforce an arbitration clause that does not meet the requirements set out by Article V of the New York Convention, due to the formal validity requirements of the arbitration agreement and the public policy of the forum. For instance, a party may challenge an award at court 'being obtained by fraud or the award or the way in which it was procured being contrary to public policy' under s 68(2)(g) UKAA. An arbitration award may not be enforceable in England according to s 103(3) UKAA 'if the award is in respect of a matter which is not capable of settlement by arbitration, or if it would be contrary to public policy to recognise or enforce the award'. Equally, an arbitral award may be set aside and reviewed in Spain according to Article 41(1)(f) SAA.

4 Conclusion

Mandatory rules, overriding mandatory rules and public policy provisions can restrict party autonomy. The parties to a contract for the carriage of goods by sea may be deprived of the recognition and enforcement of the choice of forum or arbitration clause.

Two circumstances must be distinguished: the incompatibility of an imperative norm with a jurisdiction agreement; and the incompatibility of a choice of law agreement affecting its

---

62 UNCITRAL Secretariat, *Guide on the Convention on the Recognition and Enforcement of Foreign Arbitral Awards 1958* (UN 2016) 240. The exceptional nature of the defence can be demonstrated in the Comments of the Netherlands Government, *Travaux préparatoires, Recognition and Enforcement of Foreign Arbitral Awards: Comments by Governments on the draft Convention on the Recognition and Enforcement of Foreign Arbitral Awards* E/2822/Add.4, 2. See also the Comments of the representative of the French Government, Mr Holleaux, *Travaux préparatoires*, Summary Record of the Eleventh Meeting E/CONF.26/SR.11, 7; see also Jan Paulsson, *The New York Convention in International Practice Problems of Assimilation International Practice – Problems of Assimilation in The New York Convention* (ASA Special Series No 9 1996) 100, 113.

63 *Deutsche Schachtbau-und Tiefbohrgesellschaft mbH v. Shell International Petroleum Co Ltd* [1990] 1 AC 295; UNCITRAL Secretariat, *Guide on the Convention on the Recognition and Enforcement of Foreign Arbitral Awards* (n 62) 242.

64 Virginia Allan and Victor Bonnin Reynes, 'Spanish courts' concept of public policy within the meaning of article V(2)(b) of the NY Convention – preliminary findings' (Memorandum to the IBA Arbitration Committee 2014) 2.

substantive validity under the Rome I Regulation. Article 9(2) can only restrict the application of the Hague–Visby Rules when these are not mandatorily applicable. One of the main consequences of the lack of harmonisation from a comparative perspective is that it serves as a legal loophole to avoid substantive rules of liability. For instance, the choice of venue under Article 22(1) of the Hamburg Rules poses a major limitation to party autonomy, by reducing the effect of an exclusive jurisdiction or arbitration agreement. Equally, the choice of an extra-EU venue could represent a manoeuvre to circumvent mandatory rules.

Parties may exclude certain foreign national rules by agreement unless Article 3(3) and 3(4) of the Rome I Regulation apply. Mandatory rules of an EU Member State under Article 3(3) of the Rome I Regulation and EU mandatory rules of Article 3(4) cannot be excluded by the contracting parties. Furthermore, foreign law provisions incompatible with the public policy of the forum according to Article 21 of the Rome I Regulation represent a limitation on party autonomy. The level of protection provided by Belgian law to commercial agents was greater than the Bulgarian law agreed by the parties in *Unamar*. The Belgian laws could be considered public policy provisions.

The overriding mandatory rules cannot be derogated by agreement. The public policy provisions of Article 45(3) of the Brussels I Regulation (recast) do not apply to jurisdiction agreements in favour of any EU Member State court. As explained in *The Morviken*, overriding mandatory rules of the forum restricted parties' autonomy by the choice of Dutch law that provided for the application of the Hague Rules, while COGSA 71 incorporated the Hague–Visby Rules. Such choice of law could not serve as a loophole to reduce the responsibility of the defendant. However, the CJEU overruled *The Morviken* in *Castelletti*, when the Brussels I Regulation (recast) (the Brussels Convention at the time the case was decided) applies.

English courts have a liberal approach concerning the incorporation of arbitration clauses and the limitations of the restrictive Articles 468 and 251 SAMN are overcome since Article VII of the New York Convention precludes their applicability. The 'public order exception' to refuse the recognition and enforcement of an award or an arbitration clause of Article V(2)(b) of the New York Convention does not have a uniform interpretation since it varies from the wider *ordre public international* to the domestic *ordre public nationale*. The concept is subject to national interpretation. England has not clearly defined the concept of public policy that the judges reviewing the arbitration or award may define, case by case. In contrast, Spain has a restrictive concept based on judicial control and the national and international principles of the legal regimes that apply to the case. However, the arbitration clause will effectively operate as a valid agreement when the formal validity and public policy requirements are met. It is widely understood that the enforcement of the clause by a judge does not contravene the core values of the forum or the legal systems involved; due process is ensured once the parties are directed to the chosen institutional or ad hoc arbitration venue and no circumvention of mandatory rules is envisaged during such procedure.

CHAPTER 7

Conclusions and a new perspective

Articulating contractual or extra-contractual provisions through preventive advocacy provides legal certainty to the parties in case of future cargo claims. Preventive advocacy is common in all sectors. It is recommended when there is a lack of material and interpretative harmonisation along with varied interpretations of treaty provisions by national courts, based on their individual legal systems. The range of national jurisprudential interpretations complicates the analysis of the provisions. The alternatives offered by procedural, material and conflictual party autonomy are not enough to overcome the lack of harmonisation affecting the global shipping market.

To provide a perspective that encompasses various national legal frameworks, this work has considered legal frameworks of European, English and Spanish legal systems to review the validity of third parties in bilateral agreements, which are included in any charterparty and B/L.

1 Procedural matters

There is a lack of legal certainty about the recognition and enforcement of jurisdiction and arbitration clauses inserted in charterparties and B/Ls, and this author has proposed an approach to obtaining legal certainty for the shipping market by analysing party autonomy, allowing for the results of a conflicting contractual or extra-contractual cargo claim to be procedurally or materially anticipated from a PIL perspective.

Article 25 of the Brussels I Regulation (recast) clearly states the formal conditions for the validity of jurisdiction clauses, while Article II of the New York Convention sets out the formal conditions for the validity of arbitration agreements. The substantive or material validity of jurisdiction and arbitration clauses may be subject to the national law applicable to the contract for carriage of goods by sea. The substantive validity of choice of forum agreements follows a 'uniform conflict rule' relying on the *lex fori* of a chosen EU Member State. However, substantive domestic law does not determine consent and only applies to the legal capacity of the parties, offer and the acceptance and, in case of fraud, duress or mistake. Article V(1) of the New York Convention states that the substantive validity of arbitration clauses is governed by the law chosen by the parties. In the absence of that choice the court first seised will decide whether it is governed by the *lex fori* or the governing law of the contract.

Validity of jurisdiction or arbitration clauses is subject to domestic law, but the minimum general requirements ascertained from the analysis set out in Chapter 3 include sufficient individualisation of charterparties, especially if they incorporate generic or by-reference charterparty forms. The incorporation of dispute resolution clauses demands greater predictability of where and under which legal framework any future cargo dispute will be resolved, and more effective application when switching from traditional sources of law to institutional ones. General words of incorporation are not sufficient in the UK; however, incorporation by appropriate reference to a charterparty in the B/L is sufficient. In EU or international law, certain limitations on recognition and validity of party autonomy must be considered, such as public order exceptions, the right to effective judicial protection and overriding mandatory rules. The interpretation of Article 25 of the Brussels I Regulation (recast) varies Spanish and English case law, although EU case law has been uniformly interpreted in the UK and Spain.

There is no single international maritime convention that enforces conflictual party autonomy or regulates conflict norms. The Hamburg Rules have not been ratified by the majority of EU Member States, and the Rotterdam Rules are (still) not in force. International maritime conventions do not include conflict rules and such rules only apply in the EU through domestic regulations enforced by judges with jurisdiction on matters related to procedural party autonomy. Asymmetry exists between conflictual, substantial and procedural party autonomy, *in toto*, that provide elements of projectable analysis due to disparate procedural actions. Material party autonomy (how far parties can go when negotiating contractual clauses) is influenced by the extent to which public policy or overriding mandatory rules can be applied to the carriage of goods by sea in commercial law. Another restriction on party autonomy may be imposed by the correct identification of the contractual carrier in order to recover damages to the cargo.

The *ad intra* and *ad extra* perspectives concerning the procedural aspects of the SAMN are inadequate and non-adapted to EU law and conventional instruments, such as the Hague, Hague–Visby and Hamburg Rules, which diminishes the practical repercussions of the admission of jurisdiction or arbitration agreements. The SAMN is not adapted to the singularities of international maritime law and normative hierarchies, but it is desirable for unification, in terms of material party autonomy. This is because it takes into account public and private interests in standard contracts and clauses, model laws, legal guidelines and principles of conduct.

When third parties are subrogated in a contractual chain or participate in a contractual relationship in ancillary ways, it can be difficult to determine their function. The SOLJ allows the setting-up of jurisdiction contracts but embraces party autonomy. It must be read in conjunction with the SAMN, that supports translational efficiency of endorsements as well as transfers. However, in order to avoid abusive practices by imposing contract clauses on the weaker party, express acceptance is required. As stated in the *Tilly Russ* and other CJEU cases, if commercial usage in a sector is validated by precedent, an approach that takes into account scope and content should be used to add third parties to a contractual relationship.

2 Privity of contract

Privity of contract restricts the shipowner from relying on a jurisdiction or arbitration clause contained in a B/L that it did not negotiate. An agent's authority in continental legal systems like Spain requires a 'reasonable test' present in national civil codes and resembles case law in common law jurisdictions. It must be stressed that any inconsistency or manipulation of

B/L clauses intended to reduce the carrier's liability is forbidden under Article III.8 of the Hague–Visby Rules, and this includes jurisdiction or arbitration clauses. The correct incorporation of the dispute resolution clause in a B/L and its validity is subject to national law or Article 25 of the Brussels I Regulation (recast) in cases of submission to an EU Member State court. In the case of Article 468 SAMN, the individualisation and separate negotiation requirements collide with the international practices of the shipping sector. However, it is debatable whether Article 468 operates in conjunction with Article 251 SAMN in light of Article 22 *bis* (2) and *ter* (4) SOLJ, when the parties select a non-EU state court.

3 Forum shopping, irreconcilable judgments and *lis alibi pendens*

Procedural unification is needed for the arrest of ships to avoid 'forum shopping', irreconcilable judgments and *lis alibi pendens*. An analysis of how the arrest of the ship can frustrate the jurisdiction or arbitration agreement of the parties reveals a lack of international substantive legal harmonisation in choice of court or arbitration clauses, as discussed in Chapter 5. The court can stay proceedings in common law jurisdictions, if a jurisdiction clause affects third-party rights, by applying the *forum non conveniens* doctrine, through Article 7(2) of the 1952 Arrest Convention. *Forum non conveniens* does not apply to arbitration clauses as the UK and Spain are bound by the New York Convention. English courts are obliged to stay unless the arbitration agreement is null and void (s 9 UKAA). There is no discretion. There is also no question of *forum non conveniens* if the parties have chosen the court of an EU Member State, as Article 25 of the Brussels I Regulation (recast) does not permit any discretion. The English court will have a discretion if the parties have chosen the court of a non-EU and non-Lugano contracting state but will stay its proceedings in favour of the court chosen unless there is strong cause not to do so.

'Forum shopping' operates with more efficiency in the 1999 Arrest Convention by allowing the proactive forum shopper to choose a forum clause written in the contract. However, any change of the company name before the claimant applies for the arrest allows the defendant to avoid the arrest of the vessel. The 1999 Arrest Convention restricts the reactive forum shopper that aims to chase the debtor's ship in any port in the world where the claimant is confident of recovery. Article 7(1) of the 1999 Arrest Convention allows an arrest in the jurisdiction where the ship is located, enhancing party autonomy by allowing the dispute on the merits of the case where agreed by the parties according to the dispute resolution clause. Article 7(5) of the 1999 Arrest Convention provides for the enforcement of the judgment on the merits where the ship is arrested. The 1952 Convention (and, doubtfully, the 1999 Arrest Convention) on jurisdiction for arrest by virtue of Article 71 of the Brussels I Regulation (recast) allows the avoidance of the *lis alibi pendens* rules of the Regulation when granting an order for arrest of a vessel located in a non-EU state. Moreover, a Member State court has discretion to order such arrest of a vessel outside the EU or, conversely, to recognise an order for arrest of a vessel inside its territory by a non-EU state if bilateral or multilateral treaties are applicable.

4 Restrictions on jurisdiction and arbitration clauses

Jurisdiction and arbitration clauses are subject to restrictions imposed by the law of the court or arbitral tribunal that first hears the case. Parties can exclude certain foreign rules by agreement within the limitations prescribed by Articles 3(3) and 3(4) of the Rome I Regulation. Article 21 of the Rome I Regulation restricts the application of foreign law provisions that are incompatible with the public policy of the forum. Public policy does not apply to jurisdiction agreements in favour of EU Member State courts under Article 45(3) of the Brussels I Regulation (recast).

The recognition of arbitration clauses has been effectively and consistently delivered through the application of the New York Convention. However, the restrictions on party autonomy that may arise when a cargo claimant initiates judicial proceedings in breach of an arbitration agreement pose challenges. The judge *ex officio* or the defendant will have to raise their concerns and request the enforcement of the valid arbitration clause. Such clause may be contained in the charterparty or be incorporated into the B/L.

The rights of the parties enshrined in Article VII of the New York Convention restrict the applicability of Articles 468 and 251 SAMN. The 'public order exception' to refuse the recognition and enforcement of an arbitration agreement lacks an international homogeneous interpretation. The 'public order exception' of Article V(2)(b) of the New York Convention has not resulted in a uniform concept of public policy. The interpretation, whether international or domestic, varies from country to country. English courts have not defined the concept of public policy, but the core values of the English legal system reflect a pragmatic, case-by-case approach, based on laws, statutes and case law referring to constitutional matters. By contrast, Spain has consistently relied on a restrictive concept of public policy relying on judicial control based on the domestic and international principles of the applicable legal regimes.

5 Perspectives for a new specialised convention on maritime matters

Certain norms are used for subjective characterisation of the carriage of goods by sea to show that it is inherently international. Substantive or material party autonomy in agreements concerning maritime carriers and other relevant actors in the carriage of goods by sea is necessary in order to achieve international harmonisation. Ideally, global leaders among maritime states should agree on a new independent and specialised convention on jurisdiction and the recognition and enforcement of judgments in maritime matters. The proposed instrument could be negotiated under the auspices of the UNCTAD, the CMI or the Hague Conference on Private International Law.

Inspiration to propose a new international instrument comes from examining the Hague Choice of Court Convention. The convention contains exclusions and specific ad hoc limitations in its scope of application, based on the objectives of the convention, which do not conflict with practice in the maritime sector. In contrast, other sectors include protective dimensions (e.g., consumers' rights or insurance) in relation to the scope of party autonomy. The main problem with the Hague Choice of Court Convention is that its scope of application does not cover certain maritime matters: it does not apply to the carriage of goods by sea, the limitation of liability for maritime claims and voyage charterparties. The Hague Choice of Court Convention is only applicable to exclusive and, not asymmetric, choice of court agreements as set out by Article 3(a):

> "Exclusive choice of court agreement" means an agreement concluded by two or more parties that meets the requirements of paragraph (c) and designates, for the purpose of deciding disputes which have arisen or may arise in connection with a particular legal relationship, the

courts of one Contracting State or one or more specific courts of one Contracting State to the exclusion of the jurisdiction of any other courts.

It requires that the choice of court agreement must be 'concluded or documented' 'in writing' or 'by any other means of communication which renders information accessible so as to be usable for subsequent reference'.

The jurisdiction of the chosen court under Article 5(1) of the Hague Choice of Court Convention must be exercised by 'the court or courts of a Contracting State designated in an exclusive choice of court agreement … unless the agreement is null and void under the law of that State'. The designated court of a contracting state cannot decline jurisdiction to hear the case, according to Article 5(2). Consequently, the court not chosen in an exclusive jurisdiction agreement 'shall suspend or dismiss proceedings to which an exclusive choice of court agreement applies' (Article 6). The grounds for ignoring such compelling obligations under Article 6 are that:

(a) The agreement is null and void under the law of the State of the chosen court;
(b) A party lacked the capacity to conclude the agreement under the law of the State of the court seised;
(c) Giving effect to the agreement would lead to a manifest injustice or would be manifestly contrary to the public policy of the State of the court seised;
(d) For exceptional reasons beyond the control of the parties, the agreement cannot reasonably be performed; or
(e) The chosen court has decided not to hear the case.

The new international convention should also include a *lis alibi pendens* rule that precludes the enforcement of judgments by EU and non-EU courts that do not give effect to arbitration agreements agreed by the litigants between the parties. The Brussels I Regulation (recast) does not provide for such mechanism. *The Wadi Sudr* is an example of *lis alibi pendens* between English and Spanish courts where the latter judged the substance of the claim, disregarding a London arbitration clause. The CJEU in *The Front Comor* banned anti-suit injunctions restraining a party from starting proceedings in the EU. However, the parties could pursue litigation in non-EU state courts. An anti-suit injunction issued by an arbitral tribunal was held valid by the CJEU in *Gazprom* since it was out of the scope of the Brussels I Regulation (recast). This is because EU courts are not allowed to assess the validity of arbitration clauses, according to Recital 12 of the Brussels I Regulation (recast). The New York Convention has precedence over the Brussels I Regulation (recast).

The new convention on jurisdiction and the recognition and enforcement of judgments in maritime matters should apply to voyage charterparties and B/Ls, as well as to time and bareboat charters. Such convention would include an article conferring jurisdiction in maritime disputes (including cargo claims) in similar terms to Article 25 of the Brussels I Regulation (recast) and Article 3 of the Hague Choice of Court Convention. Overcoming the lack of a uniform *lis alibi pendens* rule between conflicting arbitral awards and judgments based on merits in Article II(3) of the New York Convention (that only refers parties to arbitration in cases that include existing valid agreements) would also be desirable in the new convention.

The lack of substantive validation rules to prove the existence of an arbitration agreement makes such *lis alibi pendens* rule necessary to avoid conflicting decisions and consequential forum shopping. The inclusion of a uniform interpretation of conflict of laws rulings could lead to a uniform application. The international uniformity achieved would provide for consistent arbitral awards and judgments based on merits, surpassing the scope of application of the Brussels I Regulation (recast) and the restrictive one of the Hague Choice of Court Convention on maritime matters.

This work has not analysed the recognition and enforcement of judgments and arbitral awards but rather jurisdiction and arbitration agreements. However, compliance with *lis alibi pendens* and mutual trust principles between EU Member States is required when a declaratory judgment is rendered to enforce an arbitration agreement or an award. In such case, the enforcement of an arbitral award may be restricted if the dispute has been already judged by an EU Member State court (*res judicata*).

Jurisdiction agreements in favour of EU Member State courts are not subject to public policy restrictions according to Article 45(3) of the Brussels I Regulation (recast). The *ordre public international* exception of Article 45(1)(a) applies to non-EU state court judgments but not to ones issued by EU Member State courts. However, the *ordre public international* exception of Article V(2)(b) of the New York Convention can only be raised by EU Member State courts when the recognition and enforcement of a judgment are sought, having been an award with *res judicata* effect (Article III of the New York Convention) rendered by any EU or non-EU court under Article VII(1) of the New York Convention. For the reasons mentioned above, the new convention on jurisdiction and the recognition and enforcement of judgments in maritime matters should contain a rule incorporating the *res judicata* effect given to judgments on the merits issued by EU Member State courts that ignore a valid arbitration agreement.

Compatibility rules regarding jurisdiction for the arrest of ships are contained in Article 7(1) of the 1952 Arrest Convention, which states that 'the Courts of the country in which the arrest was made shall have jurisdiction to determine the case upon its merits if the domestic law of the country in which the arrest is made gives jurisdiction to such Courts'. Article 7(3) notes the following:

> If the parties have agreed to submit the dispute to the jurisdiction of a particular Court other than that within whose jurisdiction the arrest was made or to arbitration, the Court or other appropriate judicial authority within whose jurisdiction the arrest was made may fix the time within which the claimant shall bring proceedings.

It would be desirable to include a clause ordering a court to stay proceedings if a valid jurisdiction clause is included in the contract for the carriage of goods, in cases of a cargo claim dispute under which an arrest is ordered. Moreover, this article would enhance jurisdiction for the arrest of vessels, enforcing any choice of forum or arbitration clause included in the contract for the carriage of goods by sea. The provision would mitigate conflicting decisions and better coordinate arbitral tribunals and courts, avoiding reactive and proactive forum shopping, while protecting the interests and choices of parties resolving disputes.

Such compatibility clause would reinforce Article 7(1) of the 1999 Arrest Convention, which provides for the arrest in the jurisdiction where the ship is located, enhancing party autonomy by explicitly allowing the dispute on the merits of the case when the parties have agreed a jurisdiction or arbitration clause. The judgment or award should be enforced by the courts where the ship has been arrested under Article 7(5) of the 1999 Arrest Convention.

The application of the *lis alibi pendens* rules of the Brussels I Regulation (recast) is avoided if a ship is located outside the territory of an EU Member State when the 1952 Convention (and potentially the 1999 Arrest Convention) applies. The proposed new convention would avoid the application of the *forum non conveniens* doctrine in the case of jurisdiction agreements present at the dispute. It is acknowledged that the doctrine does not apply to arbitration clauses, because the UK and Spain are bound by the New York Convention. In any case, once a judgment or award has been rendered it would be enforced where the ship has been arrested.

Thus, there is a strong need for uniform rules in order to ensure legal certainty. Possible obstacles to successful negotiations on the proposed new specialised convention for maritime matters, and subsequent approvals/ratifications, are likely to be rooted in political and legal reasons. The unilateralism of national legislators, such as the drafters of the Spanish SAMN, ignores the inherently international nature of the maritime sector and the subjective characterisation of its actors. However, there are contradictory examples in areas such as non-contractual liability caused by oil pollution, where there is strong harmonisation. The proposed new convention would be difficult to accomplish in practice. The shipowner's interests in the EU (as opposed to shippers located outside Europe in 'cargo countries') could be one reason along with political interests. The reasons are acute and would require the EU to support and authorise Member States to ratify such a new convention in maritime matters that would be prevalent over the Brussels I Regulation (recast).

What are the main obstacles for the approval of the proposed new instrument? First, Article 5 of the Hague Choice of Court Convention does not require parties to reside in a contracting state, unlike in the Brussels I Regulation (recast). Second, any contracting state may refuse to be competent (Article 19) when the residence of the parties and all the elements of the dispute, except the location of the chosen court, have no link to that state. Third, any contracting state may refuse the recognition and enforcement of a judgment of another contracting state (Article 20) when the residence of the parties and all the elements of the dispute, except the location of the chosen court, are located in the requested state. Consequently, if the choice of forum in maritime matters between non-EU and EU Member States is liberalised, EU Member States would be obliged to recognise jurisdiction agreements in favour of non-EU countries in cases of cargo dispute. This could lead to the application of the Hamburg or Rotterdam Rules, which do not generally recognise exclusive jurisdiction agreements (the Rotterdam Rules do in specific circumstances). This author believes that the negotiation of such an international instrument, despite current legal, political and economic constraints, would transform a static and descriptive playing field into a dynamic terrain.

Despite attempts made with the UN Convention on International Transport of Goods of 1980, a unified multimodal transport regime has not yet been put in place, and the still-not-in-force Rotterdam Rules offer a limited scope regarding exclusive dispute resolution agreements on volume contracts. A new international instrument should include exclusive jurisdiction and arbitration agreements, including multimodal transport, in its scope of application, and ideally, such an instrument would be ratified by both the UK and the EU. There are no clear answers as to what the future will bring in 2021 and beyond, after the expiration of the Brexit transition period, but the questions posed following the analysis of the status quo lay the ground for future research and reflection. A new instrument would represent a substantive contribution to the creation of a new regime that would benefit not just the UK and EU, but other nations around the globe. Precisely as some of the matters previously expressed have not been resolved by the time this book has been drafted, future scholars can consider and pontificate.

ANNEX I

Bibliography

Books

Abou-Nigm VR, *The Arrest of Ships in Private International Law* (Oxford University Press 2011) 78–91.

Aikens R, R Lord and M Bools, *Bills of Lading* (CRC Press 2015).

Albrecht H-C and others (eds), *Maritime Law Handbook* (Kluwer Law International 1998).

Alfons C, *Recognition and Enforcement of Annulled Foreign Arbitral Awards: An Analysis of the Legal Framework and Its Interpretation in Case Law and Literature*, Vol 12 (Peter Lang 2010).

Álvarez Rubio JJ, *Derecho Marítimo y Derecho Internacional Privado: Algunos Problemas Básicos* Vitoria-Gasteiz (Servicio de Publicaciones Gobierno Vasco 2000).

———, *The Legal Lessons of the Prestige Case: Prevention, Management and Sanction Against Marine Pollution by Hydrocarbons* (Aranzadi 2011).

Andrews N, *Arbitration and Contract Law: Common Law Perspectives*, Vol 54 (Springer 2016).

Arizon F and D Semark, *Maritime Letters of Indemnity* (CRC Press 2014).

Baatz Y and others (eds), *Maritime Law* (4th edn, Informa Law from Routledge 2018).

Bagheri M, *International Contracts and National Economic Regulation: Dispute Resolution Through International Commercial Arbitration*, Vol 11 (Kluwer Law International 2000).

Barendt EM, *An Introduction to Constitutional Law* (Oxford University Press 1998).

Batiffol H, *Les conflits de lois en matière de contrats: étude de droit international privé comparé* (Sirey 1938).

Baughen S, *Shipping Law* (Routledge 2018).

Beck G, *The Legal Reasoning of the Court of Justice of the EU* (Bloomsbury Publishing 2013).

Belintxon Martín U, *Derecho europeo y transporte internacional por carretera* (Aranzadi 2015).

Joshua S Force and Robert J Zapf (eds), *Benedict on Admiralty* (7th edn, LexisNexis 2011).

Berger KP, *International Economic Arbitration* (Deventer 1993).

Berlingieri F, *International Maritime Conventions (Volume 1): The Carriage of Goods and Passengers by Sea* (CRC Press 2014a).

———, *International Maritime Conventions (Volume 2): Navigation, Securities, Limitation of Liability and Jurisdiction* (CRC Press 2014b).

———, *Berlingieri on Arrest of Ships Berlingieri on Arrest of Ships Volume I: A Commentary on the 1952 Arrest Convention* (Informa Law from Routledge 2017a).

———, *Berlingieri on Arrest of Ships Volume II: A Commentary on the 1999 Arrest Convention* (Informa Law from Routledge 2017b).

Blackaby N, C Partasides, A Redfern and M Hunter, *Redfern and Hunter on International Arbitration* (5th edn, Oxford University Press 2009).

Blake SH, J Browne and S Sime, *A Practical Approach to Alternative Dispute Resolution* (2nd edn, Oxford University Press 2012).

Bogdan M, *Concise Introduction to EU Private International Law* (Apollo Books 2012).

Born GB, *International Arbitration: Law and Practice* (2nd edn, Wolters Kluwer Law & Business 2016).

Briggs A, *Agreements on Jurisdiction and Choice of Law* (Oxford University Press 2008).

———, *Civil Jurisdiction and Judgments* (Informa Law from Routledge 2015).

Bunikowski D, *Historical and Philosophical Foundations of European Legal Culture* (Cambridge Scholars Publishing 2016).

Bureau D and H Muir Watt, *Droit international privé*, Vol 2 (Presses Universitaires de France 2007).

Calvo Caravaca A-L and J Carrascosa González, *Derecho Internacional Privado* (Comares 2016).

———, *Tratado de Derecho internacional privado* (1st ed, Tirant Lo Blanch, València 2020).

Calvo Caravaca A-L and JD González Campos, *La sentencia extranjera en España y la competencia del juez de origen* (Tecnos 1986).

Carballo Piñeiro L, *International Maritime Labour Law* (Springer 2015) 34.

Carbone SM and F Munari, *Regole e organizzazione dei trasporti marittimi internazionali* (Giuffrè Editore 1990).

Caron DD and LM Caplan, *The UNCITRAL Arbitration Rules: A Commentary* (Oxford University Press 2013).

Carr I and P Stone, *International Trade Law* (5th edn, Routledge-Cavendish Taylor and Francis Group 2013).

Carrascosa González J, *La ley aplicable a los contratos internacionales: el Reglamento Roma I* (Colex 2009).

Chitty J, *Chitty on Contracts: General Principles*, Vol 1 (31st edn, Sweet & Maxwell 2012).

Coipel–Cordonnier N, 'Les conventions d'arbitrage et d'élection de for en droit international privé' (1999) Bibl. dr. priv. LGDJ 314.

Corcione C, *Third Party Protection in Shipping* (Taylor & Francis 2019).

Cordero Moss G, *International Commercial Arbitration: Party Autonomy and Mandatory Rules* (Tano Aschehoug 1999) 53.

Craig P and G De Búrca, *EU Law: Text, Cases, and Materials* (6th edn, Oxford University Press 2015).

Dalhuisen J, *Dalhuisen on Transnational Comparative, Commercial, Financial and Trade Law*, Vol 1 (6th edn, Bloomsbury 2016).

Davis CM, *Maritime Law Deskbook* (Compass Publishing Company 1997).

Derrington SC and JM Turner, *The Law and Practice of Admiralty Matters* (Oxford University Press 2007).

DiMatteo LA (ed), *International Sales Law: A Global Challenge* (Cambridge University Press 2014).

Dunt J, *Marine Cargo Insurance* (2nd edn, Informa Law from Routledge 2015).

Emparanza Sobejano A and JM Martín Osante (eds), *Comentarios Sobre la Ley de Navegación Marítima* (Marcial Pons 2015).

Emparanza Sobejano A and A Recalde Castells, *El contrato de transporte internacional de mercancías por ferrocarril* (Thomson Civitas 2008).

Falkanger T, HJ Bull and L Brautaset, *Scandinavian Maritime Law: the Norwegian Perspective* (4th edn, Universitetsforlaget 2017).

Fellmeth AX and M Horwitz (eds), *Guide to Latin in International Law* (Oxford University Press 2009).

Fernández Rozas JC, SA Sánchez Lorenzo y G Stampa, *Principios generales del arbitraje* (Tirant lo Blanch 2018) 24.

Fitzmaurice M, O Elias and P Merkouris (eds), *Treaty Interpretation and the Vienna Convention on the Law of Treaties: 30 Years On* (Martinus Nijhoff 2010).

Force R, M Davies and AN Yiannopoulos, *Admiralty and Maritime Law* (abr edn, Beard Books 2006).

Gabaldón García JL and JM Ruiz Soroa, *Manual de Derecho de la Navegación Marítima* (Marcial Pons 2006).
Gaudemet-Tallon H, *Compétence et exécution des jugements en Europe: Règlement no 44-2001, conventions de Bruxelles 1968, et de Lugano 1988* et 2007 (LGDJ 2010).
Gillespie A and S Weare, *The English Legal System* (6th edn, Oxford University Press 2017).
Glass DA, *Freight Forwarding and Multi Modal Transport Contracts* (Taylor & Francis 2013).
González Campos J, *Diversification, Spécialisation, Flexibilisation et Matérialisation des Règles de Droit International Privé: Cours Général, Recueil des Cours*, Vol 287 (Martinus Nijhoff 2002).
Gray JW, *Shipping Futures* (Informa Pub 1990).
Grigera Naón HA, *Choice-of-Law Problems in International Commercial Arbitration*, Vol 29 (Mohr Siebeck 1992).
Guerra M and F Nectali, *Le Conflit de Lois en Droit des Transports de Marchandises par Mer* (University of Bourgogne 2013).
Güner-Özbek MD, *The Carriage of Dangerous Goods by Sea* (Springer 2008).
Harley ST, *How to Secure a Maritime Lien: A Study* (Lampert & Selway Publishing 1981).
Hartley TC, *International Commercial Litigation: Text, Cases and Materials on Private International Law* (Cambridge University Press 2009).
———, *Choice-of-Court Agreements Under the European and International Instruments: The Revised Brussels I Regulation, the Lugano Convention and the Hague Convention* (Oxford University Press 2013).
———, *The Foundations of European Union Law* (Oxford University Press 2014).
———, *International Commercial Litigation: Text, Cases and Materials on Private International Law* (Cambridge University Press 2020).
Hervey T and others, *Research Methodologies in EU and International Law* (Bloomsbury Publishing 2011).
Hess B, *Europäisches Zivilprozessrecht* (CF Müller Verlag 2010).
Hill J, *The Law Relating to International Commercial Disputes* (Lloyd's of London Press New York 1994).
Holleaux D, J Foyer and G de Geouffre de La Pradelle, *Droit International Privé* (Masson 1987).
Houtved A, *Shipping* (Danmarks Skibsmæglerforening 2005).
Hueck A and C-W Canaris, *Recht der Wertpapiere* (12th edn, Vahlen 1986).
Jackson DC, *Enforcement of Maritime Claims*, 4th edn (Informa Law from Routledge 2006).
Jacquet J-M, *'Retour sur la règle de conflit de lois en matière de contrats' 3 JDI* (Clunet 1991).
———, *Le contrat international* (1st edn, Dalloz 1992) 112–120.
———, 'Contrats', in *Repertoire de droit international*, Vol 1 (Encyclopedie Dalloz 1998).
Jodłowski J, *'Les conventions relatives à la prorogation et à la dérogation à la compétence internationale en matière civile' 143 Rec. des Cours ADI* (Martinus Nijhoff 1974).
Joseph D, *Jurisdiction and Arbitration Agreements and Their Enforcement* (Sweet & Maxwell 2005) 108–109.
Kelsen H, *Pure Theory of Law*, translated by Max Knight (University of California Press 1967).
Kiestra LR, *The Impact of the European Convention on Human Rights on Private International Law* (Springer 2014).
Lorente Martínez I, 'Competencia Judicial Internacional y Compraventa Internacional de Mercaderías: Un Estudio de Meta Jurisprudencia Analítica' (Doctoral dissertation, Universidad de Murcia 2016).
Lundmark T, *Charting the Divide Between Common and Civil Law* (Oxford University Press 2012).
Mackie KJ, Miles D, Marsh W and Allen T, *The ADR Practice Guide* (3rd edn, Tottel Publishing 2007).
Maduro M, K Tuori and S Sankari (eds), *Transnational Law: Rethinking European Law and Legal Thinking* (Cambridge University Press 2014).

Malintoppi A, *Diritto Uniforme e Diritto Internazionale Privato in Tema di Transporto* (Guiffrè Editore 1955).

Mandaraka-Sheppard A, *Modern Maritime Law (Volume 1): Jurisdiction and Risks* (CRC Press 2013).

Mayer P and V Heuzé, *Droit international privé* (Montchrestien 2004).

Meeson N and J Kimbell, *Admiralty Jurisdiction and Practice* (Taylor & Francis 2013).

Merkin R and L Flannery, *Merkin and Flannery on the Arbitration Act 1996* (Taylor & Francis 2019).

Møllmann A, *Delivery of Goods Under Bills of Lading* (Routledge 2016).

Moses ML, *The Principles and Practice of International Commercial Arbitration* (2nd edn, Cambridge University Press 2012).

Munari F, *Il Diritto Comunitario dei Trasportti* (Guiffrè Editore 1996).

Murray C, D Holloway and D Timson-Hunt, *Schmitthoff's Export Trade: The Law and Practice of International Trade* (12th edn, Sweet and Maxwell 2012).

Mustill MJ and SC Boyd, *Commercial Arbitration: Companion Volume* (Butterworths 2001).

Neumayer KH, *Autonomie de la volonté et dispositions impératives en droit international privé des obligations* (4th edn, Revue Critique de Droit International Privé 1957).

Özdel M, *Bills of Lading Incorporating Charter Parties* (Bloomsbury Publishing 2015).

Pachecker HH, *Nafa's Blue Book: Legal Terminology, Commentaries, Tables and Useful Legal Information* (Xlibris Corporation 2010).

Park WW, *Arbitration of International Business Disputes: Studies in Law and Practice* (2nd edn, Oxford University Press 2012).

Peláez del Rosal M, *La competencia territorial en el proceso civil. El acuerdo de sumisión expresa* (Ariel 1974).

Petrochilos G, *Procedural Law in International Arbitration* (Oxford University Press 2004).

Raape L, *Internationales Privatrecht* (5th edn, Verlag Franz Vahlen 1961).

Recalde Castells A, *El Conocimiento de Embarque y Otros Documentos del Transporte. Función Representativa* (Citivas 1992).

Reimann M and R Zimmermann, *The Oxford Handbook of Comparative Law* (Oxford University Press 2006).

Reithmann C and D Martiny (Hrsg), *Internationales Vertragsrecht, Das Internationale Privatrecht der Schuldverträge* (8th rev edn, Otto Schmidt, Köln 2015).

Rodríguez Mejía M, *Medidas Cautelares en el Proceso Arbitral* (Universidad Externado de Colombia 2014).

Rogers A, J Chuah and M Dockray, *Cases and Materials on the Carriage of Goods by Sea* (Routledge 2013).

Ross A, *On Law and Justice* (University of California Press 1959).

Rowley JW (ed), *Arbitration World: Jurisdictional Comparisons* (European Lawyer Reference 2012).

Ruiz Abou-Nigm V, *The Arrest of Ships in Private International Law* (Oxford University Press 2011).

Sanchez Aristi R and N Moralejo Imbernón, *Property and Trust Law in Spain* (Kluwer Law International BV 2011).

Sánchez-Gamborino FJ, *El contrato de transporte internacional CMR* (Tecnos 1996).

Schoenbaum TJ, *Admiralty and Maritime Law*, Vol 1 (4th edn, Thomson/West 2004).

Schwab KH and G Walter, *Schiedsgerichtsbarkeit: systematischer Kommentar zu den Vorschriften der Zivilprozeßordnung, des Arbeitsgerichtsgesetzes, der Staatsverträge und der Kostengesetze über das privatrechtliche Schiedsgerichtsverfahren* (Beck 2005).

Scrutton TE and others, *Scrutton on Charter Parties and Bills of Lading* (23rd edn, Sweet & Maxwell 2015).

Seriki H, *Injunctive Relief and International Arbitration* (Informa Law from Routledge 2015).

Singh L, *The Law of Carriage of Goods by Sea* (Bloomsbury Professional 2011).
Spurin CH, *The Law of International Trade and Carriage of goods* (Nationwide Mediation Academy for NADR UK Ltd 2004).
Steingruber AM, *Consent in International Arbitration.* Oxford International Arbitration Series (Oxford University Press 2012).
Stopford M, *Maritime Economics* (3rd edn, Routledge 2009).
Tang ZS, *Jurisdiction and Arbitration Agreements in International Commercial Law* (Routledge 2014) 71.
Tetley W, *Maritime Liens and Claims* (2nd edn, Les Éditions Yvon Blais Inc 1998).
Treitel GH, FMB Reynolds and TG Carver, *Carver on Bills of Lading* (4th edn, Sweet & Maxwell 2017).
Tuori K, *European Constitutionalism* (Cambridge University Press 2015).
Twining W, *Globalisation and Legal Theory* (Cambridge University Press 2000).
Van Calster G, *European Private International Law* (Bloomsbury Publishing 2016).
Van Hoecke M (ed), *Methodologies of Legal Research: Which Kind of Method for What Kind of Discipline?* (Bloomsbury Publishing 2011).
Virgós Soriano M and F Garcimartín Alférez, *Derecho procesal civil internacional: litigación internacional* (Thomson Civitas 2007).
Vischer F, *Internationales Vertragsrecht. Die kollisionsrechtlichen Regeln der Anknüpfung bei internationalen Verträgen* (Stämpfli 1962).
von Bar L, *The Theory and Practice of Private International Law* (W Green & Sons 1892).
von Savigny FC, *System des heutigen römischen Rechts* (Leipzig 1840).
Westwood J, *Building Your Business Through Export* (Kogan Page Publishers 2012).
Zournatzi C, *Arbitrato e Contratti di Trasporto Marittimo* (Cedam 2014).
Zweigert K, H Kötz and T Weir, *Introduction to Comparative Law*, Vol 3 (Clarendon Press Oxford 1998).

Contributions to edited books and journal articles

Abarca Junco AP (dir), 'La competencia judicial de los tribunales españoles: Foro de la autonomía de la voluntad' (2013), *Derecho Internacional Privado*, Madrid, UNED 134.
Albors Méndez E and J Portales Rodríguez, 'Capítulo 4 Cuestiones jurisdiccionales en el Derecho Marítimo. Los Casos "FRONT COMOR" y "WADI SUDR"', in JL García-Pita y Lastres, MR Quintáns-Eiras and A Díaz de la Rosa (eds), *Estudios De Derecho Marítimo* (Thomson Reuters-Aranzadi 2012) 121–140.
———, 'Embargo Preventivo De Buques', in Emparanza Sobejano and others (eds), *Comentarios sobre la Ley de Navegación Marítima* (Marcial Pons 2015).
Álvarez Rubio JJ, 'Hacia un nuevo Derecho Marítimo Comunitario: Breves Reflexiones en el Marco de las Tendencias Actuales del Derecho Internacional Privado', in Julio D González Campos (ed), *Pacis Artes. Obra Homenaje al Profesor Julio D González Campos*, Vol 2 (Edifer 2005) 1165.
———, 'La regla de especialidad como cauce para superar los conflictos normativos entre el Derecho comunitario y los Convenios internacionales en materias especiales', 7499 *Diario La Ley* (2010) 2.
———, 'Comentario a la sentencia del TJUE de 4 de mayo de 2010, Asunto C-533/08 TNT Express Nederland BV c. AXA Versicherung AG', 1 *Revista Jurídica de Catalunya* (2011) 266.
———, 'La Dimensión Procesal Internacional en la Ley de Navegación Marítima', 159 *Anuario Español de Derecho Internacional Privado* (2014–2015) 14–15.
Álvarez Rubio JJ and U Belintxon Martín, 'La Nueva Ley de Navegación Marítima desde la Perspectiva del Derecho Internacional', in E Sobejano and others (eds), *Comentarios sobre la Ley de Navegación Marítima* (Marcial Pons 2015).

———, 'Entre La Haya, Hamburgo y Rotterdam: La compleja opción legislativa interna ante las cuestiones de jurisdicción y arbitraje en el derecho marítimo', 17 *Spanish Yearbook of Private International Law* (2017) 596.

———, 'A Correct Jurisprudential Orientation in Relation to the Validity and Scope of the Submissive Clause in Favour of a Foreign Court Contained in a Bill of Lading. Commentary on the Judgment of February 13, 2019 of the Provincial Court of Barcelona (Section 15)', 11(2) *Cuadernos de Derecho Transnacional* (2019a) 388.

———, 'Una aproximación jurisprudencial a la Ley de Navegación Marítima desde la óptica del derecho internacional', in A Emparanza Sobejano and JM Martín Osante (eds), *Ley de Navegación Marítima: Balance de su aplicación práctica* (Marcial Pons 2019b).

Añoveros Terradas B, 'Restrictions on Jurisdiction Clauses in Consumer Contracts within the European Union', 1 *Oxford University Comparative Law Forum* (University of Oxford 2003), available at: <https://ouclf.iuscomp.org/restrictions-on-jurisdiction-clauses-in-consumer-contracts-within-the-european-union/#fn180sym> (accessed 15 January 2018).

Baatz Y, 'Jurisdiction and Arbitration', in TD Rhidian (ed), *New Convention for the Carriage of Goods by Sea-the Rotterdam Rules: An Analysis of the UN Convention on Contracts for the International Carriage of Goods Wholly or Partly by Sea* (Lawtext Publishing 2009) 258.

———, 'Jurisdiction and Arbitration', in TD Rhidian (ed), *The Carriage of Goods by Sea Under the Rotterdam Rules* (Lloyd's List 2010a) 319.

———, 'A Jurisdiction Race in the Dark', *Lloyd's Maritime and Commercial Law Quarterly* (2010b) 364.

———, 'Forum Selection in Contracts for the Carriage of Goods by Sea: The European Dimension', 2 *Lloyd's Maritime and Commercial Law Quarterly* (2011a) 208.

———, 'Jurisdiction and Arbitration in Multimodal Transport', 36 *Tulane Maritime Law Journal* (2011b) 643.

———, 'Chapter 14 Jurisdiction' and 'Chapter 15 Arbitration', in Y Baatz, C Debattista, F Lorenzon, A Serdy, H Staniland and MN Tsimplis, *The Rotterdam Rules: A Practical Annotation* (CRC Press 2013).

———, 'Thirty Years of Europeanisation of Conflict of Laws and Still all at Sea?', in M Clarke (ed), *Maritime Law Evolving: Thirty Years at Southampton* (Hart Publishing 2015a).

———, 'Should Third Parties Be Bound by Arbitration Clauses in Bills of Lading?', 1 *Lloyd's Maritime and Commercial Law Quarterly* (2015b) 85.

———, 'Charter Party Arbitration Clause in a Bill of Lading and Its Effect on Third Parties', in M Goldby (ed), *Role of Arbitration in Shipping Law* (Oxford University Press 2016) 107.

———, 'The Conflicts of Laws, in Y Baatz and others (eds), *Maritime Law* (4th edn, Informa Law from Routledge 2018) 1.

———, 'Choice of Jurisdiction in Bills of Lading and Cargo Insurance', in Jason Chuah (ed), *Research Handbook on Maritime Law and Regulation* (Edward Elgar Publishing 2019).

Badia A, 'Jurisdicción y competencia', in JC Fuentes Gómez and others (eds), *Comentarios a la Ley de Navegación Marítima* (Dykinson 2015) 415–428.

Basedow J, 'Exclusive Choice-of-Court Agreements as a Derogation from Imperative Norms', in P Lindskoug, U Maunsbach, G Millqvist, P Samuelsson and H-H Vogel (eds), *Essays in Honour of Michael Bogdan* (Juristförlaget i Lund 2013) 15–31, Max Planck Private Law Research Paper No 14/1.

Batiffol H, 'Subjectivisme et objectivisme dans le droit international privé des contrats', in *Choix d'Articles rassemblés par ses amis* (Librairie General de Droit et de Jurisprudence 1976) 249–263.

———, *Unilatéralisme et contrats en droit international privé*, Liber amicorum AF Schnitzer (Librairie de l'Université de Genève 1979) 7–31.

Baughen S, 'Bailment's Continuing Role in Cargo Claims', *Lloyd's Maritime and Commercial Law Quarterly* (1999) 393.

———, 'Misdelivery and the Boundaries of Contract and Tort', *Lloyd's Maritime and Commercial Law Quarterly* (2003) 413.

Beck G, 'The Macro Level: The Structural Impact of General International Law on EU Law: The Court of Justice of the EU and the Vienna Convention on the Law of Treaties', 35 *Yearbook of European Law* (2016) 1.

Belintxon Martín U, 'Derecho internacional privado y Derecho marítimo internacional: competencia judicial internacional y acuerdos atributivos de jurisdicción en la LNM', 12(1) *Cuadernos de Derecho Transnacional* (2020).

Bell AP, 'Sub-Bailment on Terms', (chapter 5), in N Palmer and E McKendrick (eds), *Interests in Goods* (Lloyd's of London Press 1993).

Berlingieri F, 'Uniformité du Droit Maritime. Quelques Problems', 3 *Il Dir Mar* (1992) 796.

———, 'The History of the Rotterdam Rules', in Meltem Deniz Guner-Özbek (ed), *The History of the Rotterdam Rules, The United Nations Convention on Contracts for the International Carriage of Goods Wholly or Partly by Sea—An Appraisal of the Rotterdam Rules'* (Springer Science & Business Media 2011) 1–63.

Binocoli F, 'Note e osservazioni a sentenza. La disciplina applicabile al lavoro portuale temporaneo. La sfera di applicazione del CCNL unico' (comments and critics to the Italian judgment of the *Corte di Cassazione* Judgment of 17 January 2005, No 731, *SGL Carbon SPA v Agenzia Marittima La Rosa SRL*), 108 *Diritto marittimo* (2006) 1–221.

Böger O, *The Case for a New Protocol to the Cape Town Convention Covering Security Over Ships* (Taylor & Francis 2016).

Bonassies P, '*La Responsabilité du Transporteur Maritime dans les Règles de la Haye et dans les Règles de Hambourg*', *Il Dir Mar* (1989) 949.

Born GB, 'The Law Governing International Arbitration Agreements: An International Perspective', 26 *S Ac L J* (2014) 814.

Borrás A, 'La Comunitarización Del Derecho Internacional Privado: Pasado, Presente y Futuro', 1 *Cursos de Derecho Internacional y Relaciones Internacionales de Vitoria-Gasteiz* (2001) 285.

Breitenmoser S and L Wildhaber, 'The Relationship Between Customary International Law and Municipal Law in Western European Countries', 48 *Zeitschrift für ausländisches öffentliches Recht und Völkerrecht* (1988) 163–207.

Brekoulakis S, 'The Relevance of the Interests of Third Parties in Arbitration: Taking a Closer Look at the Elephant in the Room', 113 *Penn St L Rev* (2008) 1165.

Briggs A, 'The Validity of 'Floating' Choice of Law and Jurisdiction Clauses', *Lloyd's Maritime and Commercial Law Quarterly* (1986) 508.

———, 'The Subtle Variety of Jurisdiction Agreements', 3 *Lloyd's Maritime and Commercial Law Quarterly* (2012) 364.

Calvo Caravaca AL and J Carrascosa González, 'Medidas cautelares y comercio internacional', 18 *Cuadernos de derecho judicial* (2004) 409.

Carbone SM, 'Art. 2', in F Pocar and S Bariatti (eds), *Commentario del nuovo diritto internazionale privato* (CEDAM 1996) 8.

Carrillo Pozo LF, 'La ley aplicable al contrato en defecto de elección: un análisis de la jurisprudencia', 74 *Revista del poder judicial* (Consejo General del Poder Judicial 2004) 11.

Chan FWH, 'Anti-Suit Injunctions and the Doctrine of Comity', 79(2) *The Modern Law Review* (2016) 341.

Coldwell R, 'Jurisdiction and the UN Convention on Contracts for the International Carriage of Goods: Where the Freedom of Contract Prevails', 17 *Int'l Trade & Bus L Rev* (2014) 108.

Cordero Moss G, 'International Contracts between Common Law and Civil Law: Is Non-State Law to Be Preferred? The Difficulty of Interpreting Legal Standards such as Good Faith', 7(1) *Global Jurist* (2007) 1.

Davies M, 'Forum Selection Clauses in Maritime Cases', 27 *Tulane Maritime Law Journal* (2002) 367.
———, 'Litigation Fights Back: Avoiding the Effect of Arbitration Clauses in Charterparty Bills of Lading', 35 *J Mar L & Com* (2004) 617.
De Borja Langelaan Osset F, 'Jurisprudencial Examination on the Legal and Procedural Regime of Jurisdiction Clauses Inserted in Bills of Lading: Current Situation and Foreseeable Future', 11(1) *Cuadernos de Derecho Transnacional* (2019) 408, 432–433.
De Miguel Asensio PA, 'El nuevo Reglamento sobre competencia judicial y reconocimiento y ejecución de resoluciones', *La Ley* 34(8013) (2013).
———, 'The Rome I and Rome II Regulations in International Commercial Arbitration', in F Ferrari (ed), *The Impact of EU Law on International Commercial Arbitration* (JurisNet 2017) 177–243.
Debattista C, 'Cargo Claims and Bills of Lading', in Y Baatz and others (eds), *Maritime Law* (4th edn, Informa Law from Routledge 2018) 187.
Delaume GR, 'Clauses d'élection de for et clauses compromissoires : évolution et gestation d'un nouveau droit américain en gestation', *JDI* (1975) 486.
Diamond A, 'The Rotterdam Rules', 4 *LMCLQ* (2009) 445.
Dickinson A, 'Territory in the Rome I and Rome II Regulations', in *The Hamburg Lectures on Maritime Affairs 2011–2013* (Springer Berlin Heidelberg 2015) 69.
Diena G, *Principes du Droit International Privé Maritime*, *Recueil des Cours*, Vol 51 (Martinus Nijhoff 1935I) 405.
Dorbeck-Jung BR, 'Comparative Legislative Studies', in E Attwooll and P Comanducci (eds), *Sources of Law and Legislation, Proceedings of the 17th World Congress of the IVR*, ARSP-Beiheft 69, Steiner, 1995 (1998).
Dutoit B and F Majoros, 'Le lacis des conflits de conventions et leurs solutions possibles', 565 *Rev. crit. DIP* (1984) 577.
Echebarria Fernández J, 'La Política Marítima Comunitaria : Interacción Entre Derecho Público-Privado y los Diferentes Bloques Normativos en Presencia', 12 *Revista de Derecho del Transporte: Terrestre, Marítimo, Aéreo y Multimodal* (2013) 173.
———, 'Action Research and Efficient Maritime Transport Contract Negotiation', in PA Nielsen, PK Schmidt and K Dyppel Weber (eds), *Erhvervsretlige Emner* (Djøf/Jurist-og Økonomforbundet 2015) 49.
———, 'Party Autonomy and the Arrest of Ships from a Comparative Perspective', in José Manuel Martín Osante and Olga Fotinopoulou Basurko (eds), *New Trends in Maritime Law: Maritime Liens, Arrest of Ships, Mortgages and Forced Sale* (Thomson Reuters 2017) 498.
———, 'Limitations on Jurisdiction and Arbitration Agreements Based on Applicable Law and the Identity of the Carrier in Cargo Claim Disputes: Who and Where to Sue?', 11(1) *Cuadernos de derecho transnacional* (2019a) 306.
———, 'The European Union's Post-"Brexit" Decisión-Making Capacity in the Development of International Maritime Law', 22 *Revista de derecho del transporte: Terrestre, marítimo, aéreo y multimodal* (2019b) 207.
———, 'Paramount Clause and Codification of International Shipping Law' 50(1) *Journal of Maritime Law & Commerce* (2019c) 45.
Espinosa Calabuig R, 'Las Cláusulas Arbitrales Marítimas a la Luz de los Usos del Tráfico Internacional', 13 *Revista Electrónica de Estudios Internacionales* (2007) 2.
———, 'Cuestiones de jurisdicción y la ley aplicable al transporte maritimo tras las "Reglas de Rotterdam" y el reglamento "Roma I"', 113(1) *Dir Mar* (2011) 18.
Feliu Álvarez de Sotomayor S, 'Nulidad de las cláusulas de jurisdiccion y ley aplicable a la luz de la ley 3/2014 por la que se modifica el texto refundido de la ley general para la defensa de consumidores y usuarios', 29 *Revista electrónica de estudios internacionales (REEI)* (2015) 5.

Fernández Rozas JC, 'El Arbitraje Comercial Internacional entre la Autonomía, la Anacionalidad y la Deslocalización' 57(2) *Revista Española de Derecho Internacional* (2005) 605.

———, 'La Comunitarización del Derecho Internacional Privado y Derecho Aplicable a las Obligaciones Contractuales' 140 *Revista española de seguros: Publicación doctrinal de Derecho y Economía de los Seguros privados* (2009) 595.

———, 'La ordenación de las relaciones privadas internacionales a través de tratados en las postrimerías de su ciclo histórico', in Santiago Torres Bernárdez and others (eds), *El Derecho internacional en el mundo multipolar del siglo XXI. Obra homenaje al profesor Luis Ignacion Sánchez Rodríguez* (Iprolex 2013) 54.

———, 'Alternatives and Uncertainties of the Dispute Settlement Clauses in International Maritime Contracts', 10(2) *Cuadernos de Derecho Transnacional* (2018) 333.

Ferrari F, 'Have the Dragons of Uniform Sales Law Been Tamed? Ruminations on the CISG's Autonomous Interpretation by Courts', in CB Andersen and Ulrich G Schroeter (eds), *Sharing International Commercial Law across National Boundaries: Festschrift for Albert H Kritzer on the Occasion of his Eightieth Birthday* (Wildy, Simmonds & Hill Publishing 2008).

Force R and M Davies, 'Forum Selection Clauses in International Maritime Contracts', in M Davies (ed), *Jurisdiction and Forum Selection in International Maritime Law* (Wolters Kluwer 2005) 32.

Forner-Delaygua Q, 'Changes to Jurisdiction Based on Exclusive Jurisdiction Agreements Under the Brussels I Regulation Recast', 11(3) *Journal of Private International Law* (2015) 379.

Francq S, 'Article 34', in U Magnus and P Mankowski (eds), *Brussels I Regulation – European Commentaries on Private International Law* (Sellier, 2012).

Franzina P, 'Lis Pendens Involving a Third Country Under the Brussels I-bis Regulation: An Overview', *Rivista di diritto internazionale privato e processuale* (2014) 23.

Garau Sobrino FF, 'Los acuerdos atributivos de jurisdicción en Derecho Procesal Civil Internacional español' 2(2) *Cuadernos de Derecho Transnacional* (2010) 52.

Garcimartín Alférez F, 'The Judgments Convention: Some Open Questions', 67(1) *Netherlands International Law Review* (2020) 19.

Gayán Rodríguez E, 'El Arbitraje Internacional en las Pólizas de Fletamento y en los Conocimientos de Embarque', *Revista de la Corte Española de Arbitraje* (1996) 22.

Giardina A, 'La lex mercatoria e la certezza del diritto nei commerci e negli investimenti internazionali', 28 *Rivista di diritto internazionale privato e processuale* (1992) 461.

Giaschi CJ, *Canadian Law of Carriage of Goods by Sea: An Overview* (Giaschi & Margolis November 2004), available at: <www.admiraltylaw.com/papers/carriage_of_goods_outline.pdf> (accessed 8 June 2018).

Gómez Jene M, 'Las Cláusulas de Jurisdicción y Arbitraje en la Nueva Ley de Navegación Marítima', 6(2) *Cuadernos de Derecho Transnacional* (2014) 112.

———, 'El convenio arbitral: statu quo = The arbitration agreement: statu quo', 9(2) *Cuadernos de derecho transnacional* (2017) 7.

González Pellicer JM, 'Sobre el Artículo 468 del Proyecto de Ley de Navegación Marítima y la Nulidad de las Cláusulas de Elección de Foro en los Conocimientos de Embarque', 8354 *Diario La Ley* (2014) 6.

Gorton L, 'The Liability for Freight', in U Bernitz and J Ramberg (eds), *Festskrift Till Jan Ramberg* (Juristförlaget 1996) 165.

Graffi LD, 'Securing Harmonized Effects of Arbitration Agreements Under the New York Convention', 28 *Houston Journal of International Law* 2006 663 [768].

Gürses Ö and J Hjalmarsson, 'Marine Insurance', in Yvonne Baatz and others (eds), *Maritime Law* (4th edn, Informa Law from Routledge 2018) 489.

Hausmann R, 'Einheitliche Anknüpfung internationaler Gerichtsstands– und Schiedsvereinbarungen?', in Werner Lorenz, Bernhard Pfister and Michael R Will (eds), *Festschrift für Werner Lorenz zum siebzigsten Geburtstag* (Mohr Siebeck 1991).

Honnold JO, 'Uniform Laws for International Trade: Early Care and Feeding for Uniform Growth', 53 *Int' L Trade & Bus LJ* (1995) 1.

Iráculis Arregui N, 'La controvertida negociación individual y separada de las cláusulas de jurisdicción y arbitraje en la Ley de Navegación Marítima', 19 *Revista de Derecho del Transporte: Terrestre, Marítimo, Aéreo y Multimodal* (2017) 173.

Jambu-Merlin R and others, 'L'Arbitrage Maritime', in *Etudes Offertes à Renè Rodière* (Dalloz 1981) 401.

Jessen H and G Theocharidis, 'National Translations of the Arrest Conventions: European Civil Law Jurisdictions', in P Myburgh (ed), *The Arrest Conventions International Enforcement of Maritime Claims* (Hart, 2019).

Jiménez Blanco P, 'La Aplicación del Foro Contractual del Reglamento Bruselas I a los Contratos de Transporte Aéreo de Pasajeros', 7294 *La Ley Unión Europea* (30 November 2009) 1.

Johnson A, A Pertoldi, N Peacock and H Ambrose, 'The Recast Brussels Regulation: Implications for Commercial Parties', 26(1) *PLC Mag* (2015) 19–26.

Kahn-Freund O, 'La notion anglaise de la proper law of the contract devant les juges et devant les arbitres. Ses développements récents et des affinités avec l'avant-projet européen d'unification des regles de conflit en la matiere', *Revue Critique de Droit International Privé* (1973) 607.

———, 'Jurisdiction Agreements: Some Reflections', 26(4) *International and Comparative Law Quarterly* (1977) 825.

Kaufmann-Kohler G, 'La Clause D'Élection De for dans les Contrats Internationaux', in *Schriftenreihe des Instituts für Internationales Recht und Internationale Beziehungen*, Vol 29 (Helbing und Lichtenhahn 1980).

———, 'How to Handle Parallel Proceedings: A Practical Approach to Issues such as Competence-Competence and Anti-Suit Injunctions', 2 *Disp Resol Int'l* (2008) 110.

Kavussanos MG and AH Alixadeh-M, 'Seasonality Patterns in Dry Bulk Shipping Spot and Time Charter Freight Rates', 37(6) *Transportation Research Part E: Logistics and Transportation Review* (2001) 443.

———, 'The Expectations Hypothesis of the Term Structure and Risk Premiums in Dry Bulk Shipping Freight Markets', *Journal of Transport Economics and Policy* (2002a) 267.

———, 'Seasonality Patterns in Tanker Spot Freight Rate Markets', 19(5) *Economic Modelling* (2002b) 747.

Keenan RT, 'Charter Parties and Bills of Lading', *Marq L Rev* 42 (1958) 346.

Kessedjian C, 'Mandatory Rules of Law in International Arbitration: What Are Mandatory Rules?', 18(1–2) *Am Rev Int'l Arb* (2007) 147.

Lagarde P, 'Première Partie. -Doctrine et Chroniques-Remarques sur la proposition de règlement de la Commision européenne sur la loi applicable aux obligations contractuelles (Rome I)', 95(2) *Revue critique de droit international privé* (2006) 331.

Lagoudis IN, CS Lalwani and MM Naim, 'A Generic Systems Model for Ocean Shipping Companies in the Bulk Sector', *Transportation Journal* (2004) 56.

Lando O, 'Private International Law: Contracts', in Kurt Lipsten (ed), *International Encyclopedia of Comparative Law*, Vol III (Martinus Nijhoff Publishers 1976a).

———, 'Contracts, Chapter 24', in Kurt Lipsten (ed), *International Encyclopedia of Comparative Law*, Vol III (Martinus Nijhoff Publishers 1976b).

Leible S, 'La importancia de la autonomía conflictual para el futuro del Derecho de los contratos internacionales', 3(1) *Cuadernos de Derecho Transnacional* (2011) 214.

Lewins K and A Nair, 'International Recent Developments: Australia', 37 *Tulane Maritime Law Journal* (2012) 559.

Li L, 'Binding Effect of Arbitration Clauses on Holders of Bills of Lading as Non-Original Parties and a Potential Uniform Approach through Comparative Analysis', 37 *Tulane Maritime Law Journal* (2012) 107.

Luzzatto R, *Metodi di Unificazione del Diritto Marittimo e Interpretazione Uniforme* (Dir Mar 1999I) 147.

Lynn RW, 'A Comment on the New International Convention on Arrest of Ships, 1999', 55 *U Miami L Rev* (2000) 453.

Lyridis DV and others, 'Optimizing Shipping Company Operations Using Business Process Modelling', 32(4) *Maritime Policy & Management* (2005) 403.

Magallón Elósegui, N, 'Agreements Conferring Jurisdiction in Favour of a Foreign Court Included in a Bill of Lading: Customs and Contractual Freedom in the Maritime Sector: Commentary on the Order of 5 July 2019 of the AAP de Madrid (Section 28)', 12(1) *Cuadernos Derecho Transnacional* (2020) 619.

Maher G and BJ Rodger, 'Provisional and Protective Remedies: The British Experience of the Brussels Convention', 48(2) *International and Comparative Law Quarterly* (1999) 302.

Mankowski P, 'Rom I-VO und Schiedsverfahren', 57(1) *Recht der internationalen Wirtschaft* (2011) 30.

Martiny D, 'vor Artikel 27', in Franz Jürgen Säcker and Kurt Rebmann (eds), 7 *Münchener Kommentar zum Bürgerlichen Gesetzbuch* (CH Beck 1990) NM 50.

Mayer FC, 'Art. 19 EUV', in E Grabitz, M Hilf and M Nettesheim (eds), *Das Recht der Europäischen Union* (Beck 2011).

Meisel F, 'The Mareva Injunction-Recent Development', *Lloyd's Maritime and Commercial Law Quarterly* (1980) 38.

Michaels R, 'The Functional Method of Comparative Law', in Mathias Reimann and Reinhard Zimmermann (eds), *The Oxford Handbook of Comparative Law* (Oxford University Press 2006).

Micklitz H-W, 'The Internal vs. the External Dimension of European Private Law – A Conceptual Design and a Research Agenda', EUI Working Paper LAW 2015/35, ERC-ERPL Project, European University Institute (2015).

Møllmann A, 'International Recent Developments: Denmark', 38(2) *Tulane Maritime Law Journal* (2014) 613.

Mora Capitán B, 'El embargo preventivo de buques: (Título IX. Normas Procesales. Capítulo I)', in A Emparanza Sobejano and JM Martín Osante (eds), *Estudio sistemático de la propuesta de Anteproyecto de Ley General de la Navegación Marítima* (Servicio Central de Publicaciones del Gobierno Vasco 2006) 709.

———, 'Unificación internacional del embargo preventivo de buques del convenio de Bruselas de 1952 al convenio de Ginebra de 1999', 24 (Anuario de Derecho Marítimo 2007) 91.

Muir Watt H, 'Party Autonomy in International Contracts: From the Makings of a Myth to the Requirements of Global Governance', 6(3) *European Review of Contract Law* (2010) 250.

Mukherjee PK and AB Bal, 'A Legal and Economic Analysis of the Volume Contract Concept Under the Rotterdam Rules: Selected Issues in Perspective', 77(1) *Journal of Transportation Law, Logistics & Policy* (2010) 27.

Nielsen PA, 'The Hague Judgements Convention', 80 *Nordic J Int'l L* (2011) 95.

———, 'The Hague 2019 Judgments Convention – From Failure to Success?', *Journal of Private International Law* (2020) 1.

Niklasson A-K, *A Comparison Between the Jurisdictional Rules in the EU and the US in the Light of the Arrest Convention and the Possibility to Shop for Forum* (School of Economics and Commercial Law, Department of Law, Göteborg University 2003).

Nossal S, 'The Bailment on Terms and the Carriage of Goods by Sea: The Mahkutai', 24(1) *Hong Kong Law Journal* (1994) 19.

Olesen TR, *Value Creation in the Maritime Chain of Transportation* (CBS Maritime 2015).

Ortolani P, 'Anti-Suit Injunction in Support of Arbitration Under the Recast Brussels I Regulation', MPI Luxembourg Working Paper Series No 6 (2015).

Özdel M, 'Enforcement of Arbitration Clauses in Bills of Lading: Where Are We Now?', 33(2) *Journal of Int'l Arbitration* (2016) 151.

Palmer N, 'Ambulatory Bailments', 36(1) *Current Legal Problems* (1983) 91.

———, 'Sub-Bailment on Terms', *Lloyd's Maritime and Commercial Law Quarterly* (1988) 466.

Paulsson J, 'The New York Convention in International Practice Problems of Assimilation International Practice – Problems of Assimilation', in *The New York Convention* (ASA Special Series No 9 1996).

Paz Ares C, 'Naturaleza Jurídica de la Letra de Cambio', in Aurelio Menéndez-Menéndez (ed), *Derecho Cambiario Estudios sobre la Ley Cambiaria y del Cheque* (Cívitas 1986).

Pejovic C, 'Civil Law and Common Law: Two Different Paths Leading to the Same Goal', 32 *Victoria U Wellington L Rev* (2001) 817.

Pryles M, 'Comparative Aspects of Prorogation and Arbitration Agreements', 25(3) *International and Comparative Law Quarterly* (1976) 543.

———, 'Limits to Party Autonomy in Arbitral Procedure', 24 *Journal of Int'l Arbitration* (2007) 327.

Quiñones Escámez A, 'Evolución de la admisibilidad de la cláusula atributiva de competencia internacional en Derecho español y comparado', 86(3) *Revista jurídica de Catalunya* (1987) 657.

Rabel E, 'Das Problem Der Qualifikation', *Zeitschrift Für Ausländisches Und Internationales Privatrecht* (1931) 241.

Ramberg J, 'Freedom of Contract in Maritime Law', *Lloyd's Maritime and Commercial Law Quarterly* (1993) 178.

———, 'Unification of Transport Law: Difficulties and Possibilities', *Il Dir Mar* (2010) 813.

Rares S, 'The Far from Halcyon Isle: Maritime Liens, Renvoi and Conflicts of Law', 28 *Australian and New Zealand Maritime Law Journal* (2014) 1.

Reinhardt F, R Casadesus-Masanell and F Nellemann, 'Maersk Line and the Future of Container Shipping.' *Harvard Business School Case* 712–449 (May 2012, revised February 2015).

Requejo Isidro M, *Recognition and Enforcement in the New Brussels I Regulation (Regulation 1215/2012, Brussels I recast): The Abolition of Exequatur* (The European Judicial Training Network [EJTN] 2014).

Reynolds, F, 'The Hague Rules, the Hague-Visby Rules, and the Hamburg Rules', 7 *Australian and New Zealand Maritime Law Journal* (1990) 16.

Rheinstein M, R von Borries and H-E Niethammer, *Einführung in die Rechtsvergleichung*, Vol 31 (Beck 1987).

Rigaux F, 'Examen des Quelques Questions Laissees Ouvertes par la Convention de Rome sur la Loi Applicable aux Obligations Contractuelles', *Cahiers de droit européen* (1988) 306.

Rodrigo de Larrucea J, *Aspectos Jurídicos de las Terminales Portuarias: El Tratamiento de los Riesgos y Responsabilidades Portuarias* (Polytechnic University of Catalonia 2008) 1.

Rogerson P, 'Lis Pendens and Third States: The Commission's Proposed Changes to the Brussels I Regulation', in E Lein (ed), *The Brussels Review Proposal Uncovered* (British Institute of International and Comparative Law 2012) 101–124, 118.

Romano GP, 'Le Choix des Principes UNIDROIT par les Contractants à l'Épreuve des Règles impératives', in *The UNIDROIT Principles 2004, Their Impact on Contractual Practice, Jurisprudence and Codification*, Vol 134(2) (Journal du droit international 2007) 473.

Salachová B and B Vitek, 'Interpretation of European Law, Selected Issues', 61(7) *Acta Universitatis Agriculturae et Silviculturae Mendelianae Brunensis* (2013) 2717.

Samuel A, 'Separability of Arbitration Clauses Some Awkward Questions About the Law on Contracts, Conflict of Laws and the Administration of Justice', 9 *ADRLJ* (2000) 36, available at: <www.adamsamuel.com/pdfs/separabi.pdf> (accessed 20 February 2017).

Samuel G, 'Comparative Law and its Methodology', in Dawn Watkins and Mandy Burton (eds), *Research Methods in Law* (Routledge 2013) 100–118.

Sánchez-Horneros Adán AM, 'La Ley 14/2014, De 24 De Julio, De Navegación Marítima: Última Llamada Para La Jurisdicción Española En Asuntos Marítimos', 8802 Diario La Ley (2016) 2.

Schlechtriem P, 'Deliktsansprüche und die Sonderordnung der Haftung aus Fracht- und ähnlichen Verträgen' *Zeitschrift für das Gesamte Handels-und Konkursrecht* (1970) 105.

Siehr K, 'Die Parteiautonomie im Internationalen Privatrecht', in P Forstmoser, H Giger and others (eds), *Festschrift für Max Keller* (Schulthess 1989) 485.

Sparka F, 'Hamburg Studies on Maritime Affairs', in Jürgen Basedow and others (eds), *Jurisdiction and Arbitration Clauses in Maritime Transport Documents* (19th edn, Springer 2010).

Strong SI, 'What Constitutes an Agreement in Writing in International Commercial Arbitration-Conflicts between the New York Convention and the Federal Arbitration Act', 48 *Stan J Int'l L* (2012) 47.

Sturley MF, 'Can Commercial Law Accommodate New Technologies in International Shipping?', in Barış Soyer and Andrew Tettenborn (eds), *New Technologies, Artificial Intelligence and Shipping Law in the 21st Century* (Informa 2019).

Sturley MF, 'Jurisdiction and Arbitration Under the Rotterdam Rules', 14 *Unif L Rev* (2009) 945.

Suderow J, 'Nuevas normas de litispendencia y conexidad para Europa: ¿el ocaso del torpedo italiano? ¿flexibilidad versus previsibilidad?', 5(1) *Cuadernos de Derecho Transnacional* (2013) 184.

Tarman ZD, 'Jurisdiction and Arbitration Under the Rotterdam Rules', in MD Güner-Özbek (ed), The United Nations Convention on Contracts for the International Carriage of Goods Wholly or Partly by Sea: An Appraisal of the 'Rotterdam Rules' (Springer 2011) 265.

Tay A E-S, 'The Essence of Bailment: Contract, Agreement or Possession?', *Sydney Law Review* (1966) 239.

Tetley W, 'Arrest, Attachment, and Related Maritime Law Procedures', 73 *Tul L Rev* (1998) 1895.

———, 'Maritime Transportation', in Herber (ed), *XII International Encyclopedia of Comparative Law* (Mohr Siebeck 2001).

———, 'Maritime Liens in the Conflict of Laws', in *Essays in Honour of Arthur T. von Mehren, Ardsley, New York* (Transnational Publishers Inc. 2002) 439.

Theocharidis GD, 'Jurisdiction for Provisional Relief under the Brussels Convention in the Maritime Context', 55 *RHDI* (2002) 453.

———, 'Mechanisms of Protection from Non-Contractual Modes of Recovery in Sea Carriage: A Comparison between Common Law and Civil Law Systems', 44 *J Mar L & Com* (2013) 219.

Todd P, 'The Hague Rules and the Burden of Proof', 2 *Lloyd's Maritime and Commercial Law Quarterly* (2019) 183.

Topaloğlu B, 'The Validity of Jurisdiction and Arbitration Clauses as Against Third Party Holders of Bills of Lading – A Comparative Study Under French, English and EU Law', 44(61) *Annales de la Faculté de Droit d'Istanbul* (2012) 492.

Treitel GH, chapter 17 'The Contracts (Rights of Third Parties) Act 1999 and the Law of Carriage of Goods by Seas', in Francis Martin Baillie Reynolds and Francis D Rose (eds), *Lex Mercatoria: Essays on International Commercial Law in Honour of Francis Reynolds* (Informa Law 2000).

Treves T, 'Il Nuovo Diritto del Mare e le Convenzioni Internazionali Sulla Protezione dell' Ambiente Marino', 101(1) *Diritto Marittimo* (1999) 219.

Troshchenovych O, JB Huebert and others, 'Brussels I Regulation and Arbitration – Trading Torpedoes for Trust?', in *Commission's Proposal on Brussels I Regulation, Judical Cooperation in Civil Matters* (European Judicial Training Network's Themis Competition 2011), available at: <www.ejtn.eu/Documents/Themis%202012/Written%20paper%20Lisbon/Written_paper_Germany_2_International_Cooperation_in_Civil_Matters%20%20%20.pdf> (accessed 15 December 2017).

Tsimplis M, 'The Liabilities of the Vessel', in Y Baatz and others (eds), *Maritime Law* (4th edn, Informa Law from Routledge 2018) 232.

Tuo CE and L Carpaneto, '*Connections and Disconnections between Brussels IA Regulation and International Conventions on Transport Matters*', 66 *Zbornik PFZ* (2016) 141.

Turci S, 'Riflessini in Tema di Responsabilitá Vettoriale Secondo le Convenzioni di Bruxelles–Visby e di Amburgo', *Il Dir Mar* (1990) 33.

Vogenauer S, 'Introduction', in S Vogenauer and J Kleinheisterkamp (eds), *Commentary on the UNIDROIT Principles of International Commercial Contracts (PICC)* (Oxford University Press 2009).

Wagner G, 'The Economics of Harmonization: The Case of Contract Law', 39 *Common Market Law Review* (2002) 1006.

Wengler W, *Les principes généraux du droit en tant que loi du contrat* (RCDIP 1982) 467.

———, *IPR-Rechtsnormen und Wahl des Vertragsstatuts: Parteiautonomie im internationalen Privatrecht, insbesondere unter der Rom-Konvention vom 19.6.1980: Vortrag vor dem Europainstitut der Universität des Saarlandes, Saarbrücker, den 26 April 1991* (Europa-Institut/Universität des Saarlandes 1991).

Yiannopoulos AN, *The Unification of Private Maritime Law by International Conventions, Law and Contemporary Problems* (Duke Law School 1965) 370.

Zurimendi Isla A, 'Capítulo 2 Responsabilidad del Porteador Frente al Adquirente de un Conocimiento de Embarque con Cláusulas de Jurisdicción y Arbitraje', in PJ Baena Baena and N López Santana (eds), *Estudios sobre la Responsabilidad de los Operadores de Transporte en la Ley de Navegación Marítima* (Aranzadi 2017) 239–263.

Conference proceedings

Heinze CA, 'Antisuit Injunctions in Support of Arbitration Proceedings and the Brussels Regulation – The Approach to Be Expected from the ECJ', *Seminar Series on Private International Law* (British Institute for International and Comparative Law, 11 July 2007).

Myburgh P, 'Recognition and Enforcement of Foreign Maritime Judgments and Arbitration Awards. Private International Law (Conflicts) Issues in Maritime Litigation', *2nd Advanced Seminar on International Maritime Law* (University of Athens School of Law, 28 May 2016).

Pamel PG and RC Wilkins (Borden Ladner Gervais, LLP), 'Bills of Lading vs Sea Waybills, and The Himalaya Clause', *NJI/CMLA, Federal Court and Federal Court of Appeal, Canadian Maritime Law Association Seminar* (Ottawa, 15 April 2011).

Pérez Benítez JJ, 'Algunas cuestiones sobre jurisprudencia marítima', *University of the Basque Country, VIII Maritime Law Conference* (Bizkaia Aretoa, Bilbao, 30 October 2017).

Sandiforth A, 'Jurisdiction/Arbitration Agreements and Anti-Suit Injunctions, London – A Safe Haven for Resolving Disputes?', *University of Southampton Institute of Maritime Law Conference* (Reed Smith LLP, London, 27 January 2017).

Tetley W, 'Transports de Cargaison par Mer, les Règles de Rotterdam, Leur Adoption par les États-Unis, le Canada, l'Union Européenne et les Pays Transporteurs du Monde?', *Conference on the Responsibility, Fraternity, and Sustainability in Law. A Symposium in Honour of Charles D Gonthier* (McGill University Faculty of Law, Center for International Sustainable Development Law, 20–21 May 2011).

Reports

Alba M and others, 'Montevideo Declaration: The Facts' (2010), available at: <https://comitemaritime.org/wp-content/uploads/2018/05/Montevideo-Declaration-The-Facts.pdf> (accessed 25 May 2020).

Allan V and V Bonnin Reynes (Allen & Overy), *Spanish Courts' Concept of Public Policy Within the Meaning of Article V(2)(b) of the NY Convention – Preliminary Findings* (Memorandum to the IBA Arbitration Committee 2014).

Collins of Mapesbury, Lord LA (Rapporteur), Members: JM Arrighi, M Bogdan, AA Cançado Trindade, L Damrosch, M Dogauchi, CJ Greenwood, G Guillaume, F Matscher, K Keith, PM North, R Ranjeva, G Ress, S Torres Bernárdez, H van Loon, A Yankov, S Yee, *Provisional Measures*, Preparatory Work of the 3rd Commission, The Institute of International Law (23 December 2016).

Oxford Economics, *The Economic Value of the EU Shipping Industry* (European Community Shipowners' Associations 2014).

Restatement (Second) of Conflict of Laws, s 80 (American Law Institute 1988).

Newsletters

Tettenborn A, 'The Nuts and Bolts of Maritime Contracts: BREXIT and Choice of Law and Choice of Court Agreements', *Tribuna Profesional ANAVE* (Spanish Shipowners' Association January 2018), available at: <www.anave.es/images/tribuna_profesional/2018/tribuna_bia0118.pdf> (accessed 15 January 2018).

Press releases

Jim Brunsden and others, 'Britain Risks Losing Access to Valuable European Legal Pact', *Financial Times* (London 20 April 2020).

Websites and blogs

Barten SH, 'Arresting Vessels and Attachment of Other Assets throughout Europe by 'Going Dutch' under the Revised Brussels Regulation' (2015), *Lexology*, available at: <www.lexology.com/library/detail.aspx?g=91b758d6-c590-47de-99c9-8328ba89db3f> (accessed 20 August 2017).

'Demise and Identity of Carrier Clauses', in *Policy and Compliance Information* (Freight Transport Association [FTA] of the UK), available at: <www.fta.co.uk/policy_and_compliance/sea/long_guide/demise_identity.html> (accessed 5 December 2017).

Fernández Rozas JC, 'Cláusula de sumisión a tribunal extranjero en conocimiento de embarque (AAP Barcelona 13 febrero 2019)' (2019), El Blog de José Carlos Fernández Rozas, available at: <https://fernandezrozas.com/2019/02/24/clausula-de-sumision-a-tribunal-extranjero-en-conocimiento-de-embarque-aap-barcelona-13-febrero-2019/> (accessed 14 May 2020).

Garcimartín Alférez F, 'Competencia judicial internacional y autonomía de la voluntad' (2 August 2017), Lecciones de Derecho Internacional Privado, Almacén de Derecho, available at: https://almacendederecho.org/competencia-judicial-internacional-autonomia-la-voluntad/ (accessed 14 May 2020).

Krishna B, 'Chartering, Education PP' (2012), available at: <http://www.slideshare.net/bharath_krishna/chartering?related=2>.

Lorenzon F and TM Cunningham, 'Volcafe: The UK Supreme Court Rules on the Burden of Proof in Cargo Claims' (27 March 2019) Gard News Insight, available at: <http://www.gard.no/web/updates/content/27345515/volcafe-the-uk-supreme-court-rules-on-the-burden-of-proof-in-cargo-claims> (accessed 8 December 2019).

Ratification Status of the Hamburg Rules Is Available on the UNCITRAL Website, available at: <https://uncitral.un.org/en/texts/transportgoods/conventions/hamburg_rules/status> (accessed 26 December 2019).

Ratification Status of the Rotterdam Rules Is Available on the UNCITRAL Website, available at: <https://uncitral.un.org/en/texts/transportgoods/conventions/rotterdam_rules/status> (accessed 26 December 2019).

UNIDROIT Website, available at: <https://www.unidroit.org/about-unidroit/overview> (accessed 6 December 2019).

The Standard Bulletin (July 2015), available at: <https://www.standard-club.com/media/1813954/standard-bulletin-latin-america-special-edition-july-2015.pdf>

United Nations Treaty Collection, available at: <https://treaties.un.org/Pages/ViewDetails.aspx?src=TREATY&mtdsg_no=XI-D-3&chapter=11&clang=_en>

'Hague, Hague-Visby and Hamburg Rules package limitation values – Eastern Europe', Gard.com, available at: <http://www.gard.no/web/updates/content/52959/hague-hague-visby-and-hamburg-rules-package-limitation-values-eastern-europe>

Oxford Reference, available at: <https://www.oxfordreference.com/view/10.1093/acref/9780195369380.001.0001/acref-9780195369380-e-1303>

Oxford Reference, available at: <https://www.oxfordreference.com/view/10.1093/acref/9780195369380.001.0001/acref-9780195369380-e-1282>

Jorgensen, Rasmus Nord, 'Bimco And Asba Join Forces To Develop Gas Tanker Voyage Charter Party' (17 May 2019) available at: <https://www.bimco.org/news/priority-news/20190527-asbagasvoy>

Guides

ICCA's Guide for the Interpretation of the 1958 New York Convention: A Handbook for Judges, International Council for Commercial Arbitration (2011), available at: <www.arbitration-icca.org> (accessed February 2017).

Circulars

BIMCO, 'BIMCO General Clause Paramount – Revised' (29 October 1997) Special Circular No 4.

———, 'Revised Himalaya Clause for Bills of Lading and Other Contracts' (17 September 2010) Special Circular No 6.

ANNEX II

Additional legal sources

National legislation

United Kingdom

Contracts (Rights of Third Parties) Act 1999.

European Union (EU)

Primary sources

Treaty of Amsterdam amending the Treaty on European Union, the Treaties establishing the European Communities and Related Acts [1997] OJ C340/1.

Treaty of Nice amending the Treaty on European Union, the Treaties establishing the European Communities and certain related acts [2001] OJ C80/01.

Treaty of Lisbon, amending the Treaty on European Union and the Treaty establishing the European Community [2007] OJ C306/01.

Council Convention, signed at Luxembourg on 9 October 1978, on the accession of the Kingdom of Denmark, of Ireland and of the United Kingdom of Great Britain and Northern Ireland to the Convention on Jurisdiction and the Enforcement of Judgments in Civil and Commercial Matters, and to the Protocol on its interpretation by the Court of Justice (78/884/EEC) [1978] OJ L 304/1.

Proposals and communications

Commission explanatory memorandum regarding the Proposal for a Council Regulation (EC) on jurisdiction and the recognition and enforcement of judgments in civil and commercial matters (1999/C 376 E/01) COM (1999) 348 final 1999/0154(CNS).

ANNEX III

Official reports and preparatory works

International

United Nations reports

UNCITRAL Secretariat, *Guide on the Convention on the Recognition and Enforcement of Foreign Arbitral Awards* (first published 1958, UN 2016).

UNCTAD Secretariat, *Charter Parties* (United Nations 1974), Doc TD/B/C.4/ISL/13.

Hague Conference of Private International Law

Dogauchi M and TC Hartley, 'Preliminary Draft Convention on Exclusive Choice of Court Agreements, Draft Report', Preliminary Document 26 (2004), available at: <www.hcch.net/index_en.php?act=publications.details&pid=3512&dtid=35> (accessed 18 September 2018).

Preparatory Works ('Travaux préparatoires') of the International Convention on the Arrest of Ships 1999

'Preparation and adoption of a Convention on arrest of ships. Compilation of comments and proposals by Governments and by intergovernmental and non-governmental organizations on the draft Articles for a Convention on arrest of ships.' Diplomatic Conference on Arrest of Ships of the United Nations/International Maritime Organization, Document A/CONF.188/3 (Geneva, 25 November 1999), Addendum 1 (11 January 1999), addendums 2 and 3 (of 23 February 1999).

Report of the Chairman of the CMI International Sub-Committee: Revision of the International Convention for the Unification of Certain Rules Relating to the Arrest of Sea-Going Ships—Report of the Chairman of the International Sub-Committee, Document Arrest 31/II-1985 Lisboa I, p 146.

Proceedings of the Main Committee Documents CRP.1-17: Document A/CONF.188/CRP.1-17 Mar 12, 1999, UN Doc A/CONE 188/6 (Mar 19, 1999) (entered into force 14 September 2011).

Preparatory Works ('Travaux préparatoires') of the 1958 New York Convention

Comments of the Netherlands Government, *Travaux préparatoires*, Recognition and Enforcement of Foreign Arbitral Awards: Comments by Governments on the draft Convention on the Recognition and Enforcement of Foreign Arbitral Awards E/2822/Add.4.

Comments of the representative of the French Government, Mr. Holleaux, *Travaux préparatoires*, Summary Record of the Eleventh Meeting, E/CONF.26/SR.11.

European Union

Reports

Hess B, T Pfeiffer and P Schlosser, *Report on the Application of Regulation Brussels I in the Member States* ('Heidelberg Report') [2008], Study JLS/C4/2005/03.

Official explanatory report on the Lugano Convention by Professor Fausto Pocar ([2009] OJ C319/1).

Schlosser P, *Report by Professor Dr Peter Schlosser on the Convention of 9 October 1978 on the Association of the Kingdom of Denmark, Ireland and the United Kingdom of Great Britain and Northern Ireland to the Convention on Jurisdiction and the Enforcement of Judgments in Civil and Commercial Matters and to the Protocol on Its Interpretation by the Court of Justice* ('Schlosser Report') [1979] OJ C59/71.

Virgós Soriano M and others, *Comparative Study of 'Residual Jurisdiction' in Civil and Commercial Disputes in the EU; National Report for Spain* (European Commission 2007).

Woodruff C and K Reed, *Comparative Study of 'Residual Jurisdiction' in Civil and Commercial Disputes in the EU; National Report for England* (European Commission 2007).

European Commission studies

Cole T and others, *Legal Instruments and Practice of Arbitration in the EU* (Directorate General for Internal Policies, Policy Department C: Citizens' Rights and Constitutional Affairs, Committee of Legal Affairs, European Parliament 2014).

European Parliament resolutions

European Parliament resolution of 7 September 2010 on the implementation and review of Council Regulation (EC) No 44/2001 on jurisdiction and the recognition and enforcement of judgments in civil and commercial matters (2009/2140(INI)).

National reports

England

Law Commission and the Scottish Law Commission, *Rights of Suit in Respect of Carriage of Goods by Sea* (1991), HC 250 1990-91.

Departmental Advisory Committee on Arbitration Law, *New Arbitration Act? The response of the Departmental Advisory Committee to the UNCITRAL Model law on International Commercial Arbitration*, Lord Justice MJ Mustill (chair) (Her Majesty's Stationery Office 1989).

The Departmental Advisory Committee on Arbitration Law (Lord Justice MO Saville, chair), *Report on the Arbitration Bill (1996).*

Additional cases

National Courts

United Kingdom

Adler v. Dickson [1954] 2 Lloyd's Rep 267.
Brandt v. Liverpool, Brazil & River Steam Navigation Co Ltd [1924] 1 KB 575.
British Airways Board v. Laker Airways Ltd [1985] AC 58.
Donoghue v. Stevenson [1932] AC 562.
Dresser UK v. Falcongate Freight Management Ltd (The Duke of Yare) [1992] QB 502.
Elder, Dempster & Co and Others v. Zochonis & Co [1924] AC 522.
GH Renton & Co Ltd v. Palmyra Trading Corp of Panama (The Caspiana) [1957] AC 149; [1957] 2 WLR 45; [1956] 3 All ER 957; [1956] 2 Lloyd's Rep 379, HL.
Gilchrist Watt & Sanderson Pty Ltd v. York Products Pty Ltd [1970] 2 Lloyd's Rep 1.
Hain Steamship Company Ltd v. Tate & Lyle Ltd [1936] 2 All ER.
J I MacWilliam Co Inc v. Mediterranean Shipping Co SA (The Rafaela S) [2003] EWCA Civ 556; [2003] 2 Lloyd's Rep 113.
Leigh & Sillavan Ltd v. Aliakmon Shipping Co Ltd (The Aliakmon) [1986] AC 785, [1985] QB 350.
Mitsui & Co Ltd v. Novorossiysk Shipping Co (The Gudermes) [1993] Lloyd's Rep 311
Moller v. Young [1855] 25 LJQB 94.
Morris v. CW Martin & Sons Ltd [1966] 1 QB 716; [1965] 2 All ER 725; [1965] 3 WLR 276; [1965] 2 Lloyd's Rep 63.
Nippon Yusen Kaisha v. Int'l Import & Export Co Ltd (The Elbe Maru) [1978] 1 Lloyd's Rep 206.
Nisshin Shipping Co Ltd v. Cleaves & Co Ltd [2003] EWHC 2602 (Comm); [2004] 1 All ER (Comm) 481.
OT Africa Line Ltd v. Magic Sportswear Corp [2005] EWCA Cov 710, [2006] 1 1 All ER (Comm) 32.
Scruttons Ltd v. Midland Silicones Ltd [1962] AC 446.
Singer v. Tees & Hartlepool Port Authority [1988] 2 Lloyd's Rep 164.
Starlight Shipping Co v. Allianz Marine & Ors (The Alexandros T) [2013] UKSC 70; [2014] 1 All ER 590; [2014] 1 All ER (Comm) 337; [2014] Bus LR 873; [2014] 1 Lloyd's Rep 223; [2013] 2 CLC 713; [2014] Lloyd's Rep IR 327.
Starlight Shipping Co v. Allianz Marine & Aviation Versicherungs (The Alexandros T) [2014] EWCA Civ 1010.
Sze Hai Tong Bank Ltd v. Rambler Cycle Co Ltd (the SS Glengarry) [1959] AC 576.

The Berge Sund [1993] 2 Lloyd's Rep 453.
The Captain Gregos (No 2), Compañia Portorafti Commerciale SA v. Ultramar Panama Inc [1990] 2 Lloyd's Rep 395.
The Eschersheim [1976] 2 Lloyd's Rep 1.
The Forum Craftsman [1985] Lloyd's Rep 291.
The Glendarroch [1894] P 226.
The Owners of Cargo lately Laden on Board the Ship Aramis v. Aramis Maritime Corp ('The Aramis') [1989] 1 Lloyd's Rep 213.
The Phonizen [1966] 1 Lloyd's Rep 150.
The Pioneer Container [1994] Lloyd's Rep 593.
Volcafe Ltd v. Compania Sud Americana De Vapores SA (Trading as CSAV) [2015] EWHC 516 (Comm), 1 Lloyd's Rep 639.
Volcafe Ltd v. Compania Sud Americana De Vapores SA (Trading as CSAV), [2016] EWCA Civ 1103, [2017] 3 WLR 1, [2017] 1 All ER (Comm) 751, [2017] 1 Lloyd's Rep 32.
Volcafe Ltd v. Compania Sud Americana De Vapores SA (Trading as CSAV), [2018] UKSC 61, [2018] 3 WLR 2087, [2018] 1 Lloyd's Law Rep Plus 97, [2019] 1 Lloyds Law Rep 21.

Court of Justice of the European Union (CJEU)

Maersk Olie & Gas A / S v. Firma de Haan en W. de Boer (Case C-39/02) [1991] ECR I-9657.
Wagner v. Fohrmann and Krier (Case 101/63) [1964] ECR 195.

Index

Page numbers in *italic* denote figures.

For Product Safety Concerns and Information please contact our EU
representative GPSR@taylorandfrancis.com
Taylor & Francis Verlag GmbH, Kaufingerstraße 24, 80331 München, Germany

www.ingramcontent.com/pod-product-compliance
Ingram Content Group UK Ltd.
Pitfield, Milton Keynes, MK11 3LW, UK
UKHW050232200926
475702UK00020B/2997
* 9 7 8 0 3 6 7 6 7 4 8 0 9 *